THE LAW OF
THE COMMONWEALTH AND
Chief Justice Shaw

". . . the absolute power of a crag vitalized by
a human spirit."

THE LAW OF
THE COMMONWEALTH AND
Chief Justice Shaw

The Evolution of American Law, 1830-1860

LEONARD W. LEVY

HARPER TORCHBOOKS ❦ The Academy Library
Harper & Row, Publishers
New York, Evanston, and London

To my wife, ELYSE

THE LAW OF THE COMMONWEALTH AND
CHIEF JUSTICE SHAW

First HARPER TORCHBOOK edition published 1967 by
Harper & Row, Publishers, Incorporated, 49 East 33rd
Street, New York, N.Y. 10016.

Library of Congress Catalog Card Number: 57-6350.

CONTENTS

ACKNOWLEDGMENTS

In some respects this book is the product of a joint enterprise. I am fortunate to have had the aid and friendship of a great teacher, Professor Henry Steele Commager of Columbia University, who first introduced me to constitutional and legal history, suggested Shaw as a subject of study, and guided the early stages of this work. Although he provided counsel, criticism, and confidence, his most important contribution was his example of intellectual rectitude and his ability to induce self-teaching. I have also incurred a deep obligation to Professor Mark DeWolfe Howe of Harvard Law School who read the whole manuscript. He knows how much time he so generously volunteered to the task of evaluation, but he cannot know how grateful I am for his searching questions and incisive comments which provoked me to rethink several chapters I had previously believed satisfactory. Professor Richard B. Morris of Columbia University is another who furnished substantial and beneficial assistance. I deeply appreciate his interest and encouragement. The help which I received from my dear friend, Dr. Harlan B. Phillips of Columbia University, has been incomparable. With his patient ear, Socratic tongue, and corrosive wit, he was the midwife to many of my ideas and co-author of the chapter on segregation as originally published in article form in the *American Historical Review*. Professors Noel T. Dowling and Dumas Malone of Columbia University and Professor Oscar Handlin of Harvard University also offered constructive suggestions. Others through their writings, chiefly Justice Felix Frankfurter and Professors Max Lerner, Edward S. Corwin, and Roscoe Pound, contributed much to my thinking. The fact that I do not always concur in the judgments of those for whom I have the highest regard does not lessen my sense of debt to them.

Columbia University, by the award of a University Fellowship, enabled me to initiate my research. Brandeis University not only provided an additional grant-in-aid, but handsomely subsidized publication. Financial support has not alone earned my gratitude to Brandeis University. It has also helped make this volume possible by being an institution where, in the words of Justice Brandeis, "research is pursued, books written, and the creative instinct is aroused, encouraged, and developed in its faculty and students."

Harvard Law School, the Boston Social Law Library, and the Massachusetts Historical Society offered unfailing courtesy in the use of their facilities. Portions of this book, sometimes with premature premises and conclusions, appeared in the *Columbia Law Review, Boston University Law Review, American Historical Review, American Quarterly, New England Quarterly, and Journal of Negro History*. I am thankful to the editors of those journals for permission to use material from their pages. The *Columbia Law Review* also granted permission to quote from the article by Walter Nelles, cited in Chapter 11. W. H. Auden's "Law Like Love" is quoted from his *Collected Shorter Poems* by permission of the publishers, Faber and Faber, Ltd., and Random House.

I wish finally to thank members of my family. My parents, Mr. and Mrs. Albert Levy of St. Louis, Missouri, and my parents-in-law, Mr. and Mrs. Albert Gitlow of New York City, have helped in ways that far transcended familial obligations and cannot be adequately acknowledged. The dedication to my wife, Elyse, is a grossly insufficient tribute to her for her creative companionship and interest, for cheerfully exempting me from duties I should have shared, and for intelligent suggestions as to style and content. It would take a book bigger than this one to express my indebtedness to her and my appreciation for her incommensurable aid.

June 1956   Leonard W. Levy

INTRODUCTION

During his thirty years as Chief Justice of the Supreme Judicial Court of Massachusetts, from 1830 to 1860, Lemuel Shaw wrote approximately 2,200 opinions, probably a record number. They extend through fifty-six volumes of the *Massachusetts Reports* and if collected separately would fill twenty volumes, covering nearly every legal subject. His domain was the whole field of jurisprudence, excepting admiralty. No other state judge through his opinions alone had so great an influence on the course of American law. A critical study of his work can illuminate much of the history of that law in its formative stage.

Legal history, though one of the oldest subjects of historical scholarship, is one of the most neglected in this country. Except for federal constitutional law and institutional developments of the colonial period, the history of our law is in its infancy. Yet a society reveals itself in its law and nowhere better than in the reports of the decisions of the state courts. The state reports are, however, the wasteland of American legal history. Not even our constitutional law can be placed in proper perspective without considering them. The almost exclusive concern of scholars with the opinions of the Supreme Court of the United States may distort the true picture. For example, the traditional emphasis on the contract-clause decisions of Marshall and Taney gives the misleading impression that the states were prevented from effectively regulating corporations. But the state decisions show otherwise.

Biography as a literary form flourishes in democratic societies that strongly value individual human endeavor. But with few exceptions even the great state judges of the nineteenth century, despite their creative and influential roles, have been neglected in favor of lesser figures from the fields of politics, war, literature, or business. Isaac Blackford, John Boyle, Thomas Cooley, Charles Doe, John B. Gibson, Peter Hitchcock, Joel Parker, Theophilus Parsons, Isaac Redfield, William Richardson, Spencer Roane, Thomas Ruffin, William Sharkey, and William Tilghman are little more than names, their work undeservedly unstudied. So long as that condition exists, there can be no history of American law, and without it, no adequate history of this nation's civilization.

Frederic Hathaway Chase, in his appreciative biography of Shaw, paid scant attention to the Chief Justice's judicial career. "It is plain," wrote Chase, "that this is no place in which to catalogue or describe his opinions. His work is accessible to all, and it speaks for itself." [1] This book will at least serve to supplement Chase by describing and evaluating many of those opinions.

Chase has written about the man. I have not tried to duplicate his work because scanty as it is, he used the available biographical materials. They are a source of disappointment to the would-be biographer. Shaw's manuscript remains are bulky but of minor value in getting at the man. He left little to reveal his mind and character except his judicial opinions. But they, after all, are the reason for his significance.

Through them we may discern what his generation thought about the relation of the individual to the state and of the states to the nation; about rights, duties, and liabilities; about the roles of government; and about the character of law itself. We may also learn how liberty and order were comparatively valued; which interests were deemed important enough to secure in legal form; and where the points of social tension, growth, and power were.

I believe that a good approach to an understanding of our legal history is through the intensive analysis of major cases. Sometimes this is best done by narrating the whole historic episode of which the case was merely a part; sometimes by dissecting the legal ideas and concepts of public policy implicit in the governing "rule." Shaw believed that "the Law" was a symmetrical and scientific system of principles, based on "reason, natural justice, and enlightened public policy," from which a rule could be deduced and adapted for every case.[2] As an appellate judge his function was preëminently a rational one: to offer formally reasoned explanation why a case should go this way rather than that. It is also important, therefore, to examine the logic of his opinions, particularly if we are to understand the adjudicatory method by which we attempt the peaceable resolution of social conflict.

Whether I use Shaw's opinions as a point of departure or a point of focus — and that depends upon the character of the case — I have tried to make each chapter stand as a selected aspect of American legal history. Some chapters treat the response of

[1] Frederic Hathaway Chase, *Lemuel Shaw* (Boston, 1918), p. 145.
[2] Norway Plains Co. v. Boston & Me. RR., 1 Gray 263, 267 (1854).

the law to a great social issue, such as Unitarianism, fugitive slavery, or trade unionism. Others attempt to show concretely how and why changes in American industrial life, such as the advent of the railroad, necessitated accommodations in the law. Still other chapters are primarily concerned with the growth of legal doctrines of great consequence, such as the police power. The last chapter is an effort to extract some unity out of diversity.

If American law is an "occult science," as Tocqueville called it, only the initiate can fathom its history. Though my own lack of legal training has sorely handicapped me in evaluating Shaw's career, I am convinced that historians should not abandon legal history to the lawyers. But because of my handicap, which will be readily apparent to the initiate, I have passed over many matters on which Shaw made his influence felt but which seemed too formidable for me to undertake. Moreover, I prefer depth on a few matters rather than breadth of coverage, on the theory that painstaking detail is a greater service to scholarship in a neglected field than summary generalizations.

1

LEMUEL SHAW

The Pre-Court Years

When Lemuel Shaw's appointment to the Chief Justiceship was announced in 1830, a Jacksonian paper commented
acidly that he was a "respectable lawyer" whose chief qualification
appeared to be his Federalist convictions.[1] In truth, though Shaw
possessed sufficient qualifications to recommend him to the position, there was little in his fifty years to suggest that he would
become Massachusetts' greatest Chief Justice, and one of the most
massive and influential figures in the history of the American judiciary. Just as his opinions were slow in maturing, so too the
passing years were slow in revealing his genius.

Shaw grew to manhood with as little promise of distinction
as there was fertility in the soil of his birth. West Barnstable in
Cape Cod was a land of scrub pines, sand, and marshes. The community was too poor, or backward, to support a schoolmaster, let
alone a school. Young Shaw was fortunate, however, to have a
minister for his father. The Reverend Oakes Shaw, a Congregationalist, educated his son in English, the Bible, and the rudiments
of the classics. At the age of twelve, in 1793, the boy wrote to his
elder brother that his chores on the farm attached to the parson-
age prevented him from studying "more than half the time." [2]
Two years later he was sent to Braintree, his mother's home, for
additional instruction to prepare him for Harvard.

It was characteristic of Shaw that despite an inauspicious be-

[1] *Boston Statesman*, Aug. 28, 1830. The legal profession warmly approved of
Shaw's appointment. See *United States Law Intelligencer and Review*, 2:368–370
(Philadelphia, Oct. 1830).
[2] Lemuel Shaw to John H. Shaw, April 18, 1793, Shaw Papers, Box 1794–1809,
Massachusetts Historical Society; printed in Samuel S. Shaw, "Lemuel Shaw, Early
and Domestic Life," *Memorial Biographies of the New England Historic Genealogical Society* (Boston, 1885, 9 vols.), IV, 203. This article by Shaw's son is very
useful for the Chief Justice's early years.

ginning at college, he finally attained high standing. Having
failed his entrance examinations on his first try, he succeeded in
his second in the fall of 1796, and demonstrated sufficient com-
petence in the next four years to make Phi Beta Kappa and be
awarded a part in a Greek dialogue at his graduation ceremonies.
While in college he supplemented his meagre allowance from
home by teaching school during the winter vacations. His friends
at Harvard were young men of average abilities; none was marked
for future fame, like William E. Channing and Joseph Story,
among the upperclassmen, or Washington Allston, Joseph Buckminster, or Loammi Baldwin of Shaw's own class of 1800.

Shaw left college undecided about his future, but inclining
towards law. Writing to his brother who had inquired what profession he expected to pursue, Shaw replied, "It is indeed a secret
which I have not yet discovered myself"; but he added that he
was considering teaching in Boston where he would be "advanta-
geously situated for studying law. It is a profession I must confess
to which I have a partiality." [3] This was the plan he followed,
in spite of his parents' desire that he enter the ministry. Late in
1800 Shaw became an assistant in the Boston South Reading
School, and "worried through" a year of teaching, which his son
said he regarded as drudgery.

But the young schoolmaster combined teaching with more
congenial pursuits. In Boston he found pleasure and instruction
in the home of his uncle, the prosperous physician, Dr. Lemuel
Hayward. Shaw's uncle introduced him to David Everett, a lawyer
(who was a better success as a dramatist and poet), and to Thomas
O. Selfridge, a Federalist politician who was Everett's law partner. Both men were frequent contributors to the *Boston Gazette,*
as were their friends, Fisher Ames and Robert Treat Paine, Jr.
Through Everett's influence, Shaw became the paper's assistant
editor and proof-reader. Unfortunately his articles in the Federalist organ cannot be identified; all contributions were signed
with pseudonyms and appear to have been written by Bay State
Romans.

Shaw's confessed partiality for the law and his frequent association with Everett and Selfridge finally convinced him to enter
the former's office as a law student in the fall of 1801. In those
days three years' study under a legal practitioner was generally
required before admittance to the bar. An industrious student,
Shaw plunged into the mysteries of the common law, and quickly

[3] Letter of Feb. 19, 1800, Shaw Papers.

revealed a grasp of legal principles that brought from his teacher a prediction of future greatness. Although Everett kept him busy reading, copying, and abstracting, Shaw still found time for an occasional article in the *Boston Gazette*. He also studied French and became proficient enough to translate a contemporary work on Napoleon.

When late in 1802 Everett moved from Boston to Amherst, New Hampshire, to open a new office, Shaw accompanied him. For the next two years he continued his law studies, attending the courts, when in session, to observe the older men. But like his teacher, he still evinced no singleness of purpose, for he had not abandoned his interest in literature. Whether his pieces appeared in the local paper over the name of "Caius" or "Cato" is unknown, but presumably it was he who translated the frequent French articles.

Nor was literature his sole distraction at Amherst. He fell in love with the daughter of Major Thomas Melville whose old-fashioned habits and costume inspired Holmes's poem, "The Last Leaf." The untimely death of Nancy Melville left a void that could not be filled by his consequent absorption in study. For the remainder of his life he carried in his wallet two love letters from her.[4] The intimacy between Shaw and the Melville family was also lifelong. In 1847 his daughter, Elizabeth Shaw, married the Major's grandson, Herman Melville.

As his legal apprenticeship drew to a close, Shaw began to consider the most advantageous place to practice. "I have thought of about fifty different places to settle in," he wrote home, "and am still as much at a loss as ever."[5] After his admission to the bar in New Hampshire, in September 1804, he went to Boston to seek his uncle's advice, and there he stayed. Then twenty-three years old, he was admitted as an attorney at the November session of the Court of Common Pleas, and took an office in Congress Street, Boston. This same year in which the future Chief Justice began his legal practice, Massachusetts, in an apt coincidence, instituted its plan to report the decisions of the Supreme Judicial Court.

Distinction in his profession, even recognition, was still a long way off for Shaw. Business came so slowly that he had ample time to deepen his legal knowledge by continued and systematic study. Winter almost passed without bringing a client; at last,

---

[4] The wallet and letters are in the possession of the Boston Social Law Library.
[5] Letter to his mother, July 20, 1804, Shaw Papers.

early in March 1805, the young attorney received two dollars for writing a will. His gross receipts for the first year barely exceeded two hundred dollars.[6] At the close of 1805, a thousand-dollars-a-year post as clerk of the New Hampshire Supreme Court seemed attractive enough for him to make inquiries, but a friend dissuaded him from actively seeking it. Instead, Shaw sought to increase his business by moving into the office of his old friend, Thomas O. Selfridge, who had an established practice. Selfridge was an extremely partisan Federalist and a man of exaggerated personal honor. Less than a year after Shaw became associated with him, Selfridge was involved in a political squabble and killed the son of a man whom he believed to have insulted him. At the trial, which was colored by party rancor, Shaw testified in his behalf. Selfridge was acquitted, making good his plea of self-defense, but shortly thereafter he left the state, and Shaw inherited some of his business. Even so, for several years, Shaw's practice mainly consisted of drawing documents, validating titles, instituting actions, and trying small criminal cases.

This experience was supplemented by his frequent attendance at the courts, where clients as well as knowledge could be acquired. Writing to his mother that there was usually one court or another in session at Boston, he said that he managed to attend almost every day: "It is true that I have not business in them constantly, but it is necessary, in a place where competition is great, to be always in the way of business. Besides, in the Supreme Court, there is always much useful information to be obtained." [7] During this period he was a member of a small club formed by young lawyers to sharpen their wits by arguing moot questions. For his own edification, he also assigned himself legal exercises in which he wrote out the arguments pro and con. It was this period of his life to which Chief Justice Bigelow referred in his eulogy on Shaw: "In early life, before professional avocations engrossed his time, he was a profound student of the old authors. He drank deep at the fountains of the law, and there filled his mind with an abundant learning." [8] In these ways he gradually developed a broad comprehension of the principles of law, in addition to the technical skills required for practice. His progress was slow but firmly founded.

Not till he had been at the bar for six years did he argue a

[6] Shaw's account books and notes of cases are in the Boston Social Law Library.
[7] Letter of March 9, 1801, Shaw Papers.
[8] Proceedings of Bench and Bar, April 9, 1861, in Supplement, 82 Mass. 604.

case before the Supreme Judicial Court. Even here he made an insignificant beginning, for the case involved the sum of five dollars, and the Court decided against his client.[9] In the same year, 1810, Shaw was appointed Justice of the Peace for Suffolk County, a minor position indeed, but recognition of a sort. In 1810 he also made what appears to have been his first political address, a rousing endorsement of Christopher Gore for governor, dedicated to "good old fashioned, sound principles of Washingtonian Federalism." [10] The address is important merely as signaling Shaw's formal debut in politics. A year later he was elected to serve in the lower house of the state legislature as a Federalist representative from Boston. A month after his election, he delivered the annual lecture on "progress" before the Humane Society of Massachusetts, addressing himself to abolition of the slave trade, humane treatment of the insane, and life-saving methods. Good Federalist that he was, he could not forbear incongruous strictures on the "ferocious despotisms" of Napoleon.[11]

From 1811 to 1815 Shaw was preoccupied with politics. In the General Court, he voted with his party on every important issue. He opposed the religious freedom act, by which the taxes exacted from dissenter groups were turned back for the support of their own churches; opposed the Gerrymander and the State Bank; and supported measures by which Massachusetts obstructed the successful prosecution of Mr. Madison's war. If his record was not impressive, it faithfully reflected the policies of his party.

Among his manuscripts of this period are several speeches, untitled and undated, that suggest he was infected with the unsavory localism currently endemic among Federalist partisans, but Shaw never voiced the treasonable sentiments that marked several of his extremist associates. That he was achieving political prominence is apparent from his connection with the Washington Benevolent Society and from the fact that he was chosen by the town authorities to deliver the annual Fourth of July Address in 1815.

The Washington Benevolent Society of Boston was founded in 1812. It was one of a network of powerful Federalist clubs dedicated to preserving the purity of the Constitution from violation by Jeffersonian principles. An early conservative writer

---

[9] Young v. Adams, 6 Mass. 182 (1810).
[10] Untitled manuscript speech, dated 1810, Shaw Papers.
[11] Lemuel Shaw, *A Discourse Delivered Before the Officers and Members of the Humane Society of Massachusetts, 11 June, 1811* (Boston, 1811).

stated that the Hartford Convention owed its origin even more to this organization than to the Essex Junto.[12] Allowing for probable exaggeration of the statement, it nevertheless suggests the tone of the Washington Benevolent Society. Lemuel Shaw was its first secretary and wrote the first draft of its constitution. The society was only sporadically active after the War of 1812, and soon after died out, indicating that it was primarily a vehicle for opposition to the war.

At the end of the war, speaking as Boston's town orator on July 4, 1815, Shaw emphasized Anglo-American ties and urged a reconciliation with England, although he took occasion, once again, to belabor the "contaminating influence of French principles." He explained that the war had been opposed, as had the embargo, because it had aided the French, and he predicted that history would pronounce a "sentence of censure and condemnation" on those who had involved us against England. "Let us hope," he added, "that the day of idle theory, of frivolous experiment, and of dangerous trifling with our great national interests, which commenced with the Administration of Mr. Jefferson, has passed away . . ."[13]

Shaw did not return to the House of Representatives until 1820. In the interim he married Eliza Knapp, the daughter of a wealthy Boston merchant, and gradually increased his own prosperity. He had, since 1813, assumed the directorship of the New England Bank. In 1819, he was recommended by almost the entire membership of the Suffolk Bar Association, including Webster and Otis, for appointment to the Court of Common Pleas; but inasmuch as the letter of recommendation remained in Shaw's possession, he may have been unwilling to accept the position.[14] In any event, the letter is significant for showing the high regard which Shaw's colleagues held for him. He was, at this time, thirty-nine.

When he was returned to the legislature in 1820, his most notable service consisted in his successful prosecution of James Prescott, Judge of Probate for Middlesex County, who was im-

[12] James Spear Loring, *The Hundred Boston Orators* (Boston, 1853), pp. 368–369. See also Samuel Eliot Morison, *The Life and Letters of Harrison Gray Otis* (Boston, 1913, 2 vols.), I, 300–302; Edward Warren, *The Life of John Collins Warren* (Boston, 1859, 2 vols.), I, 107–115; and William A. Robinson, "The Washington Benevolent Society in New England," *Proceedings*, Massachusetts Historical Society, 49:274–286 (1916).

[13] Loring, *Boston Orators*, pp. 375–376; Chase, *Lemuel Shaw*, p. 309.

[14] Letter of Suffolk Bar Association, April 22, 1819, Shaw Collection, Boston Social Law Library.

peached before the state Senate for corrupt practices. Shaw acted as chief manager for the lower house in the case against Prescott. The senior counsel for the defense was Daniel Webster, whose magnificent eloquence was not calculated to impress the Senate, acting as judges, as much as Shaw's patient, factual presentation. Prescott was convicted and removed from office.[15]

In addition to his membership in the House, Shaw was also a member of the Massachusetts Constitutional Convention of 1820. His role was distinctly a minor one, for he spoke rarely, and not at all on the two major issues with which the convention was confronted: extension of the suffrage and separation of church and state. Moreover, Shaw's views on most questions cannot be determined because roll-call votes were seldom recorded. One such vote was on a proposal to abolish the constitutional requirement[16] of public taxation for the support of religious worship, a requirement which in effect established the Congregational Churches, both Trinitarian and Unitarian. Unfortunately, a majority of the Congregationalist-dominated convention — Shaw included — voted against the proposal for disestablishment.[17] Ironically, an early opinion by Shaw as Chief Justice contributed indirectly to the ending of state-supported religion, by driving the Trinitarian Congregationalists into the ranks of the non-conformist groups arraigned against the Unitarians and the establishment.[18]

It is sufficient to note, with regard to Shaw's part in the convention debates, that he was with the majority in recommending an amendment to provide for the incorporation of towns, and in opposing a proposition to make bank stockholders personally liable. He was with the minority in favoring a resolution of the judiciary committee, of which he was a member, aimed at securing judges against removal except by a two-thirds vote of the legislature. He also spoke briefly against the right of an accused person to address the jury by himself as well as by counsel. The only other occasions on which he spoke were in conjunction with his duties as chairman of the committee on rules for the governance of the convention.[19] In sum, Shaw was not as important to the convention as it was to him: merely being present, listening to the

---

[15] Octavius Pickering and William H. Gardiner (eds.), *Report of the Trial by Impeachment of James Prescott* (Boston, 1821).

[16] Article III, Declaration of Rights, Massachusetts Constitution of 1780.

[17] *Journal of Debates and Proceedings in the Convention of Delegates, Chosen to Revise the Constitution of Massachusetts, November 15, 1820–January 9, 1821. Reported for the Boston Daily Advertiser* (Boston, 1853, 2nd ed.), p. 559.

[18] Stebbins v. Jennings, 10 Pick. 172 (1830), discussed in Chapter 3.

[19] See *Journal of Debates*, pp. 192, 542; 475–476; 566; 14, 15–18, 35, 36–38.

debates, and working with men like Daniel Webster, Joseph Story, Levi Lincoln, Josiah Quincy, and Isaac Parker, gave him such experience and first-hand knowledge of constitutional principles as would be invaluable to him on the bench.

Similarly, Shaw's career in the legislature might be said to have provided him with that working insight into legislative problems and public needs which was one of his distinguishing marks as a jurist. His most fruitful years in the legislature were 1821 and 1822, when he served as state senator. He wrote the joint committee report disassociating Massachusetts from a public land-grab scheme by which several of the original thirteen states claimed an equivalent for lands that had been set aside in the newer states, under federal policy, for public purposes. Shaw's report, which was adopted, was an objective review of the illegality of the state claims against the national government. His judicial temperament showed in his insistence upon settling the issue honestly — and therefore unfavorably to his own state — by waiving all considerations of state interest and expediency.[20] As state senator, too, Shaw was commissioner for the revision of the laws of the Commonwealth, in association with Asahel Stearns of Harvard Law School and Theron Metcalf, who in later years was Shaw's associate on the bench.[21] Doubtless this laborious work was of inestimable value to Shaw as lawyer and judge. Finally, as state senator Shaw made his most constructive public contribution in his pre-Court years: he was mainly responsible for converting the antiquated town government of Boston into a modern city system.

Shaw always took a strong interest in municipal affairs. He served repeatedly as fire-warden, selectman, and member of the school board. At the Constitutional Convention, he delivered the major address on the desirability of incorporating Boston, arguing that town government was neither deliberative, representative, nor efficient for a population of over forty thousand. His argument must have been persuasive, for the convention drew an amendment to the state constitution providing for city governments. Ratification of the amendment made the incorporation of Boston possible, and in 1821, the town appointed a committee of thirteen to draw up a new plan of government.

[20] For a good account of the land question and Shaw's report, see Frederic H. Chase, *Lemuel Shaw* (Boston, 1918), pp. 103–109.

[21] Asahel Stearns and Lemuel Shaw, commissioners, and Theron Metcalf, ed., *The General Laws of Massachusetts from the Adoption of the Constitution to February, 1822* (Boston, 1823, 2 vols.).

On the committee with Shaw, who drafted the first report, were Josiah Quincy, Daniel Webster, John Phillips, Charles Jackson, William Sullivan, and William Prescott. Their task was difficult; the few American precedents, principally the charters of New York and Philadelphia, could not be used as guides because their English cast made them unacceptable to Boston. Following a town meeting that recommended additional changes, a second report was drafted, debated, passed, and recommended to the legislature over the signature of Shaw and others. In the legislature Shaw sat on the joint committee for the incorporation of towns and wrote the charter for Boston's city government. This charter provided for the division of the City of Boston into twelve wards and distributed the powers of government among a Mayor, a Board of Aldermen, and a Common Council. The system prevailed until 1913 with only one material change, the vesting of a veto power in the Mayor in 1856 — which was done after consultation with Chief Justice Shaw.[22]

After his two terms in the state Senate, Shaw returned to his neglected legal practice. Perhaps his wife's death at this time awakened him to the necessity of providing for the future of his infant son and daughter, as well as for the care of his mother. He began to devote himself almost exclusively to his legal practice. Early in 1825, he wrote in explanation of his seeming neglect of social obligations, "The truth is I visit nobody, I am entirely out of society . . . I really lead a solitary life." [23] Not till two years later did he remarry. By then his practice was prosperous enough to permit him to resume political activity, though in a limited degree. In 1828 he campaigned for Adams against Jackson, and was a member of a committee to get out the vote in Suffolk County. Early in the next year he headed a committee of merchants and leading citizens of Boston who favored free trade, and wrote their petition to Congress in opposition to the Tariff of Abominations.[24] In 1829, too, he served once again in the General Court.

[22] This outline on the evolution of city government has been constructed from James Bugbee, "Boston under the Mayors," in J. Winsor, ed., *The Memorial History of Boston* (Boston, 1881, 4 vols.), III, 217-224, 293-294; Henry H. Sprague, *City Government in Boston: Its Rise and Development* (Boston, 1889), pp. 5-29; *Journal of Debates*, pp. 192-195, 615, 631, 634; and Chase, *Lemuel Shaw*, pp. 110-118.
[23] Letter to Mrs. Cochran, undated, "early in 1825" penciled at head, Shaw Papers.
[24] *Memorial to Congress against the Tariff Law of 1828, by Citizens of Boston* (Boston, 1829).

But after 1822, Shaw's career was largely given over to his law practice. As of that time, he was forty-one, a well-known lawyer and politician, though not a wealthy one. But, he had built his career on sure foundations, and just as surely he rose in his profession when he devoted himself to it. He took as a partner Sidney Bartlett, a brilliant young man who had studied law with him, and who in the next fifty years became a leader of the American bar. Bartlett possessed the one capacity which Shaw lacked: he could undertake the most exhaustive research on a case. Shaw, on the other hand, always disdained the hunting of precedents; his forte lay in his talent for seizing upon the basic principle involved in a case and exploring its legal ramifications. With his practice uninterrupted by extraneous matters and a junior partner to do his drudge work, Shaw was free to prosper, and prosper he did.

During his first twenty years at the bar, he had argued twenty-three times before the Supreme Judicial Court; in the last six years before his accession to the bench in 1830, he appeared before that Court sixty-two times. In contrast to the insignificance of his first appearance, one of his last cases was a landmark in constitutional law: *Charles River Bridge v. Warren Bridge.*[25] This case is too familiar to require more than perfunctory notice of Shaw's part in it. Although Daniel Webster was associated with him as senior counsel for the plaintiff — the "monopoly" — Shaw was connected with their cause at a very early date, apparently as a lobbyist. He was the reputed author of a pamphlet, published about 1824,[26] setting forth the views that became the property of the Charles River Bridge in the arguments of counsel before the Massachusetts Court and the United States Supreme Court, and which were adopted by a minority of the judges on both Courts.[27] More than a year before the legislature chartered the competing Warren Bridge, Shaw wrote to Hope Savage, who was shortly to become his wife:

[25] 6 Pick. 376 (1828), and 7 Pick. 344 (1829). The case was first heard on a petition for an injunction against defendants. Shaw wrote the bill of complaint. When the petition was rejected, the cause was argued on its merits.

[26] Widener Library, Harvard University, has a rare pamphlet, lacking the title page, attributing its authorship to Shaw. See *A Concise View of Some of the Facts and Arguments Respecting Another Bridge, to South Boston. Respectfully Addressed to the Citizens of Boston*, n.d. (1824?).

[27] Charles River Bridge v. Warren Bridge, *supra*, note 25. See especially Shaw's arguments at 7 Pick. 344, 391–402. See also Charles River Bridge v. Warren Bridge, 11 Pet. (U.S.) 420, 442 ff. and 583 ff. (1837), and the history of the case in Charles Warren, *History of Harvard Law School* (Boston, 1908, 2 vols.), I, 507–543.

I have finally finished the long case, which has so engaged me, and which has been protracted to a most unexpected length. The subject, is an application for a new bridge between Charlestown and Boston, the effect of which would be to destroy the whole value (about $300,-000) of the present bridge. The great amount of property involved, induces all parties interested to engage in the controversy with great zeal and perseverance.[28]

Briefly, Shaw was responsible for the view that the plaintiff s charter must be construed as an exclusive contract which was unconstitutionally impaired by the state act incorporating the defendant's bridge company. Fortunately for the economic development of the country, these views were not adopted by a majority of either court in which the cause was argued.

Shaw's prominence at the bar in his last years of practice is only suggested by the great frequency of his appearances before the Supreme Judicial Court. Because his practice was largely given over to commercial law, much of his work consisted of advising clients, keeping them out of the courts, and representing them before legislative committees. He was chief counsel as well as director of the New England Bank from 1813 to 1830, and the bank was never a party to a case in the Supreme Judicial Court during those years.

From 1823 on, Shaw became a man of considerable affluence, holding a fairly large amount of insurance company and bank stock. Whether he retained his investments after 1830 cannot be determined, but they earned a good income for him before then. In 1825, for example, "installments" on his shares in just the Boylston Fire and Marine Insurance Company and the Washington Bank came to $4,000. Webster stated that Shaw's last years of practice brought him $15,000 to $20,000 annually, a phenomenal sum in those days.[29] His savings and investments made it possible for him to accept the Chief Justiceship and live comfortably on the salary of $3,500. In 1855 he paid $269.50 in personal estate taxes and $604.55 in real estate taxes, and five years later his taxes totaled more than one-half of his salary. He also held several thousand acres of Kentucky lands.

Besides his income in the pre-Court years, the surest proof of his success at the bar is that he was chosen to deliver the address

[28] Letter of Feb. 14, 1827, Shaw Papers.
[29] Peter Harvey, *Reminiscences and Anecdotes of Daniel Webster* (Boston, 1890), p. 127.

at the annual meeting of the Suffolk Bar Association in 1827,[30] and served as President of that organization in 1829 and 1830. By the age of fifty, he had achieved all that was possible as a lawyer in his state. It was then, when he was at the head of his profession, that the highest recognition was accorded him: the Chief Justiceship.

[30] Lemuel Shaw, "Profession of the Law in the United States. Influence of the Form of Government and Political Institutions upon the Law and Its Professors." Extract from an Address Delivered before the Suffolk Bar, May, 1827. *American Jurist and Law Magazine*, 7:56–69 (Jan. 1832).

2

THE CHIEF JUSTICE

Appointment and Judicial Character

I

When Isaac Parker, who had been Chief Justice of the Supreme Judicial Court since 1814, suddenly died, Governor Levi Lincoln offered the position to Justice Joseph Story of the United States Supreme Court. Though Story was tempted to accept, he was unwilling to let the choice of his successor to the national tribunal rest with President Jackson.[1] Lincoln then decided upon Shaw for the position. After consulting with Daniel Webster and finding him in agreement, the Governor sent Webster to offer Shaw the appointment. Webster's own account of the meeting, which took place on August 22, 1830, is fascinating:

> I approached him upon the subject. He was almost offended at the suggestion. "Do you suppose," said he, "that I am going at my time of life to take an office that has so much responsibility attached to it for the paltry sum of three thousand dollars a year?" "You have some property," I replied, "and can afford to take it." "I shall not take it under any circumstances," was his answer. I used every argument I could think of. I plied him in every possible way, and had interview after interview with him. He smoked and smoked, and, as I entreated and begged and expostulated, the smoke would come thicker and faster. Sometimes he would make a cloud of smoke so thick that I could not see him. I guess he smoked a thousand cigars while he was settling the point. He would groan and smoke. He declared, by all that was sacred he would resist the tempter. I appealed to his patriotism. I said he was a young man, and should take it for that reason. A long judicial life was the only useful one to the State. His decisions would give stability to the government, and I made him believe it was his duty, — as I think it was under the circumstances.[2]

[1] *Boston Statesman,* Aug. 28, 1830.
[2] Harvey, *Daniel Webster,* pp. 127–128.

In spite of his entreaties, Webster got no more from Shaw by the end of the first interview than a promise not to refuse conclusively without giving the matter greater thought. That night, alone — for Mrs. Shaw was in Barnstable — Shaw came to a decision. In the morning, as he wrote to her, he "peremptorily declined." [3] The Governor, learning of the refusal, immediately sent Webster with a note saying that he was "entirely overwhelmed," and would call on Shaw at his study.[4] Only a promise to reconsider was exacted.

Alone again, Shaw wrote to his wife: ". . . the nomination is postponed till to-morrow. I have given the subject the deepest attention. The considerations are very strong on both sides. I must decide today. It is a most important crisis in my life." [5] To the pleas of the Governor and of Webster were added the urgings of leading members of the bar. Gravely Shaw drew up a "Memorandum": "Whether I shall accept the appointment of Judge." [6] Against acceptance he listed financial loss, sacrifice of ease and independence, and prolonged absences from home. "In favor," he listed the fact that at fifty, "the labors of the Bar begin to become irksome," and his practice might decline; judicial emolument was regular and permanent. He also considered the honor and usefulness of the position, *if* he could ably discharge its duties. "The above 'if,'" he humbly confessed to himself in the "Memorandum," "is with me the great cause of apprehension and alarm";

Upon this I confess I am influenced more by the judgment of others than my own. I am conscious that I cannot thus discharge the duties; they assure me that I can. I have only one consolation, that I have often thought the same in regard to other arduous undertakings and yet upon trial have found my strength equal to the occasion. If I undertake this great office, God grant it may be so.

The next morning he accepted, but with the "greatest reluctance." [7] On the twenty-fifth he wrote to his wife that he had received many congratulations, "but," he added, "those who have given them know little of the solicitude and anxiety which I feel on the subject." [8] Within a month Chief Justice Shaw assumed

[3] Letter to Mrs. Shaw, Aug. 23, 1830, Shaw Papers.
[4] Lincoln to Shaw, letter of Aug. 23, 1830, "carried by Hon. Mr. Webster," Shaw Papers.
[5] Letter to Mrs. Shaw, Aug. 23, 1830, Shaw Papers.
[6] Undated "Memorandum," Shaw Papers, Box 1828–1830.
[7] Harvey, *Daniel Webster*, p. 128.
[8] Letter to Mrs. Shaw, Aug. 25, 1830, Shaw Papers.

the duties that he discharged with such distinction during the next thirty years.

Daniel Webster always boasted that he was responsible for Shaw's acceptance. "Massachusetts is indebted to me for having Judge Shaw at the head of her judiciary . . . ," claimed Webster. Shaw

never would have taken the place had it not been for me. Although he accepted the office with the greatest reluctance, he has filled it with unsurpassed ability; and to-day there is not in the world a more upright and conscientious and able judge than Chief Justice Shaw. He is an honor to the ermine. For that, I repeat, the people of Massachusetts owe me a debt of gratitude, if for nothing else.[9]

II

When Shaw came to the bench, American law was in its formative period. There were but twenty-five volumes of the *Massachusetts Reports* and only a few more for the reported decisions of the United States Supreme Court. The range of subjects covered in these volumes was narrow. Not even the principles of real property law, pleading, or admiralty were thoroughly grounded and understood. Whole areas of law were largely uncultivated, many unknown. Several leading decisions had been handed down in constitutional law, but the future of the police power for the promotion of the general welfare was as yet obscure. The concept of eminent domain was vaguely understood; indeed the term itself was still to be used in an American decision. The law of common carriers dealt with wagoners, coaches, and sailing ships, and there was as yet no American book on the subject.[10] Nor had an American book been written on corporation law, which was still in its most rudimentary stages.[11] The law of copyrights, trade names, and trade-marks was almost unheard of in the courts; patent law was in its infancy. Insurance law was unchartered except in marine cases. Actions for negligence were few and elementary: the first volume to treat it as a special subject would not be published until after Shaw left the bench.[12] In fact, it was not until

[9] Harvey, *Daniel Webster,* 128.
[10] Joseph K. Angell's *A Treatise on the Law of Common Carriers* (Boston, 1849) was the first one.
[11] Joseph K. Angell and Samuel Ames published the first *Treatise on the Law of Corporations* (Boston), in 1832.
[12] Thomas G. Shearman and Amasa A. Redfield, *A Treatise on the Law of Negligence* (New York, 1869).

the year before he resigned that there appeared an American treatise on the subject of torts.[13] Radical changes were to come in the law of evidence. Labor law was dominated by the doctrine of criminal conspiracy; the fellow-servant rule was unheard of. Except for matters involving watermills and turnpikes, the whole field of public service corporations was judicially unexplored. Thus it is doubtful whether anything in American law was conclusively settled, not even something so fundamental as the meaning of "malice" and the manner of its proof in a murder case. Nor was the acceptance of the English common-law system in America at all certain: the great problem of adapting that system to American needs and ideals was still unsolved.[14] And new problems were constantly arising.

During the three decades of Shaw's judicial career, Massachusetts experienced a period of unprecedented economic activity and social reform. Out of the older rural, agrarian-merchant society was evolving a complex, urban-industrial one. Thousands of great manufacturing enterprises came into existence, bringing with them the factory system. Steam began to supplant water power, and scores of inventions revolutionized the age. Turnpikes, canals, bridges, and especially railroads metamorphosed communication and transportation. Public service corporations were formed, and the private corporation was becoming the dominant form of business organization. All of these developments precipitated new problems for legal adjudication, insuring for Shaw an unrivaled opportunity to mold the law.

Although the strategy of time and place worked in his favor, it was Shaw's genius in accommodating the law to the shifting conditions and requirements of the community that made him preëminent. But for his qualities of mind, his impress would have been unworthy of notice. He was, first of all, temperamentally receptive to change. Speaking before the Suffolk Bar Association, in 1827, he said:

[13] Francis Hilliard, *The Law of Torts and Private Wrongs* (New York, 1859).
[14] My description of the condition of American law at about 1830 is based primarily upon Charles Warren, *A History of the American Bar* (Boston, 1911), pp. 288–290, 448–462, 471–474, 485, and 492–499; and upon Roscoe Pound, *The Formative Era of American Law* (Boston, 1938), *passim*. An excellent study on a specialized topic is Edwin Merrick Dodd, *American Business Corporations until 1860* (Cambridge, 1954). There is no adequate general history of American law. For the problem of the common law, see Pound, pp. 6–7, 95–97, 108–109, and 142–145. On p. 143, he says, "In 1833, it was still not wholly settled that we should receive the common law . . ."

There are, no doubt, many persons, fond of ease and quiet, who would desire to pursue the tranquil tenor of their lives, in the same steps with their fathers, because their fathers walked in them, and yield a ready submission to any laws, which were the laws of their fathers. Of this class there are no doubt lawyers, educated in a profound reverence for things established, who could never think of questioning the authority of a black-letter maxim, and who would regard a rule of law found in a dictum of Coke or Lord Hobart, as much sounder and wiser than any new rule, though drawn by the most exact deduction from a series of well established principles of natural justice. But were we to sympathize ever so deeply in the tastes and feelings of those, with whom a love of repose, and an abhorrence of all changes are predominant sentiments, still it would be useless to regret the existence of changes which are now irrevocable, or to lament over a state of things, which we can neither alter nor control. We can no more bring back past institutions, with the maxims and habits which belong to them, than we can restore past time.

And in the same address, he added: "It is due to the spirit of the age, that whilst a rapid progress is [in] making in every other department of knowledge, as much should be done for the science of law, as the subject will admit." [15]

The second distinguishing characteristic of Shaw's mind was his constant preoccupation with basic principles. He had a knack for knifing to the heart of a controversy and explaining the principle that governed it, and he had, too, that capacity for bold and simple generalization so often the mark of a trail-blazing judge. To Shaw the law was a science founded on reason. Accordingly, he strove in his opinions to impart to the law system and symmetry. He would not ordinarily dispose of a case on the ground that "the law is so established, that so it was enacted by the statute of Edward I. or so it was ruled in the Year Books." The rule might be a good one, but Shaw looked for a better reason: "The question will still be put," he declared, " 'upon what principle is it founded?' This question must be fairly met and answered." [16] In his first utterance on the bench, a eulogy of his predecessor, he summed up his conception of the judicial function, emphasizing the importance of principles:

The ultimate object of all laws, and of all jurisprudence, is, to do justice between parties; and the judge who, by patient research and persevering investigation, can unravel a complicated case, seek out its governing principles with their just exceptions and qualifications, and,

---

[15] Shaw, "Profession of Law," pp. 64-65, 67.
[16] *Ibid.*, p. 66.

without violating the rules, or weakening the authority of positive law, can apply those principles in a manner consistent with the plain dictates of natural justice, may be considered as having accomplished the most important purpose of his office.[17]

The infrequent use of citation — often its total absence — was habitual with Shaw. Although he was duly respectful of the value of old formulas, he was more often compelled to make them serviceable. Consequently, his opinions give the impression of an imperious scorn for precedent. But it was his conception of the law as a *growing* science that made him impatient with mere authority for its own sake. He could not content himself with precedent, well though he could conscript it to his service when he wished. His inventive spirit would not permit him to be the prisoner of someone else's opinions. For him the vigor of the law depended upon its keeping abreast of the changes wrought by human endeavor. Therefore he constantly searched for ways to adapt the old to the new, reconcile conflicting doctrines, and so restate the law as to make it practical and plastic.

Shaw was a poor stylist. His opinions were discursive, comprehensive, and ponderously written. Possessing weight rather than brilliance, they do not readily lend themselves to quotation, but must be read through for the total effect. His mind was full to overflowing with argument and illustration; consequently, the range of discussion was too broad, if an opinion is to be considered as a mere decision of the question presented by a case. But in his diffuseness lay much of his strength. The judge who confines his opinion to the issue and decides on narrow grounds performs his immediate duty — and may be forgotten to jurisprudence. Shaw's tendency, however, was to write a treatise on the subject before him. "If the simplest motion were made," recalled Senator Hoar, who practiced before him, "he had to unlimber the heavy artillery of his mind, go down to the roots of the question, consider the matter in all possible relations, and deal with it as if he were besieging a fortress." [18] In the course of his elaborate discussions, he often explained principles in terms of public policy or social advantage, and placed his decisions on the broadest possible ground. When he retired after thirty years, his judg-

---

[17] "A Sketch of the Life and Character of the Hon. Isaac Parker, Late Chief Justice of This Court. An Address Delivered before the Bar of Berkshire, by Lemuel Shaw, C.J., September term 1830, at Lenox," Appendix, 9 Pick. 577–578.

[18] George F. Hoar, *Autobiography of Seventy Years* (New York, 1903, 2 vols.), II, 388.

ments had cast illumination on almost every branch of law within his jurisdiction.

Shaw performed his work with the utmost seriousness. Every case, regardless of the importance of the parties or the amount involved, was a matter of equal concern with him. Justice and the principle involved were what attracted him. Once, in a petty action on whether a calf worth a few dollars was exempt from attachment against a debtor, laughter from the bar impelled the Chief Justice to cut in with great emotion: "Gentlemen, this may seem to you a trifling case, but it is a very important question to a great many poor families." [19] The copious notes he took for every case indicate the care he gave to his work; his manuscript *Minutes of the Massachusetts Supreme Judicial Court* fill fifty-two large volumes. His capacity for prodigious labor prompted Webster's remark that Shaw could "do the work of ten men, and at night eat ham enough to raise the market price in Cincinnati." [20]

In spite of his energies, he sometimes put off delivering the opinion of the Court until he was certain that every facet of a case had been exhaustively discussed. Judge Thomas, who practiced before Shaw and sat beside him on the bench, spoke of his great patience and willingness to be instructed.[21] Another associate, Judge Bigelow, recalled that in conference, Shaw's aim was to seek advice rather than to "urge and enforce his own opinions. . . . Anxious only to arrive at just conclusions, he listened with candor to the arguments of others. He had no pride of opinion or overweening confidence in his own judgment. No one could be more open to conviction or more ready to yield his own views, when concession involved no sacrifice of principle." [22]

Yet no man could be more firm when principle was at stake. Though he would listen and consider, his own opinions held sway over the Court because of the weight of his reasoning. Of some 2,200 opinions that he wrote in three decades, only one was a dissent;[23] and rarely did Shaw's associates dissent from his opin-

---

[19] Proceedings of the Bench and Bar, April 9, 1861, Supplement, 82 Mass. 598. See also, Hoar, *Autobiography*, II, 388. The case was Carruth v. Grassie, 11 Gray 211 (1858).

[20] Joseph A. Willard, *Half a Century with Judges and Lawyers* (Boston, 1895), p. 134.

[21] Benjamin F. Thomas, "Sketch of the Life and Judicial Labors of Chief-Justice Shaw," *Proceedings*, Massachusetts Historical Society, 10:70–71 (2nd ser., Boston, 1867).

[22] Proceedings of Bench and Bar, April 9, 1861, Supplement, 82 Mass. 606. See also Thomas, "Sketch of Shaw," p. 72.

[23] Herrick v. Johnson, 11 Metc. 26 (1846).

ions. In all but three of his fifty constitutional opinions he had
the unanimous concurrence of the Court. By comparison, Marshall, who was certainly a strong judge, carried his whole Court
with him in only twenty-three of his thirty-six constitutional opinions.

Just as his opinions dominated his Court, so Shaw dominated
the court room by his presence. He was a formidable-looking
man, squat, and powerfully built. A contemporary once said of
his huge, peculiarly magnificent head that "Michael Angelo . . .
would have made a Moses of it." [24] He had strong, coarse features
— a wide, grim mouth, piercing eyes under heavy brows, and a
great nose — and deep lines etched his grave face. His hair, worn
extremely long, was like a shaggy mane. To everyone, he gave the
impression of strength and dignity. Senator Hoar was reminded
of "the statues of Gog and Magog in the Guildhall in London";
and Rufus Choate, watching a sculptor at work on a lion, declared, "Why that's the best likeness of Chief Justice Shaw that
I ever saw." [25] On another occasion, Choate exclaimed that he
regarded Shaw as the Indian did his wooden idol, knowing that
he was ugly, but feeling that he was great.[26]

Shaw's manner on the bench was austere and gruff. He had
an unfortunate faculty of expressing disapproval by sharp rebuke.
He brooked neither levity, interruption, nor pointless argument.
An impulsive lawyer once inadvertently interrupted Shaw and
proposed a motion to amend. He was cut short with "There is
one amendment you can make without a motion, your *manners*,
sir." [27] The Chief Justice played no favorites. The leaders of the
bar and younger men alike experienced the lash of his tongue.
Senator Butler, when asked where he was taking his huge mastiff
dog, replied that he was going down to the Court House to show
him the Chief Justice "so as to teach him to growl." [28] Shaw once
delivered the perfect squelch to a verbose lawyer who made a
long introduction. When the lawyer replied, after being cautioned, that "We have quite a broad sea before us, Your Honor,"
Shaw responded, "So much the more need of keeping close-hauled

[24] Quoted in Chase, *Lemuel Shaw*, p. 275.
[25] Hoar, *Autobiography*, II, 388; and Samuel G. Brown, *The Life of Rufus
Choate* (Boston, 1891, 6th ed.), p. 438, note.
[26] For different versions of this story, see Brown, p. 438, note; Edward G. Parker,
Reminiscences of Rufus Choate (New York, 1860), p. 201; and Hoar, *Autobiography*,
II, 388.
[27] Willard, *Half Century with Judges*, p. 131.
[28] Benjamin F. Butler, *Autobiography of Personal Reminiscences. Butler's Book*
(Boston, 1892), p. 1002.

on the wind then." [29] Judge Emory Washburn dreaded the law term of the Court, and said he sometimes felt that he would rather lay his head on a railroad track than argue a case before Shaw.[30]

In spite of his manners, the Chief Justice had the respect of everyone. Men used the word "reverence" when they spoke of him, and Senator Hoar recalled that he was revered by the people as if he were a demigod. Their confidence in him was accounted the principal reason for the defeat of the amendment proposed by the Constitutional Convention of 1853 for an elective judiciary. Speaking of this, Judge Thomas told the story of a friend who asked one of the members of the convention, "What are they doing down at the State-House?" "Discussing the question whether Chief-Justice Shaw is a divine institution or a human contrivance." [31] Though Shaw had "growled . . . rather savagely" [32] at Rufus Choate on many an occasion, when a lawyer rose in anger at a remark of the Chief Justice, Choate restrained him, whispering, "Do not reply hastily. Remember that with him, and under him, life, liberty, and property are safe." [33]

After his appointment as Chief Justice, Shaw scrupulously avoided all political activity. Not even in his private correspondence, except once in a while to his sons, would he commit himself on politics. Though he was known to be a staunch Whig, and was invited to participate at Whig functions, he consistently refused. He would not even attend the Constitutional Convention of 1853 "on account of my judicial position which is quite aloof from political controversy." [34] But the law, though a "jealous mistress," did not monopolize his time. He read widely and was well informed on a great variety of matters. His memberships in a dozen societies suggest his broad interests: at various times he was active in the Massachusetts Historical Society, the Berkshire Agricultural Society, the Friday Evening Club, the American Academy of Arts and Sciences, the Boston Athenaeum, The Society for Propagating the Gospel Among the Indians, Phi Beta Kappa, the Harvard Board of Overseers, and the American Unitarian Association, among others.

[29] Willard, *Half Century with Judges*, p. 133.

[30] Hoar, *Autobiography*, II, 388–389.

[31] Thomas, "Sketch of Shaw," pp. 72–73.

[32] Parker, *Choate*, p. 201.

[33] Quoted in Chase, *Lemuel Shaw*, p. 289. For expressions of the same sentiment from others see Proceedings of Bench and Bar, April 9, 1861, Supplement, 82 Mass. 598 and 605.

[34] Shaw to Lemuel Shaw, Jr., March 5, 1853, Shaw Papers.

But it is Shaw the Chief Justice, not Shaw the man, who is remembered. For thirty years he configured the law so that it could serve the exigencies of changing times, and his mind was always fresh and inventive. In his seventies, when his body grew weak and his eyes failed him, when his wife instructed his sons to take care of him, wash his ears, comb his hair, he handed down leading opinions on the police power, the right to be free from unreasonable searches and seizures, common-carrier liabilities, jury trials, negligence, and many other subjects.[35] At the age of eighty, he delivered one of his greatest opinions, demonstrating once again in an entirely novel case his remarkable power to forecast the needs of the future and mold ancient common-law principles to what he called, "new institutions and conditions of society, new modes of commerce, new usages and practices, as the progress of society in the advancement of civilization may require." [36]

[35] Commonwealth v. Alger, 7 Cush. 53 (1851); Fisher v. McGirr, 1 Gray 1 (1854); Norway Plains Co. v. Boston and Maine R.R., 1 Gray 263 (1854); Commonwealth v. Anthes, 5 Gray 185 (1855); Jones v. Robbins, 8 Gray 329 (1857); Shaw v. Boston and Worcester R.R., 8 Gray 45 (1857).

[36] Commonwealth v. Temple, 14 Gray 69, 74 (1859), decided June, 1860, on a question for the first time involving a horse-drawn street car.

3

THE UNITARIAN CONTROVERSY

Church, State, and Court

I

The Reverend Jedidiah Morse met the challenge of Unitarianism with the stunning query: "Are you of the Christian or the Boston religion?" John Lowell, a champion of the new theology, replied in kind to Puritan orthodoxy. "Are you," he retorted, "a Christian or a Calvinist?" [1] Such was the tone of the theological disputes among Congregationalists during the early nineteenth century. The period was one of religious turbulence, and the harsh metaphysical dogmas of Orthodoxy were vulnerable to new and rationalistic heresies.

Unitarianism, nurtured by the Age of Reason, proved congenial to the restless self-reliance of eastern Massachusetts. At its core, the optimistic faith was "a human protest against a lop-sided doctrine of divine sovereignty which robbed man of all real freedom and worth." [2] It disavowed a God of predestination in favor of a God of love; rejected the doctrine of total depravity in return for a belief in the native dignity of man; stressed the humanity of Christ and the irrationality of the Trinity; and regarded as superfluous the idea of regeneration, since the divine appeared in everyone. The tone of Unitarianism was coolly intellectual but distinctly ethical. As it liberated men's minds from the incubus of scholastic creed, it quickened free inquiry and romantic impulses. New England's "flowering" owed much to Unitarianism.

The movement spread quickly through coastal society. The venerable Pilgrim church in Plymouth adopted Unitarianism in 1800, and eight years later, of all Boston's colonial churches, only

---

[1] The Morse-Lowell altercation occurred in 1815. See Ferris Greenslet, *The Lowells and Their Seven Worlds* (Boston, 1946), p. 168.

[2] William W. Fenn, "The Unitarians," in John W. Platner, *et al., The Religious History of New England* (Cambridge, 1917), p. 125.

the Old South persevered. Liberal gains — some of them temporary — were vehemently opposed by a besieged Orthodoxy which,
content with the beliefs that had served so well over two centuries,
refused to give up the ghost. The ensuing controversy divided
Congregationalists into two contesting parties, Unitarian and Trinitarian. The liberals had won an early skirmish over the Hollis
Professorship of Divinity at Harvard in 1805, and shortly after,
the Orthodox abandoned that institution as godless, establishing
Andover Theological Seminary as a citadel of Calvinism. Party
publications entered the lists, and stalwarts on each side fired
theological broadsides which evoked acrimonious reply and
counter-reply.

Enduring hostilities were perpetuated by a legal question:
which body constituted the true church when divided loyalties
resulted in schism? The question, a complex one upon which reasonable men might honestly disagree, was passionately contended
at law, because the victor's prize included the name, records, and
property of many a wealthy "first" church. This secular aspect of
the Unitarian-Trinitarian controversy affected political attach-
ments and the civil establishment of religion in the Commonwealth. Before Lemuel Shaw became Chief Justice of the Supreme
Judicial Court, the dispute over the rights to church property in
instances of schism had drawn the judiciary into the fray. Chief
Justice Isaac Parker, when subjected to Trinitarian animadversions against his famed Dedham decision,[3] indiscreetly published
his vindication of the Court in the official Unitarian organ.[4]

The Dedham decision in the case of *Baker v. Fales* (1820) established a precedent that was persistently maintained against
furious Orthodox assaults. Schism had ruptured the church in
Dedham parish. The Orthodox majority of the church had seceded when the parish implemented its changed religious views
by electing a Unitarian minister. Two bodies within the parish
claimed title, as the true church in Dedham, to the property rights
of that church.[5]

[3] Reverend Parsons Cooke, *Unitarianism an Exclusive System, or the Bondage of
the Churches Planted by the Puritans* (Boston, 1828), pp. 6–7.

[4] "Reply to the Reverend Parsons Cooke," *Christian Examiner* (Boston), 5:277–
283 (July–August 1828).

[5] The Dedham controversy may be followed in Erastus Worthington, *The History of Dedham . . . to 1827* (Boston, 1827), pp. 112–15; "Letters on the Introduction and Progress of Unitarianism in New England," *Spirit of the Pilgrims* (Boston),
3:507–509 (Oct. 1830); *Christian Disciple* (Boston), 2:257–280 *passim* (July–Aug.
1820). An excellent secondary account is Charles Warren, *Jacobin and Junto* (Cambridge, 1931), pp. 286–311.

The Supreme Judicial Court held unanimously that the exclusive constitutional right of the parish to elect its religious teacher established an organic relationship between parish and church. "A church," declared Chief Justice Parker, "cannot subsist but in connection with some corporate parish or religious society." Unconnected to some society, a church was devoid of "legal qualities" and could not control property that it might have held "in trust" for the society or parish to which it had formerly been attached. Hence, when a majority of the members of a Congregational church separated from the majority of the parish, the remaining church members, although a minority, constituted the church in such a parish and retained the rights and property belonging to it.[6]

The fratricidal clashes of the Congregationalists were aggravated by the Dedham decision and acquired political ramifications. In 1823, these were revealed in an unprecedented voting alliance between the orthodox Congregationalists, heretofore Federalists, and the nonconformist denominations who were usually Democrats.[7] The Federalist "Indian Summer" in Massachusetts, an eleven-year respite, was permanently frozen by the defeat of Harrison Gray Otis, the Unitarian-supported Federalist candidate for governor. Religion was a prominent issue in the election. "Calvinists and Republicans," newly allied, voted against Unitarians and Federalists. Thus the Orthodox, constrained to secede from their churches, also seceded from the Unitarian-Trinitarian Congregationalist bloc formerly bolstering the Federalist party at the polls. But for the schism within Congregationalism, Otis might have won the election.[8]

[6] Baker v. Fales, 16 Mass. 487, 505 (1820). An interminable semantic, historic, and legal exegesis on the case may be followed in sectarian debates. See "The Congregational Churches of Massachusetts," *Spirit of the Pilgrims*, 1:57–74 (Feb. 1828); *ibid.*, 113–140 (March 1828); the reply in "Review of the 'Vindication of the Rights of the Churches . . . ,'" *Christian Examiner*, 5:298–316 (May–June 1828); *ibid.*, 478–505 (Nov.–Dec. 1828); and the counter-reply in "Review of the Rights of the Congregational Churches," *Spirit of the Pilgrims*, 2:370–403 (July 1829). For an authoritative account of the legal issues, see Edward Buck, *Massachusetts Ecclesiastical Law* (Boston, 1866).

[7] On denominational political behavior, see William A. Robinson, *Jeffersonian Democracy in New England* (New Haven, 1913), pp. 128–150; and Jacob C. Meyer, *Church and State in Massachusetts, 1740–1833* (Cleveland, 1930), pp. 137–159.

[8] On the election of 1823, see Samuel E. Morison, *Life and Letters of Harrison Gray Otis* (Boston, 1913, 2 vols.), II, 241–243; and Arthur B. Darling, *Political Changes in Massachusetts, 1824–1848* (New Haven, 1925), pp. 24–25. It was the *Boston Statesman*, March 27, 1823, quoted by Darling, which coupled "Calvinists and Republicans." The Reverend Parsons Cooke said that "democracy or Calvinism" was opposed to "Federalists and Unitarians," in *Spirit of the Pilgrims*, 3:642 (Dec.

The "warfare," as it was called by both sects, continued throughout the decade. In the election year of 1828, the Reverend Parsons Cooke, a young orthodox firebrand, preached a sermon that was published as a political pamphlet.[9] He urged that all Christians unite to purge Unitarians from the state offices which they "monopolized." The chief object of Cooke's attack was the Dedham decision, which he likened to the faggot and the flame used to suppress churches and freedom of conscience. Worse still, the case had been decided in a partisan spirit:

> It deserves seriously to be questioned whether our courts have been entirely free from sectarian influence. For while, with one exception, all the seats in both our courts have been filled by Unitarians, decisions have come out, clothed with the authority of laws . . . exerting a most oppressive influence in favor of that denomination . . . And this fact induces the presumption, and it is not uncandid to indulge it, that the court must have been influenced in coming to their convictions of right in the case, by their wishes for the prosperity of their party.[10]

II

Ten years after the Dedham decision, a similar case came before the Court, now presided over by Lemuel Shaw. He was a conservative and devout Unitarian. As a member of the Massachusetts Constitutional Convention of 1820–21, he had joined in voting down a radical proposal to sever church and state. But his second opinion as Chief Justice, in *Stebbins v. Jennings,* the Brookfield case,[11] was to contribute indirectly to that very end.

1830). The Reverend Lyman Beecher, Orthodoxy's leader, exultant after the 1823 victory of the Jeffersonian candidate, wrote that the political influence of the "evangelical population" defeated the "Unitarian political party." Lyman Beecher, *Autobiography and Correspondence,* ed. by Charles Beecher (New York, 1864, 2 vols.), I, 517–518; see also II, 144–146.

Additional insight into the political realignment of religious groups may be afforded by the hypothesis that evangelism had its stronghold among the middle and lower classes as contrasted with the appeal of rationalistic Unitarianism to upper classes. Moreover, all Christians, excepting Universalists, condemned Unitarianism as a hellish abandonment from revealed religion and from Trinitarian doctrines.

[9] *Unitarianism an Exclusive System* (12 pp.). See note 3, *supra.*

[10] *Ibid.,* pp. 6–7. As mentioned, the vindication of the supreme bench — and of the Unitarian position on many critical issues — came from Chief Justice Parker himself in his denomination's journal. See also "Remarks on a 'Letter to the Reverend Parsons Cooke,'" *Spirit of the Pilgrims,* 1:67–72 (Dec. 1828). The fullest secondary account of the Cooke-Parker affair is in George Punchard, *History of Congregationalism from about A.D. 250 to the Present Time* (Boston, 1881, 5 vols.), V, 661–673.

[11] 10 Pick. 172 (1830).

During the preceding decade, there had been at least thirty instances of Congregationalist schisms. In every church affected, it was the Trinitarians who seceded; in twenty-three of the thirty, the seceders constituted an overwhelming preponderance of the church membership. Without exception they lost the properties of the churches involved, once to the Universalists and on all other occasions to the Unitarians.[12] It was a controversy arising from one of these thirty schisms that was brought before Shaw in 1830, and the consequences of the case were of a larger import than the "certain tankards, and other articles of church furniture" immediately concerned. The Chief Justice, consenting to full arguments by counsel as if the issue were unsettled, in effect reopened the Dedham case. This action brought into question the validity of all the transfers of church properties in the past decade.[13]

The controversy in the Brookfield case had a familiar pattern. A majority of the inhabitants of the Third Precinct in Brookfield had become disenchanted with Orthodoxy. Following dissolution, by mutual consent, of the contract between the parish and the Trinitarian pastor, a representative of the liberal theology had been settled. The majority of the church membership, faithful to traditional doctrines, seceded and followed the old pastor to another meetinghouse in the vicinity — an ancient Protestant practice of maintaining the faith by separation from the erring body. Out of the original membership, only two men were in accord with the views of the parish and had not accompanied the seceders. This minority of two claimed to be the Church in the Third Precinct of Brookfield. Thus there were two bodies within the parish lines, each asserting itself as the true church.

The case reached the Supreme Judicial Court in an action brought by the Unitarian plaintiff, who claimed the church property in his official capacity as deacon of the church in Brookfield. The Trinitarian defendant insisted upon his right to retain the property as deacon of the same church. Each relied on a statute of 1786 providing that all "grants and donations, whether real or personal," made to churches should vest in the deacons in their official capacities, to be held for the use and benefit of the churches.[14]

The argument by the plaintiff's counsel was founded squarely

---

[12] "The Exiled Churches of Massachusetts," *Congregational Quarterly* (Boston), 5:216–240 (July, 1863).

[13] There were five more cases of schism in 1830.

[14] St. 1786, ch. 51, reënacting Prov. Laws, 1754, ch. 12, sec. 1.

on the decision given in the Dedham case, but the defendant attempted to distinguish the case at bar. He maintained that the only point which had been decided previously concerned property devised to a church in trust for the benefit of a parish or precinct. He then introduced historical evidence to prove that churches had subsisted entirely distinct from the parishes with which they had been associated in public worship; and he contended that they sustained a corporate character at least to the extent of insuring their perpetuity and controlling their property, whether or not they were dependent upon parishes.[15] The argument was described by the Chief Justice as "able, and very elaborate."

At the outset, Shaw indicated his intention to review the entire controversy, as if the Dedham decision did not constrain the Court. His opinion for the full bench was daring in its admissions and recondite in doctrine. He admitted validity in the proposition that a church might be distinct from the parish with which it was associated; ". . . yet it by no means follows," he contradicted counsel, "that a church, as such, in legal contemplation, can exist, except as incident to, or connected with some parish or religious society." [16] The church was composed of those members of the parish who united to celebrate Christian ordinances. Deacons, by statute expressly declared to be a corporation, would by the very act of secession cease to be members of the church, their powers vesting in their successors. It followed, reasoned Shaw, that though they were distinct bodies in their corporate capacities, the deacons were "incident to and indissolubly connected with the churches from which they emanate."

Shaw had reduced the church to a mere appendage of the parish, which he lauded as the soil for the roots of a Christian vine. Next, he sought to rebut the contentions that churches held a corporate character and could subsist and act without dependence on or connection with any parish or society. Admission of the possible truth of these contentions was immediately followed by the inevitable "but":

But to be of any avail in the argument, it must be shown that the churches are corporations, or possess corporate powers known to the law at least to the extent of enabling them to have an independent existence and perpetual succession, and to hold and exercise some control over property.[17]

[15] The report of the defense's argument in 10 Pick. 172 is supplemented by "A Review of the Brookfield Case," *Spirit of the Pilgrims*, 5:402–406 (July, 1832).

[16] 10 Pick. 172, 181.

[17] *Ibid.*, at 186.

He denied this, adding that to found such an argument "it must appear that the exercise of corporate powers are necessary for the rights and powers conferred on the church." In the absence of necessity, such powers are not, as claimed, given by implication. Inference from history revealed that before 1754 churches had not legally been deemed corporations competent to take and hold property. Therefore, since no such powers could be attributed by implication after 1754,[18] churches were "effectually rendered . . . legally incapable of either taking or holding property." [19]

How then, if churches were not corporations, could they preserve their own perpetual succession? The answer appeared obvious. The parish to which the church was necessarily attached was itself a corporation with perpetual succession, and the existence of the church was guaranteed by its identification with that corporation. Moreover, property given to the church vested in the incorporated deacons. Then corporate powers could not be attributed to churches by implication from their supposed need. Even conceding corporate status to a church, it was still unable to secede and act alone.

The Chief Justice concluded with a reaffirmation of the principles enunciated in the Dedham decision. Judgment was awarded for the plaintiff, the deacon of the Unitarian church connected to the third precinct in Brookfield and regarded by the Court as the church of that society.

III

This opinion was of vital significance to the status of the churches of the two antagonistic parties.[20] The actions of the Court affected at least eighty-one churches involved in parish separations,[21] according to statistics gathered by a committee of

[18] Date of the first statute vesting deacons with corporate powers. See note 14, *supra.*

[19] 10 Pick. 172, 189.

[20] The opinion confirmed and supported in the extreme a precedent that was never again questioned by the state's courts. See Sawyer v. Baldwin, 11 Pick. 492 (1831); Page v. Crosby, 24 Pick. 211 (1839); Tibballs v. Bidwell, 1 Gray 399 (1854); Parker v. May, 5 Cush. 336 (1850); Weld v. May, 9 Cush. 181 (1852); and Jefts v. York, 10 Cush. 392 (1852). The last three cases cited also affirmed that a church is not a corporation, nor a quasi corporation. As late as 1920, the Supreme Court held that the corporation was the legal entity holding title to real and personal estate used for religious purposes, whereas the church was merely the body of communicants gathered in membership for religious observances. McNeilly v. The First Presbyterian Church in Brookline, 243 Mass. 331.

[21] Punchard, V, 686, gives the total as one hundred and twenty-six. See also Warren, p. 309.

twenty-three Orthodox ministers between 1833 and 1836, "when the facts were fresh." Their report, "The Exiled Churches of Massachusetts," concerned

those Orthodox Congregational churches of Massachusetts, which were driven from their houses of worship by town or parish action prompted by the Unitarian movement, and sustained by decisions of Unitarian judges upon the bench of our Supreme Courts; — decisions to which all concerned submitted as being technically the law of the land, for the time being, but which the Orthodox portion of the community have steadfastly believed will one day be legally set aside on account of the manifest injustice that is in them.[22]

The report uncharitably implied that the decisions provided the "ruling motive in sustaining the system of oppression" — the motive being an unprincipled lust for property gain.[23] So unduly harsh a view was compounded by the accusation that Unitarian measures to achieve ascendency in the parishes were downright wicked and dishonest.

Though no proof exists that the Brookfield church was a victim of unfair play, it was one of the 110 out of 130 Unitarian churches in the Massachusetts of 1843 which were of Trinitarian origin.[24] One critic of the Court's religious decisions, with a felicity for imagery, likened its distinction between church and society to "the cockatrice's egg out of which those great judges, Parker and Shaw, successively sitting thereon, afterwards hatched dire mischief to the churches." [25] The extent of this "mischief" may be approximated by Orthodox computations, mainly from the figures presented in the "The Exiled Churches of Massachusetts." As a result of the Dedham decision and its extension in the Brookfield decision, it was determined that 3,900 members of the eighty-

[22] "The Exiled Churches of Massachusetts," p. 216. The churches won by the Unitarians through a procedure assented to by the courts were known to the Orthodox as the "Juridical Churches."

[23] The Orthodox ministers included in their report examples of what they claimed were Unitarian measures. Representative samples: "One man was hired to vote by having his town tax paid for him; another for two shillings, besides as much as he could drink. . . . To secure voters against the Orthodox, flattery, threats, brandy, rum, gin and other like irresistible arguments were employed, in abundance. . . . Voters were brought in who were legal voters in other societies. . . ." (*ibid.*, pp. 233–235).

[24] Estimate by Episcopal Bishop George Burgess, *Pages from the Ecclesiastical History of New England, 1740–1840* (Boston, 1847), pp. 121–122. Albert Dunning, *Congregationalists in America* (Boston, 1894), p. 302, stated that of the 361 Congregational (Orthodox) churches in Massachusetts in 1810, the meetinghouses and other property of 126 of them were eventually lost to Unitarianism.

[25] Charles E. Stevens, "Essay on Church and Parish," quoted in Paul E. Lauer, *Church and State in New England* (Baltimore, 1892), p. 105.

one "exiled" churches were forced to surrender their interest in church properties valued at more than $600,000 to only 1,282 members.[26] It is little wonder that the indignant Orthodox should have fulminated against what they conceived to have been a great injustice wrought by the Court's rulings.

As late as 1856, an unkind article in the *Puritan Recorder* charged that the whole procedure was little more than legalized theft. The anonymous critic wrote in part:

. . . church after church was plundered of its property, even to its communion furniture and records. We called this procedure *plunder* thirty years ago. We call it by the same hard name now. And we solemnly call upon those Unitarian churches which are still in possession of this plunder, to return it. They can not prosper with it. And we call upon the courts of Massachusetts to revoke these unrighteous decisions, and put the Congregational churches of the state upon their original and proper basis.[27]

Similarly, Dean Fenn of Harvard Divinity School, a Unitarian, in a lecture in 1917, recalled that "The Unitarians who fell heir to the property of the ancient churches were accused of robbery and plunder." He reminisced further:

As a boy in one of the Congregational churches in Boston I used to hear, although not from the pulpit, that "the Unitarians stole our churches" and it was not until many years afterward that I learned that the "robbery" was by order of the Supreme Court of the Commonwealth.

Drawing a distinction "between law and justice," Dean Fenn advised that the decisions did "not seem equitable." [28] Earlier, one of the ablest spokesmen for Unitarianism, while staunchly defending the judicial doctrines of the Dedham and Brookfield cases, admitted frankly:

We do not feel perfectly satisfied with the legal decisions in the two cases bearing on the ownership of church property, though we admit that the issue raised was a perplexing one.[29]

[26] See also Joseph S. Clark, *Historical Sketch of the Congregational Churches, 1620–1858* (Boston, 1858), p. 271–272; Henry M. Dexter, *The Congregationalism of the Last Three-Hundred Years* (New York, 1880), p. 619; and Punchard, V, p. 686.

[27] Quoted in George Ellis, *A Half-Century of the Unitarian Controversy* (Boston, 1857), p. 415.

[28] "The Unitarians," in Platner, pp. 109, 110–111.

[29] Ellis, p. 31. Ellis gives an excellent account of the legal aspects of the decisions, the best from the Unitarian point of view. See Appendix IV, "The Legal Decisions in Cases of Church Property," pp. 415–432.

There was good reason for not feeling "perfectly satisfied" with these decisions. They do not withstand close legal scrutiny.[30] Moreover, Shaw in 1850 handed down another opinion that contradicted the earlier ones at crucial points.[31] Though on a different issue, this later opinion was virtually a treatise on the relationships and powers of churches and religious societies or parishes. Churches were indeed corporations, at least to the extent of sharing with deacons the power of taking and holding all property in perpetuity, subject to no trust on behalf of the parish; managing and disposing of property; and suing and defending all actions touching their property. Shaw sought briefly to distinguish his 1850 holding from the earlier ones, but the distinction did not distinguish. His 1830 and 1850 opinions cannot both be right. Perhaps his Orthodox critics were correct in some degree when they attributed his Brookfield opinion to his Unitarianism.[32] Given the intensity of denominational partisanship in 1830, he would have been more than human if predilections deep below consciousness did not color his understanding of the law of the case.

Much later, in 1877 when religious passions had long since subsided, a case involving the same issue and with similar statutory and constitutional provisions to construe arose in New Hampshire.[33] Chief Justice Doe, another very able Unitarian judge, decided the case against his own denomination. He explicitly repudiated for New Hampshire the Dedham and Brookfield decisions which he thought unsupported by any ground of law or history. Doe's opinion, in time of calm, leaves little to be said for the acumen of Shaw's.

IV

But whatever its acumen, Shaw's opinion had far-reaching consequences, affecting not only the churches of the Congregational-

[30] For a critical point-by-point analysis of the Brookfield opinion, see my article, "Chief Justice Shaw and the Church Property Controversy in Massachusetts," *Boston University Law Review*, 30:219 ff. (April 1950), pp. 229–234.

[31] Parker v. May, 5 Cush. 336 (1850), discussed in the article cited at note 30, *supra*.

[32] Shaw's associates on the Court, except for Marcus Morton, were also Unitarian. Morton, a Baptist and a champion of religious liberty (Oakes v. Hill, 10 Pick. 333, 1830), may have joined his Unitarian brethren in the Brookfield case not only because he agreed with their legal views, but because he believed that parishioners ought to have a church of their faith, particularly if they had to be taxed for its support.

[33] Holt v. Downs, 58 New Hamp. 170 (1877).

ist denominations, but also the entire structure of church-state relationships in Massachusetts. Probably unintended, these consequences were generally liberal except in one respect. By subordinating churches to parishes, instead of permitting the independent existence of churches, the opinion bolstered the territorial parish system upon which the Commonwealth's establishment of religion was based. The constitution and legislation enacted in pursuance of it had hamstrung freedom of conscience and equality of sects by requiring compulsory, tax-supported public worship on a parish basis.[34] The parish was a public corporation empowered to levy and collect taxes for, and compelling attendance at, public worship. Since the parish was a "body politic," a subdivision of the state, the subordination of church to parish in effect produced an amalgamation of church and state, irreconcilable with religious liberty.

The territorial parish system for many years virtually established Congregationalism as the state church, and the Supreme Judicial Court was its constant bulwark.[35] When a modification of the system made the taxes of other sects payable to their own churches,[36] Chief Justice Parker pointedly lamented, "The mischief to be dreaded is the breaking up of the parochial religious system." [37] Not until after religion and government were divorced by an amendment to the state constitution did the territorial parish cease to be a public corporation.[38]

But the "breaking up of the parochial religious system" actually began as a result of Parker's own Dedham decision which split the Congregationalist-Federalist alliance, making possible the Democratic victory of 1823. The new legislature provided[39] that any ten or more legal voters, whether dissenters or seceders, might form a "poll" parish and be relieved of the burden of supporting the territorial parish church. Therefore, their taxes would go instead to the church of the poll parish. These new poll parishes weakened the old territorial system, which from a legal

[34] Article III, Declaration of Rights, Massachusetts Constitution of 1780; and St. 1786, ch. 10 and St. 1799, ch. 87.
[35] See Edward Buck, *Massachusetts Ecclesiastical Law* (Boston, 1866), pp. 41 ff. Under the rule of Barnes v. First Parish of Falmouth, 6 Mass. 401 (1810), the taxes of non-conformists who belonged to unincorporated religious societies were made payable to the Congregational church of the parish.
[36] St. 1811, ch. 6, enacted to wipe out the distinction between incorporated and unincorporated societies. See note 35, *supra*.
[37] Adams v. Howe, 14 Mass. 340, 348 (1817).
[38] Chase v. Merrimac Bank, 19 Pick. 564 (1837).
[39] St. 1824, ch. 106.

standpoint, was propped up by Shaw's Brookfield decision that a church could not subsist apart from a parish.[40]

Yet his decision, like Parker's in the Dedham case, had the effect of advancing the cause of religious and political liberty even as it subordinated church to body politic. As a matter of usage, the Congregational churches had controlled the ordination of ministers and the admission of members. "Where the minister held to an unabated Calvinism and his church sympathized with him," wrote Charles Warren, "no new member could pass the ordeal of covenant without acceding to the terms required of a member of the congregation for securing the privilege of church communion. Thus all the parishioners who held liberal views were excluded from the church." [41]

The Dedham and Brookfield decisions democratized this system by giving political control of the church to a majority of the parish, who alone could elect the minister of the parish church. To be sure, Orthodox church members were forced between hammer and anvil. Had they remained in the church, with no power to choose their minister, they would have been exposed to "blasphemous" teachings supported by their own taxes. If they seceded to form a poll parish, they committed ecclesiastical suicide in the sense that they forfeited the name, records, and properties of their church. Yet the alternative decision would have been worse, because the losers would have been the majority of the parish, who paid most of the taxes and were not even admitted to church membership. Shaw's Brookfield decision meant that after two centuries, the democratic principle of congregationalism had fulfilled its promise by permitting the majority of parishioners to govern their church and be not merely attendants but members. Thus freedom of religion was promoted.

This same result was brought about in still another way. Just as the Dedham decision unintentionally provoked the passage of the poll-parish law of 1824, the Brookfield decision contributed to the separation of church and state. No longer could any one denomination accrue the benefits of an establishment of religion,

[40] Between 1824 and 1830, sixty poll parishes were incorporated. Twenty-seven were Orthodox Congregationalist, one Unitarian, and the rest divided among other denominations. The existence of sixty poll parishes, a figure based on my own count of the statutes of incorporation between 1824 and 1830, hardly bears out a Unitarian estimate that nine-tenths of the parishes of the state by 1830 were of the poll type. "Difficulties in Parishes," *Christian Examiner*, Vol. 9, No. 40 (Sept. 1830), pp. 4–5.

[41] Warren, *Jacobin and Junto*, pp. 301–302.

or escape the price of subordination where it was a minority. With the old territorial parish churches completely in the hands of the majority of the parish, a system of local option prevailed. Thus in some parishes, particularly in western Massachusetts, the Orthodox dominated, while in the east, particularly in Suffolk County, they were in a minority.

Consequently the Orthodox abandoned their historic position shortly after the Brookfield decision, but not until then. They accused the Unitarians of usurping their liberties, as well as their churches and taxes. In 1831 the Reverend Parsons Cooke issued a violent *Remonstrance Against an Established Religion in Massachusetts,* excoriating Unitarianism as the "state religion." An "injured community" was implored to "rise and put down this odious monster."

I see not what security we now have, except in the ballot boxes, that the climax of abuses will not soon be headed by an act of uniformity. . . . It has become the sacred, the religious duty of every citizen, who wields power of a vote, to employ it now on the side of religious freedom and equal rights.[42]

During that same year, 1831, the journal that had been founded to explain the Orthodox position, arrived for the first time at a most belated conclusion. The editor, writing on the "Third Article in the Declaration of Rights," discovered that it created "a legal, religious establishment," which was "repugnant . . . to the rights of conscience." Thus was announced Orthodoxy's support for the overthrow of the "whole system of taxation, by which our laws require religion to be supported . . ."[43]

Although the logic of the Baptists and Quakers had at last been adopted by Calvinism's progeny, there is an unavoidable inclination to credit a Unitarian assertion that

It was only when church property was given by the courts to the parish in preference to the church, and when the "standing order" churches had been repeatedly foiled in their efforts to retain the old prerogatives, that a majority could be secured for religious freedom . . .[44]

The alliance between the Orthodox and the dissenter sects jelled into a widespread popular front movement for disestablishment,

[42] Cooke, *Remonstrance* (Boston, 1831), pp. 20, 23-24.
[43] *Spirit of the Pilgrims*, 4:631, 635 (Dec. 1831).
[44] George W. Cooke, *Unitarianism in America* (Boston, 1902), p. 121.

except in Suffolk County, the stronghold of Unitarianism. With passage of the Eleventh Amendment to the state constitution, adopted November 11, 1833, religion was disengaged as "an engine of the state." [45] The land that cradled Puritanism had at last swung abreast of the rest of the nation. But the property settlements, which figured in the advance, remained unaffected.

[45] Oakes v. Hill, 10 Pick. 333 (1830).

4

SATAN'S APOSTLE AND FREEDOM
OF CONSCIENCE

I

Abner Kneeland was a heretic — a cantankerous, inflexible heretic. He was regarded as an immoral being who had crawled forth from some Stygian cave to menace Massachusetts in the 1830's. Not the least of his infamy is that his career provoked one of the worst opinions ever written by Chief Justice Shaw. Respectable men may have been right in believing that Kneeland polluted everything he touched. Yet if one believed Kneeland, he was merely a harbinger of free thought and a noble exponent of liberty of conscience. His name might now be shrouded in oblivion but for the fact that an outraged community, upon which he inflicted his opinions, retaliated by inflicting martyrdom upon him. He was the last man to be jailed by Massachusetts for the crime of blasphemy.[1]

In the *Bible of Reason* which Kneeland preached to his audiences, Samuel Gridley Howe, the humanitarian, had read with alarm "that infidelity is spreading like wild-fire, and that in fifty years Christianity will be professed only by a miserable minority of male bigots and female fools." With the reformer's urgency, Dr. Howe had reached for his pen "to make the public aware of the leprosy that is creeping over the body politic." He demonstrated that Kneeland, "the hoary-headed apostle of Satan," had characterized the rich as tyrants; judges and lawyers as knaves; the clergy as hypocrites; and the Holy Bible as a string of lies. Kneeland also incited class hatreds, counseled a union of farmers and workingmen, railed against property, complained of high

[1] I am indebted to the urbane article by Henry Steele Commager, "The Blasphemy of Abner Kneeland," *New England Quarterly*, 8:29–41 (March 1935), which first broke ground on the Kneeland trial.

prices, derided the sacredness of marriage, and taught sex education.[2]

What made Kneeland a danger was not his views alone, but the fact that his lectures at Boston's Federal Street Theatre attracted throngs of two thousand, and a like number subscribed to his *Investigator*. This periodical, according to a political enemy, was "a lava stream of blasphemy and obscenity which blasts the vision and gangrenes the very soul of the uncorrupted reader."[3] Samuel Parker, who prosecuted Kneeland for the Commonwealth, pointed out that the *Investigator* sold *cheaply* and was favored with a large circulation among the *poor;* and Judge Peter Thacher in Municipal Court, when charging the jury that first convicted Kneeland, warned of fatal consequences should religious restraints disintegrate: no longer would the laboring classes be consoled to their humble position or be respectful of authority.[4]

It was the *Investigator*[5] that got Kneeland into the legal controversy which agitated Massachusetts for four years. Orthodox descendants of the Puritans, erecting their government during the Revolution, had apparently thought it necessary to appease the vanity of God by implementing a constitutional recognition of His existence with an act against blasphemy, passed in 1782. Under this statute, an indictment was brought against the editor of the *Investigator* for having "unlawfully and wickedly" published, on December 20, 1833, a "scandalous, impious, obscene, blasphemous and profane libel" of and concerning God.[6]

The penalties admissible under the anti-blasphemy act justified Kneeland's belief that the indictment recalled witch-hunting days.[7] Any person wilfully blaspheming the name of God by denying Him, or by cursing or contumeliously reproaching Him or

---

[2] Samuel Gridley Howe, "Atheism in New England," *The New England Magazine,* 7:500–509 (December 1834) and 8:53–62 (January 1835).

[3] John Barton Derby, *Political Reminiscences, Including a Sketch of the Origin and History of the "Statesman Party" of Boston* (Boston, 1835), p. 144.

[4] (Samuel D. Parker) *Report of the Arguments of the Attorney of the Commonwealth at the Trials of Abner Kneeland, for Blasphemy, in the Municipal and Supreme Courts, in Boston, January and May, 1834.* Collected and published at the request of some Christians of various denominations (Boston, 1834, 93 pp.), pp. 13 and 16. Thacher's charge is available in John D. Lawson, editor, *American State Trials* (St. Louis, 1921, 20 vols.) XIII, 495–512.

[5] The *Investigator* of Boston, founded by Kneeland in 1831, was the first rationalist periodical in America (Joseph McCabe, editor, *Biographical Dictionary of Modern Rationalists,* London, 1920, p. 405).

[6] Commonwealth v. Kneeland, 20 Pick. 206 ff. (1838).

[7] Letter from Abner Kneeland to Lemuel Shaw, June 1, 1838, Shaw Papers, Boston Social Law Library Manuscript Collection.

any part of the Trinity or the Bible, could be punished "by Imprisonment not exceeding Twelve Months, by sitting in the Pillory, by Whipping, or sitting on the Gallows with a Rope about the Neck, or binding to the good Behaviour, at the discretion of the Supreme Judicial Court." [8]

The indictment contained three counts based on articles published in the *Investigator*. The first count alleged a gutter obscenity relating to the miraculous conception of Christ; the second, an irreverent ridicule of prayer; the third was based on part of a published letter to the editor of the Universalist *Trumpet* — the only article written by Kneeland himself — in which the variations of blasphemy had been contemptuously exhausted. He had written:

1. Universalists believe in a god which I do not; but believe that their god . . . is nothing more than a chimera of their own imagination. 2. Universalists believe in Christ, which I do not; but believe that the whole story concerning him is as much a fable and fiction as that of the god Prometheus. . . . 3. Universalists believe in miracles, which I do not; but believe that every pretension to them is to be attributed to mere trick and imposture. 4. Universalists believe in the resurrection of the dead, immortality and eternal life, which I do not; but believe that all life is material, that death is an eternal extinction of life.[9]

This was evidence enough for the state to conclude that the flag of atheism had been planted in its midst, in preparation for "an exterminating warfare" against Christianity.[10]

The case against the incarnate Robespierre also had a political character. In 1835, John Barton Derby, who had once been "a nut of old Hickory," revealed that Abner Kneeland was a leader of the Democratic radicals:

I assert, as a fact beyond contradiction, that nineteen-twentieths of the followers of Abner Kneeland were and are now Jacksonmen, . . . I venture to declare that if any person will procure the Boston Anti-Bank Memorial, he shall find among its subscribers nearly every man who attends the Infidel orgies at the Federal-street Theatre. I have no doubt that the Infidel party constitutes at least one-third of the Jackson party of the City at this moment. Kneeland is an avowed Jackson-

---

[8] "An Act Against Blasphemy," Mass. St. 1782, ch. 8. The blasphemy laws of the seventeenth century included the death penalty and such grisly means of punishment as boring through the tongue with hot irons.

[9] *American State Trials*, XIII, 453.

[10] Parker, *Report*, p. 60.

man, — and advocated his re-election in his newspaper; the leading men of his society are avowed Jacksonmen, and many of them the most active and influential members of the party.[11]

Appropriately enough, Kneeland was represented by Andrew Dunlap, a high-ranking member of the Massachusetts Democratic Party and formerly state attorney general.[12]

Whiggery had small occasion for regret at the conviction of the *Investigator's* editor by the dozen God-fearing men who sat as a jury in Judge Thacher's court. But only the first of five trials had been completed. Kneeland appealed his cause, and in the spring of 1834, the second trial began before Judge Samuel Putnam of the Supreme Judicial Court. Putnam, like Thacher, was a Whig.

For the Commonwealth, prosecutor Parker, the son of an Episcopal bishop, repeated at the second trial the arguments he had used at the first.[13] He thought it necessary to support the constitutionality of the anti-blasphemy act by defending Christianity from "every . . . enemy who had attacked it," Hobbes, Hume, Gibbon, Voltaire, Rousseau, and Paine included. Christianity, Parker declared, was part and parcel of the state constitution and of the common law; if Jefferson, that "Virginian Voltaire," had believed otherwise, his remarks were an "imbecile dart" at Christianity, proof of his notorious hostility toward it! The trial was not an Inquisition, nor were those "hackneyed topics, the liberty of the press, the liberty of conscience, and freedom of inquiry" at stake. If there was persecution, it came from the defendant against "Religion . . . and the very foundations of civil society." Blasphemy was no lawful exercise of freedom; its repression signified no intolerance. The guarantee of a free press referred simply to political topics.

The article in the *Investigator* relating to the Virgin Birth, Parker thought "too obscene . . . too revolting" to bear discussion. As for the article on prayers, God had been called an "Old Gentleman," indecently and with unbecoming levity, and most irreverently had been compared with President Jackson — any person "one grade above an idiot" could see that God had been exposed to blasphemous derision.

Although Parker argued that Kneeland, as editor, was liable

---

[11] Derby, p. 143.

[12] Derby, pp. 12, 13, 15, 44, and 82. For a sketch of Dunlap, see James Spear Loring, *The Hundred Boston Orators* (Boston, 1853), pp. 504–505.

[13] The following account of Parker's argument is based on the *Report of the Arguments*.

for the first two articles, they had been only reprints from the New York *Free Inquirer*. He made his strongest case on the public letter, arguing that Kneeland had criminally blasphemed by his wilful denial of God, his remarks on the history of the Saviour as a fable, and his reference to miracles as a trick. Fanny Wright and Robert Dale Owen would reproach Kneeland as a renegade if he disavowed his atheism.

Blasphemy, Parker asserted, was but one part of the system introduced by the disciples of Owen and Wright. Not only was atheism to be enthroned, but moral restraints removed, illicit sexual relations encouraged, the laws of property repealed, and the horrible experiments of New Harmony and Nashoba introduced in Boston itself. Kneeland, as Lieutenant-General of this system, sought converts for it among the young and the poor "with a view first to demoralize them, and then to make them apt instruments to root up the foundations of society, and make all property common, and all women as common as brutes." This peddler of obscenity spread "revolutionary and ruinous" principles, among which Parker counted a knowledge of contraceptive methods and the "Physiology of the Female Genital System." This amounted to a "Complete Recipe" for teaching the young "how they could have intercourse with safety and without discovery." Parker also insinuated that the meeting-house of the infidels was little more than a brothel. "I have been informed," he lecherously advised the court, that "there are beds in the Dressing Rooms at the Federal Street Theatre." It was as plain as the shield of morality which he clasped over his righteous breast that he considered Kneeland guilty not merely of blasphemy, but also of lasciviousness, atheism, adultery, communism, and other varieties of "moral and *political* poison." The prosecutor had paraded his imagination before the court and found the defendant guilty by association.

The most conspicuous feature of Judge Putnam's charge,[14] like Judge Thacher's before it — and Judge Wilde's yet to come — was the haze of partiality enveloping it. The jurors made indecent haste to do their duty as requested; all but one lined up on the side of the angels in only ten minutes. As noted by "some friends of religion and law," on whose behalf Parker's arguments were published, "A personal and political friend of the Defendant's Counsel was the dissentient Juror. He did not regularly belong on that Jury, and was put there by means of Mr. Dunlap's

[14] *American State Trials*, XIII, 533–535.

exertions." The dissentient juror was Charles Gordon Greene, Jacksonian editor of *The Morning Post*.[15]

The third trial in November 1834, before Judge Samuel Wilde of the Supreme Judicial Court, also ended in a hung jury.[16] David Henshaw, boss of the Democratic party of Massachusetts, now wrote a pamphlet which exhibited the biased charges in each trial and espoused the cause of civil liberties.

Among all the incidents of awakening interest [Henshaw wrote] which have exacted the action, and called forth the opinion of the public during the past year, there is none which has occurred more vitally affecting, for good or evil, according to its final termination, the civil liberties of the country, than the trial of Abner Kneeland, on an indictment for blasphemy. It strikes at the root of the liberty of conscience, and the freedom of the Press; and involves in its consequences the preservation or the destruction of the free institutions of this country.[17]

But a fourth trial in November 1835, again before Judge Wilde, ended in a conviction.[18]

A sentence of sixty days hung over Kneeland. He had preached God's word for over thirty years, first as a Baptist and long as a Universalist, but he had passed to skepticism and then to free inquiry.[19] He had been called an atheist — what had he not been called! — but he was determined to show the justice of his cause. He would make a final appeal to the full bench of the Supreme Judicial Court.

II

The case of *Commonwealth v. Kneeland* was heard in March 1836. Dunlap was dead. Only one man could act as Kneeland's counsel: himself. He was a scriptural scholar, a carpenter, a minister, a phonetics expert, a legislator, a philosopher, author of common-school spellers, and something of an obstetrician. Why not the advocate of his own cause? He had represented himself at his last trial, and he could do so again before Chief Justice Shaw and the Supreme Judicial Court.

[15] Derby, p. 145.
[16] *American State Trials*, XIII, 536–537, notes.
[17] *Review of the Prosecution Against Abner Kneeland for Blasphemy*. By (David Henshaw) a Cosmopolite (Boston, 1835, 32 pp.), p. 1. See also Andrew H. Ward, "David Henshaw," *Memorial Biographies of the New-England Historic and Genealogical Society* (Boston, 1880–1908, 9 vols.), I, 492.
[18] *American State Trials*, XIII, 575.
[19] William H. Allison, "Abner Kneeland," *Dictionary of American Biography*.

The state was represented by its attorney general, James T. Austin, who had won lasting fame for deprecating the murder of Elijah Lovejoy, and for having accused the seraphic Dr. Channing of inciting insurrection.[20] Austin emulated Parker's argument, forcing Kneeland to complain to the court that "every species of personal abuse . . . which our language could furnish" was heaped upon him.[21]

Kneeland appeared before the court, he said, "like a lofty oak that has braved the storms of more than sixty winters, and yet remains . . . pure as the mountain snow. . . ." He repeated all of Dunlap's arguments and more, first arguing that the charges as recorded in the indictment constituted no offense. Judge Putnam had admitted that even an atheist might propagate his opinions, and Judge Wilde had admitted that the truth of the Scriptures might be denied, although both annexed the condition of speaking decently. Were his crimes, then, merely an offense against delicacy? Yet he had by no means transcended the usual ferocity and extremism of theological controversy — a fact for which he offered proof.

There was no blasphemy in the article on the miraculous conception; the Virgin was not even named in the statute. Moreover, where was the obscenity that had made strong men blench? There was merely a quotation from Voltaire's *Philosophical Dictionary*, which circulated in the respectable Athenaeum and in the Harvard library.[22] If an indelicate word (testicle), derived from a classical language and found in any school dictionary, was regarded by some as obscene — well, shrugged Kneeland, "Evil to him who evil thinks."

There was no blasphemy in that article on prayers. Certain modes of prayers had been satirized, yes, but the Puritans had disparaged prayers, too. Chauncey, the second President of Harvard, had attacked them as a "hell-bred superstition," an ebullition of bitterness not poured forth in the *Investigator*. Why had Christians taken offense at the *Investigator's* satire? "Birds do not generally flutter till they are hit."

Nor was there blasphemy in the public letter he had addressed to the Universalist editor, the count in the indictment

[20] John W. Chadwick, *William Ellery Channing* (Boston, 1903), pp. 277, 285–286.

[21] (Abner Kneeland) *Speech of Abner Kneeland Delivered Before the Full Bench of Judges of the Supreme Court, In His Own Defense, for the Alleged Crime of Blasphemy. Law Term, March 8, 1836* (Boston, 1836, 44 pp.), p. 30.

[22] Voltaire had derided the idea of the Virgin Birth by suggesting the improbability of conception without the intervention of the male genitals.

mainly relied upon by the attorney general. That letter had been written in the mildest of language, without cursing or contumelious reproach. A disbelief in the doctrines of Christianity was not prohibited by the statute. Anyway, Kneeland continued, he had simply expressed a disbelief in the creed of the Universalists, a fact which he sought to prove by an elaborate grammatical analysis of his words, "Universalists believe in a god which I do not . . ." Yet, even if his words should be construed to express a general disbelief in the existence of God, it would not be a *denial* of God within the meaning of the statute. A disbelief is an expression of doubt; a denial is a positive assertion without any doubt; and the statute referred only to wilful denial. "I do say," Kneeland declared, "and shall until my dying breath, I never intended to express even a disbelief in, much less a denial of, God."

Was this Boston's Robespierre speaking, Satan's apostle? In that same letter to the Universalist editor he had written, "I am not an Atheist but a Pantheist." He did believe in God; God was everything, Nature, the Universe. "I believe," he had written, "that it is in God we live, move, and have our being; and that the whole duty of man consists . . . in promoting as much happiness as he can while he lives." [23] Here was a creed as spiritual and benevolent as that of the Transcendentalists!

Having argued that he had not blasphemed even under that law "as cruel as the laws against witchcraft," Kneeland proceeded to argue its unconstitutionality. He proposed that it violated Article II of the Massachusetts Declaration of Rights, which declared that no subject would be restrained "for worshipping God in the manner and season most agreeable to the dictates of his own conscience; or for his religious professions and sentiments." Judge Wilde's instructions in the former trial had stripped Kneeland of this protection by holding that his atheistic denial of God's existence was an *irreligious* profession. Kneeland had appealed his case because of this charge.

To Kneeland, Article II should be interpreted broadly, under the maxim of Jefferson, that "error of opinion may be safely tolerated, when reason is left free to combat it." Here was proclaimed the principle of "universal toleration." His own sentiments, urged the defendant, were religious, not irreligious, but the article protected *all* sentiments respecting religion. If the court could brand his sentiments as irreligious, this

[23] *Speech of Abner Kneeland*, p. 42; *American State Trials*, XIII, 555.

discreditable quibble would destroy the whole object of the provision in the Bill of Rights, leaving it in the power of the Legislature and Courts to harass by penal prosecutions all who might maintain a profession or sentiment in or respecting religion which the Legislature and Courts might choose to consider irreligious.

Conformists were in no danger of being persecuted; Article II was intended for those who needed protection, those who professed unpopular sentiments respecting religion. Concluding, Kneeland said: "I stand on a ground as broad as space, and as firm as the rock of ages; to wit, on the right of conscience, together with the privilege of the freedom of speech and the liberty of the press."

More than two years passed before the Court gave its opinion. But the case was not forgotten. There were men in Massachusetts who valued "the right of conscience." William Lloyd Garrison could recall that when every Christian church in Boston turned him down, Kneeland had offered him the use of his meeting-house. Emerson, working on his Divinity School Address, might have remembered that George Ripley had been censured by the Orthodox for teaching transcendentalism. Theodore Parker knew that George Noyes, the biblical scholar, had once been threatened by Attorney General Austin with prosecution for heresy.[24] Almost all who were given to heterodox ideas — utopians, abolitionists, transcendentalists — balked at using the strong arm of the state to silence Kneeland. In March 1839, Dr. Channing wrote to Ellis Gray Loring, the abolitionist lawyer: "My intention is to see and converse with Judge Shaw on the subject. That a man should be punished for his opinion would be shocking, — an offense at once to the principles and feelings of the community." [25]

III

All was in vain. In April, Chief Justice Shaw delivered the opinion of the Court, sustaining Kneeland's conviction.[26] His opinion did not so much reveal his greatness as it confirmed Richard Henry Dana's observation that Shaw, a conservative Unitarian

[24] *William Lloyd Garrison, 1805–79, The Story of His Life, Told by His Children* (New York, 1885, 4 vols.), II, 142; Henry S. Commager, *Theodore Parker* (Boston, 1936), pp. 64–69; Chadwick, pp. 277, 285–286.
[25] William Henry Channing, *The Life of William Ellery Channing* (Boston, 1899), p. 506.
[26] Commonwealth v. Kneeland, 20 Pick. 206 (1838). Shaw's opinion is at pp. 211–225.

and Whig, was "a man of intense and doting biases." [27] It was no coincidence that the one judge who dissented from Shaw's opinion was Marcus Morton, the only Jacksonian on the bench.

Shaw explained that the delay in handing down the decision was occasioned by the "intrinsic difficulty attending some of the questions raised in the case, and a difference of opinion among the judges." He thought the first question for decision was whether the language of the defendant as set forth in the indictment constituted blasphemy within the meaning of the statute. Blasphemy, wrote Shaw, may be described as

speaking evil of the Deity with an impious purpose to derogate from the divine majesty, and to alienate the minds of others from the love and reverence of God. It is purposely using words concerning God, calculated and designed to impair and destroy the reverence, respect, and confidence due to him . . . It is a wilful and malicious attempt to lessen men's reverence of God.

The offense to be prohibited by the statute was the "wilful denial of God . . . with an intent and purpose to impair and destroy the reverence due to him." The Chief Justice had "no doubt" that Kneeland's public letter amounted to the offense. Although Kneeland had couched his language in the form of a disbelief, "if" he had intended a wilful denial of God's existence, his disbelief constituted a denial. Whether his language was, in fact, used with unlawful intent

was a question upon the whole indictment and all the circumstances, and after verdict, if no evidence was erroneously admitted, or rejected, and no incorrect directions in matter of law were given, *it is to be taken as proved,* that the language was used in the sense, and under the circumstances, and with the intent and purpose, laid in the indictment, so as to bring the act within the statute.[28]

For more than two years this decision had been in the making, and in the end, the fundamental question — had Kneeland blasphemed? — was settled without reasoned consideration; it was "taken as proved" simply by accepting the verdict of guilty. Furthermore, Shaw neglected to determine whether Kneeland was liable for the articles which he had not written. What then had been the purpose of hearing the cause on the "whole indictment and all the circumstances" as the Court itself had ordered

[27] Charles Francis Adams, *Richard Henry Dana* (Boston, 1891, 2 vols.), I, 354.
[28] 20 Pick. 206, 213, 216–217. Italics added.

at the very beginning? All that Shaw had offered was a definition of blasphemy which could meet with no disagreement; Kneeland himself had proposed the same definition to prove that he had committed no offense.[29] Thus far, Shaw's opinion was, and remained, a neatly orchestrated abstraction at no point touching the realities of the case.

The Chief Justice next addressed himself to the argument that the statute was repugnant to the constitution. He cited with approval a decision by Kent that blasphemy was a *common-law* crime not to be abrogated by a constitution carrying the doctrine of unlimited tolerance.[30] Here was an implication that in spite of the state constitution, and whether or not the statute was valid, Kneeland was guilty at common law because Christianity was incorporated therein. Shaw proceeded, however, to examine the provisions of the Massachusetts Declaration of Rights supposedly violated by the statute.

Article XVI provided that "the liberty of the press is essential to the security of freedom in a state; it ought not therefore to be restrained in the Commonwealth." Shaw construed this to mean only that individuals would be at liberty to print, although responsible for the matter printed, without previous permission of any officer of the government. Kneeland's argument relative to the liberty of the press, said Shaw, was best refuted by reformulating it: "every act, however injurious or criminal, which may be committed by the use of language, may be committed with impunity if such language is printed."

Not only would the article in question become a general license for scandal, calumny, and falsehood against individuals, institutions and governments . . . but all incitation to treason, assassination, and all other crimes however atrocious, if conveyed in printed language, would be dispunishable.[31]

There was not the least basis for this characterization of Kneeland's argument. On the contrary, he is officially reported to have said: "I do not contend, however, that a man who slanders his neighbor in print, shall not be answerable for the injury he

[29] *American State Trials,* XIII, 539.

[30] People v. Ruggles, 8 *Johnson's Reports* (New York) 290 ff. (1811). The facts of this case differed from Kneeland's in that Ruggles had blasphemed beyond doubt, by calling Jesus Christ a "bastard" and Mary a "whore." Ruggles' case is discussed in John T. Horton, *James Kent, A Study in Conservatism* (New York, 1939), pp. 188–193.

[31] Commonwealth v. Kneeland, 20 Pick. 206, 210 (1838).

inflicts"; he had only contended that Article XVI guaranteed him the right to propagate his sentiments on religion or on any other subject. Nevertheless, Shaw ruled that Article XVI was no ground for excusing publication of the articles specified in the indictment or for invalidating the statute. Shaw's construction of the article as a mere prohibition of prior restraints upon publication emasculated its guarantee of liberty of the press, by reading into it the very common-law definition of a free press which its framers sought to supplant.

Nor did Shaw find any violation of Article II, which guaranteed religious liberty. The statute merely made it punishable wilfully to blaspheme the name of God. "Wilfully," said Shaw, meant "with a bad purpose"; in this statute, an intent "to calumniate and disparage the Supreme Being." But, Shaw added, the statute did not prohibit the fullest inquiry and freest discussion for "honest" purposes; it did not even prohibit a "simple and sincere avowal of a disbelief in the existence and attributes of God." So construed, the statute did not restrain the profession of any religious sentiments; it was intended merely to punish acts which have "a tendency to disturb the public peace." [32]

This section of the opinion possessed the dubious distinction of ignoring the case at bar of a man who had at worst quoted Voltaire, satirized prayer, and denied God. If the statute did not prohibit free discussion, Kneeland should have been tending his presses instead of anticipating jail. If his purposes were not honest, and if he had disturbed the peace in a manner not protected by the guarantees of civil liberties, then Shaw was evading reasoned judgment on the particulars.

Blasphemy is of course a verbal crime, like libel, in that mere words constitute a criminal act. Nevertheless, it is questionable whether Kneeland committed the crime. Given a statute construed by Shaw to prohibit only "acts" which have a "tendency to disturb the public peace," Kneeland was really convicted for expressing opinions which fell far short of immediate criminal incitement, attempt, or solicitation. The dangers to freedom inherent in a test of remote bad tendency of speech — the test employed by Shaw — were long familiar to civil libertarians in both England and America. For example, Virginia's "Bill for Establishing Religious Freedom," drafted by Jefferson and enacted in 1785, asserts:

[32] *Ibid.*, at 221.

that to suffer the civil magistrate to intrude his powers into the field of opinion and to restrain the profession or propagation of principles, on supposition of their ill tendency is a dangerous fallacy, which at once destroys all religious liberty, because he being of course judge of that tendency will make his opinions the rule of judgment, and approve or condemn the sentiments of others only as they shall square with or differ from his own; that it is time enough for the rightful purposes of civil government for its officers to interfere when principles break out into overt acts against peace and good order . . .[33]

Dr. Phillip Furneaux, the English liberal, also believed that expression should be unfettered until it results in dangerous action. Punishing utterances relating to religion "because of their tendency," would, he predicted, bring religious liberty "entirely at an end . . . Punishing a man for the tendency of his principles, is punishing him before he is guilty, for fear he should be guilty." [34] Shaw's opinion in the Kneeland case was wholly at variance with any true freedom of discussion.

That opinion grieved Judge Morton, a champion of the laboring classes and civil liberties. He regretted that he was driven to lengthy dissent, but he had strong convictions on the matter.[35] He considered as illiberal the view that Article II embraced only religious, as contrasted to irreligious, professions. To Morton the article was a "general proposition" enacted "for the protection of the rights of the people." "Being interwoven in the frame of the government, it was intended to continue in force as long as that should endure. It should . . . receive a liberal construction, unrestrained by the prevailing tenets of any particular time or place." Thus, all beliefs and *disbeliefs* concerning religion were protected to the extent that no individual was responsible to any human tribunal for his opinions on the existence of God; "operations of the human mind especially in the adoption of its religious faith" are "entirely above all civil authority," added Morton. Religious truths did not need the "dangerous aid" of legislation.

The act against blasphemy Morton considered constitutional only when construed not to penalize a mere denial of God. "No one may advocate an opinion which another may not controvert." Criminality depended upon motive, a fact which provided a broad boundary between liberty and license. The denial "must be

---

[33] Preamble to 12 Hening (Va.) *Statutes* 84.

[34] 5 Bl. *Comm.*, App. 34.

[35] Morton's opinion is at 20 Pick. 206, at 225–246. On Morton, see Scott H. Paradise, "Marcus Morton," *Dictionary of American Biography*.

blasphemously done": there must be a denial inspired by corruption and malice for the purpose of injuring others. A wilful denial imparted no crime because "wilful" at worst, meant *obstinately:* "Every person has a constitutional right to discuss the subject of a God, to affirm or deny his existence. I cannot agree that a man may be punished for *wilfully* doing what he has a legal right to do." Morton concluded, "This conviction rests very heavily upon my mind."

The case had closed with a lone opinion that Abner Kneeland had not received justice from the Commonwealth of Massachusetts. But at least the State and Civilization and Religion had been saved — not, however, without converting the central figure into an embittered martyr.

IV

On June 1, 1838, Kneeland wrote a letter to Shaw cruelly attributing the death of his infant son to the severe shock of the mother, as a "consequence of my being again summoned to Court after more than two years silence, to hear the decision and probable sentence which would have left her unprotected in the critical and most trying hour." In spite of his grief, Kneeland informed Shaw, he was as prepared as he ever would be "to undergo the penalty of that barbarous, cruel, absurd law, of witchcraft memory." He wanted it known that he refused to say anything to mitigate his punishment, since his son's death had made him "totally indifferent as to the amount of punishment." He was fortified in the knowledge that

the current of public opinion is turned so much against this odious persecution, that every iota of suffering which I shall have to endure . . . will help the cause in which I am engaged; for which cause, if need be, I am willing to suffer; yea, more willing, if I can understand the account, than was the pattern of christian [*sic*] patience; for even should my agony cause me to sweat blood . . . I shall never offer up the fruitless prayer, "if it be possible let this cup pass from me;" much less would I *blasphemously* say, "My God, my God, why hast thou forsaken me?"

The arrogant letter closed with the information that Kneeland would submit proudly and endure the penalty indignantly, but he requested that his sentence begin early: " 'whatever thou dost, do quickly.' " [36]

---

[36] Kneeland to Shaw, June 1, 1838, Shaw Papers, Boston Social Law Library.

Shaw had delayed entering judgment on the verdict. It was within his power to suspend sentence and bind Kneeland to good behavior, but the latter's letter scarcely stimulated magnanimity. On August 8, Theodore Parker wrote to George Ellis:

. . . Abner was jugged for sixty days; but he will come out as beer from a bottle, all foaming, and will make others foam. . . . The charm of all is that Abner got Emerson's address to the students, and read it to his followers, as better infidelity than he could write himself.[37]

Abner was not jugged, however, without a remonstrance by certain persons who felt strongly about civil liberties.

George Bancroft received from Ellis Gray Loring a copy of a petition in circulation about Boston, which Loring advised he had drawn and Dr. Channing had revised. "Many of the Unitarians and Baptists sign — none of the Orthodox Congregationalists. Garrison and the leading abolitionists sign." The petition requested the Governor to grant Kneeland's unconditional pardon, because, among other reasons,

. . . religion needs no support from penal law . . . opinion should not be subjected to penalties . . . the assumption by government of a right to prescribe or repress opinions has been the ground of the grossest depravations of religion, and of the most grinding despotisms . . . the freedom of speech and the press . . . is never to be restrained by legislation.[38]

Channing's name headed the list, followed by one hundred and sixty-seven others, including Parker, Emerson, Ripley, Garrison, and Alcott.[39] The names read like a "Who's Who" among the reformers — dangerous intellectuals and eccentrics all. What impress could they have made upon Chief Justice Shaw's friend, the Whig Governor Edward Everett, whose Democratic rival in the past four elections had been the Jacksonian dissenter, Marcus Morton? The petition for a pardon, which competed with a counter-petition from the conservative clergy, was rejected. Lemuel Shaw, a minister's son who was too quick to see a "bad purpose" in a man who held "bad views" on religion, has the precarious

[37] Franklin B. Sanborn and William T. Harris, *A. Bronson Alcott: His Life and Philosophy* (Boston, 1893, 2 vols.), I, 281.

[38] Loring's letter to Bancroft is written on the reverse side of a copy of the petition, dated June 13, 1838. Bancroft Papers, Massachusetts Historical Society. The petition is reprinted in Channing, pp. 504-505.

[39] Channing, p. 504, and Allison, p. 457.

honor of having been the last Chief Justice of Massachusetts to have sent a man to prison for blasphemy.

Abner Kneeland served his time. Upon his release from prison, he emigrated, with members of his First Society of Free Inquirers, to the free air of frontier Iowa. There he established an unsuccessful utopian community, "Salubria," and became active in Democratic politics. He died unreconstructed at seventy-one, in 1844, surrounded by portraits of great rationalists and mourned by the child whose name he had suggested, Voltaire Paine Twombly.[40]

[40] On Kneeland's later life, see Mary R. Whitcomb, "Abner Kneeland: His Relations to Early Iowa History," *Annals of Iowa*, Series 3, 6:340–363 (1904), and H. S. Commager "The Blasphemy of Abner Kneeland."

5

THE LAW OF FREEDOM

Emancipating Slaves in Transit

I

As Chief Justice, Shaw defined the law of freedom and bondage in Massachusetts. Before his accession to the bench, when he could freely express himself as an individual, he had with real conviction exercised his outraged sensibilities against slavery. In 1811, while serving his first term as a representative in the General Court, he delivered a discourse on "progress" before the Humane Society of Massachusetts. Alluding to the traffic in human flesh as "one continued series of tremendous crimes," he lauded its abolition as vindicating "the righteous cause of the injured African" and furthering "the cause of humanity." [1] Nine years later, when the nation was agitated by the contest over the admission of Missouri, Shaw contributed an article on the subject to the *North American Review*.[2] This article is important for an understanding of his thought on slavery: even as a judge, he did not waver from the essentials of his stand of January 1820.

Shaw believed that because slavery was a subject affecting the security of the nation, it should be approached "with great calmness and good temper in which the eager pursuit of a desirable end will not blindly overlook the only practicable means in arriving at it." He condemned reproaches upon those who owned slaves and appeals to the passions of those who did not. But his plea for moderation was coupled to a recognition that American profes

---

[1] *A Discourse Delivered Before the Officers and Members of the Humane Society of Massachusetts, 11 June, 1811* (Boston, 1811), p. 11.

[2] "Slavery and the Missouri Question," *The North American Review and Miscellaneous Journal* (Boston), 10:137-168 (Jan. 1820), p. 139.

sions of the "purest principles of natural and civil liberty" were contradicted by practices whereby "a large proportion of human beings are utterly deprived of all their rights." [3]

He then sounded a conservative note: "Slavery, though a great and acknowledged evil, must be regarded, to a certain extent, as a necessary one, too deeply interwoven in the texture of society to be wholly or speedily eradicated." He would not alarm the inhabitants of the slave states. He regarded their condition more in sorrow than in anger, feeling no hostility, uttering no condemnation.

The question whether slavery shall continue in those states, or whether it shall in any way be modified or limited, we consider as exclusively a question of local jurisdiction, belonging to those states respectively: and whatever may be our wishes and hopes on the subject, we expressly disclaim any legal or constitutional authority on the part of any other state or of the United States, to interfere in any arrangements respecting slavery, which those states respectively may think fit to adopt.

Although Shaw portrayed the conditions of the slaves as an abolitionist might, he believed that in states where slavery had long prevailed, a sudden or general emancipation would ruin the community and cause misery to the Negroes. "The principles of self-defense, therefore, and powerful considerations of national safety, constituting a case of political and moral necessity, require at least the continuance of this great evil."

Shaw wanted it remembered, however, that a practice wrong in itself but justified by necessity must be limited to that necessity. He considered it to be the duty of the slave states to provide for liberation as speedily as their internal safety would permit. After emphasizing the dangers of slavery to the prosperity and strength of the nation as a whole, he expressed gratification, not alone for humanitarian reasons, that enlightened men in the slave states had proposed ameliorative measures. He believed that if he were mistaken in thinking that a "safe and gradual abolition" would be achieved, there would be a "great national calamity." After elaborately defending the constitutional power of the national government to prevent the extension of slavery into the territories, he concluded his essay with the thought that the fate of millions of men, plus the fortunes of the American

[3] All quotations, to next footnote, are from "Slavery and the Missouri Question," pp. 138, 141, 143, 145, 147.

republic, would be determined by a settlement of the question.

Shaw's views, which anticipated Lincoln's by three decades, were statesman-like. Although the condition of the South invited his compassion, his faith was vested in the future of freedom. Only his pride and love for the Union exceeded his honest concern for the natural and human rights of slaves; accordingly, the imperatives of national security were given transcendent weight in his scheme of values.

II

Shaw sat as Chief Justice for over two years without hearing a case bearing on the liberty of an alleged slave. Then on December 4, 1832, the case of *Commonwealth v. Howard* [4] came before him for adjudication. A Mrs. Howard, whose permanent residence was in Cuba, had brought with her to Massachusetts a Negro boy named Francisco, "12 or 14 years of age," whom she had purchased as a slave in Havana. Certain persons, probably abolitionists, eagerly desired the Court to agree that under no circumstances could the taint of slavery even for a moment infect a free Commonwealth.

A writ of habeas corpus was issued against Mrs. Howard in order to have the boy brought before the Court, and Samuel Eliot Sewall, Corresponding Secretary of the New England Anti-Slavery Society, was retained to argue his freedom. The defendant declared that she did not claim Francisco as a slave, that he was free and only her servant. To this plea, witnesses were produced who testified that Mrs. Howard had held the youth as a slave in Cuba, and in Massachusetts had referred to him as her property. "The evidence," reported the *Daily Atlas,* "was strong to show that Mrs. Howard intended, or had intended until this *habeas corpus* was brought, to claim him as her slave in Havana, on her return there." It was the Court's duty, claimed Sewall, to interfere so that the lad would be saved from a return to slavery.

Both parties actually agreed on the most important point: Francisco was free. They differed on the reasons for his freedom and on whether he should return with the defendant or be remanded to a guardian appointed by the Court.

[4] This case is unreported in the official reports of the Court. Its title has been surmised from the facts as given in the fullest account found, that of the Boston *Daily Atlas* for Dec. 5, 1832, which was copied verbatim by many other journals, including such diverse ones as *The Liberator* (Boston), Dec. 8, 1832, and *The American Jurist and Law Magazine,* 9:490–492 (1832).

Under the circumstances, Shaw did the most simple and sensible thing: he examined Francisco privately to determine his personal wishes, and the boy told the Chief Justice that he desired to remain with Mrs. Howard. In his opinion, Shaw recognized that a question of "great importance" was before the Court, because the writ of habeas corpus, he said, was intended for the protection of personal liberty. His decision was summarized by the *Daily Atlas* as follows:

If Mrs. Howard, in her return to the writ, had claimed the boy as a slave, I should have ordered him to be discharged from her custody. But it appears from her return to the writ, that she does not claim him as a slave. The boy, by the law of Massachusetts, is in fact free; and Mrs. Howard having by her return to the writ, disclaimed to hold him as a slave, has made a record of his freedom, and cannot make him a slave again in the Island of Cuba.

From the imperfect account available it appears that Shaw had every intention of freeing the boy had he been claimed as a slave. The importance of the case lies in its doctrine, based on the illegality of slavery in Massachusetts,[5] that a slave, brought to that state by his master, might have his status transformed from one of bondage to one of freedom. By this opinion, Shaw cast from an old rule a new mold for the law of freedom in Massachusetts.

III

The last week of August 1836 presented a more favorable opportunity for Shaw to advance the principles of a free society. There came before the Court the case of *Commonwealth v. Aves*,[6] involving the liberty of a six-year-old slavegirl, Med. Although the abolitionists applauded Shaw's decision, he probably greeted their praise with stony disdain. Yet the effect of the decision made it an anti-slavery document.

The case presented a wholly novel situation in Commonwealth history, and in point of law was without precedent in any state or federal reports. A white woman, Mary Slater, whose home was

[5] In Commonwealth v. Jennison, the Quork Walker case, 1783, it was held, *per* Cushing, C. J., that slavery was illegal in Massachusetts because it was repugnant to the Declaration of Rights of the state constitution. *Proceedings*, Massachusetts Historical Society, 2nd ser., 13:292–294 (1871). This 1783 opinion concerned only permanent residents of Massachusetts who were claimed as slaves; it did not govern the status of temporary residents.
[6] 18 Pick. 193 (1836).

in New Orleans, had come to Boston on a vacation, bringing Med with her. The little girl was by the law of Louisiana a slave owned by Mr. Slater. While in Boston, she was kept in the custody of Thomas Aves, Mrs. Slater's father. A writ of habeas corpus was sued out at the instigation of parties interested in having her declared free, principally the Boston Female Anti-Slavery Society. Aves, acting as Slater's legal agent, made the return on the writ and stated the causes of the child's confinement.

The precise question at issue was: can a slave, brought into Massachusetts by a citizen of a slave-holding state on a temporary visit, be restrained of his liberty while in Massachusetts and be taken out of the state against his consent, on the return of the master?

The law in such a case was undecided. Federal courts and state courts, even in the South, had ruled that the permanent removal of a slave to a free state liberated him from bondage. In 1822, a Pennsylvania court declared the slave Hannah Hall to be free "the moment her mistress brought her (from the District of Columbia) into Pennsylvania to reside."[7] The decisions in Mississippi, Virginia, and Louisiana were even more forceful on the point.[8] These Southern courts held that the right to freedom acquired by residence in a state whose laws forbade involuntary servitude was not forfeit even by return or by forcible removal to a slave state. The distinction between Med's case and the others cited is sharp. Mrs. Slater had acquired no domicile in Boston, and she clearly avowed her intention to take Med back to New Orleans with her. Consequently, Shaw had to decide a novel question: what was the status of a slave brought only *temporarily* into a free state?

Both parties to the dispute were represented by distinguished legal talent. For the Commonwealth, in support of the writ, the principal argument was made by Ellis Gray Loring, an officer in the Massachusetts Anti-Slavery Society, who jeopardized his social standing by his habit of pleading unpopular causes. Loring was aided by Rufus Choate and Samuel E. Sewall. For the slaveholder, young Benjamin Robbins Curtis, later famed for his dissent in

[7] Commonwealth *ex. rel.*, Hall v. Cook, 1 Watts Pa. Rep. 155 (1822). See also the decision by Bushrod Washington in *Ex Parte* Simmons, 4 Wash. C.C. Rep. 396 (1823).

[8] Harry *et al.* v. Decker and Hopkins, Walker's Miss. Rep. 36 (1818); Griffith v. Fanny, Gilmer's Va. Rep. 143 (1820); Lunsford v. Coquillon, 14 Martin's La. Rep. 401 (1824).

the Dred Scott case, upheld the right of property in slaves.[9] His partner and relative, C. P. Curtis, also represented the defendant. The efforts of counsel in this case received august commendation. Joseph Story, acknowledging receipt of a printed copy of the case, wrote to Loring: "I have rarely seen so thorough and exact arguments as those made by Mr. B. R. Curtis and yourself. They exhibit learning, research and ability of which any man may be proud." [10]

The case was heard on August 21, from nine in the morning till nearly seven that evening, with only an hour and a half recess for dinner. Benjamin R. Curtis maintained that comity between states of the Federal Union compelled legal effect to be given to Louisiana laws and institutions, regardless of their inconsistency with Massachusetts policy. Lord Mansfield's great decision in Sommersett's case[11] was inapplicable, he argued, by reason of this peculiar and intimate relationship among sister American states. Reminding the judges of the full bench that their opinions "as men or as moralists" were without bearing on the question, he ventured that the Court's decision should be based on what *the law* deemed moral or immoral. The Court could hardly deny to a master the limited right claimed, on ground that slavery was immoral, when at any moment it might be called upon by an owner of a fugitive slave to grant a certificate, under the United States Constitution, which would put the entire force of the state at his disposal to remove his slave. Curtis also pointed out that New York, Pennsylvania, New Jersey, and Rhode Island gave statutory permission to masters to carry their slaves with them when visiting.[12]

A week later, the Chief Justice gave the opinion of the unanimous Court, freeing Med. Pending appointment of a probate guardian, she was remanded to the custody of the law.[13] As a judicial decision bearing on a quasi-political issue, Shaw's was a diplomatic performance. He managed to voice northern opinion resolutely, but without rebuke to the South. With a like

[9] In his dissent, Justice Curtis reversed his 1836 position and stated and followed Shaw's decision in this case. Scott v. Sanford, 19 How. 393, 564, 591 (1857).

[10] Wm. W. Story, *Life and Letters of Joseph Story* (Boston, 1851, 2 vols.), II, 235.

[11] 20 Howell's *State Trials* 1 (1772). Sommersett was freed by Mansfield when his master, a Virginian, brought him to England.

[12] 18 Pick. 193, 195–201.

[13] She was later adopted by Isaac Knapp, publisher of *The Liberator*. See issue of Oct. 15, 1836.

calm, he attended carefully to the intricacies of comity so as not to afford a sensitive section reason to think its legal rights were being impaired.

After stating the case, Shaw sketched the history of slavery in Massachusetts, concluding that by the constitution and laws of the Commonwealth, slavery was illegalized "upon the ground that it is contrary to natural right and the plain principles of justice." Evidence of the point he derived, in part, from a literal reading of Article I of the 1780 Massachusetts Declaration of Rights, which pronounced the free and equal status of all men by birth. He thought it would be difficult "to select words more precisely adapted to the abolition of negro slavery" — surely a reading persuaded by strong Yankee predilections.[14]

Because slavery had no legal status in Massachusetts, it was necessary to determine what respect could be meted out to claims from communities that validated the institution. For the best authorities,[15] he asserted, held that slavery is not contrary to the law of civilized nations; nor indeed was it proper for one state to treat the laws of another as void because they were contrary to its own views of morality and policy. Yet slavery was so odious that it could not be introduced and sustained except by positive law. This was especially so since it was a relation founded in brute force, not in right.

What then was to be made of the argument that rights in personal property, acquired by the local law of domicile, follow the owner everywhere, in accord with the comity of nations? Such rights, said the Chief Justice, were severely limited. They pertained "only to those commodities which are everywhere and by all nations, treated and deemed subjects of property." But slavery was based on mere local or municipal law, and speaking "with strict accuracy," it was not correct to say "that a property can be acquired in human beings," even by local laws.[16] These laws, while they might operate within their own jurisdiction, could not operate in full vigor out of that jurisdiction.

As a result of this reasoning, Shaw ruled out application of the law arising from the comity among nations. For if comity applied, the consequences would have been inadmissible, as he pointed out. Slavery would extend to every place where slaves

[14] 18 Pick. 193, 210.

[15] Shaw cited Marshall in the case of the *Antelope*, 10 Wheaton 121 (1822) and Mansfield in Sommersett's case (*supra*, note 11).

[16] 18 Pick. 193, 216; quotes following are at pp. 218, 217, 219, 221.

might be carried. Masters might bring their slaves into Massachu setts and exercise over them all the rights and powers of property owners "for any length of time . . ." — an application of the law "wholly repugnant to our laws, entirely inconsistent with our policy and our fundamental principles. . . ."

It was a general rule, Shaw stated, that all persons arriving within the limits of a state became subject to all its municipal laws and were entitled to such privileges as those laws conferred. The rules applied "as well as to blacks as whites," he declared, so far as concerned Massachusetts:

. . . if such persons have been slaves, they become free, not so much because any alteration has been made in their *status,* or condition, as because there is no law which will warrant, but there are laws, if they choose to avail themselves of, which prohibit their forcible detention or forcible removal.

The one exception to this rule was in the case of fugitives. Nevertheless, Article IV, section 2, of the United States Constitution, providing for the return of escaped slaves, together with the Fugitive Slave Law of 1793, could not be construed to apply to the case of a slave who had not fled, but had been brought into Massachusetts by his master. The force of the Constitution and laws of the United States on the subject of fugitives must be limited to the plain meaning and intent of the language used.

Shaw insisted that this strict construction of the clause on fugitives protected the owners of slaves. While certain "overzealous philanthropists" might contend that the article in the federal Constitution and the laws made pursuant to it were not binding because they were contrary to natural right, he could not perceive the force of the objection. He had already shown that slavery was not contrary to the law of nations, and could be the proper subject of agreement among sovereign states. The clause in question was introduced into the Constitution as a result of compromise in the Convention of 1787. It was intended "to secure future peace and harmony," said Shaw. But it was also intended "to fix as precisely as language could do it, the limit to which the rights of one party should be exercised within the territory of the other. Thus national law required the states to return slaves only in cases of escape. Upon such reasoning, Shaw offered the Court's opinion that a master voluntarily bringing a slave into Massachusetts had no authority to detain him against his will, or to carry him out of the state against his consent, for the purpose of holding him in slavery.

Shaw had picked his words with caution, because the constitutional issues he grappled with were not only combustible, but perplexing. He settled the legal status of slavery in Massachusetts, ruled on comity as it pertained to slavery, and construed the Fugitive Slave Law — in each instance his judgment approached impeccability. While his opinions as an individual perceptibly suggested the disposition of the case, they were shrouded by his solemn effort to decide fairly and in harmony with known legal principles.

The "rational, just and noble decision of this eminent judge" thrilled Garrison and his "overzealous philanthropists." [17] But only they would describe the decision as having effected for Massachusetts Cowper's metaphysical transformation:

> Slaves cannot breathe in England; if their lungs
> Receive our air, that moment they are free,
> They touch our country, and their shackles fall.

If the shackles fell from a slave brought to Massachusetts, it was not because he trod upon free soil and inhaled free air, but only because there was no law in the Commonwealth by which the master might restrain him of his liberty. Moreover, Shaw had offered the dictum that if a slave waived the protection afforded by the laws of Massachusetts, his condition was unchanged. Shaw also made it evident that he had every intention of enforcing the Fugitive Slave Law if the occasion to do so arose. Yet he had candidly condemned property in human beings, and so Charles Sumner praised the judiciary, "always pure, fearless, and upright," for having inflicted the "brand of reprobation upon slavery." [18]

On the basis of the sampling of press opinion quoted in *The Liberator*, the newspaper response to the decision seems to have been sectional. Northern journals cheered the opinion, though there were some sour editorials which worried over the Court's light concern for property, and feared Southern reactions. One of these, the Boston *Columbian Centinel*, called the decision "the MOST IMPORTANT" ever made in any one of the free states. On the whole, Southern opinion divided only in its degree of

[17] *The Liberator*, Sept. 24, 1836. See also, for other press opinion, the issues of Sept. 3, Oct. 8, Oct. 15, and Oct. 22, 1836.
[18] Sumner's *Complete Works* (Boston, 1900, 20 vols.), I, 308.

disapprobation, although the Louisville *Advertiser* sensibly saw nothing in the decision "to irritate or alarm the South"; its editor expressed wonderment at the way the Supreme Judicial Court of Massachusetts "has been so bitterly and harshly condemned." The Baltimore *Chronicle* fumed over judicial confiscation of property and declared that whereas the Constitution had provided for the restoration of slaves fleeing from one state to another, "the decision of Chief Justice Shaw virtually annuls this security . . ." Irrationality reached a pitch in the deep South. The Augusta *Sentinel,* for example, editorializing on the "outrage of Southern Rights," exclaimed that the Union was worthless if its members were able to destroy the right of private property and to deprive the people of the South "of what is justly theirs." "This is the strongest and boldest step ever yet taken against the rights of the South, and leaves the puny efforts of the abolitionists at an immeasurable distance in the rear," the paper trumpeted, as it demanded of Southerners whether they would submit to the outrage. One New England journal, the *Hampshire Republican,* in a reply which defended Massachusetts against such tirades, wondered if Southerners had not been hypocritical about their devotion to state's rights.

IV

By his opinion in Med's case, Chief Justice Shaw had established a monumental precedent in law, and the antislavery party was not lax in taking advantage of its liberality. Through their efforts, a number of actions were brought and won to secure the liberty of slaves whose masters had voluntarily carried them to Massachusetts.[19] Invariably Shaw employed the rule that such slaves became free because slavery was local and liberty general.

In cases like Francisco's,[20] where the master not only disclaimed chattel ownership, but admitted the individual's right to freedom and consented to his voluntary decision to return South or remain in Massachusetts, it was Shaw's custom to retire to his private chambers with the person, inform him of the fact of his freedom, and ascertain his choice as to his future. Shaw first satisfied himself, however, that the former slave was intelligent

[19] See Anne v. Eames (1836), *Report of the Holden Slave Case,* Holden Anti-Slavery Society pamphlet (1839); Commonwealth v. Ludlum, *New Bedford Mercury* as excerpted in *The Liberator,* Aug. 31, 1841; Commonwealth v. Porterfield, *Law Reporter* 7:256 ff. (Boston, Aug., 1844); Commonwealth v. Fitzgerald, *Law Reporter* 7:379 ff. (Dec., 1844); and "Betty's Case," *Law Reporter* 20:455 ff. (Nov. 1857).

[20] Commonwealth v. Howard. See note 4, *supra.*

enough to judge his own interests.[21] In the case of Anson, an eight-year-old Negro boy, the Chief Justice ruled that the consent of so young a child would not authorize his removal from a free state to one where he would again be held in slavery.[22] The apparent distinction between this case and Med's was that the claimant did not insist that property rights in Anson authorized his removal as a slave; instead, she agreed to acknowledge the child's will in the matter. Shaw rejected the distinction because "a child of such tender years has no will, no power of judging . . . his will and choice are to be wholly disregarded." Little Anson was discharged from the custody of his mistress and given over to the care of guardians appointed by the Probate Court. "The Supreme Court of our Commonwealth," reported the Massachusetts Anti-Slavery Society, "to its honor be it told, has made an advance . . . on the decision in the Med case, and that in regard to a point of considerable practical importance. Nothing is more common than for the wives of slaveholders to bring with them from the South young slaves, as attendants during their Northern tours." [23]

In 1844, the Chief Justice pushed to its limits the logic of his opinion in Med's case, by an unreported decision affecting the status of slave seamen in the service of the United States Navy.[24] Robert Lucas, a Negro, was taken from the frigate *United States,* commanded by Captain Stribling, and brought before Shaw at chambers by a writ of habeas corpus. At the hearing it appeared that Lucas' Virginia master, Fitzgerald, a purser in the navy, had obtained authority from the Secretary of the Navy to take his slave with him on duty. Lucas had been entered on the muster roll of the frigate as a landsman at nine dollars a month; his wages went to his master. At sea, where he was under Stribling's command, he waited on Fitzgerald as a servant, in accord with usual naval practice. After a Pacific voyage, the *United States* returned on orders to Boston, her first American port of entry. Two shipmates of Lucas informed Shaw that the slave

[21] In one case, Commonwealth v. Porterfield, *Law Reporter* 7:256 ff. (1844), the freedman elected to enjoy his liberties in Boston rather than return with his former master to New Orleans, even though his parents were there. Yet in "Betty's Case," *Law Reporter* 20:455 ff. (1857), Betty admitted strong attachment to her owners and preferred to return with them to Tennessee where her husband lived.

[22] Commonwealth v. Taylor, 3 Metc. 72 (1841).

[23] *Eleventh Annual Report, Presented to the Massachusetts Anti-Slavery Society, by its Board of Managers* (Boston, 1843), p. 46.

[24] Commonwealth v. Fitzgerald, *Law Reporter,* 7:379 ff. (1844).

desired freedom, and they gave the information under which the writ issued.

Benjamin F. Hallett, for the purser and the captain, argued against Lucas' freedom, making much of the contention that this case was not covered by the Med decision, in which Shaw had pointedly refused to give an opinion in regard to a slave brought to Massachusetts *involuntarily* by the master because of "accident or necessity . . . remaining no longer than necessary." [25] Defense also argued the obligation of a contract: Lucas' enlistment into the service of the United States, in Virginia, was by the law of that state a contract that could not be invalidated when he left its limits and involuntarily entered Massachusetts.

In an "elaborate opinion," [26] Shaw ruled that while enlistment was a contract, slaves cannot be enlisted in the United States Navy because ". . . none but a free person can enter into a contract." The United States might contract for the employment of a slave, but acquired no greater rights over the slave than the master himself had. So, declared Shaw, even if the government's contract with the purser was initially valid,

yet as slavery is local, the instant the frigate went out of Virginia, the slave became free, and Fitzgerald's authority over him as master ceased, and of course the authority of the United States over him, which depended on Fitzgerald's, ceased at the same time.

To defense's disclaimer of voluntarily bringing Lucas to a free state, Shaw replied that by putting him aboard a United States vessel, Fitzgerald had consented to his slave's being carried anywhere the ship might be sent.[27] Discharging Lucas from the service of both his master and the federal government, Shaw concluded with a precise and sweeping formulation of the law on the subject at issue: "Where a slave is in Massachusetts casually, not being a runaway, whether he is brought here voluntarily by his master or not, there is no law here to authorize his restraint." [28]

These words clearly show that the Chief Justice was prepared to insure the freedom of any slave, not a fugitive, who reached

[25] Commonwealth v. Aves, 18 Pick. 193, 225 (1836).
[26] *Law Reporter* 7:380 ff. p. 382.
[27] In a recent case, Shaw had ruled that a master, putting a slave aboard a private vessel bound for Trinidad, gave legal consent to that slave's being brought to Boston, when so brought by the ship's captain who was the master's agent (Commonwealth v. Porterfield, *Law Reporter* 7:256 ff., 1844).
[28] *Law Reporter*, 7:380 ff., p. 382.

his Commonwealth. The opinion is also noteworthy because in effect it served notice on *all* sea captains, not just naval officers, that they possessed no legal claim to the services of slaves in their crews — at least, not within the jurisdiction of Massachusetts where Shaw could enforce the law of freedom. "This decision," reported the *Boston Post,* "greatly enlarges all the previous decisions in similar cases and may be regarded as limiting the claim of the master strictly to the case of a fugitive." [29]

Med's case was the leading one in a group beginning with Francisco's and ending with Lucas'. In none of these cases was the Chief Justice constrained by statute or precedent to decide as he did: by his opinions he made and defined the law. In each of these cases he set free a human being. All the opinions were given several years before the sectional controversy over the extraterritorial operation of the law of property in slaves had assumed its violent character in the 1850's. None of them involved the status of fugitive slaves.

[29] Quoted in *The Liberator,* Oct. 18, 1844.

6

THE FUGITIVE SLAVE LAW

Remanding Runaways

I

The fugitive-slavery issue was freighted with perils to the nation. Shaw's thought on the subject was filled with apprehension for the security and harmony of the Union. He was earnestly a man of peace who would not consciously aggravate a situation offering the menace of a "great national calamity." To persons of like sensibilities, the histrionics of extremists, who rasped unceasingly on the sinful nature of slavery, were exasperating. In October 1835, two months after conservatives in a mass meeting at Faneuil Hall had apologized to the South for the abolitionism in Boston, a mob of several thousands, including many "gentlemen" from State and Milk Streets, stormed a meeting of the Boston Female Anti-Slavery Society, cowed the defenseless praying women, and nearly lynched William Lloyd Garrison. A quietus on agitation was devoutly wished by persons of standing. Frenzied provocateurs, vowing obedience not to law and order and the Constitution, but to an unwritten "higher law" of conscience, endangered the political stability that came from allegiance to the sound nationalist doctrines of Marshall and Webster. Article IV, section 2, of the United States Constitution had provided for the return of fugitive slaves, and Congress had passed the Act of 1793 to that end. As a judge, Shaw felt duty-bound to enforce the Constitution as law regardless of whatever moral twinges he may have experienced. When the abolitionists hurled their barbs at him, they aimed at a man who reluctantly regarded the return of runaways as a legal necessity.

II

It was not until 1842 that the first bona fide case of a fugitive slave came before Shaw; but in 1836 there occurred a case that clearly indicated his desire to avoid giving effect to the Fugitive Slave Act unless the facts at issue presented no other recourse. In August 1836, Philadelphians reading about the new slave case in Boston learned that two fugitives had been rescued in the very presence of the Supreme Judicial Court of Massachusetts — an insult "without parallel in the history of that state."

Even the insurgents in Shays' rebellion were polite and courtly in comparison with the mob in the present case. — One might expect the very bodies of Parsons, Dana, and Parker to rise out of their graves and reprove the lawless spirit of the times for such an outrage against the majesty of the laws. Truly we are fallen upon evil days when such things can be perpetrated, — and with impunity. The most strenuous assertions . . . can offer no apology for this barefaced insult to the laws of Massachusetts and the Constitution of the United States.[1]

The monstrous event that caused a thrill of outrage to run down editors' spines occurred on a Monday, the first day of the month, before Chief Justice Shaw himself. On the preceding Saturday, the brig *Chickasaw*, Henry Eldridge, Captain, had sailed into Boston harbor carrying two Negro passengers, Eliza Small and Polly Ann Bates. Both women had with them legal documents as proof of their free status. While the *Chickasaw* lay in the stream, she was boarded by one Matthew Turner who represented himself to the captain as the agent of John B. Morris, a wealthy slave-holder of Baltimore. The women were asserted by Turner to be fugitives from Morris' service. At this point in the story, contemporary versions differ. Two newspapers, both of which voiced the politics of the State Street merchants, agreed that the women "freely admitted that they were the property of Mr. Morris, and gave him (Turner) reasons for making their escape." [2] That they carried evidence of their freedom was not mentioned by either paper. Another journal carried the information that Turner, on being shown such evidence by one of them, "pocketed it and refused to return it." [3] The inimitable *Liberator* reported on August 13: "We learn that Turner, the woman catcher, when he

---

[1] The *National Gazette*, Philadelphia, quoted in the *Columbian Centinel* (Boston), Aug. 9, 1836. Dana, Parsons, and Parker were Shaw's predecessors. The account here of the case of Commonwealth v. Eldridge, which was not reported by Pickering, the court reporter, has been reconstructed by piecing together versions from several Boston newspapers for the week beginning August 1, 1836. The papers used are the *Daily Evening Transcript, The Liberator,* and the *Columbian Centinel,* which also carried long excerpts from the *Mercantile Journal.*

[2] *Mercantile Journal,* Aug. 1; see also the *Columbian Centinel,* Aug. 2.

[3] *Daily Evening Transcript,* Aug. 1.

first met his intended victims on board the vessel pretended to be very friendly, and under the assumed name of James Wilson, by his professions of friendship obtained the free papers of one of the women." Failing to get the papers of the other woman by this ruse, continued *The Liberator,* Turner disclosed his real identity and design. Eliza and Polly Ann, hearing that they were to be forcibly returned, broke down; whereupon "the *kindhearted* and *pious* kidnapper read to them from the Bible for their consolation . . ." Thus, from the evidence, it is not clear whether the women were fugitives or whether they were the victims of a mean plot by their former master to repossess them.

In any case, Captain Eldridge detained his passengers on the brig at the request of Turner until the latter obtained a warrant for their arrest as escaped slaves. News of the events on the *Chickasaw* quickly circulated. A large and excited group of Negroes collected on the wharf. During Turner's absence, a Negro citizen appeared before Chief Justice Shaw and secured a writ of habeas corpus directed against Eldridge, forcing him to release the unfortunate women pending a hearing on the question of his authority to hold them in restraint. Deputy Sheriff Huggerford, who served the writ, found the women in a state of agitation, locked in their cabin. One of them, a mulatto of about thirty, upon learning that friendly proceedings had been instituted, burst into tears, crying that "She knew God would not forsake her and send her back to the South." [4]

Shaw was no longer available in Court that same afternoon, and on the technical objection that the writ had been signed by him, Justice Wilde postponed the hearing till nine o'clock the following Monday morning. As the Court opened that August first, the Chief Justice took the bench, sitting alone. Spectators, mostly Negroes, packed the room. The few whites present were, in the main, abolitionists concerned with the freedom of two of God's children. If there were any in the audience friendly to the cause of Eldridge or the slaveowner's agent, they were lost in a sea of sympathizers for the alleged slaves.

On the basis of the writ and the return to it by Eldridge, the question before the Court was restricted to the captain's right to detain the women. The arguments of counsel, however, ranged further afield, into the constitutional issue over fugitive slavery. A. H. Fiske, on behalf of the captain, read an affidavit by Turner, who was present in court, to the effect that the women were the

[4] *Daily Evening Transcript,* Aug. 1.

property of the Baltimore citizen whom he represented. Then Fiske launched into a defense of the Fugitive Slave Law of 1793, under which the claim to the women was made. He moved for a postponement of the hearing so that evidence might be brought from Baltimore to prove that they were slaves. Samuel Eliot Sewall, the abolitionist lawyer so frequently a volunteer on behalf of any Negro's liberty, addressed the Court in opposition to the motion. He argued that Eldridge had no claim to the women, that all human beings were free-born and had a natural right to the enjoyment of their liberties. When he had finished, the larger part of the audience, much excited, burst into applause.

The Chief Justice, rising to give his opinion, stated the issue simply: "Has the captain of the brig *Chickasaw* a right to convert his vessel into a prison?" [5] He decided that the defendant had not the least right to hold the women. They had been detained in his custody in a most unlawful manner, since he in no way brought himself within the provisions of the federal statute of 1793. Shaw concluded his opinion by saying "the prisoners must therefore be discharged from all further detention." [6]

Turner, the agent, then arose and implied that he would make a fresh arrest under the provisions of the Fugitive Slave Law, and he inquired of the Court whether a warrant would be necessary for that purpose.[7] At the same moment a constable was sent to lock the door leading downstairs. These actions created a wave of excitement among the spectators. The general impression was that the slave-hunter was about to make a fresh seizure right on the spot, even though the prisoners appeared to have been discharged by the Chief Justice.

Tension charged the air for a moment. Before Shaw could answer Turner, word was passed to the women informing them that they were discharged and advising that they clear out before the agent got them again. "The Court room now exhibited one of the grossest outrages of public justice that we have ever before witnessed." Could the respectable property owners in State Street have had foreknowledge of the violence that broke loose the next moment, "five-hundred men could have been rallied to the Court . . . prepared to sustain the supremacy of the laws." Someone called to the people in the room, "Take them." A chant of "Go —

[5] *Right and Wrong in Boston in 1836* (Third) *Annual Report of the Boston Female Anti-Slavery Society* (Boston, 1836), p. 51.

[6] *Daily Evening Transcript*, Aug. 1.

[7] In Commonwealth v. Griffith, 2 Pick. 11, 18 (1822), Parker, C. J., upholding the Act of 1793, had ruled that seizure might be made without a warrant.

go!" rang out. Instantly, the tumult broke: the spectators, both white and colored, turned into a disorderly mob, rushed over the benches, and stormed down the aisle toward Eliza and Polly Ann. Shaw protested, "Stop, stop," but the mob tore on, yelling "Don't stop." Shaw climbed down out of his bench and endeavored vainly to hold the door against them. Huggerford, the only officer in the room, was grabbed, throttled, and "maltreated to the peril of his life." The crowd, bearing away the prisoners, disappeared through the private passageway of the judiciary and dashed down the stairs of the Court House. In Court Square, the fugitives were shoved into a carriage and driven out of the city, followed for a short distance by the screaming mob. Huggerford and a posse took up the pursuit. The carriage crossed over Mill Dam — where toll money was thrown out while the horses were driven at a gallop — and was gone.[8]

The story of the shocking rescue was a sensation in Boston's newspapers. The *Columbian Centinel* excoriated the seditious "Abolition Riot," and estimated that ninety percent of the public shared its views. "A Friend of the Union," in a letter to the editor, wrote heatedly that if a few fanatics and Negroes were suffered to browbeat and put down the highest tribunals of the nation, "then adieu to its peace and union." Only exemplary punishment of the leaders and abettors of the mob, stated the writer, would "satisfy our Southern brethren, and convince them that their *rights* and *property* will be protected, at least here in New England . . ."[9] But the fugitives were never recaptured; nor were their rescuers ever brought to trial, because, most curiously, no one came forward to identify any of them. The editor of the merchants' paper sputtered furiously:

The prisoners have been forcibly rescued, at noonday, from our highest court, sitting in the heart of a populous city. The outrage was committed by a mob of several hundreds, and after three days search, neither the prisoners nor one of the rioters have been arrested. Is there no person who was present who can identify one of the offenders? Could such a scene be enacted, and the Chief Justice be assailed *vi et armis* (with force of arms!) in the face of day, and in open court, and no person be able to detect one of a hundred? The case has not its parallels in the annals of crime . . . All the money in the Treasury is but as dross compared to the importance of sustaining the dignity and supremacy of the public tribunals in whom depend

[8] *Mercantile Journal*, August 1, 2, 3.
[9] *Columbian Centinel*, Aug. 3.

not only the rights and peace of the citizens, but the very existence of the state.[10]

It was generally agreed that a monstrous event had happened for which Garrisonism was somehow responsible.

But only *The Liberator* carried the story that only two days after the "Abolition Riot" occurred, the Massachusetts Anti-Slavery Society had held a special meeting, during which resolves were voted expressing on the part of the members their "deep regret and decided disapprobation." *The Liberator* (August 6) also made clear its disapproval of the tumultuous conduct of the persons involved. The "incident" was an "unjustifiable" one, but the abolitionist society and the organ of the cause agreed that it was "not unpardonable," because it developed out of ignorance and misapprehension. It is true that the mob and Sewall, who was censured for "instigating" it,[11] deserve exculpation from accusation of having planned a "rescue," that is, of having conspired to seize the prisoners from the custody of the law. The event was unforeseeable, and the friendly audience acted under the impulse of fear to get the women out of the clutches of the slave hunter *after,* it was thought, they had been released by Shaw.

The Chief Justice himself seems to have recovered his judicial composure almost at once. In spite of his active part in trying to quell the outbreak, there was, fortunately, no report of his having been physically abused. On August first, the *Daily Evening Transcript* said: "The Judge stated that they (the women) must be brought back to be regularly discharged in open court"; but two days later informed its readers that "the Chief Justice considers the prisoners as *virtually discharged* — " and regarded the disturbance as one that could not reasonably have been anticipated. Judge Wilde, his associate, was of the same opinion.

Shaw, it should be noted, had not only refused, under the facts of the case, to allow the alleged fugitives to be held at the agent's pleasure; he had not granted a postponement of the hearing as requested, so that evidence could be brought from Baltimore to prove that they were the property of Morris. Obviously Shaw was disinclined to enforce the Fugitive Slave Law except in a case of unavoidable necessity. His opinion was based on the facts as legally brought: not on a claim to the women by Turner,

[10] *Ibid.,* Aug. 5.
[11] *Ibid.,* Aug. 3.

but on their unlawful detention by Eldridge. Shaw never had an opportunity to reply to Turner's request for a warrant to make a new arrest, for it was at that moment that the wild rush began. The *Mercantile Journal* was confident, however, that he would have remanded the women to Turner's custody.

There was a shocking postscript to this first "rescue" of alleged fugitive slaves in Boston.[12] Four weeks later, a United States naval officer from Baltimore entered Samuel Eliot Sewall's office and after announcing that he was a relative of Morris the slaveowner, proceeded to insult the abolitionist lawyer "with opprobrious epithets," and then struck him "a number of blows with the butt end of a horsewhip." [13] The assailant, who immediately thereafter left town, had informed his victim that he had no right to interfere with Southern property rights. It was the very week of Med's case,[14] when the Chief Justice himself had indulged in similar interference which reduced Sewall's to insignificance.

III

Six years later the famous Latimer case occurred. On October 19, 1842, a Constable Stratton, furnished with a warrant issued by the Boston Police Court, arrested George Latimer, "a fine looking colored man." [15] A complaint of theft in Virginia had been brought against him by James B. Gray, a Norfolk slavemaster, who simultaneously claimed the fugitive from justice as his slave. Soon a crowd of "nearly three-hundred, mostly male blacks," [16] assembled before the Court House where the prisoner was held. To defeat a rescue, he was slipped out by the back door and locked up in the Leverett Street jail. Coolidge the jailer, like Stratton, was by Gray's written authority his legal agent. Fearing that Gray and his men might smuggle Latimer out of the city

---

[12] The first attempt to enforce the Act of 1793 was in Massachusetts that same year. The slave escaped from the court room in the midst of proceedings against him. There appears to be no evidence that he was rescued, though a sympathetic crowd opened to allow him through. Letter of Josiah Quincy, quoted in the Boston *Atlas*, Oct. 15, 1850, and cited by M. G. McDougall, *Fugitive Slaves (1619–1865)* (Boston, 1891), p. 35. In the only other case in Massachusetts before 1836, Commonwealth v. Griffith, 2 Pick. 11 (1823), the slave evaded rendition, but by what means remains undetermined.

[13] *Daily Evening Transcript*, Aug. 29.

[14] Commonwealth v. Aves, 17 Pick. 193 (1836). See Chapter 5.

[15] *Boston Post*, Oct. 20, 1842.

[16] Letter from Gray's counsel, City Attorney E. G. Austin, "To the Public," Nov. 21, quoted in full with an abolitionist critique by the *Emancipator and Free American* (Boston), Dec. 1, 1842.

late at night, parties interested in freedom's cause successfully petitioned Chief Justice Shaw for a writ of habeas corpus.

The following evening, Stratton, in compliance with the writ, produced Latimer before Shaw in the Supreme Court room. The Court was not officially in session, but since the judges were present for other purposes, they also heard this case. At the time, "immense crowds" were milling about the Court House "in a very feverish state of anxiety . . ." [17] Gray's attorney, E. G. Austin, defended the seizure of Latimer under the terms of the Fugitive Slave Law. Stratton justified himself by showing the police court warrant, Gray's claim to Latimer as a slave, and his own appointment as Gray's agent. Samuel Eliot Sewall and Amos Merrill, for the prisoner, argued from *Prigg v. Pennsylvania*[18] on the illegality of all proceedings against Latimer done under color of state or local authority.

After consultation with the other judges, Shaw discharged the writ and ordered Latimer returned to the custody of his captors. In his opinion he confined himself strictly to the fugitive-slavery question, ignoring the contention that the police court warrant was void because of federal legislation on fugitives from justice.[19] He ruled that Gray and Stratton showed sufficient authority to detain the prisoner under the Act of 1793, which the United States Supreme Court had recently upheld in Prigg's case. State courts could not interfere with the operation of a constitutional statute under whose terms Gray as claimant was entitled to arrest Latimer wherever he fled, prove his ownership before a federal court, and obtain therefrom a certificate to carry his slave away with him. Shaw also thought that Gray should be allowed reasonable time to take the necessary measures to get a certificate of rendition. Since the prisoner had been arrested only

[17] *The Atlas* (Boston), quoted by *The Liberator,* Oct. 28, 1842.

[18] 16 Peters 539 (1842). In this case, at pp. 617–618, it was held, *per* Story, J., that the Constitution vested exclusive authority in Congress to legislate on fugitives from slavery, in consequence of which, the states could not legislate on the subject. By way of dictum Story added that the states could not be required to enforce federal legislation in a case of exclusive Congressional authority.

[19] Shaw gave an opinion on this point in Commonwealth v. Tracy, *et al.,* 5 Metc. 536 (1843). The case involved three Negroes who had been convicted for riotous assault in the abortive rescue of Latimer on the night of Oct. 20, 1842, immediately following Shaw's dismissal of a writ of habeas corpus on his behalf. Defense alleged the unconstitutionality of Rev. Sts. 1835, ch. 142, sec. 8, which provided for the arrest of persons liable to extradition. The argument was based on the Prigg dictum. Shaw's opinion on the right of the states to provide machinery for the arrest of fugitives from justice became the law in every state in the country.

the day before, and his master made oath to apply before a federal court, Shaw found no legal ground to remove Latimer from custody.[20] When Stratton and his assistants escorted the slave back to jail, they were riotously attacked by the mob outside the Court House. The rescue attempt failed, but one officer was given "a touch of the nose bleed" and another was "struck by a brickbat, and severely hurt . . ."[21] Eight of the mob were arrested, all of them Negroes.

On the next day, the twenty-first, the opposing counsel agreed to postpone examination on the larceny charge in order to settle the fugitive slave question. Bail was fixed at $200 for Latimer's appearance in police court ten days later. Austin then decided that if Latimer were released on bail, a new question would arise: who was to hold him in custody in the interval? To save trouble, Austin quashed the complaint against him as a fugitive from justice, because he could then be held by Stratton as a fugitive slave in accordance with Shaw's order.[22] As events showed, this move not only confirmed abolitionist suspicions that the larceny charge was originally a fictitious device to apprehend Latimer; it also created a circumstance which led eventually to the slave's freedom, for he was now being held in jail, at Gray's convenience and jailer Coolidge's profit, without the police court warrant. Gray's next move, an application before Justice Story, on circuit duty, for a certificate of rendition, did not strengthen his action in jailing Latimer. Story, holding the case over for two weeks to give Gray time to obtain evidence of his title from Norfolk, did order that he legally detain Latimer in the interim. The United States, however, had rights to use a Boston jail by permission of Massachusetts only to hold persons committed by authority of a federal court. Story did not order Latimer's commitment; he simply remanded him to Gray's personal custody. The abolitionists now began to rake the city with angry protests against the illegal and abusive use of its jail. A mass meeting was called for October 30 in Faneuil Hall.[23]

On October 24, a final legal effort was made by Latimer's friends to free him. They sued out a writ of personal replevin, under a state personal liberty law of 1837, passed to guarantee

[20] *The Atlas,* excerpted by *The Liberator,* Oct. 28, 1842; *Emancipator and Free American,* Nov. 3 and Dec. 1, 1842.

[21] *Boston Post,* Oct. 21 and Oct. 24, 1842.

[22] Austin's "Letter to the Public."

[23] *The Liberator,* Nov. 4 and Nov. 24, 1842; *Law Reporter,* 5:482 (Boston, March 1843).

trial by jury "on questions of personal freedom." This law did not exclude fugitive slaves from its protection.[24] It read in part: "If any person is imprisoned . . . unless it be in the custody of some public officer of the law, by force of a lawful warrant . . . he shall be entitled, as of right, to a writ of personal replevin . . ." [25] The writ was served on Coolidge, commanding him to produce Latimer before the Court of Common Pleas, there to submit the cause of his detention before a jury. Coolidge, however, refused to acknowledge the writ. Latimer's attorneys again applied to the Chief Justice for relief, and again he issued a writ of habeas corpus, this one commanding the jailer to show why he had rejected the writ of personal replevin. The hearing was held immediately, in Coolidge's parlor adjoining the jail.[26]

After Sewall and Merrill had argued Latimer's rights under the personal liberty law, Shaw remarked to Austin, Coolidge's counsel, that no reply would be necessary because his own judgment was fixed and required no confirmation.[27] In the account of Shaw's opinion as reported by Garrison, who was one of the few outsiders present, an important paragraph reveals much of Shaw's thought on the fugitive-slavery question. He said, "in substance," reported *The Liberator* (November 4), that

. . . he probably felt as much sympathy for the person in custody as others; but this was a case in which an appeal to natural rights and the paramount law of liberty was not pertinent! It was decided by the Constitution of the United States, and by the law of Congress, under that instrument, relating to fugitive slaves. These were to be obeyed, however disagreeable to our own natural sympathies and views of duty! . . . By the Constitution, the duty of returning runaway slaves was made imperative on the free states, and the act of Congress . . . was in accordance with the spirit of that instrument. He repeatedly said, that on no other terms could a union have been formed between the North and the South . . .

To the contentions that Latimer could not be held without a warrant or evidence of his status as a slave, and that presumption was in favor of his freedom, Shaw replied by holding to his sworn obligation to support the Constitution. This obligation could be

---

[24] J. C. Hurd, *The Law of Freedom and Bondage in the United States* (Boston, 1862, 2 vols.), II, 32, note.

[25] St. 1837, ch. 211, sec. 1.

[26] *Law Reporter*, 5:483 (1843). There are no official Court Reports of the proceedings had under either habeas corpus in the Latimer affair.

[27] Austin's letter "To the Public," and *The Liberator*, Nov. 4.

met only by protecting Gray's right under law to have sufficient time for producing evidence to his claim.

As to Latimer's rights under the Massachusetts Personal Liberty Law of 1837, they were non-existent, ruled Shaw. That law had been passed by state officers sworn to support the Constitution and laws of the nation; they could not pass any law in conflict with these superior obligations. Therefore, the statute relied upon by the prisoner could not be construed to embrace runaways. Such persons must be regarded as exceptions to its provisions. The statute, Shaw concluded, citing Prigg's case, was unconstitutional and void insofar as it concerned fugitive slaves.[28] Accordingly, the writ of personal replevin was inapplicable in Latimer's case. Shaw then ordered that the slave once more be remanded to the custody of the agents of Gray, whose claim was properly pending before a federal court.[29]

The abolitionists countered this opinion with abuse most galling. At their Faneuil Hall meeting on October 30, Sewall imputed to Shaw the "basest motives of personal feeling." [30] Wendell Phillips pronounced his famous curse upon the Constitution, and Francis Jackson, Frederick Douglass, and Edmund Quincy did their best to incite a crowd to rescue. The intemperate Garrison wrote that Shaw's opinion proved his readiness to aid "in kidnapping a guiltless and defenseless human, and to act the part of Pilate in the Crucifixion of the Son of God . . ." Where, asked Garrison, did Shaw's guilt differ "from that of the slave pirate on the African coast . . . ?" [31] When "A Subscriber" protested that it was "unchristian" to classify with slavers "one of the best men in the community," Garrison replied that Chief Justice Shaw had betrayed the honor of Massachusetts "when Liberty lay bleeding." The Chief Justice was also subjected to derision because he held "court" in the jailor's parlor while police stood guard.[32] Shaw, of course, was free to hold a hearing on a writ of habeas corpus wherever he judged expedient. Moreover, according to Peleg Chandler, editor of the conservative *Law Re-*

[28] This was the first case in which Shaw invalidated a statute, in whole or in part.

[29] *Boston Post,* Nov. 1, 1842; *Law Reporter,* 5:483; Austin's letter, "To the Public."

[30] Boston *Daily Bee,* quoted in *The Liberator,* Nov. 4, 1842.

[31] *The Liberator,* Nov. 4.

[32] *The Liberator,* Nov. 11; *Emancipator and Free American,* Nov. 3 and Dec. 1, 1842.

porter, the suggestion to hold the hearing at the jail came from Latimer's counsel.[33]

Chandler undertook "to deal a blow" against the "false morality, born from the sophistry of fanaticism" which sought to undermine public confidence in the judiciary and the laws of the nation. He referred indignantly to critics who insisted that Shaw should have freed Latimer in accordance with the "law" of conscience, in spite of the Constitution and Congress. Did not the abolitionist know, asked Chandler,

that a judge has nothing to do with the moral character of the laws which society chooses to make, and which, when made, it places him upon the bench to apply the facts before him? Does he not know that the judiciary is the mere organ of society, to declare what the law is, and having ascertained, to pronounce what the law requires?[34]

In his defense of Shaw, and of Story too, Chandler sketched an image of the neutral judge who, exercising no personal discretion, allowed none of his own considerations of morality or conscience to intrude upon the performance of his duties. The zealots who made civil disobedience sound doctrine, however, had their own image of the ideal judge. He was a Judge Harrington of Vermont who, rejecting documentary proof that a Negro claimed was in fact a fugitive slave, had allegedly remarked: "If the master could show a bill of sale, or grant, from the Almighty, then his title to him would be complete: otherwise it would not." [35]

With such a judge in mind, Garrisonians were not given to pause in a scrupulous regard for fact or moderation when discussing Lemuel Shaw. They meant to whip public opinion into a froth of hysteria, and fortune favored them. Justice Story was too ill to hear the case as scheduled on the fifth of November, and the date when Gray might apply before a federal court for a certificate was advanced to the twenty-first. The abolitionists made the most of the opportunity which time gave to them. They bellowed animadversions at mass meetings up and down the state. A propaganda sheet, the *Latimer Journal and North Star,* rife with a sense of bitter injustice, was published tri-weekly, beginning with November 11. The editors, Dr. Henry I. Bow-

[33] *Law Reporter,* 5:483.
[34] *Ibid.,* 5:481 and 493.
[35] S. E. Sewall, "Harrington's Decision," letter printed in *The Liberator,* Jan. 3, 1843.

ditch and William F. Channing, sons of famous fathers, circulated twenty thousand copies of each issue. "The slave shall never leave Boston even if to gain that end our streets pour with blood," they wrote.[36] The judiciary was their special target. "The whole of the Latimer Journal," stated the *Law Reporter,* "was largely devoted to the most positive assertions, that the chief justice's decision upon the *habeas corpus* was grossly illegal, and he and Mr. Justice Story are accused of using their offices to oppress their fellow men." [37]

Bowditch, Channing, Charles Sumner, and others of similar persuasion got up a petition threatening the Sheriff of Suffolk County with removal from office if he did not order his subordinate, jailor Coolidge, to release Latimer. Sheriff Eveleth did not himself consider Latimer to be properly jailed without a warrant. Spurred by the threat of removal and by public demonstrations against the use of the jail by Gray and his agents for their personal advantage, Eveleth ordered Latimer's release by noon of the eighteenth. This new development, just a few days before the slaveowner could get a certificate, put Gray in a quandary. He still had legal custody of Latimer, but if he held him privately, his slave would be rescued from him.[38] As his counsel, Austin, explained in his letter "To the Public," "to attempt to keep Latimer in any other place than the jail, was to raise at once a signal for a riot, if not bloodshed." Consequently Gray consented to sell his claim for $400. Immediately after the sale, Latimer was set free.

The Fugitive Slave Law was yet to be enforced in Massachusetts. Whittier stated its defiance in "Massachusetts to Virginia": "No fetters in the Bay State, — no slave upon our land!" An immense petition for repeal of the law, bearing 51,862 Massachusetts signatures, rolled up into the size of a barrel, was presented in Congress by "Old Man Eloquent," John Quincy Adams. Under "gag law," the petition was not received. The state legislature, however, favorably responded to anti-slavery protests. Outraged citizens had held meetings in every county and in almost every town "to demand that their ancient Commonwealth should never again be insulted by the conversion of her jails into barracoons, and her sworn servants and judicial officers into the minions of the slave catcher." [39] On February 17, 1843, following a great

[36] Quoted in *Law Reporter,* 5:491.
[37] *Ibid.,* 5:492.
[38] *The Liberator,* Nov. 25, 1842.
[39] *Twelfth Annual Report, Presented to the Massachusetts Anti-Slavery Society* (Boston, 1844), pp. 4–5.

demonstration in Faneuil Hall, a petition with 65,000 names, borne on the shoulders of six men, was delivered to the State House where it was presented by Charles Francis Adams. The "Latimer Law," an act "further to protect Personal Liberty," was passed. It prohibited state judges from recognizing the Act of 1793 or issuing certificates of rendition; it prohibited officers of the Commonwealth from assisting in the arrest of alleged fugitive slaves; and it prohibited the use of state jails for the confinement of fugitives.[40] Such a law had been made legally possible by the opinion in Prigg's case[41] by Justice Story who had, ironically, been subjected like Shaw to obloquy in the abolitionist press. Other northern states also passed personal liberty laws, converting the Act of 1793 into a nullity by the withdrawal of state aid in its enforcement.

IV

Southern anxiety for the loss of runaways was allayed by a new Fugitive Slave Law passed by Congress, with Webster's endorsement, as part of the Compromise of 1850. The peculiar ingenuity of the new legislation was that it brought the law of bondage home to a free state. It was a law of flint, providing federal officials for its effective enforcement. When hateful scenes of slavery were transferred from the South and enacted in the streets of Boston, the old city was confronted with a choice among cherished alternatives: liberty or union? freedom or property? The new law produced a curious moral spectacle, for the question which distracted the minds of free men was whether to catch slaves or not to catch slaves.

To the anti-slavery hotspurs, fanatically devoted to a "higher law" than the Constitution, the measure was diabolical; it violated the purest promptings of conscience and Christianity. Wendell Phillips resolved for "the Abolitionists of Massachusetts" that "CONSTITUTION OR NO CONSTITUTION, LAW OR NO LAW" they would fight the sins which Black Daniel symbolized.[42] Those who praised Webster's patriotism and defended the Act of 1850 denied that the Theodore Parkers and Charles Sumners had

---

[40] *Ibid.;* V. I. Bowditch, *Life and Correspondence of Henry Ingersoll Bowditch* (Boston, 1902, 2 vols.), I, 134; *Emancipator and Free American*, March 24, 1843; and St. 1843, ch. 69.

[41] Prigg v. Pennsylvania, 16 Peters 539 (1842).

[42] *Nineteenth Annual Report, Presented to the Massachusetts Anti-Slavery Society* (Boston, 1851), p. 99.

a monopoly on moral justification. If the conservatives like the Chief Justice had retreated from the cause of individual freedom, it was in an anxious regard for even greater moral values: peace and Union. Or so they reasoned.

Charles Francis Adams wrote that while a shallow veneer of anti-slavery sentiment had been fashionable among them, it was "mere sentiment," without roots either in conviction or in material interests. "On the contrary," contended Adams, "so far as material interests were concerned, a great change had recently taken place. The manufacturing development of Massachusetts had been rapid, and a close affiliation had sprung up between the cotton spinners of the North and the cotton producers of the South, — or as Charles Sumner put it, between 'the lords of the loom and the lords of the lash.' " [43]

By mid-century a great majority of Boston's "best people" no longer concealed their warmness toward Southern interests. Their eagerness to keep on the best of terms with the South was later recalled by Edward L. Pierce, a student at Harvard Law School (1850–52). "A southern slave holder, or his son at Harvard," he wrote, "was more welcome in society than any guest except a foreigner . . . The deference to rich southern planters was marked." [44] Almost all the wealth of the city was controlled by the "Cotton Whigs," and as social and business Boston gradually became "almost avowedly a pro-slavery community," [45] its self-justification of loyalty to the Constitution and to national security approached hysteria. When the news came from Washington that the Fugitive Slave Act had been safely passed, one hundred guns roared a joyous salute across the Common.

A few weeks later, opponents of the law swelled Faneuil Hall to fire their invective against its supporters, to pledge their aid to Negro fellow-citizens, and to demand "INSTANT REPEAL." A group of fifty — it soon grew to two hundred and ten — was appointed to act as a Committee of Vigilance and Safety which determined to render the abominable act a nullity. Then in the same hall, in November, defenders of the law swore their allegiance to it at a "Constitutional Meeting." [46]

---

[43] C. F. Adams, *Richard Henry Dana* (Boston, 1891, 3rd ed., 2 vols.), I, 127.
[44] Pierce, *Memoir and Letters of Charles Sumner* (Boston, 1893, 4 vols.), III, 6.
[45] Adams, *Dana*, I, 127.
[46] *Nineteenth Annual Report*, pp. 31–32, 42–43. The complete membership list of the vigilance committee is in Austin Bearse's *Reminiscences of Fugitive-Slave Law Days in Boston* (Boston, 1880), pp. 3–5.

V

In the furious climate of irreconcilable loyalties and thunderous rallies engendered by the Act of 1850, men waited apprehensively to see whether a solemn act of Congress would be honored, or be superseded by the resolves of a Gideon's army of lawless agitators. A month after the law was passed, slave-hunters arrived in Boston searching for William and Ellen Craft, fugitives from a Georgia planter. Here was the first test — and the vigilance committee, led by the indomitable Parker, tracked down the slave-hunters and chased them out of town. Then on February 15, 1851, the Shadrach affair began.

From Norfolk there came to Boston a "hired kidnapper," [47] with documents prepared in Virginia, claiming a waiter at Taft's Cornhill Coffee House as a slave. George Ticknor Curtis, "Cotton Whig" and Commissioner of the United States Circuit Court, issued a warrant for the arrest of the alleged runaway, one Frederick Wilkins, alias Shadrach. Seized as he unsuspectingly served breakfast to United States Deputy Marshal Patrick Riley, Shadrach was hustled through a back street to the Court House. Riley notified City Marshal Francis Tukey and Mayor Bigelow that he "got a nigger," [48] sent for Commissioner Curtis and the claimant's counsel, and directed the doors of the United States Court Room to be locked and guarded. Shadrach, finally informed of the charges against him, requested counsel. In the meantime, word had spread that the marshal had captured a fugitive slave. Vigilance men Samuel Eliot Sewall, Charles Davis, Ellis Gray Loring, Charles List, Robert Morris, and Richard Henry Dana — he who had sailed before the mast — all volunteered for the defendant.

As a turbulent crowd, increasing by the moment, assembled in Court Square, Dana prepared a petition for habeas corpus addressed to Chief Justice Shaw. Morris, in Loring's presence, had obtained verbal authority from Shadrach to apply for the writ and swore before Dana that the petition was accurate. It stated that the prisoner was held by Deputy Marshal Riley on pretence of his being a fugitive slave, and that he did not know whether there was a warrant for his arrest. With this petition Dana sought out Shaw, whom he found in the lobby of the Supreme Judicial Court Room with Associate Justice Metcalf, and explained that

[47] *The Commonwealth*, Boston, Feb. 17, 1851.
[48] Tukey's letter, dated Feb. 17, quoted in *The Liberator*, Feb. 21, 1851.

with the writ he hoped to bring a test case on the constitutional power of a commissioner to issue a warrant under the Act of 1850. Shaw flatly refused to grant habeas corpus in Shadrach's behalf, revealing a positive disapproval of the anti-slavery efforts. In his diary, under the entry for that Saturday, February 15, the ardently partisan Dana recorded in detail his conversation with the Chief Justice.[49] In what Dana considered "a most ungracious manner," Shaw had replied after reading the petition, "This won't do. I can't do anything on this." And laying it on a table, he turned away to busy himself with something else; but he was not rid of Dana so easily. To an inquiry into the defects of the petition, Shaw gave the impression of trying to "bluff" off his questioner. Finally he yielded to Dana's persistence with the objection that Shadrach had not signed the petition. The lawyer then reminded the judge that state law permitted the petition to be made on behalf of the petitioner. Dana thought to himself that the Chief Justice certainly knew that in extreme cases, when the writ was most needed to protect personal liberty, circumstances might make it impossible for the prisoner to sign personally. Shaw was obstinate:

"There is no evidence that it is in his behalf. There is no evidence of his authority."

"Do you require proof of his authority? What proof do you require, sir?"

"It is enough for me to say that the petition is not sufficient. The petition shows on its face that the writ cannot issue. It shows that the man is in legal custody of a United States marshal."

Again the lawyer instructed the judge: the fact of legal custody must appear on Riley's return to the writ *after* it was granted. Shaw tried another tack, this time complaining that Shadrach could not properly swear ignorance of the charge against him. Dana called attention to the fact that the petition stated fully the pretence of arrest. Finding this to be true, Shaw fell back on his original objection that there was want of evidence from the prisoner. He then added his final objection — "and not made," wrote Dana, "until after he had positively refused to issue the writ" — that the petition required an appended copy of the warrant of arrest or a statement that a copy had been applied for and could not be obtained. Yet the petition clearly stated that Shadrach did not know whether his imprisonment was under a warrant or not. Moreover, the Act of 1850 permitted arrests without a warrant.

[49] Adams, *Dana*, I, 179–182.

Dana was disconsolate: "I felt that all these objections were frivolous and invalid, but seeing the temper the Chief Justice was in, and his evident determination to get rid of the petition, I left him for the purpose of either procuring the evidence he required or of going before another judge." [50]

Dana returned to the United States Court Room. Extending from its door into the street was a crowd of about two hundred Negroes.[51] Inside the court room, Shadrach's counsel requested time to consult with him and to prepare the defense. Commissioner Curtis held the proceedings over until the following Tuesday. Officiously, Riley ordered the room cleared of spectators, reporters, and attorneys so that Shadrach might be left alone with his guards. At about two o'clock the door was unlocked to let out the last few persons, Charles G. Davis, Robert Morris, Elizur Wright, editor of *The Commonwealth*, all members of the abolitionist Committee of Vigilance and Safety.

As the door was opened a yell went up from the Negroes milling in the passageways. Instantly a tug of war began over the door, the officers inside straining to keep it shut, the crowd pressing to force it open. Shadrach headed for the unguarded opposite exit, and as about fifteen men streamed into the room, jamming Riley into a corner behind the door, the marshal screamed from his place of safety, "Shoot him! Shoot him!" But the rescuers had already escorted Shadrach out of the room, down the stairs, and into the streets. Dana, working in his office opposite the Court House, rushed to his window at the sound of shouting in time to see two huge Negroes, bearing Shadrach between them, dash off toward Cambridge "like a black squall," the mob cheering as they departed.[52]

The amazing rescue threatened the success of "peace measures," and the nation protested. The Washington correspondent of the New York *Journal of Commerce* telegraphed from the capital: "Some sensation was produced here by the intelligence of the negro insurrection in Boston." [53] Secretary of State Webster thought the rescue was "a case of treason." [54] On February 17, President Fillmore called a special cabinet meeting to discuss

[50] Adams, *Dana*, I, 181.
[51] *Daily Evening Transcript*, Feb. 17, 1851.
[52] The account of the rescue has been followed in Elizur Wright's eye-witness story in *The Commonwealth*, Feb. 17, 1851; Riley's deposition in *The Liberator*, Feb. 21, 1851; *Daily Evening Transcript*, Feb. 15 and Feb. 17, 1851; Adams, *Dana*, I, 182–183.
[53] Quoted in the *Daily Evening Transcript*, Feb. 19, 1851.
[54] C. M. Fuess, *Daniel Webster* (Boston, 1930, 2 vols.), II, 270.

measures to be taken, and on the next day, issued a proclamation commanding all civil and military officers to assist in recapturing Shadrach and to prosecute all persons who took part in the "scandalous outrage" committed against the laws of the United States. On the Senate floor, Henry Clay demanded to know whether a "government of white men was to be yielded to a government by blacks." [55] Boston's reputation had been "bady damaged," especially in the South. The *Savannah Republican* scourged the city as a "black speck on the map — disgraced by the lowest, the meanest, the BLACKEST kind of NULLIFICATION." [56]

In Boston, the press fulminated against the "mischief which mad Abolitionism will wantonly perpetrate." On February 18, the Board of Mayor and Aldermen expressed regret that the Commonwealth's dignity had been criminally insulted, and ordered the City Marshal to make "the whole police force" available to quell a similar breech of law should one be anticipated. Two days later, the Common Council approved unanimously the Board's action and "cordially" endorsed the President's proclamation.[57]

The abolitionists, in their turn, ridiculed the furor which the rescue had occasioned. "Warrington" attacked as Tories the leading citizens who pretended outrage: "State-street brokers and Milk-street jobbers who . . . hold mortgages on slave property . . . dared not to disturb the good understanding between the planters and the manufacturers . . ." [58] And was not the rescue for the greater glory of God and His children? Dr. Bowditch marked down the day in his calendar as "a holy day," and Parker thought the rescue was "the noblest deed done in Boston since the destruction of the tea in 1773." [59] Impishly, vigilance men recalled that Mrs. Glasse, the celebrated cook, had prudently premised in her recipe for cooking a hare, "First, *catch* your hare!"

Richard Henry Dana shared the rejoicing of his fellows, but in the aftermath of the rescue, he set down in his diary the one event that marred the day and disturbed not only him, but Judge Metcalf too. "The conduct of the Chief Justice, his evident disin-

[55] *The Liberator*, Feb. 21 and Feb. 28, 1851.

[56] Quoted in *The Liberator*, April 11, 1851. See the same issue for comment by the *New Orleans Picayune*.

[57] *Boston Courier*, April 12, 1851, *The Liberator*, Feb. 21, 1851. See *The Liberator* and *The Commonwealth*, Feb. 17, 1851, for a characterization of the city's press comment.

[58] *Lowell American*, Feb. 21, 1851, quoted in Mrs. W. S. Robinson (ed.), *"Warrington" Pen-Portraits* (Boston, 1877), p. 191.

[59] Bowditch, I, 212; H. S. Commager, *Theodore Parker* (Boston, 1936), p. 219.

clination to act, the frivolous nature of his objections, and his insulting manner to me, have troubled me . . ." wrote Dana. Shaw's conduct, he concluded perspicaciously, "shows how deeply seated, so as to affect, unconsciously I doubt not, good men like him, is this selfish hunkerism of the property interest on the slave question." [60]

Shaw's Whiggery was indeed robust, and he never lost his admiration for Webster's politics or principles. There exists no statement from Shaw that he, like Webster, Choate, and Curtis, approved of the Fugitive Slave Law as an expedient to cement the sectional differences that menaced the Union; yet there is nothing in the cast of the man's mind, temperament, or associations suggesting that his judicial obligation to enforce Congressional law necessarily conflicted with his personal opinions. Four months before the death of Webster, his lifelong friend, Shaw wrote that it would have been "a glorious thing to have so distinguished a man as Mr. Webster elected Prest [*sic*] of the U.S." [61] With the passing years, the intensification of the slavery controversy made the security and peace of the Union Shaw's passion; long ago these values had been elevated in his mind to a case of political and even "moral" necessity.[62] He remained an old-line Whig when less conservative men drifted to the new Republican banner; by 1860 he was advocating appeasement of the South and supported the Constitutional Unionists, heirs to the traditional compromise party. While Dana and his friends — "overzealous philanthropists" Shaw had called them[63] — predicated their position on the natural rights of man, the Chief Justice responded to motives also worthy of respect: love for the Union and national harmony. Translated into the political values of the 1850's, this meant a love for law and order, for "peace measures," for maintaining inviolate the North's pledge to remand fugitive slaves.

VI

It was notorious that no fugitive slave had ever been returned from Boston. Webster Whigs were dismayed that the whole state of Massachusetts was known as the cradle of "mad Abolitionism." It had become a matter of pride, not alone in the South, that a

[60] Adams, *Dana*, I, 183. "Now, hunkerism," wrote Dana, "making material *prosperity and ease* its pole star, will do nothing and risk nothing for a moral principle" (p. 125).

[61] Letter of June 15, 1852, to Lemuel Shaw, Jr., Shaw Papers.

[62] Shaw, "Slavery and the Missouri Question," p. 143.

[63] Commonwealth v. Aves, 18 Pick. 193, 219 (1836).

fugitive should be seized in Boston and taken back to slavery. Then, on Thursday evening, April 3, 1851 — before the excitement of the Shadrach case had subsided — the city government of Boston was presented with an opportunity to make good on its promises of loyally enforcing the Fugitive Slave Act: Thomas Sims was taken into custody as a fugitive slave belonging to Mr. James Potter, a rice planter of Chatham County, Georgia.

Sims spent that night, and the rest of his nights in Boston, confined to the jury room of the Court House which was reserved for use in federal cases. He was thus technically imprisoned in a federal jail. This expedient was resorted to, as in Shadrach's case, because there was no United States prison in Massachusetts, and because the 1843 "Latimer Law" of the state prohibited the use of its prisons for detaining any person accused of being a fugitive slave. In the court-room prison, Sims was kept under close guard by the men of Charles Devens, the United States Marshal.

On the next morning, Boston awoke to witness one of the most extraordinary spectacles in its existence. During the night, the Court House had been barricaded. Under the direction of City Marshal Francis Tukey, iron chains had been girded entirely around the building. Its approaches were cleared by a belt of ropes and chains along the sidewalks, and heavy links stretched across its doorways. The Court House was in fetters, "bound . . . to the Georgia cotton presses." Here was a visible answer, thought Bronson Alcott, to the question, "What has the North to do with slavery?" Tukey had concentrated his men on the scene. The entire regular police force, reinforced by great numbers of special police, patrolled the area and were stationed around and within the building. Wendell Phillips estimated the total number of police at no less than five hundred! Only authorized persons could get within ten feet of the Court House and pass the armed cordon.[64] In effect, this meant that the city government of Boston had temporarily suspended the right of an ordinary citizen in a free Commonwealth to attend public sessions of its courts.

News of the arrest and of the exceptional scenes at the Court House hurried about the city. Several hundred people, infected

[64] *The Commonwealth,* April 14, 1851; Odell Shephard (ed.), *The Journals of Bronson Alcott* (Boston, 1938), p. 234; *The Commonwealth,* April 5, 1851; Phillips' speech at Faneuil Hall, Jan. 30, 1852, reported in the *Twentieth Annual Report, Presented to the Massachusetts Anti-Slavery Society, By Its Board of Managers* (Boston, 1852), p. 112 (T. W. Higginson put the figure at "one or two hundred" in his *Cheerful Yesterdays,* Boston, 1899, p. 140); *Daily Evening Transcript,* April 5, 1851.

with curiosity, clogged Court Square from early morning till ten at night. There was no organized attempt at disturbance, although the police were jeered at and scolded by women; on the other hand, repeated cheers were given for the Union. Not till midnight was the square emptied of the crowds for that day.[65] Word of the whole affair reached Longfellow, who recorded in his journal: "April 4, 1851. There is much excitement in Boston about the capture of an alleged fugitive slave. O city without soul! When and where will this end? Shame that the great Republic, the 'refuge of the oppressed,' should stoop so low as to become the Hunter of Slaves." [66]

Low indeed was the stooping, for the chains across the door of the temple of justice were neither low enough to step over nor high enough to walk under. Those who entered the Court House on special business, lawyers, city officers, members of the press (who could enter if their views on the slavery question were safe enough[67]), commissioners, and judges — even the judges — all had to bow their backs and creep beneath the chains. Tukey, the satrap in charge, had ordered it so. Chief Justice Lemuel Shaw of the Supreme Judicial Court, the great Shaw, venerated for his wisdom and for his advanced age, was among the first that morning to stoop beneath the chains.[68] Decades before, Shaw himself had commented that one of the many evils in legally sanctioning slavery was that it degraded ministers of the law and profaned the sanctuary of justice.[69] Senator Joseph T. Buckminster told the Massachusetts Senate that day about the Chief Justice's performance. "We are a law-and-order loving people," he declared. "With such an illustrious example of submission to law and order before them, I cannot believe that the citizens will commit any treason or violence." [70]

At nine that same Friday morning, Commissioner Curtis opened his court to hear the case of young Thomas Sims. The scene was the United States Court Room, up two high and narrow flights of stairs. Six guards were at the door. The prisoner sat with two policemen on each side of him and five more directly behind. Only his counsel could approach him from the front.[71] His counsel

[65] *Daily Evening Transcript*, April 5, 1851; *National Intelligencer*, April 12, 1851.
[66] S. Longfellow (ed.), *Life of Henry Wadsworth Longfellow, with Extracts from His Journals and Correspondence* (Boston, 1936, 2 vols.), II, 192.
[67] *The Commonwealth*, April 5, 1851.
[68] *The Liberator*, April 11, 1851.
[69] "Slavery and the Missouri Question," p. 139.
[70] Quoted in the *Daily Evening Transcript*, April 7, 1851.
[71] Higginson, p. 141.

were men of first eminence — the vigilance committee had wasted no time in sounding out legal aid. Robert Rantoul was there, a volunteer in Sims' defense who was a United States Senator, and Webster's successor at that. In little more than a year Rantoul would be dead, and Whittier would write in "Rantoul": "We saw him take the weaker side, And right the wronged, and free the thrall." Charles G. Loring, a leader of the Boston bar, also appeared for the prisoner. Seth Thomas was present for the Southern claimants, such "despicable wretches" Dana had never beheld — "cruel, low-bred, dissolute, degraded beings!" [72]

Thomas produced documents to prove that Sims belonged not to himself, but to James Potter of Georgia. Bacon, the agent, whom he had brought from Savannah as witness, took the stand to identify Sims as Potter's slave.[73] There was no testimony on behalf of the defendant. It would have taken weeks before witnesses might be found in Georgia and brought to Boston to speak in court for him. But the law of 1850 envisioned no such delays, only an informal hearing in which the fate of the alleged fugitive was to be decided in a "summary manner," as the law said. The claim of the slave-catcher, made by affidavit or testimony, was in effect sufficient proof to identify the prisoner as the person in fact owing service.[74]

Sims' attorneys moved to introduce as evidence for their client his sworn statement that he was born in Florida; that he had been free as long as he could remember; that his free papers were probably with Mr. Morris Potter of Savannah; and that he never knew nor heard of James Potter, the man who claimed him, until after his arrest. Curtis, however, rejected this affidavit by refusing to entertain the motion on ground that the law of 1850 stated: "In no trial or hearing under this Act shall the testimony of such al-

[72] Adams, *Dana,* I, 185.

[73] *Daily Evening Transcript,* April 4, 1851; *The Liberator,* April 11, 1851.

[74] Section 6, Fugitive Slave Act, in H. S. Commager (ed.), *Documents of American History* (New York, 1946, 3rd ed.), I, 322. Andrew C. McLaughlin states that if Webster himself had been haled before a commissioner by a slave-holder who produced "affidavits," he could not deny his obligation to serve as a slave. And, argues McLaughlin, if it be answered that the act was not directed against white men, does that mean that the Constitution presumed slavery to be the natural status of Negroes and all Negroes to be slaves? Indeed, was the presumption so conclusive that a Negro could not even deny his slavery; and did the Constitution establish a white man's government in which Negroes were not afforded protections of the law? ". . . On the face of the Constitution such does not appear to be the fact" (*Constitutional History of the United States,* New York, 1935, pp. 536–537).

leged Fugitive be admitted as evidence." [75] Curtis then held the case over till the next day, Saturday.[76]

On the same Friday morning, when the hearing before Curtis had just begun, Samuel E. Sewall appeared before the Supreme Judicial Court and appealed to Chief Justice Shaw for a writ of habeas corpus to bring Sims before the Court on ground of illegal detention. After consulting with his associates a few moments, Shaw announced his decision to refuse the petition. He stated that if the writ were issued and the prisoner should be brought before the Court, its duty would be to remand him to the custody from which he was taken, by reason of no jurisdiction to decide whether he was or was not a fugitive. Sewall then requested permission to argue on the unconstitutionality of the law of 1850. Again Shaw refused, informing him, somewhat crustily, that the Court had already passed its judgment.[77] "When a Court of Justice sits in fetters . . . the ancient and prescriptive safeguards of personal liberty must of course give way," recorded the abolitionist society.[78]

Discouraged but resourceful, Sims' friends shifted to the familiar technique of agitation. Perhaps public opinion might pressure the courts to a more friendly view of the matter, or a crowd might even be incited to a rescue. The vigilance committee decided to hold a public meeting. The anti-slavery forces convened on the Common, and in the evening, reassembled in Tremont Temple, one thousand strong. Samuel Gridley Howe presided. Speeches of "the most extravagant character" were delivered. Wendell Phillips, the principal speaker was "treasonably violent"; he "maligned Chief Justice Shaw in terms that a gentleman would hardly apply to a pickpocket" for Shaw's refusal to grant the writ. Phillips advised resistance to the Fugitive Slave Act and declared that before a slave should be carried out of Massachusetts, its railroads and steamboats should be destroyed. He also counseled the Negro men of the city to arm and defend themselves.[79]

[75] Section 6, Fugitive Slave Act. "But constitutional provisions and legal practices are in many respects directed to the protection of the innocent; an act making it quite legal and possible to deny a free man (indeed, white or black) ordinary protection, and forbidding him to deny his guilt, or his alleged status, can not be looked upon as wholly free from an unconstitutional stain" (McLaughlin, p. 537).

[76] *Law Reporter* 14:3–4; *The Liberator*, April 11, 1851.

[77] *The Liberator*, April 4, 1851; *National Intelligencer*, April 8, 1851.

[78] *Twentieth Annual Report*, p. 21.

[79] *Daily Evening Transcript*, April 5, 1851.

The law-and-order element of the city was badly frightened. The *Daily Evening Transcript* (April 5) stigmatized the abolitionists as an "imbecile faction" and promised that the overwhelming majority of citizens were resolved at all hazards "to uphold the laws, the Constitution, and the Union." Because of the inflammatory appeals of the agitators, Mayor Bigelow and Marshal Tukey feared a repetition of the Shadrach affair. They doubtless considered the city police incompetent to deal with the poets, preachers, lawyers, and physicians who composed the vigilance committee. While the Tremont Temple meeting was in progress, three companies of the military were ordered out by the mayor: the City Guards, the New England Guards, and the Boston Light Guards. In addition, two hundred and fifty United States troops, with two pieces of ordnance, were kept on the alert at the Charlestown Navy Yard. All that Friday night, members of the vigilance committee, including the gentle Bronson Alcott, "beat the streets," in a gesture of supreme defiance, to protect other fugitives from being arrested.[80]

On Saturday, April fifth, the Sims affair provoked sharp action in the state Senate. Sims requested by petition that the legislature intervene in his favor by passing a special law requiring a writ of habeas corpus to be issued to him. His petition stated that the writ had been refused by the Supreme Judicial Court, that he was a citizen of Massachusetts, and that he ought not to be "surrendered, exiled, or delivered to bondage, until proved to be a slave by a 'due process of law.' " Senator Keyes spoke at length in Sims' favor, declaring that as a result of Shaw's decision, the noble writ of habeas corpus lay a dead letter at the feet of the Fugitive Slave Act. Senator Robinson echoed these sentiments and claimed that the judiciary should be made responsible by popular election. He even hinted at Shaw's impeachment. However, the Chief Justice and his associates had many supporters who believed them to be "the purest and most incorruptible judiciary in the world." In the end, Sims' petition was laid on the table.[81]

In Court Square, the events of Saturday — and of the following week — resembled those of the preceding day. Again there appeared the crowds, the armed cordon, and the judges passing under the chains. In the United States Court Room, Curtis lis-

[80] *Ibid.* Every night while Sims was in Boston, a few companies of the Boston Brigade, thereafter styled the "Sims Brigade," were detailed to prevent a forcible rescue. *National Intelligencer,* April 8 and 10, 1851; *Twentieth Annual Report,* p. 22; *The Journals of Bronson Alcott,* p. 244.

[81] *The Commonwealth,* April 8, 1851; *Law Reporter* 14:14.

tened to additional evidence that Sims was Potter's slave. That night, readers of the *Commercial Gazette* in New York learned that "The whole Union will probably know in a few days whether a fugitive slave can be arrested in the capital of Massachusetts, and in case the claim is made out, be delivered safely to his master in another State." [82] And a sensitive poet added another entry in his journals: "April 5. Troops under arms in Boston; the court house guarded; the Chief Justice of the Supreme Court forced to stoop under chains to enter the temple of Justice! This is the last point of degradation. Alas for the people who cannot feel an insult!" [83]

Over the weekend, a number of gentlemen of high standing, including Charles Loring, spoke privately to Shaw and his associates, persuading them to reconsider their refusal to hear an argument. Monday morning, Richard Henry Dana appeared with Rantoul before the Supreme Judicial Court.[84] They presented Sims' petition for a writ of habeas corpus, which set forth that Sims was imprisoned in the Court House by Marshal Devens on pretense of a warrant, issued by Curtis, describing him as a fugitive slave. Sims stated that he was free and prayed to the court to have him brought before it to be discharged. Shaw demanded that the court be satisfied of the unconstitutionality of the warrant before granting the writ, thereby rejecting Dana's plea that the writ should issue as of right.[85]

Rantoul then argued, first that Curtis, who was a federal officer but not a judge, exercised under the Act of 1850 a judicial power which Congress was empowered to confer only upon a judge appointed for good behavior and with a fixed compensation;[86] second, that the act itself was unconstitutional because Congress, which could exercise only powers expressly delegated, had no power to legislate at all on the subject of fugitive slaves,

[82] Quoted in the *National Intelligencer*, April 8, 1851.

[83] Longfellow, II, 193.

[84] Dana proudly recorded in his diary that he had never been under the chains: "I either jump over it," he wrote near the close of the case, "or go around to the end, and have the rope removed, which they have at last graciously substituted for the last few links of the chain" (Adams, *Dana*, I, 192).

[85] *Ibid.*, 185; "Thomas Sims's Case," 7 Cush. 285, 287 (1851).

[86] Curtis held office at the pleasure of a U.S. Circuit Court and was compensated by a fee which varied according to his decision: $5 if he found against the claimant and double if against the fugitive. This provision of the act, section 8, was assailed by Anson Burlingame for having fixed the price of a slave at $1000 and the price of a Yankee's soul at $5. Henry Wilson, *History of the Rise and Fall of the Slave Power in America* (Boston, 1872, 3 vols.), II, 309.

no such power being vested.[87] As Dana remarked, Rantoul made "a very striking and forcible argument, considered as a . . . piece of abstract reasoning, but not one calculated to meet the difficulties in the minds of the court." [88]

The unanimous judgment of the Court, given at three o'clock the same Monday, was a denial of the writ. Shaw's opinion was the first full-dress sustention of the constitutionality of the Fugitive Slave Act of 1850 by any court. A decade later, Hurd, the historian of the law of bondage, wrote that the opinion was thereafter regarded as "the highest authority — to the degree that in opinions of judges in later cases who have maintained the action of commissioners in like circumstances, it has been taken to preclude all further juristical discussion." [89]

That the Chief Justice had reasoned through his stand on the controversial law before that Monday may be surmised from the length and maturity of an opinion written in only a few hours. As early as the Med case of 1836, he had indicated his intention of giving effect to Congressional enactment should the duty of remanding a fugitive slave arise.[90] In the 1842 Latimer case, he had voided a state personal liberty law in so far as it applied to fugitives, and had remanded Latimer to his master's custody. Shaw's conduct in the Shadrach case was also revealing. It would have been contrary to the man had his opinion in the Sims case taken any other turn than it did.

In that opinion, Shaw first disposed of the petition for a writ of habeas corpus, stating that the writ could not be awarded when there was insufficient ground for discharge and the prisoner would have to be remanded. Thus he obviously implied that if a cause bearing on Sims' right to a discharge were to be argued before the court — a procedure which would have followed the issuance of the writ — he would find against Sims' freedom.[91]

Addressing himself to the argument on the alleged unconstitutionality of the law of 1850, Shaw found there were two questions before the Court: first, whether Congress was empow-

[87] 7 Cush. 285, 287–291. Article 4, section 2, paragraph 3 of the U.S. Constitution states: "No Person held to Service or Labour in one State, under the laws thereof, escaping into another shall, in Consequence of any Law or Regulation therein, be discharged from such Service or Labour, but shall be delivered up on claim of the Party to whom such Service or Labour may be due."

[88] Adams, *Dana*, I, 185.

[89] J. C. Hurd, *The Law of Freedom and Bondage in the United States* (Boston, 1862, 2 vols.), II, 653.

[90] Commonwealth v. Aves, 18 Pick. 193, 219–221 (1836).

[91] 7 Cush. 285, 292–293.

ered to pass any law on the subject of fugitive slaves; and second, whether the law actually passed violated the provisions of the federal Constitution. He thought it necessary for the disposition of the first question to consider the historical circumstances under which the Constitution was framed and the objects of its adoption. He was obsessed with the fiction that it would never have come into being had it not provided for the return of runaways. It was an appalling picture he sketched of thirteen disunited states embroiled in "constant border wars" that would result from hostile incursions of one sovereignty into another's territory for the purpose of recapturing escaped slaves. Before the thirteen states compacted to relinquish part of their independence and join in a union, their differences on slavery "must first be provided for." The clause in question must therefore be construed as a treaty entered into on the highest considerations of reciprocal benefit and to secure peace. Such was Shaw's view of the matter. The important point, of course, is not that his history was wrong but that it was considered essential to a decision of the case for reasons of high policy: the necessity for maintaining peace in the Union.[92]

In the light of his history, Shaw found that the fugitive slave clause of the United States Constitution was bedrock upon which Congressional authority to legislate might be erected. He was satisfied that even if the Constitution did not direct in detail how the rights and benefits of the clause were to be secured, Article I, section 8, granted to Congress authority to make all laws necessary and proper to carry into execution those powers specifically vested.[93]

It may be presumptuous to criticize such logic in view of its precedent by Story in Prigg's case.[94] Yet the provisions of the clause dealing with fugitives from service patently vest no power in Congress to which that body, under Article I, section 8, the "necessary and proper" clause, might give effect by legislation. Rantoul had elaborated on this point, which Shaw chose to ignore. Instead, the Chief Justice drew sweeping implications that permitted him to turn to the Fugitive Slave Act of *1793* with the assurance that its intent was to implement "the power and duty of Congress to secure and carry into effect a right confirmed by the Constitution. . . ."[95]

[92] *Ibid.*, 295–297.
[93] *Ibid.*, 299.
[94] 16 Peters 539, 620 (1842).
[95] 7 Cush. 285, 300.

This first Fugitive Slave Act he described as having authorized a summary and informal proceeding adapted to the exigency of the occasion. No regular suit at law was provided for. The fugitive was simply seized, brought before a United States judge or state magistrate, and on proof that he owed labor to the claimant, it was made the duty of the judge or magistrate to give a certificate warranting the removal of the fugitive to the state from which he had fled.[96] But to *describe* the Act of 1793, as Shaw did, was not to join issue with the challenge that the Act of 1850 was unconstitutional because it made no provision for a trial by jury. As to the mode of trial contemplated, Shaw remarked: "The law of 1850 stands, in this respect, precisely on the same ground with that of 1793, and the same grounds of argument which tend to show the unconstitutionality of the one, apply with equal force to the other; and the same answer must be made to them." [97] That answer, to repeat, was that the laws had not described a suit, but a summary proceeding.

Shaw next rejected the contention that the Act of 1850 was unconstitutional because of Congressional inability to confer judicial authority upon Circuit Court Commissioners. The duties and powers of these commissioners he considered "very similar" to those delegated to justices of the peace by the Act of 1793. It was manifest to him that Congress had not deemed the functions of the justices of the peace, as they related to escaped slaves, to be judicial. And he pointed to the difficulty in marking "minute shades of difference" between judicial and non-judicial powers, because under every government there were functions exercised which, requiring "skill and experience, judgment and even legal and judicial discrimination," resisted precise classification. They were "partly judicial and partly administrative." In consequence of this line of reasoning, he refused to distinguish between the powers granted to justices of the peace and those to commissioners. He also refused to consider on its own merits the question whether the powers exercised by commissioners under the Act of 1850 were constitutionally delegated. This was not a new question, he declared, "but one settled and determined by authorities which it would be a dereliction of official duty, and a disregard of judicial responsibility, to overlook." With this last remark, Shaw launched into extensive quotations from the various authorities, state and

[96] *Ibid.,* 301.
[97] *Ibid.,* 310.

especially federal, which had upheld the first fugitive slave law.[98]

The conclusion of the opinion is of interest because Shaw suggested some of the premises that underlay his logic. Not often do judges touch on the larger grounds of decision, their own views on public policy, which can sway their judgment in a case. Shaw did not, of course, crudely offer his personal endorsement of the Fugitive Slave Act of 1850 as a wise and necessary enactment. He did hint at his reluctance to decide Sims' case. He as much as informed counsel that he preferred them to bring their petition before United States judges; *they* would determine whether Sims was being illegally held. As for himself, he recognized "no necessary occasion for drawing the authority of the State and United States Judiciary into conflict with each other." He had relied on Supreme Court precedent, in a case depending upon the Constitution, because such a procedure was "absolutely necessary to the peace, union and harmonious action of the State and General Governments." It would be a grave move to invalidate an act of Congress passed under a clause of the Constitution which was not only "the best adjustment" which could be made of conflicting interests in the Convention of 1787; this fugitive slave clause was also an "essential element" in the formation of the Union, "necessary to the peace, happiness and highest prosperity of all the states." Concluded Shaw: "In this spirit [of compromise], and with these views steadily in prospect, it seems to be the duty of all judges and magistrates to expound and apply these provisions in the constitution and laws of the United States. . . ."[99]

Many of the city's first merchants were present in the court room to hear Shaw's opinion — only a favored audience was permitted entry. George Bancroft, the historian, testified before a committee of the state Senate that while a plain citizen of Massachusetts could not obtain admittance within her halls of justice, he could do so by saying to the officers at the door, "I am a gentleman from the South!" When the opinion was read, the merchants in attendance, "who had swallowed their dinner in a hurry to get this as the dessert," muttered, "Good, good." The anti-slavery men grieved over the decision; "most painful," reported Elizur Wright's paper, the *Commonwealth*. "What a moment was lost when Judge Shaw declined to affirm the unconstitutionality of the Fugitive Slave Law!" exclaimed Emerson: "This filthy enactment

[98] *Ibid.*, 303–308.
[99] *Ibid.*, 310, 318–319.

was made in the nineteenth century by people who could read and write. I will not obey it, by God." Theodore Parker wrote to Charles Sumner that he never had had any confidence in the Supreme Judicial Court anyway, adding with spiteful glee: "But think of old stiff-necked Lemuel visibly going under the chains! That was a spectacle!" [100]

For public consumption, however, the abolitionists trumpeted the theme of the ermine having been dragged in the dust, and they libeled Shaw for having "spit in the face of Massachusetts . . ." [101] Benjamin Thomas, later Shaw's associate on the high bench, was much closer to the truth in his estimate. He wrote that although there were "portions of that opinion which did not command our assent . . . it is not difficult to understand or to respect the position of the Chief Justice on the subject." Thomas added that Shaw "was so simple, honest, upright, and straightforward, it never occurred to him there was any way around, over, under, or through the barrier of the Constitution, — that is the only apology that can be made for him." [102] But no apology need be made for him if one accepts his debatable premise that the decisions of the United States Supreme Court sustaining the Act of 1793 must be taken as controlling precedents for the Act of 1850.

After Shaw's decision, the abolitionists frantically redoubled their activity. From pulpit, press, and platform, they thundered condemnation. The ultras among them conspired to rescue Sims by lawless means. Fantastic schemes were plotted; all but one were abandoned as impractical. The one was to have Sims jump from the window of his Court House prison to a waiting carriage. But almost at the last minute the rescue was blocked: new iron bars were fitted in the window.[103]

All week, while rescue plans were being discussed and public opinion agitated, Sims' lawyers tried to save him by due process.

[100] *Newburyport Union,* quoted in *The Liberator,* May 2, 1851; *The Commonwealth,* April 8, 1851; E. W. Emerson and W. E. Forbes (eds.), *Journals of Ralph Waldo Emerson* (Boston, 1912), VIII, 201, 236; O. B. Frothingham, *Theodore Parker* (New York, 1880), p. 416.

[101] Theodore Parker, *The Trial of Theodore Parker for the "Misdemeanor" of a Speech in Faneuil Hall Against Kidnapping* (New York, 1864), pp. 214-215; *The Commonwealth,* April 8, 1851.

[102] Benjamin Thomas, "Sketch of the Life and Judicial Labors of Chief-Justice Shaw," *Proceedings,* Massachusetts Historical Society, 2nd ser., 10:74 (1867).

[103] Adams, *Dana,* I, 188-193; Higginson, pp. 141-144; *National Intelligencer,* April 10, 1851; *Twentieth Annual Report,* p. 23; *The Commonwealth,* April 5, 1851; *The Liberator,* April 11, 1851; Bearse, pp. 24-25.

The proceedings before Curtis continued, and a bewildering number of new actions were instituted, before Judge Peleg Sprague of the United States District Court and Justice Levi Woodbury of the United States Supreme Court, on circuit. Every writ and petition was defeated. Then, on Friday, April 11, Commissioner Curtis delivered his opinion, remanding Sims to the custody of the agent who claimed him. So ended the legal proceedings against Thomas Sims.[104] During the black hours of Saturday morning, a guard of three hundred armed men led the slave through the streets of the sleeping city. At Long Wharf the brig *Acorn,* armed with cannon, received him. Before dawn, he was on the way back to his master.[105]

In Boston, most of the respectable citizenry were relieved to be done with a disagreeable but necessary job.[106] To the benefit of peace and profits, the majesty of the law had prevailed. *The Commonwealth* of April 14 accurately summed up the city's press: " 'Boston is redeemed!' shouts all hunkerdom, 'the Fugitive Slave Law has been enforced!' " The *Boston Herald* (April 14) was proud that the city had verified its mettle: "Our city has been redeemed from the opprobrious epithets which have been denounced against her, for her supposed inability and disinclination to yield to the laws of the Union, and the South will please accord us all the credit which is due therefore." As if in reply, Sims' "home town" paper, the *Savannah Republican,* acknowledged its "pleasant duty to accord to the authorities and people of Boston great credit for the firm and energetic manner in which they have demeaned themselves." [107] The paper was particularly pleased with Chief Justice Shaw's decision. Another Savannah journal, however, was most crabbed about the manner in which Sims was returned. "If our people," it declared, "are obliged to *steal their property out of Boston in the night,* it would be more profitable to adopt a regular kidnapping system at once, without regard to

[104] *The Trial of Thomas Sims* (Boston, 1851), 1–47; *Law Reporter* 14:2–15 (Jan., 1852); Parker, p. 151; *The Commonwealth,* April 8 and 11, 1851; *The Liberator,* April 8 and 18; Adams, *Dana,* I, 188–193.

[105] Bowditch, I, 216–223; *The Liberator,* April 18 and 25, 1851; *Daily Evening Transcript,* April 12, 1851; *Twentieth Annual Report,* pp. 22–23; *National Intelligencer,* April 17, 1851; *The Commonwealth,* April 23, 1851. For a detailed account of the events in this case following Shaw's decision — the other legal proceedings, the rescue plots, and the mass meetings — see Leonard W. Levy, "Sims' Case: The Fugitive Slave Law in Boston in 1851," *Journal of Negro History,* 35:39–74 (January, 1950), 61 ff.

[106] *Daily Evening Transcript,* April 12, 1851.

[107] Quoted in the *Daily National Intelligencer,* April 25, 1851.

law." The nearby *Augusta Republic* responded in much the same way, adding that the slave could never have been returned had it not been for "the countenance and support of a numerous, wealthy, and powerful body of citizens. It was in evidence that fifteen hundred of the most wealthy and respectable citizens — merchants, bankers and others — volunteered their services to aid the Marshal." [108]

Elsewhere in the nation there was much rejoicing over the vindication of the Act of 1850. Webster wrote the President that all that was needed now was to get rid of some of the "insane" abolitionists and fre-soilers.[109] In the nation's capital, the *National Intelligencer* of April 13 headlined its lead story, "SUPREMACY OF THE LAW SUSTAINED." In Virginia, the *Richmond Whig* cried, "All honor to the brave old city!" The *New York Express* praised Shaw's opinion and the way the Fugitive Slave Act had been "so beautifully" executed. And so it went in the press of other cities.[110]

Opinion was not, of course, unanimous. In New England, for example, little free-soiling dailies spoiled the festive occasion with words about "human freedom" and "conscience." The *Norfolk* (Massachusetts) *Democrat* cursed the affair as the "darkest and most disgraceful crime that has ever been perpetrated" in Boston's history. The *Massachusetts Spy* and the *Hartford Republican* recalled the "shame" of the rendition with anguish.[111] To the *Lowell American,* it was "a combination of the money and the Websterism of Boston" which was responsible for a "victory of cotton over the conscience of the people!" [112]

Whittier memorialized the humiliating case and called his poem "Moloch in State Street." And in his journals, the transcendental Alcott wrote: "I had fancied till now that certain beautiful properties were mine — by culture and the time and place I live in, if not by inheritance — namely a City, Civilization, Christianity, and a Country." [113]

[108] Quoted in Bearse, pp. 29–30.
[109] April 13, 1851, *Writings, Letters and Speeches* (National Edition, 1903), XVI, 606.
[110] Quotations from *The Liberator,* May 2, 1851, which gives extensive excerpts from the press opinion of many cities, including Albany, Buffalo, Mobile, Philadelphia, and Louisville.
[111] Quoted in *The Liberator,* May 2.
[112] Quoted in Robinson, pp. 193–194.
[113] *Journals,* p. 246.

VII

Not until the spring of 1854 was Boston again — and for the last time — convulsed by the fate of an escaped slave captured in its streets. Lemuel Shaw was not a participant in the Anthony Burns case, which was the most tragic and thrilling of its kind,[114] but his Court did not wholly escape involvement. After Transcendentalist poets and preachers attacked the Court House in a vain effort to rescue Burns, the building was converted into an armored slave-pen, guarded by a detachment of United States marines, two companies of artillery with cannon, rifles, and fixed bayonets, and the United States Marshal's guard, "a gang of about one-hundred and twenty men, the lowest villains in the community, keepers of brothels, bullies, blacklegs, convicts . . ." [115] No one was permitted into the Court House, neither judges, jurors, witnesses, nor litigants, without first passing a cordon five men deep, and proving a right to be there. During this siege, the state courts were scheduled to be in session but adjourned in most cases, while United States Commissioner Edward G. Loring, in a mockery of the canons of judicial neutrality, consigned Burns to slavery. Burns' counsel, Dana, lamented in his diary:

Thus the judiciary of Massachusetts has been a second time put under the feet of the lowest tribunal of the federal judiciary in a proceeding under the Fugitive Slave Law. Judge Shaw, who held the Supreme Judicial Court, is a man of no courage or pride, and Judge Bishop, who held the court of Common Pleas is a mere party tool, and a bag of wind at that. It was the clear duty of the court to summon before it the United States marshal to show cause why he should not be committed for contempt, and to commit him, if it required all the bayonets in Massachusetts to do it, unless he allowed free passage to all persons who desired to come into either of the courts of the State.[116]

Dana was overwrought when he made his remark about Shaw. But the Chief Justice was entitled to no credit for his tacit submission to the bayonets which closed his court. By his inaction he permitted what was in effect the rule of martial law for the sake of "Union-saving" measures. In the critical years before the Civil War, few men who labored constructively under public responsibility escaped unblemished from a compromise with slavery.

[114] A good account of the Burns case is in Commager's *Theodore Parker*, pp. 232–242.

[115] Adams, *Dana*, I, 273.

[116] *Ibid.*, p. 274.

Less than two weeks after President Pierce signed the Kansas–Nebraska Act, destroyer of sectional peace, Anthony Burns' freedom was sacrificed to the Fugitive Slave Law. A military escort of two thousand men marched the lone slave out of black-draped Boston, its flags at half-mast, while the people of the city watched in shame. Just as the rendition of Sims had helped elect Sumner to the Senate, so the rendition of Burns, together with the despised Kansas–Nebraska Act, led to a new and drastic Massachusetts Personal Liberty Law.

This statute,[117] which Shaw opposed, obligated the justices of the Supreme Judicial Court to take fugitive slaves from the custody of the federal marshal, by habeas corpus, and to have the slaveowner's claim tried by a jury in a state court. The governor, upon advisement by the Supreme Judicial Court, returned this bill unsigned, quoting the Court's opinion that state authorities could not interfere with a person in the custody of federal officers under United States law.[118] The measure, adopted without the governor's signature, provided in addition that a federal commissioner empowered to issue certificates of rendition could hold no state judicial office; nor could any lawyer who acted as a counsel to a slaveowner in a fugitive slave case practice thereafter in the courts of the state. In these provisions,[119] the personal liberty law was probably an unconstitutional bill of attainder, but neither in whole nor in part was it ever tested before the Court. The statute was partly directed against Commissioner Loring for his rendition of Burns, and under its terms he was removed from office as Judge of Probate. Popular resentment against him was so feverish that he was also dismissed from his post on the Harvard Law School faculty, despite a recommendation in his favor by Lemuel Shaw, Fellow of the Harvard Corporation.[120]

VIII

On August 21, 1860, Shaw resigned from the bench. He was free at last to express himself on public matters as a private citizen. A divided nation was facing a Presidential election. The

[117] St. 1855, ch. 489.

[118] Benjamin Curtis, *A Memoir of Benjamin Robbins Curtis* (Boston, 1897, 2 vols.), I, 345–346.

[119] They were repealed in 1858, leaving the rest of the statute intact. St. 1858, ch. 175.

[120] H. G. Pearson, *The Life of John A. Andrew* (Boston, 1904, 2 vols.), I, 72 ff.; Charles Warren, *History of the Harvard Law School* (New York, 1908, 3 vols.), II, 196–199.

"Bell-Everetts," arch-conservators of compromise and national unity, pledged to "no political principle other than the Constitution of the Country, the Union of the States, and the Enforcement of the Laws," appealed to the most respected man in Massachusetts for permission to use his name as candidate for Elector-at-Large. Alluding to the dangers of secession, the Union State Committee wrote to him:

In this state of things your appearance at the head of our electoral ticket as a revered mediator between the Northern and Southern extremes of party, would, in our humble opinion, be in entire conformity with your honored career, of vast importance to the country, and a crowning title to its grateful veneration.[121]

On the back of this letter, eighty-year-old Lemuel Shaw scrawled, "nomination declined/Sept 4." Great age may have made him reluctant to engage in politics, though the reason for his declination is unrecorded. Undoubtedly he was in sympathy with the cause of the party. In a real sense, he was all his life a Constitutional Unionist. Nomination would not likely have been officially tendered were his party views not known.

A few months later, in his final public act, Shaw headed a group of prominent conciliationists who hoped to appease the South by recommending unconditional repeal of Massachusetts' Personal Liberty Laws. In an "Address" published on December 18, the signatories, "impelled by no motive save the love of our country," warned:

The foundations of our government are shaken, and unless the work of destruction shall be stayed, we may soon see that great union . . . broken into weak, discordant, and shattered fragments; and that people, who have dwelt under its protection in unexampled peace and prosperity, shedding fraternal blood in civil war.[122]

Urging their fellow citizens first to examine their own conduct for "causes which threaten a great people with ruin," before demanding loyalty to the Constitution from the South, the signers documented their conviction that Massachusetts itself "has violated our great national compact" by its personal liberty laws. Such laws, commanding interference by the state with the laws of the national government, were "laws commanding civil war." There followed a fervent plea for sanity in the conduct of state

[121] Shaw Papers, Box 1855–61.
[122] "Address To the Citizens of Massachusetts," printed in Curtis, I, pp. 329–335.

affairs. Were Massachusetts "honestly and generously" to discharge its obligations under the Fugitive Slave Act and to repeal the provoking statutes, then secession might be given pause and the Union preserved. Five days later, South Carolina seceded.

The "Address" bore the signatures of some of the most distinguished and influential men in Massachusetts. Among the forty-two were Benjamin R. Curtis, Joel Parker, George Ticknor, Jared Sparks, Levi Lincoln, Emory Washburn, and Theophilus Parsons. The first name on the list was Lemuel Shaw's.

He who had given liberty to every slave, not a runaway, brought before him while he sat on the bench of justice, ended his public career in opposition to "An Act to protect the Rights and Liberties of the People of the Commonwealth of Massachusetts." [123] As the "national calamity" he had always dreaded became ever and ever an increasing reality, a man of his conservative temperament and Unionist views could only retreat from the cause of individual freedom in anxious regard for an even greater value, the nation itself. Were one charitably disposed to a man who with integrity compromised under fire, it might be said of Lemuel Shaw, as Tennyson said of statesmen, that he

> knew the seasons when to take
> Occasion by the hand, and make
> The bounds of freedom wider yet.

[123] St. 1855, ch. 489.

7

SEGREGATION

Origin of the "Separate but Equal" Doctrine

I

In mid-nineteenth-century Massachusetts, color prejudice sought its last legal refuge in Boston's system of public schools. Yet no institution was safe from the pitiless criticism of conscience, for the age of the Universal Reformers pulsated with the spirit of social justice. Only the vision of a perfect society delimited the imagination. Quite proper then that in William Lloyd Garrison's state the reformers should devote some measure of their energies toward improving the status of the free American Negro. The law prohibiting intermarriage had been rescinded in 1843, and railroads had been forced to abandon Jim Crow cars.[1] Separate schools for Negroes had been abolished, where they had existed, in Salem, Lowell, New Bedford, Nantucket, and in the smaller towns.[2] In the Supreme Judicial Court in 1849, Charles Sumner, arguing the cause of Sarah Roberts before Chief Justice Shaw, eloquently coupled the "civilization of the age" to an appeal for the abolition of segregated education in Boston.[3]

For half a century schools for the exclusive use of Negro children had been maintained in Boston. Both parties to the Roberts case agreed that the first school was originally established, in 1798, at the request of Negro citizens "whose children could not attend

[1] St. 1843, ch. 5; *Twelfth Annual Report, Presented to the Massachusetts Anti-Slavery Society, by Its Board of Managers, January, 1844*, pp. 5, 7; *Argument of Charles Sumner, Esq. against the Constitutionality of Separate Colored Schools, in the Case of Sarah C. Roberts vs. The City of Boston. Before the Supreme Court of Mass., Dec. 4, 1849* (Boston, 1849), p. 32 (hereafter cited as *Sumner's Argument*).

[2] See letters to Edmund Jackson from school committees of various towns on the results of abolishing separate schools, in *Report of the Minority of the Committee of the Primary School Board, on the Caste Schools of the City of Boston with some remarks* (by Wendell Phillips) *on the City Solicitor's Opinion* (Boston, 1846) Appendix, pp. 21–27.

[3] *Sumner's Argument*, p. 31.

the public schools on account of the prejudice then existing against them." [4] Boston had refused to incur the expense of the colored school, but it was made possible by the benefactions of white philanthropists. In 1806 the basement of the newly erected African Baptist Church in Belknap Street was secured as a permanent site. When Abiel Smith, "the merchant prince," died in 1815 and left an endowment of $4,000 for the school, it took his name. Not until 1812 had Boston assisted the school; the town's grant of $200 was continued yearly till 1815, when the Board of Selectmen assumed control. Five years later, after the primary school for children of four to seven had become a part of the public-school system, Boston legally fixed the pattern of segregation by establishing a separate primary school for Negroes.[5]

For more than twenty years thereafter, the Smith Grammar School and its primary-school appendages continued undisturbed. Meanwhile, the Boston Negro had been growing in political maturity. Once the battle against the Jim Crow car was won, Negro militants, urged on by the Massachusetts Anti-Slavery Society, turned their faces against the Jim Crow school, once a blessing, now a discriminatory abomination. In 1846 they petitioned the primary school committee for the abolition of exclusive schools. Despite the protests of its two abolitionist members, Edmond Jackson and Henry I. Bowditch, the committee decided against the petition. Candidly naming racial differences as the reason for their action,[6] the majority declared that segregated education for Negroes was "not only legal and just, but is best adapted to promote the education of that class of our population." [7] That very year, the white master of Smith School officially reported that the institution was shamefully neglected, desperately in need of repairs.[8]

[4] Roberts v. City of Boston, 5 Cush. 198, 200 (1849). See also *Sumner's Argument*, pp. 27–28.

[5] *Report of a Special Committee of the Grammar School Board, presented August 29, 1849, on the petition of sundry colored persons praying for the abolition of the Smith School* (Boston, 1849), pp. 18–21, 68–69.

[6] The majority report stated: "The distinction is one which the Almighty has seen fit to establish, and it is founded deep in the physical, mental, and moral natures of the two races. No legislation, no social customs, can efface this distinction." "Extracts from the Majority Report on the Caste School," in *The Liberator* (Boston), Aug. 21, 1846. To Garrison, such remarks were "flimsy yet venomous sophistries."

[7] Quoted in Roberts v. City of Boston, 5 Cush. 198, 201 (1849).

[8] "The school rooms are too small, the paint is much defaced, and every part gives evidence of the most shameful negligence and abuse. There are no recitation rooms, or proper places for over-clothes, caps, bonnets, etc. The yards, for

For over four years the issue was the occasion of discord among public officials and among the Negroes themselves, who were bitterly divided. In the press, and at public meetings, it was long debated, and no less than two majority and two minority school-committee reports were published. Without action by the legislature, which alone could end the controversy, all the circumstances were at hand for a court case.[9]

II

Benjamin Roberts was one of the Negro leaders in the fight against segregation. Four times he tried to enter his five-year-old daughter Sarah in one of the white primary schools of the district in which he resided, and as many times she was rejected by authority of the school committee, solely on the grounds of color. On the direct route from her home to the primary school for Negroes, Sarah passed no less than five other primary schools. Roberts was informed that his child might be admitted at any time to the colored school, but he refused to have her attend there.[10] Determined to test the constitutionality of the school committee's power to enforce segregation, Roberts brought suit in Sarah's name under a statute[11] which provided that any child illegally excluded from the public schools might recover damages against the city.

To argue Sarah's cause, Roberts retained Charles Sumner, a man of erudition, eloquence, and exalted moral fervor; he was to become New England's greatest senator and slavery's most implacable foe. The City of Boston was represented by its solicitor, Peleg W. Chandler, Massachusetts' foremost expert on municipal law and founder of one of the earliest legal journals, the *Law Reporter*.[12]

---

each division, are but about fifteen feet square, and only accessible through a dark, damp cellar. The apparatus has been so shattered and neglected that it cannot be used until it has been thoroughly repaired" (Remarks of Ambrose Wellington, Master of Smith School, quoted in *City Document No. 28, Reports of the Annual Visiting Committees of the Public Schools of the City of Boston*, Boston, 1846, p. 151).

[9] *Sumner's Argument*, p. 4; *Report of a Special Committee of the Grammar School Board . . . August 29, 1849*, pp. 1–10, *passim; The Liberator*, Aug. 10, Sept. 7, Dec. 7, 14, 21, 1849, Jan. 4, Feb. 8, 15, 1850.

[10] 5 Cush. 198, 200–201 (1849).

[11] St. 1845, ch. 214.

[12] Chandler's argument in the Roberts case is not reported by Cushing, the court reporter. But see *The Liberator*, Aug. 28, 1846, for the full text of his opinion as City Solicitor given three years earlier to the school committee. Much of what Chandler said on the constitutionality of segregated education was adopted by the Court.

Sumner's argument before Shaw turned on a "single proposition — *the equality of man before the law*." [13] Quoting the paragraphs of the Massachusetts Constitution which courts of a later day were to construe as meaning the same as the "equal protection" clause of the Fourteenth Amendment,[14] Sumner observed that every form of inequality and discrimination in civil and political institutions was thereby condemned. He alleged the unconstitutionality of the segregated school on the grounds of its "caste" nature, and proved that the school committee had been motivated by racial prejudice. The power of the committee, delegated by the state legislature, was merely to superintend the public schools and to determine "the number and qualifications of the scholars." [15] A power to segregate could not be implied, argued Sumner, for the committee "cannot brand a whole race with the stigma of inferiority and degradation." To imply the existence of that power "would place the Committee above the Constitution. It would enable them, in the exercise of a brief and local authority, to draw a fatal circle, within which the Constitution cannot enter; nay, where the very Bill of Rights shall become a dead letter." [16] Only factors of age, sex, and moral and intellectual fitness might be considered by the committee as qualifications, not complexion. Just as the law required the regulation and by-laws of municipal corporations to be reasonable, Sumner asserted, so must the acts of the school committee be reasonable.[17] But an *a priori* assumption by the committee that an entire race possess certain qualities which make necessary a separate classification of that race, was an unreasonable exercise of the committee's discretion, and therefore an illegal one.

Anticipating the "separate but equal" doctrine, Sumner ar-

[13] *Sumner's Argument*, p. 31.

[14] Declaration of Rights, Art. I: "All men are born free and equal, and have certain natural, essential and unalienable rights, among which may be reckoned the right of enjoying and defending their lives and liberties . . ." Art. VI: "No man, nor corporation, or association of men, have any other title to obtain advantages, or particular and exclusive privileges, distinct from those of the community, than what arises from the consideration of services rendered to the public . . ." See Lehew v. Brummell, 103 Mo. 546, 553 (1890); Gong Lum v. Rice, 275 U.S. 78, 86–87 (1927).

[15] Rev. Sts. 1835, ch. 23, secs. 10 and 15.

[16] *Sumner's Argument*, p. 21.

[17] See Commonwealth v. Worcester, 3 Pick. 462 (1826); Vandine's Case, 6 Pick. 187 (1826); City of Boston v. Shaw 1 Metc. 130 (1840). In the last-named case, as Sumner pointed out, the Court had voided a city by-law as unequal and unreasonable.

gued that the segregated school could not be an "equivalent" because of the inconveniences and the stigma of caste which it imposed, and because a public school, by definition, was for the equal benefit of all. The right of the Negro children was to "precise equality." [18]

Before closing, Sumner discussed certain matters "not strictly belonging to the juridical aspect of the case," yet necessary for understanding it. His remarks, which have been validated by modern sociological scholarship, were in part as follows:

The whites themselves are injured by the separation . . . With the law as their monitor . . . they are taught practically to deny that grand revelation of Christianity — the Brotherhood of Mankind. Their hearts, while yet tender with childhood, are necessarily hardened by this conduct, and their subsequent lives, perhaps, bear enduring testimony to this legalized uncharitableness. Nursed in the sentiment of Caste, receiving it with the earliest food of knowledge, they are unable to eradicate it from their natures . . . The school is the little world in which the child is trained for the larger world of life. It must, therefore, cherish and develop the virtues and the sympathies which are employed in the larger world . . . beginning there those relations of equality which our Constitution and laws promise to all . . . Prejudice is the child of ignorance. It is sure to prevail where people do not know each other. Society and intercourse are means established by Providence for human improvement. They remove antipathies, promote mutual adaptation and conciliation, and establish relations of reciprocal regard.[19]

III

Chief Justice Shaw, delivering the unanimous opinion of the Court, upheld to the fullest extent the power of the school committee to enforce segregation.[20] The case required for its disposition no fine analysis of difficult legal points, and Shaw confined himself, as did the counsel before him, primarily to general principles — and to predilections as well. That his opinion has had an enduring influence may be attributed in part to the sweep and force with which the principles were announced, and to the articulation given those predilections.

Pointing out that the plaintiff had access to a school for Negro children as well fitted and conducted in all respects as other

[18] *Sumner's Argument*, pp. 24-25.

[19] *Ibid.*, pp. 28-30, *passim.*

[20] Justice Richard Fletcher, who had given an opinion at the bar on the unconstitutionality of segregated schools, unexplainedly did not sit in the Roberts case.

primary schools,[21] the Court rejected the contention that she had been unlawfully excluded from public-school instruction. The issue, rather, was one of power, "because, if they [the committee] have the legal authority," said Shaw, "the expediency of exercising it in any particular way is exclusively with them." [22] The latter half of this unqualified proposition, which invested the school committee with discretionary powers to classify pupils by race, religion, economic status, or national origin, was stated as a fixed legal fact in support of which the Court risked no reasons. Similarly, other conclusions which were adopted regarding the points at issue were characterized by a singular absence of considered judgment.

For example, Shaw proceeded directly from *carte blanche* approval of the committee's discretionary powers, to an assumption — in itself, sufficient to decide the case — that all individuals did not possess the same legal rights. And whom else could he have had in mind but Negroes? His own words are given in full:

The great principle, advanced by the learned and eloquent advocate of the plaintiff, is, that by the constitution and laws of Massachusetts, all persons without distinction of age or sex, birth or color, origin or condition, are equal before the law. This, as a broad general principle, such as ought to appear in a declaration of rights, is perfectly sound; it is not only expressed in terms, but pervades and animates the whole spirit of our constitution of free government. But, when this great principle comes to be applied to the actual and various conditions of persons in society, it will not warrant the assertion, that men and women are legally clothed with the same civil and political powers, and that children and adults are legally to have the same functions and be subject to the same treatment; but only that the rights of all, as they are settled and regulated by law, are equally entitled to the paternal consideration and protection of the law, for their maintenance and security. What these rights are, to which individuals, in the infinite variety of circumstances by which they are surrounded in society, are entitled, must depend on laws adapted to their respective relations and conditions.

Stripped of its rhetoric, this paragraph set forth two contradictory propositions, perhaps more succinctly expressed by that favored class, the pigs of George Orwell's *Animal Farm:*

[21] The fact that the segregated schools provided equal facilities was not challenged by the plaintiff. Expensive but timely improvements were completed in September of 1849. The case was argued less than three months later. *Report of a Special Committee of the Grammar School Board . . . August 29, 1849,* pp. 13, 70.

[22] All quotations of Shaw's opinion are from 5 Cush. 198, at 206–210.

ALL ANIMALS ARE EQUAL
BUT SOME ANIMALS ARE MORE EQUAL THAN OTHERS

Having virtually decided the case by asserting unreasoned grounds for decision, the Chief Justice defined the question before the Court — an inversion of the order of logic. He stated the question in such a way as to make possible by his answer the "separate but equal" doctrine:

Conceding, therefore, in the fullest manner, that colored persons, the descendants of Africans, are entitled by law, in this commonwealth, to equal rights, constitutional and political, civil and social, the question then arises, whether the regulations in question, which provides separate schools for colored children, is a violation of any of these rights.

Thereupon, Shaw established in detail the undisputed facts that legal rights depend upon provisions of law; that the state constitution declared broad principles intended to direct the activities of the legislature; that the legislature, in turn, had defined only the general outlines and objects of an educational system; and that the school committee had been vested with a plenary power to make all reasonable rules for the classification of pupils. Shaw was impressed with the fact that the committee, after long deliberation, believed that the good of both races was best promoted by the separate education of their children. The Court, he said, perceived no ground to doubt that the committee formed its belief "on just grounds of reason and experience, and in the results of a discriminating and honest judgment."

In introducing into the jurisprudence of Massachusetts the power of a governmental body to arrange the legal rights of citizens on the basis of race, the Chief Justice was bound to show for the Court not only that the discrimination, in the face of an equality of rights clause, was not forbidden; he should have shown that such discrimination was reasonable. Instead, he contented himself with the thought that the prejudice which existed "is not created by law, and probably cannot be changed by law." He added, moreover, that it would likely be fostered "by compelling colored and white children to associate together in the same schools." This was the Court's answer to Sumner's contention that the maintenance of separate schools tended to perpetuate and deepen prejudice. It did not occur to Shaw to appraise the experience of other towns in Massachusetts, where children without regard to race attended the same schools with the most successful results. Thus the doctrine of "separate but equal" as a constitutional justification of racial segregation in public schools first entered American jurisprudence.

By 1855 the unceasing efforts of the abolitionists and Negroes proved to be of greater weight in Massachusetts than the opinion of its distinguished Chief Justice. A new statute was enacted which rooted out the last legal refuge of racial discriminination in Massachusetts.[23]

IV

In constitutional history, however, Shaw's opinion had a continuing vitality. It was initially cited with approval by the high court of the Territory of Nevada in 1872.[24] Two years later the California Supreme Court endorsed the doctrine by quoting most of Shaw's opinion, and concluded: "We concur in these views and they are decisive . . ." [25] The courts of New York, Arkansas, Missouri, Louisiana, West Virginia, Kansas, Oklahoma, South Carolina, and Oregon have also relied upon the Roberts case as a precedent for upholding segregated education.[26] It has been mentioned by lower federal courts twice in recent years, as well as on earlier occasions.[27]

In the United States Supreme Court, the Roberts case was first discussed by Justice Clifford in *Hall v. DeCuir* as an authority for the rule that "equality does not mean identity." [28] In

[23] St. 1855, ch. 256, sec. 1: "In determining the qualifications of scholars to be admitted into any public school or any district school in the Commonwealth, no distinction shall be made on account of the race, color or religious opinions, of the applicant or scholar."

[24] State *ex rel.* Stoutmeyer v. Duffy, 7 Nev. 342, 386, 395–396 (1872).

[25] Ward v. Flood, 48 Cal. 36, 41, 52–56 (1874).

[26] People *ex rel.* King v. Gallagher, 93 N.Y. 438, 441, 448, 453 (1883); Maddox v. Neal, 45 Ark. 121, 125 (1885); Lehew v. Brummell, 103 Mo. 546, 547, 553 (1890); *Ex parte* Plessy, 45 La. Ann. 80, 85, 87–88 (1893); Martin v. Board of Education, 42 W. Va. 514, 516 (1896); Reynolds v. Board of Education of the City of Topeka, 66 Kan. 672, 684–686 (1903); Board of Education of the City of Kingfisher v. Board of County Commissioners, 14 Okla. 322, 332 (1904); Tucker v. Blease, 97 S. Car. 303, 330 (1913); Crawford v. School District No. 7, 68 Ore. 388, 396 (1913).

[27] Claybrook v. City of Owensboro, 16 Fed. 297, 302 (1883); Wong Him v. Callahan, 119 Fed. 381, 382 (1902); Westminster School District of Orange County v. Mendez, 161 Fed. 2d. 774, 779 (1947); Corbin v. County School Board of Pulaski County, Va., 84 Fed. Supp. 253, 254–255 (1949).

[28] While his concurring opinion was directed at the unconstitutionality of La. Rev. St. sec. 1, 1870, which barred separate accommodations for Negroes on common carriers, Clifford addressed himself to the subject of education to show that, "Questions of a kindred character have arisen in several of the States, which support these views in a course of reasoning entirely satisfactory and conclusive" (Hall v. DeCuir, 95 U.S. 485, 503, 504, 505, 1877).

Plessy v. Ferguson, decided in 1896, the Court turned to Shaw's opinion as a leading precedent for the validity of state legislation which required segregation of the white and colored races "in places where they are liable to be brought into contact . . ." [29] When it is considered that the Plessy case itself became the leading authority on the constitutionality of the "separate but equal" doctrine, the influence of the Roberts case appears immeasurable. In 1927, in *Gong Lum v. Rice,* it was mentioned by a unanimous bench to support the proposition that segregation in education "has been many times decided" to be constitutional.[30] Chief Justice Taft, the spokesman in the Gong Lum case, also added that the Massachusetts court had upheld "the separation of colored and white schools under a state constitutional injunction of equal protection, the same as the Fourteenth Amendment . . ." [31]

Thus, Shaw's doctrine in the Roberts case became the law of the land and remained so more than a century after he originated it. Its uncritical acceptance by the highest courts of so many jurisdictions, in a nation whose Constitution is color-blind, long warranted its reëxamination and repudiation. This historic step was finally taken by the Supreme Court of the United States on May 17, 1954. Chief Justice Warren, for a unanimous bench, stated:

Does segregation of children in public schools solely on the basis of race, even though the physical facilities and other 'tangible' factors may be equal, deprive the children of the minority group of equal educational opportunities? We believe that it does. . . . We conclude that in the field of public education the doctrine of 'separate but equal' has no place. Separate educational facilities are inherently unequal.[32]

[29] 163 U.S. 537, 544–545 (1896). Plessy v. Ferguson was upon the right of the state to require segregation of colored and white persons in public conveyances, and "the act so providing was sustained . . . upon the principles expressed by Chief Justice Shaw" (Westminster School District of Orange County v. Mendez (161 Fed. 2d. 774, 779, 1947).

[30] 275 U.S. 78, 86 (1927). As a matter of fact, the United States Supreme Court had always assumed, but had never actually decided, the constitutionality of "separate but equal" as regards public schools. See *New York University Law Quarterly Review,* 23:298–303, note (1948); see also Leonard W. Levy, "Fallacies in the Law of Segregation," *New Republic,* 128:16–17 (March 23, 1953), and "Separate but Equal," *The New Leader,* 36:8–10 (Feb. 2, 1953).

[31] 275 U.S. 78, 86–87 (1927). For the provisions of the Massachusetts "injunction of equal protection," see supra, note 14.

[32] Brown v. Board of Education of Topeka, 347 U.S. 483, 493, 495 (1954). At p. 491, the Court noted that the "separate but equal" doctrine "apparently originated in *Roberts v. City of Boston.*"

8

THE FORMATIVE PERIOD OF RAILROAD LAW

Eminent Domain and the Public Works Doctrine[1]

I

Anyone familiar with the legal history of railroad corporations knows that they were objects of the law's solicitude. In the decades after the Fourteenth Amendment, railroads alleged that their character as private enterprises freed them from regulation. But surprisingly, during the formative period of railroad law, they claimed and received special considerations precisely because they were not private. Indeed, the Supreme Judicial Court of Massachusetts protected railroads in their extraordinary privileges and powers on the legal theory that they were public works. On the basis of this same legal theory, the Court also preserved an almost unqualified area of actual and potential state control.

More than any other judicial figure, Lemuel Shaw formulated the fundamentals of American railroad law. It was a fitting historical coincidence that he was nominated Chief Justice on the very day of the successful trial run of the first American steam-powered locomotive.[2] As late as 1930, on the centennial anniversary of Shaw's appointment, Chief Justice Rugg quoted with approval the remark of an eminent railroad attorney that "by mastering Shaw's opinions on railroads one would have a sure

---

[1] The term "railroad law" is often used loosely to encompass virtually any case to which a railroad was a party. Yet much that passes as railroad law belongs to the law of common carriers or might be best classified under tort, evidence, constitutional, or some other appropriate legal heading. But the real problem, which transcends technical classification, is the impact of a specific technological innovation upon the law generally.

[2] August 24, 1830. See the *New England Palladium* (Boston), Aug. 27, 1830; *Boston Daily Advertiser*, Aug. 30, 1830, and the excerpt therein, dated Aug. 24, from the *Baltimore Gazette*; *Columbian Centinel* (Boston), Sept. 4, 1830. The first American engine ran on the Baltimore and Ohio line.

guide in principle for the solution of modern problems in that branch of the law." [3] The statement of the legal historian Charles Warren is equally impressive: "As the number of railroad cases decided in Massachusetts practically equalled that of all the other states combined; and as the principles laid down by Chief Justice Shaw practically established the railroad law for the country, the gradual growth of that law from year to year may be substantially traced in the court decisions of that State." [4]

During the thirty years that Shaw presided over its highest court, the Commonwealth underwent transformation from a predominantly agricultural-merchant economy to a manufacturing one. The railroad was a chief factor in this change: indeed, the iron arteries of communication saved Boston from the economic ruin which the competition of New York's Erie Canal threatened. Yet the project of a railroad from Boston to the Hudson, when first presented, was ridiculed as an absurdity — "as useless as a railroad from Boston to the Moon." [5] Hostility to innovation was overcome only after a period of agitation by enterprising men who convinced the public and the legislature that the railroads would bring prosperity. Lemuel Shaw was one of these railroad educators: his last public act before becoming Chief Justice was to preside as chairman of a committee which recommended a petition to the General Court for a railroad from Boston to the interior. Only two months before his appointment, Massachusetts granted a charter for the building of its first railroad to the Boston and Lowell line.

A variety of novel and important legal questions were posed by the advent of railroads. The Supreme Judicial Court was called upon to define their status at law; construe their charters; explore the law of eminent domain; establish rules of damage in cases of injury to property and persons; determine the rights, duties, and liabilities of railroads as common carriers of passengers and freight; reconcile competing systems of internal improvements; and consider the state's regulatory powers. [6] Under

[3] Supplement, 272 Mass. 602 (1930).

[4] *A History of the American Bar* (Boston, 1911), p. 485.

[5] *Boston Courier,* June 27, 1827, quoted by C. F. Adams, "The Canal and Railroad Enterprise of Boston," in J. Windsor (ed.), *Memorial History of Boston* (Boston, 1881, 4 vols.), IV, 122; E. C. Kirkland, *Men, Cities, and Transportation* (Cambridge, 1948, 2 vols.), I, 93–97, 108, 360.

[6] Chapter 9 will deal with developments in the common law resulting from the many cases on the rights, duties, and liabilities of railroads as common carriers of passengers and freight, or resulting from the establishment of rules of damage in cases of personal injury.

Shaw, the law generally acted as a seismograph, sensitive to the tremors of social change. New questions were sometimes solved by the formulation of original doctrines, more often by applying a modified and reinvigorated existing doctrine. Only on infrequent occasion was the law deep-frozen by the ill-considered acceptance of ancient maxims.

II

Significantly, railroads and the term "eminent domain" entered the jurisprudence of Massachusetts simultaneously. The first mention of either was made by Chief Justice Shaw in 1834, when he announced that it was the incontestable right of the state to appropriate private property for public use in the case of railroads, on the ground that they were "public works." [7] In 1835, in the very first case in which a railroad was a party, Shaw pointed out that under acts of the legislature intended to promote public improvements, the railroad claimed rights "as granted by the public and to be exercised and carried into effect for the use and benefit of the public." [8] A year later he observed that while a

[7] Wellington, *et al.*, Petitioners, 16 Pick. 87, 102–103 (1834). The first and only mention of "eminent domain" in an American decision before 1834 appears to have been in Beekman v. Saratoga & Schenectady RR., N.Y. Chancery Reports, 3 Paige 45, 73 (1831). Philip Nichols, *The Law of Eminent Domain* (Boston, 1917, 2nd ed.), I, 24, note 9, incorrectly states that Shaw's opinion in the Wellington case was the first to mention "eminent domain." Before its appearance in a judicial opinion, the term had occasionally been used by counsel. Arthur Lenhoff, "Development of the Concept of Eminent Domain," *Columbia Law Review*, 42: 598, note 16, points out that the term was employed by counsel as early as 1796, in Lindsay v. Comm'rs, 2 Bay (S.Car.) 38, 46, 53. James Kent should be credited for popularizing the term; see his *Commentaries on American Law* (Boston, 1826–1830, 4 vols.), II (1827), 275. Despite these early usages, an excerpt from an argument by Daniel Webster before the U.S. Supreme Court may be put in evidence to indicate how novel was the concept itself, as well as the term, even as late as 1848. Webster said: "This power, the eminent domain, which only within a few years was first recognized and naturalized in this country, is unknown to our Constitution or that of the State. It has been adopted from writers on other and arbitrary governments. . . . But being now recognized in Court, our only security is to be found in this tribunal, to keep it within some safe and well-defined limits, or our State Governments will be but unlimited despotisms over the private citizens . . . (If) the legislature, or their agents, are to be the sole judges of what is to be taken, and to what public use it is to be appropriated, the most levelling ultraisms of Anti-rentism or agrarianism or Abolitionism may be successfully advanced" (West River Bridge Co. v. Dix, 6 How. 507, 520–521, 1848).

[8] Boston Water Power Co. v. Boston & Worcester RR., 16 Pick. 512, 526 (1836). The first case in which a railroad was a party was not decided in the U.S. Supreme Court until 1840. Philadelphia & Trenton RR. v. Simpson, 14 Peters 448. The first *Treatise on American Railroad Law* was not published until 1857 (New York). The author was Edward L. Pierce.

railroad was constructed at private expense, "The work is not the less a public work; and the public accommodation is the ultimate object." [9]

This view was probably influenced by earlier decisions sustaining the power of turnpikes, gristmills, bridges, and canals, under legislative authorization, to take or damage private property. Yet again Shaw was the first to maintain that such private enterprises were in effect public utilities. For example, not until 1834 did the Court hold that a private turnpike was, in legal contemplation, a public highway.[10] Thus, while the work of Chief Justices Parsons and Parker, Shaw's predecessors, was not without effect upon him, he went considerably further than they. It was he who established the foundation of the emerging law of public utilities.[11]

In 1842, in the first railroad tax case,[12] an extraordinary decision was given as a logical consequence of the doctrine that railroads were not ordinary private corporations in the contemplation of the law. The case developed from the fact that the Western Railroad, along with other owners of real estate, was taxed by the town of Worcester on all its property, except its franchise. The question was whether a railroad was exempt from taxation, and if so, to what extent. In his opinion the Chief Justice found it necessary to examine the Western's charter,[13] which, by the way, was typical for the period. The charter authorized the exercise of the right of eminent domain for the construction of a road not exceeding five rods wide. The duty of the corporation was to transport persons and goods. The levying of tolls was

[9] Fuller v. Dame, 18 Pick. 472, 483 (1836).

[10] Commonwealth v. Wilkinson, 16 Pick. 175 (1834). In this case Shaw declared (at 176–177): "But the principal question . . . is, whether a turnpike road in this Commonwealth, is a highway, and whether an indictment will lie against any person, for obstruction thereon as a public nuisance. We think, that a turnpike road is a public highway, established by public authority for public use, and is to be regarded as a public easement, and not as private property. The only difference between this and a common highway is, that instead of being made at the public expense in the first instance, it is authorized and laid out by public authority, and made at the expense of individuals in the first instance; and the cost of construction and maintenance, is reimbursed by a toll, levied by public authority for the purpose. Every traveller has the same right to use it, paying the toll established by law, as he would have to use any other public highway." Shaw had spoken of railroads as "public works" two weeks prior to this statement. See note 7, *supra*.

[11] See *infra*, Ch. 13, sec. IX. The statement by Shaw in note 10, *supra*, suggests what is meant by the remark that he established the foundation of the emerging law of public utilities.

[12] Inhabitants of Worcester v. Western RR., 4 Metc. 564 (1842).

[13] St. 1833, ch. 116.

authorized, but the legislature reserved the power to limit rates and profits, required annual accounting reports, and had the right to investigate the corporation's books at all times. The state also had an option to buy out the corporation on specified terms after a certain period.

The conclusions at which Shaw arrived after examining this charter merit attention as a notable judicial determination of the character of "this class of corporations," and as an inferential endorsement of the extensive control of the legislature. He said:

> From this view of the various provisions of the law, by which the rights and duties of the Western Rail Road Corporation are regulated, it is manifest that the establishment of that great thoroughfare is regarded as a public work, established by public authority, intended for the public use and benefit, the use of which is secured to the whole community, and constitutes therefore, like a canal, turnpike or highway a public easement. The only principle, on which the legislature could have authorized the taking of private property for its construction, without the owner's consent, is, that it was for the public use. . . . It is true, that the real and personal property, necessary to the establishment and management of the railroad, is vested in the corporation; but it is in trust for the public. The company have not the general power of disposal, incident to the absolute right of property; they are obliged to use it in a particular manner, and for the accomplishment of a well defined public object . . .[14]

On this view of the legal status of railroads, the Court held that the lands of the Western within the authorized width and all the structures erected thereon, if necessarily incident to the public easement, were not liable to taxation. Not exempt, however, was property not incident to the construction and maintenance of the railroad or its use by the corporation as common carriers, nor property beyond the authorized width.[15]

Shaw's rule was intended to effect a public subsidy of railroads, for the Western's charter did not expressly grant it a tax exemption. There was no intimation, however, that the legislature lacked power to reserve the right to tax a public work; indeed, the tenor of the opinion confirmed the legislature in its powers. Moreover, the decision had history on its side: the practice in Massachusetts, as Shaw pointed out, had been to exempt all public works from taxation, including bridges, turnpikes, and public buildings of all kinds.

[14] 4 Metc. 564, 566 (1842).
[15] See also Boston and Maine RR. v. City of Cambridge, 8 Cush. 237 (1851).

III

Just as taxation was related to the interlocking concepts of eminent domain and public works, so too were half of all the railroad cases before 1860. Even the principle that a railroad is liable for the acts of all its agents, whether employees, officers, or contractors, was dovetailed, most curiously, with these same concepts. *Hilliard v. Richardson*,[16] for example, substantially eliminated an employer's common-law liability for the negligence of the employees of his contractor. The Court, however, left this liability unimpaired in regard to railroads, on the theory that a railroad, entrusted by the state to appropriate property for the execution of a public work, cannot escape its duty to protect the public against danger inhering from a delegation of power to a contractor. Thus the general liability of railroads to third parties for the acts of all agents remained fixedly severe. This rule of law probably induced the selection of more careful contractors, conductors, engineers, and other employees, in accordance with the best interests of the public and railroads alike.

Two cases of magnitude imposed upon the Court the task of construing railroad corporation charters with a view to expounding the law of eminent domain in relation to public contracts.[17] In the first of these cases, *Boston Water Power Co. v. Boston and Worcester Railroad,* decided in 1839, Shaw wrote one of his greatest opinions, anticipating by almost a decade a similar ruling by the United States Supreme Court[18] that the contract clause of the federal Constitution does not restrain the state's power of eminent domain.

The question was whether the legislature could constitutionally authorize a railroad to take land and a franchise, on payment of compensation, by locating and constructing its road across the plaintiff's basins. The plaintiff, a water power company, argued: (1) that the right to the use of its land was a franchise and not property such as the land itself, which could be taken by eminent domain; and (2) that by Article I, section 10 of the federal Constitution, the state surrendered that part of eminent domain which consists in the power of vacating contracts. The first question was decided on a practical consideration:

---

[16] 3 Gray 349 (1855).

[17] Boston Water Power Co. v. Boston and Worcester RR., 23 Pick. 360 (1839); Boston and Lowell RR. v. Salem and Lowell RR. *et al.,* 2 Gray 1 (1854).

[18] West River Bridge Co. v. Dix, 6 How. 507 (1848).

although the value of the land was reduced by the location of the railroad, the franchise had not actually been taken. The legislature's grant to the railroad was only an appropriation to another public use of a portion of the land over which the water power company exercised its franchise. The right to the use of that land, declared the Chief Justice, was not outside the "liability to which all the lands of the Commonwealth are subject to be taken for public use, at an equivalent, when in the opinion of the legislature, the public exigency or as it was expressed in the case of highways, when public convenience and necessity may require it." [19] Since the franchise was impaired but not destroyed as alleged, there was no necessity to decide whether the whole of it might be taken. Yet Shaw stated, "I am not aware that it stands upon a higher or more sacred ground than the right to personal or real property." [20]

He agreed that a grant of land was a contract, but rejected the contention that the contract controlled the power of eminent domain:

And yet there can be no doubt, that land granted by the government, as well as any other land, may be taken by the legislature in the exercise of the right of eminent domain, on payment of an equivalent. Such an appropriation therefore is not a violation of the contract by which property, or rights in the nature of property, and which may be compensated for in damages, are granted by the government to individuals.[21]

This was the first decision in American jurisprudence on the point that the power of eminent domain could not be restrained by, or contracted away under, Article I, section 10, of the national Constitution.

Fifteen years later, in the second great contract clause case, *Boston and Lowell Railroad v. Salem and Lowell Railroad et al.*,[22] the Court answered two important questions: was it within the power of the legislature to grant in the charter of a railroad a thirty-year monopoly of the business between two cities; and, were the rights thus vested infringed by three other railroads who had combined their connecting roads to form a parallel, continuous route between the same *termini?*

[19] 23 Pick. 360, 392.
[20] *Ibid.*, at 393. See also Central Bridge Corp. v. City of Lowell, 4 Gray 474 (1855).
[21] 23 Pick. 360, 394.
[22] 2 Gray 1 (1854).

It is pertinent to note that the Boston and Lowell had been incorporated as the first Massachusetts railroad in 1830, only six months after the decision in the Charles River Bridge case,[23] at which time the Massachusetts Court in effect had held that in a public contract, exclusive rights are not granted by implication. Daniel Webster and Lemuel Shaw had represented the losing party in that case, the Charles River Bridge Company. Shaw, in his opinion as Chief Justice in the 1854 case, referred to the timidity of "moneyed men" in those early days when it had been impossible to estimate the costs or profits of a railroad.

With this want of experience, and with an earnest desire on the part of the public to make an experiment of this new and extraordinary public improvement, it would be natural for the government to offer such terms, as would be likely to encourage capitalists to invest their money in public improvements; and after the experience of capitalists, in respect of the turnpikes and canals of the Commonwealth, which had been authorized by the public, but built by the application of private capital, but which as investments had proved in most instances to be ruinous, it was probably no easy matter to awaken anew the confidence of moneyed men in these enterprises.[24]

Bearing in mind these circumstances at the time of plaintiff's incorporation, Shaw found it easy to construe the words of the charter as conferring exclusive rights.

To the contention that the legislature had exceeded its powers in granting such rights, he replied that it possessed full authority to regulate all public rights and to make such grants as might be useful to the public. Perspicaciously he foresaw that the public interest was best served by a strictly regulated natural monopoly, rather than by laissez-faire competition between close, parallel roads which would make "unnecessary waste" inevitable. Consequently he held that when the legislature had conferred exclusive rights in consideration of the public benefit to be gained — the public being protected by the reserved powers of the government to purchase the franchise and to control rates, profits, and service — and when the grantees had advanced their money in good faith, then the state was bound by contract. The Court was aware that a contrary ruling would have destroyed the continuing public utility of the pioneer railroad and would have inhibited or dried up capital investments in public improvements.[25]

[23] Charles River Bridge v. Warren Bridge, 7 Pick. 344 (1829).
[24] 2 Gray 1, 28.
[25] *Ibid.*, 33–34. See also *infra*, pp. 271–272.

Though the contract was held to be irrepealable by ordinary law, the Chief Justice asserted that it gave way to the extraordinary power of eminent domain, for "Whatever exists, which public necessity demands, may be thus appropriated." [26] Under color of eminent domain, the legislature might reach every species of valuable right and interest, including all real and personal property, easements, franchises, and incorporeal hereditaments. The case at the bar was concluded by holding that the defendants had illegally combined their roads in a manner infringing upon the plaintiff's charter, because the legislature had nowhere manifested an explicit intention to take any part of the rights or franchise there conferred.

In these two contract-clause cases, the public interest as determined by the legislature was the primary concern of the Court. Even the interpretation of a grant as a contract of exclusive rights, irrepealable by ordinary laws, rested on consideration of the fact that the public had obtained a benefit in return and was protected by the terms of the contract. The undiminished sovereign power over all property was supported, yet investment was secured and business encouraged. Railroad corporations were reminded that they derived all their rights from the state and held them subject to regulation. The legislature in turn was reminded, and wisely, that since "great caution" was a virtue in making grants, it should carefully estimate the cost of the reciprocal public advantage to be obtained and should provide for time's unpredictable changes by reserving extensive powers of control. Shaw's opinions reveal a man with vision enough to calculate the economic needs of Massachusetts, and boldness enough to shape the law to allow for orderly progress.

IV

The same achievement is evident in a line of cases wherein the Court harmonized competing or conflicting systems of internal improvements. Other public-service corporations whose property was taken or used by railroads contested the infringement of their vested rights. Reference has already been made to the 1839 decision — *Boston Water Power v. Boston and Worcester R.R.* — which reconciled the use of the same land by a water-power company and a railroad. The first case of this character, decided earlier the same year, was a suit for an injunction against a

[26] 2 Gray 1, 35.

railroad brought by a turnpike.[27] Had the Court enjoined the railroad in either of these cases, the new mode of transportation would have been left in a state of legally arrested development. On the other hand, the rights of the complainants merited serious respect. The Court's duty, then, was to adapt one public work to the other in the public interest.

In the Newburyport Turnpike case, the right of the railroad under color of eminent domain to raise the turnpike road so as to cross it on the same level was disputed as obstructive, because by charter and statute the railroad was empowered only to pass over or under. Shaw ruled that a railroad passed over a turnpike by crossing it on its surface as well as when crossing above it on a bridge. This answer to the question of whether charter rights were interfered with when railroads intersected highways, rested on general considerations of social advantage. Railroads and highways were public works, said Shaw,

and we are to presume, that in granting, limiting, and modifying the powers and rights of each, the legislature had in view that common public good, which is the object of them all. In cases, therefore, where some interference is unavoidable . . . such construction ought to be put upon them [legislative provisions] if possible, as that the powers and privileges of each shall be no further limited or restrained, than may be reasonably necessary to enable the other to accomplish the public purpose, for which it was established.[28]

On application of this doctrine, the law provided for the adaptation of railroads to bridges, canals, turnpikes, highways, and all other public improvements.

An allied case presented, in Shaw's words, "a very important question; one, which, in the great multiplication of railroads, is likely to affect deeply the interests of many parts of the commonwealth, and which has not yet been decided." [29] The question was whether a railroad could take the roadbed of a public highway for the location of its road. The Court enjoined the railroad from doing so without express authorization from the legislature. The Chief Justice thought it remarkable that in a matter so deeply affecting private rights and interests, the precise location of a railroad was not fixed by its charter or by a board of public officers; rather, the charter empowered the railroad to determine its route within stated *termini*. Considering "how large" were the powers thus vested in the railroad, the rule was that "they ought to be construed with a good degree of strictness, and not enlarged by construction." [30] Accordingly, it was held that in a grant to construct a railroad between fixed *termini,* no authority was given prima facie to lay it out longitudinally along an existing public highway; the two uses were inconsistent. By this rule, the Shaw Court conserved the state's highway resources and stayed railroad usurpation of the legislature's prerogative of eminent domain. The legislature was held competent to supplant one public use with another as long as its intention to do so was shown by express words or by necessary implication.

The power of eminent domain is a high prerogative of sovereignty, founded upon public exigency, according to the maxim: *Salus re-publicae lex est,* to which all minor considerations must yield, and which can only be limited by such exigency. The grant of land for one public use must yield to that of another more urgent.[31]

In another case, the city of Roxbury, to protect the lives and property of its citizens using a highway that was crossed by a railroad, sought to force the latter to comply with an order to build a bridge over the track of its road at the point of intersection. Deciding in favor of the city, the Chief Justice declared: "The same qualities [mass and speed] which render railroads useful, also render them dangerous, and require that every precaution should be taken . . ." [32] In *Commonwealth v. Nashua and Lowell Railroad,*[33] argued by Rufus Choate against Benjamin F. Butler, the question concerned the limits on the authority of local communities to prescribe expedients which might "reconcile the use of the highway and the railroad with each other." Shaw refused to fix limits and upheld the order of a town requiring the railroad to erect a drawbridge at a crossing to accommodate travel over a peculiarly situated highway. The doctrine was established that any obstruction of a public way is prima facie a public nuisance against which an indictment might lie.[34]

[30] *Ibid.,* at 70.
[31] *Ibid.,* at 71–72.
[32] City of Roxbury v. Boston and Providence RR., 6 Cush. 424, 429 (1850).
[33] 2 Gray 54 (1854).
[34] See also Commonwealth v. Proprietors of New Bedford Bridge, 2 Gray 339 (1854); Commonwealth v. Vt. & Mass. RR., 4 Gray 22 (1855); Old Colony & Fall River RR. v. Plymouth, 11 Gray 512 (1858); Commonwealth v. Old Colony & Fall River RR. 14 Gray 93 (1859).

It may be observed at this point that unlike other great conservative judges — Marshall, Story, and Kent come to mind — Chief Justice Shaw, except in the tax exemption case,[35] construed public grants in favor of the interests of the community and against those that were private. Consequently, when the chartered powers and privileges or railroads were exercised in the public interest, he interpreted them broadly;[36] but when they competed with the right of the community to protect itself or to conserve its resources in communications, life, or property, he interpreted them narrowly.

v

Controversies over alleged injuries to private property by railroads, in consequence of their exercise of the right of eminent domain, constituted the single most frequent cause of litigation in the formative period of railroad law. Varied novel cases of this nature compelled the judiciary to formulate precise rules of damage. A special problem was presented by cases not within the express requirements of Article X of the Massachusetts Declaration of Rights. The provision there made, that compensation must be paid for property "appropriated," had been implemented by a general law which established the liability of every railroad for "all damages, that shall be occasioned by laying out, and maintaining their road, or by taking any land or materials . . ."[37] Clearly, a railroad was responsible for damages when it withdrew an individual's profitable use of his property by taking it for a public use. But what of a case in which a railroad injured property not "appropriated"?

This question first arose in *Dodge v. County Commissioners of Essex,* decided in 1841.[38] The facts were that the petitioner's house, located near the railroad but not within its limits, was demolished by the blasting done by the railroad on its own land while grading its road. The new question, as defined by the Chief Justice, was "whether, under the provisions of the revised statutes respecting railroads, one can have compensation for damages whose land has not been directly taken for the site of the railroad, nor for supplying materials for its construction."[39]

[35] Worcester v. Western RR., 4 Metc. 564 (1842), *supra*, pp. 121–122.

[36] See Babcock v. Western RR., 9 Metc. 553 (1845); Brainard v. Clapp, 10 Cush. 6 (1852); Commonwealth v. Hartford & New Haven RR., 14 Gray 379 (1860).

[37] Rev. Sts. 1835, ch. 39, sec. 56.

[38] 3 Metc. 380 (1841).

[39] *Ibid.,* at 381.

The Court found the statute "broad enough" to embrace the loss which petitioner had sustained. His house could not be moved out of the way of danger from blasting; yet blasting, with due precautions, was an appropriate and justifiable means of constructing a railroad. The damage, then, was unavoidable. By such reasoning Shaw established the doctrine that railroads were responsible for damage necessarily done in the lawful execution of a public work.[40]

Decisions in cases similar to the Dodge case rested on the theory that the state, in authorizing a public work, makes provision for compensation to all vested rights that are abridged in the public interest. But unlawful damage could not be done in the name of the public; therefore, the theory precluded compensation if under color of eminent domain a railroad caused property loss by acting with carelessness or negligence, or in a manner not warranted by its charter. Though no remedy was provided by statute in a case of this nature, the Court did not leave an aggrieved party without the protection of law. As Shaw first pointed out by dictum in the Dodge case, an action of tort would properly lie if in the construction of a railroad unnecessary or unauthorized damage was done to property not appropriated.[41] In *Mellen v. Western Railroad*,[42] a tort case, this dictum was converted into law. Offering a scathing criticism of the railroad for "wanton disregard of the rights of individuals" and for its assumption of "absolute right" to injure private property with impunity at common law, the Court ruled that where a railroad is charged for tort, it has the burden of proving that its acts were strictly within conferred powers. Thus did the Court affirm that private property was adequately safeguarded from railroad encroachments, by both statutory and common law.

VI

Railroads making compensation for appropriated or damaged property naturally tried to pay as little as possible. In actions brought by holders of real estate against railroads for the recovery

[40] See also Ashby v. Eastern RR., 5 Metc. 368 (1842), and Parker v. Boston and Maine RR., 3 Cush. 107 (1849).
[41] Dodge v. County Commissioners of Essex, 3 Metc. 380 (1841). See also Proprietors of Locks and Canals v. Nashua & Lowell RR., 10 Cush. 385 (1852); Estabrooks v. Peterborough & Shirley RR., 12 Cush. 224 (1853); Blood v. Nashua & Lowell RR., 2 Gray 137 (1854); Mellen v. Western RR., 4 Gray 301 (1855); Carson v. Western RR., 8 Gray 423 (1857).
[42] 4 Gray 301 (1855).

of damages, it was common for the railroads to attempt to extinguish or diminish the claim by establishing a "set-off" or counterclaim. A railroad would offer evidence alleging that in consequence of the building of its road, the remaining property of the person whose land was damaged had increased in value; then the Court would be requested to order a proportionate reduction of the petitioner's claim.

The general rule for cases not involving public works was laid down by Shaw in an 1835 opinion.[43] He held that a manufacturing company which was liable for damages could not claim a set-off for benefits in the way of unearned increments to real-estate values that accrued from the growth in population, schools, stores, "and all the usual incidents to the establishment of a manufacturing village in a district which was before exclusively or essentially agricultural." The benefits from the general prosperity induced by the company's improvements, ruled Shaw, were "too contingent, remote and indirect, to be brought into consideration in this question of damages . . ." [44]

Railroads, however, alleged that because they were public works they were entitled to considerations not accorded merely private corporations. In *Meachum v. Fitchburg Railroad,*[45] the railroad went to the extreme of claiming a set-off for the unearned increment that its road had brought, not only to the plaintiff's property which adjoined the land appropriated but also to his other property, located at some distance away. The Court maintained that there must be some limitation to the proposition advanced in a very early case[46] that in consequence of the laying out of a public work, benefits occasioned to the remaining part of the property should be considered as reducing the damages for the land actually taken. The new view was that one whose land has been taken for a railroad "has a right, in common with his other fellow citizens, to the benefit arising from the general rise of prosperity in the vicinity, occasioned by the establishment of the railroad and the facilities connected therewith." [47] The doctrine of the decision was that collateral benefits justified a corresponding reduction of the damages to be paid by the railroad only if it could show a "direct" and "peculiar" benefit to the

---

[43] Palmer and Co. v. Ferrill, 17 Pick. 58 (1835).
[44] *Ibid.,* at 63–64.
[45] 4 Cush. 291 (1849).
[46] Commonwealth v. Coombs, 2 Mass. 489, 492 (1806).
[47] 4 Cush. 291, 297 (1849).

property through which its trains passed, or to the property adjoining the particular tract of land actually taken. Only two years later, it became necessary to restate the rule: no set-off would be allowed for benefits or increased values shared in common with the neighborhood.[48] From time to time the rule was reaffirmed, despite railroad efforts to secure its modification.[49]

VII

Although the Shaw Court demonstrated concern for private property by placing common-law checks on railroads, generously extending statutory protections, and constricting the set-off rule, it did not, however, protect property from any and all damage that might be occasioned by the exercise of eminent domain. To an enlightened Court, there was one value more privileged at law than vested rights: the public right. Several of the Chief Justice's opinions illustrate this view.[50]

In the Davidson case,[51] argued by Rufus Choate against Sidney Bartlett, the railroad had built its tracks across the flats of a tide-mill company by erecting a bridge over the mouth of a creek at the head of the mill. The mill owners sued for damages because the railroad practically wiped them out of business: the bridge obstructed the free flow of the tide water into their dam, causing the water to overflow their land, impair the operation of their mills, and prevent navigation to their wharf. In spite of these facts, the decision was against the mill owners. Shaw declared flatly: "The public have a right to regulate the use of public navigable waters for the purpose of passage; and the erection of a bridge with or without a draw, by the authority of the legislature, is a regulation of a public right, and not the deprivation of any private right, which can be a ground for damages." [52] Consequently, although the railroad's bridge was an obstruction destroying the beneficial use of private property, it was not deemed by the Court as an invasion of property rights which entitled the

[48] Upton v. South Reading RR., 8 Cush. 600 (1851).
[49] See Davis v. Charles River Branch RR., 11 Cush. 506 (1853); Browne v. Providence, Warren & Bristol RR., 5 Gray 35 (1855); Dickenson v. Inhabitants of Fitchburg, 13 Gray 546 (1859).
[50] Davidson v. Boston and Maine RR., 3 Cush. 91 (1849); Proprietors of Locks and Canals v. Nashua and Lowell RR., 10 Cush. 385 (1852); Boston & Worcester RR. v. Old Colony RR., 12 Cush. 605 (1853).
[51] 3 Cush. 91 (1849).
[52] Ibid., at 106.

owners to compensation; for in contemplation of law there had been no "taking of private property for public uses." [53]

Shaw's opinion, though limited in the application of its doctrine, was a blow to the sanctity of property. Although a private enterprise had suffered ruinous damage by — as Shaw inimitably put it — "the mere regulation of a public right, and not a taking," [54] the Court provided for no legal indemnity, and said nothing about constitutional limitations on the legislative power which, in effect, authorized the damage. The broad legal theory underlying the decision was that the loss had been suffered in common with the whole of the community for the greater good of the community, because it had been an obstruction in the use of a public right — the right to use land washed by the tide waters — which had occasioned damage. By means of this legal fiction an impairment in the enjoyment of property was sustained as a legitimate exercise of government power. Because there had been no "taking," that power, in a strict sense, must be classified within the ambit of the police powers, not eminent domain.[55]

The second of the Chief Justice's opinions which illustrate judicial limitations on private economic interests in favor of the public interest, was given in *Proprietors of Locks and Canals v. Nashua and Lowell Railroad*,[56] a leading case of great consequence. The question was whether the depreciation in the value of real estate not crossed by a railroad and not physically endangered by its construction could be considered in awarding damages.

Turnpike, bridge, steamship, and other businesses, together with certain local interests, strenuously opposed the railroads which diverted their traffic and trade.[57] If in this case the Court

[53] *Ibid.* So, too, where damages were alleged against a railroad for having built upon a wharf a bridge which impeded access by vessels, it was held *per* Shaw, C.J., that since the bridge passed over a navigable channel as authorized by the legislature, private parties suffering thereby could not sustain a claim for damages. Boston and Worcester RR. v. Old Colony RR., 12 Cush. 605 (1853).

[54] 3 Cush. 91, 106 (1849).

[55] For a clear distinction between the police power and the power of eminent domain, see Shaw's opinion in Commonwealth v. Tewksbury, 1 Cush. 520 (1846), and Commonwealth v. Alger, 7 Cush. 53, 84–86 (1851), discussed in Chapter 13, *infra*, pp. 246–254.

[56] 10 Cush. 385 (1852).

[57] For the effect of the railroad upon turnpikes and the protests of the latter, see P. E. Taylor, "The Turnpike Era in New England" (unpub. *MS.*, Yale Library, 1934), pp. 308–320. When the first railroad charter was granted by the Massachusetts legislature, it was described by the turnpike interests as "those cruel turnpike

had validated the canal company's claim against the Nashua and Lowell, then all railroads would have been saddled with a general liability crippling in its effects. The floodgates of litigation would have been thrown wide open to every owner of real estate and proprietor of private enterprise whose property values had suffered because of the location or competition of a railroad.

Shaw was rarely the technical judge who decided cases on constricted grounds. His greatness lay in what Justice Holmes described as his "accurate appreciation of the requirements of the community . . ."[58] In this opinion, Shaw treated the issue as one of high public policy. He stated without equivocation:

The law does not propose to grant indemnity for all losses occasioned by the laying of a railroad. If it did, it would extend to turnpikes and canals, the value of which is diminished or destroyed by loss of custom; to taverns and public houses deserted or left in obscurity; to stage-coach proprietors and companies; to owners of dwelling-houses, manufactories, wharves, and all other real estate in towns and villages, from which a line of travel has been diverted.[59]

Any loss arising from diversions of travel or custom, whether direct or indirect, ruled the Chief Justice, would be too remote to be evaluated as an element of damages. Only special damage, damage different in kind and peculiar from that sustained by others, warranted indemnity.

This rule reduced the question to whether diminution in the market value of land not otherwise touched or affected by a railroad was such special damage. The answer was "no," because such losses

are common to the whole community, to be borne by the public in consideration of the greater public good to be acquired. They are, however, to be well considered by the legislature before granting such a charter; and we presume that no wise government would grant a charter tending to such public inconvenience, without a great preponderance of public good to overbalance them.[60]

killers and despisers [sic] of horseflesh." Quoted by Taylor, p. 311, from J. Hayward, *Gazetteer of Massachusetts* (Boston, 1849), p. 193. For comment on the opposition of other businesses and/or their straits, see Oscar and Mary F. Handlin, *Commonwealth, A Study of the Role of Government in the American Economy: Massachusetts, 1774-1861* (New York, 1947), pp. 188, 191, 193, 231, 265; Forward v. Hampshire and Hampden Canal Co., 22 Pick. 462, 465-467 (1839); and Chase v. Sutton Mfg. Co., 4 Cush. 152, 167-168 (1849).

[58] *The Common Law* (Boston, 1881), p. 106.

[59] 10 Cush. 385, 389.

[60] *Ibid.*, at 391.

Taken together, the decisions in the varied cases on land damage arising from the exercise of the right of eminent domain by railroads reflect soundly defined doctrines that struck an equilibrium between the rights of all parties, private and public alike. Individuals were legally guaranteed an equivalent for the value of appropriated property and were shielded against set-off claims by railroads for the benefits shared in common with the community; railroads, in turn, were protected from claims for remote damages suffered by the whole public. So if railroads occasioned either general prosperity or economic distress, no party could maintain a claim. In all cases where the public right was involved it was held inviolate.

VIII

Railroad rates, which in later years were a subject of so much controversy, scarcely posed a problem for the judiciary before the Civil War. One reason is that from the time the first railroad charter was granted in Massachusetts, on June 5, 1830, the legislature reserved rate-fixing powers.[61] Indeed, government control figured so prominently in the state's railroad history from the very beginning that it was taken for granted. For example, before private enterprise prevailed as the system for building and managing the roads, the chief issue of debate was government ownership versus private ownership under strict government regulation: the right of the legislature to intervene in the economy was not questioned.[62]

Written into the very acts of incorporation were provisions for state supervision of rates. The railroads were authorized to levy tolls for profit and as compensation for the cost of construction and management, but as the Chief Justice once stated, the power to take toll "is in every respect a public grant, a franchise, which no one could enjoy but by the authority of the government. This grant of toll is subject to certain regulations, within the power of the government, if it should become excessive." [63] Specifically, the legislature reserved the right to reduce passenger and freight

[61] St. 1830, ch. 4, secs. 5, 12.

[62] Before the first charter was granted, it seemed that railroads might become an outright government project, financed and operated on public credit. Governor Levi Lincoln, the State Board of Directors of Internal Improvements, a legislative committee, and many prominent citizens supported state action. Kirkland, *Men, Cities and Transportation*, I, 105–111; Handlin and Handlin, *Commonwealth*, pp. 184-188.

[63] City of Roxbury v. Boston and Providence RR., 6 Cush. 424, 431–432 (1850).

rates, and profits as well, whenever the net income of a company exceeded ten per cent of its capital stock. For checking purposes, the legislature required yearly reports of all acts and doings, receipts and expenditures. In addition, it reserved the right to prescribe rates which might be charged by competing companies authorized to connect and enter upon each others' track.[64]

A general statute of 1845, relating to the exercise of the latter right, provided the first test of the legality of rate regulation by a state authority. Under the terms of the act, special commissioners appointed by the Supreme Judicial Court were to fix, by means of a schedule of rates, the compensation which one railroad should pay another for having its freight and passenger cars drawn over the track of the latter.[65] In 1852, the Fitchburg line, objecting to a petition for the appointment of commissioners, alleged that the act infringed its chartered right to regulate its own tolls subject only to the condition that the legislature might intervene when profits passed the maximum allowance.[66] The Court rejected this argument in a very brief opinion by upholding the statutory right of commissioners.

Eight years later, decisions of first importance were given in a brace of cases[67] bearing on state regulations of railroad rates and services. The first of these, *Boston and Worcester Railroad v. Western Railroad* [68] marked a precedent in which a rate schedule drawn by a government body came under judicial review for a determination whether that body, a special commission, had permitted a "reasonable compensation" to the complainant railroad. It was alleged that the commissioners had transcended their statutory authority[69] and had not fixed rates upon a fair and proper economic basis. Merrick's opinion for the Court was a model of judicial restraint. Referring to the commissioners, he declared that the Court

will so far supervise and control their proceedings as to see that, in the discharge of the duties thus imposed upon them, they have acted within the scope, and have neither exceeded nor failed to exercise the

[64] See Rev. St. 1835, ch. 39, secs. 45–86.

[65] St. 1845, ch. 191, sec. 2.

[66] Vermont and Massachusetts RR., v. Fitchburg RR., 9 Cush. 369 (1852).

[67] Boston and Worcester RR. v. Western RR., 14 Gray 253, and Lexington and West Cambridge RR. v. Fitchburg RR., 14 Gray 266 (1859).

[68] Argued by Justice B. F. Thomas, who had recently resigned from the Court, against Sidney Bartlett.

[69] St. 1845, ch. 191, sec. 2, as amended by St. 1857, ch. 291, sec. 2.

full measure of authority with which they are invested. In considering their return, if it be found that they have thus acted, their doings and decisions will not be interfered with. The Court will not examine any question upon which they, within the limits of their legitimate authority, have passed, nor reverse or disturb any award which they have made consequent to their determination of it. But on the contrary their award should in such case be approved and affirmed.[70]

As to what constituted a reasonable compensation and the basis upon which it was to be computed, the Court emphasized the difficulty and complicated nature of the problems. Merely as a suggestion, and not as a rule to bind regulating authorities, the Court proposed that for a prudently constructed and properly managed railroad, a sum for all services at least equal to legal interest upon the amount of investment, after payment of all current costs, would be a reasonable compensation. But formulas were for the commission, not the Court, to determine. "They [the commissioners] heard the parties, their allegations, proofs and arguments," declared the Court, "and we see no reason for believing that in deciding the questions submitted to them, they did not act in conformity either to the letter or to the spirit and purpose of their commission." [71]

In the companion case of *Lexington and West Cambridge Railroad v. Fitchburg Railroad*,[72] the Court upheld the right of commissioners to fix the number and times of trains to be run over the roads of connecting companies. The statement was made *per curiam* that as commission powers were fixed by a general law,[73] "in order that its provisions may be adapted to the various cases which may arise, the powers conferred by it are necessarily broad and unlimited, and to some extent discretionary, in order that persons suitably qualified in point of skill and experience may prescribe a rule of compensation suited to the particular case . . . the legislature by necessary implication intends to invest them with all the powers appropriate and necessary to accomplish the purposes intended." [74]

Thus government regulation was upheld to the limit. Provided that a commission followed fair procedure and confined itself to the job of fixing rates and services, the judiciary would make

[70] 14 Gray 253, 261.
[71] *Ibid.*
[72] 14 Gray 266 (1859).
[73] St. 1845, ch. 191, sec. 2, as amended by St. 1857, ch. 291, sec. 2.
[74] 14 Gray 266, 271 (1859).

no inquiry into its conclusions, or the methods by which they were reached, and the work of the commission would be accepted as final. It is impressive that these views were promulgated as early as 1859. Only after a most confusing history of judicial interference with regulatory agencies have present-day courts finally come to adopt in principle the position of the Shaw Court. This position assumes, first, that extensive controls of the economy are within the compass of legislative powers; second, that it is not the function of courts to prescribe rates or formulas for determining reasonable compensation; and third, that a rate-making agency, as the creature of the legislature, is a tribunal of final resort within the scope of its authority, as long as fair procedure (due process) is the order of the day.

IX

The role of the state courts in the history of government regulation has not yet attracted the attention of historians who are breaking new ground to correct the erroneous belief that laissez-faire prevailed before the advent of federal control in the economy.[75] Dominated by a Chief Justice who owed allegiance to the tenets of Federalism and Whiggery, the Shaw Court was friendly to the principle that the government exercised as of right a controlling role in the economy. It was not until after the Civil War that the shibboleth of laissez-faire gained real currency. Before that time, when the sovereign authority was contested in cases of public regulation, it was upheld in Massachusetts at least. The rights of property, though adequately protected, ranked

[75] *E.g.* the Handlins, after making much of the legislature's power to control the right of a railroad to discontinue its lines, offer the acute problem of 1857: whether the Fitchburg's abandonment of service to Watertown was a violation of its charter; then they comment: "Baffled, the legislative committee reached no decision and left unsolved, for the time being, the fundamental question of whether a road could slough off the unprofitable portions of its route or whether its obligations to those it served required consideration of the line as a whole" (*Commonwealth*, pp. 240–241). Had not this admirable monograph slighted the work of the Court — to which almost every issue came for adjudication — the fact might have been included that in the legislature's bafflement, the Court reached a decision of this precise question. It was held, *per* Thomas, J., that the discontinuance of a branch line when there was insufficient business to pay expenses did not forfeit a railroad's franchises. The Court brandished a wholesome rod over railroads by adding that franchises would be forfeit by a failure to meet the public wants, and also that the legislature "has reserved to itself full power to amend or alter the charters of railroad companies and regulate the exercise of powers under them" (Commonwealth v. Fitchburg RR., 12 Gray 180, 188, 1858).

second to the rights of the Commonwealth. To Chief Justice Shaw, the concept of the "Common-Wealth" meant a working partnership among government, people, and capital to build and grow together for the greater good.

9

THE FORMATIVE PERIOD OF RAILROAD LAW

Common-Carrier Liabilities and Torts

I

Originally the railroad was thought to be merely a new species of highway, literally a road of rails, public in nature because it was intended for the use and benefit of the public. As Chief Justice Shaw once remarked, in the earliest legislation the railroad was regarded "as an iron turnpike, upon which individuals and transportation companies were to enter and run with their own cars and carriages, paying a toll to the corporation for the use of the road only." [1] This conception was abandoned even before the first railroad was put into operation. In 1831 the Boston and Worcester was empowered in its charter[2] to purchase engines and cars for transportation of persons and goods; and all the subsequent legislation of the Commonwealth was based on the assumption that railroads were carriers of passengers and merchandise.

In contemplation of law, railroads were *common* carriers. Because they were built to serve the public, exercised a public employment, they enjoyed special privileges and powers. They were publicly hired at advertised terms and were obligated to transport all freight and passengers. Public favor had given them a huge volume of business. Thus their very nature, as well as the legal consequences of their actions, stamped them as common carriers and subjected them to all the pertinent rules of the com-

---

[1] Boston and Lowell RR. v. Salem and Lowell RR. *et al.*, 2 Gray 1, 28 (1854). See Sts. 1829, chs. 26, 93; 1830, ch. 4; 1831, ch. 56. See also Boston and Lowell RR. v. Boston and Maine RR., 5 Cush. 375, 383 (1850), and Commonwealth v. Fitchburg RR., 12 Gray 180, 187 (1858).

[2] St. 1831, ch. 72.

mon law.[3] But the application of those old rules to a novel mode
of transportation compelled accommodation in the law.

In an early consideration of whether railroads were common
carriers, the Supreme Judicial Court observed that the question
was of the highest importance "to our community, from the magnitude and the variety of interests concerned in it." [4] For there
was a material distinction between the legal liabilities attending
private carriers and common carriers. The former were responsible merely for ordinary care, but the law imposed extraordinary
liability upon the latter. The common carrier was deemed the
insurer of goods placed in its control and was bound to deliver
them in the same condition as received. For all losses, regardless of
cause or agency, the common carrier was liable. Exceptions to this
rule derived only from acts of God against which no human
foresight could guard, from acts of public enemies such as invad-
ing armies, or from the negligence or default of the consigner
himself. The burden of proof rested with the carrier to rebut the
legal presumption that it was liable in all cases.[5]

II

In view of the strictness of common-law rules, it was of considerable economic importance to know when and for how long
the liability of common carriers attached to railroads. Obviously,
it attached when goods were in actual transit. But unlike the old
wagoners or their successors, the express businesses, railroads
could not pick up and deliver freight door-to-door. When did
transit begin and end? It was a well-established rule that unless
shipment were delayed upon the express orders of the consignor,
common-carrier liability commenced immediately upon acceptance of goods for transportation whether or not they were temporarily stored by the carrier at its convenience in preparation
for the actual shipment: ". . . deposit is a mere accessory to the

[3] Thomas v. Boston and Providence RR., 10 Metc. 472, 475 (1845); Norway
Plains Co. v. Boston and Maine RR., 1 Gray 263, 269 (1854). See also Forward v.
Pittard, 1 Term R. (Eng). 27; 4 Doug. (Eng. K.B.R.) 287.

[4] Thomas v. Boston and Providence RR., 10 Metc. 472, 475 (1845). The question
was earlier considered in Commonwealth v. Power, 7 Metc. 596 (1844), where it was
held, *per* Shaw, C.J., that a railroad might make reasonable and suitable regulations
in regard to its facilities and all persons using them. On this point see also Cheney
v. Boston and Maine RR., 11 Metc. 121 (1846); O'Brien v. Boston and Worcester
RR., 15 Gray 20 (1860); Commonwealth v. Connecticut River RR., 15 Gray 447,
450 (1860).

[5] Thomas v. Boston and Providence RR., 10 Metc. 472, 475. See also Hastings v.
Pepper, 11 Pick. 28 (1831), and Joseph K. Angell, *A Treatise on the Law of Carriers*
(Boston, 1849, 1st ed.), pp. 144 ff. Angell's was the first American work of its kind.

carriage." [6] In contrast, the perplexing problem of when transit came to an end, and with it the discharge of common-carrier liability, required for its solution an adjustment of common-law rules to the railroad business.

This question was the subject of *Thomas v. Boston and Providence Railroad,* a case of first impression, decided in 1845[7] in an opinion by Justice Hubbard. The leading case, however, came nine years later in *Norway Plains Company v. Boston and Maine Railroad* [8] where the opinion was delivered by the Chief Justice, relaxing the extraordinary liability of railroads. Shaw's introduction to his opinion is a classic statement on the growth of the common law. He wrote:

It is one of the great merits and advantages of the common law, that, instead of a series of detailed practical rules, established by positive provisions, and adapted to the precise circumstances of particular cases, which would become obsolete and fail, when the practice and course of business, to which they apply, should cease or change, the common law consists of a few broad and comprehensive principles, founded on reason, natural justice, and enlightened public policy, modified and adapted to the circumstances of all the particular cases which fall within it. These general principles of equity and policy are rendered precise, specific, and adapted to practical use, by usage, which is the proof of their general fitness and common convenience, but still more by judicial exposition; so that, when in a course of judicial proceeding, by tribunals of the highest authority, the general rule has been modified, limited and applied, according to particular cases, such judicial exposition, when well settled and acquiesced in, becomes itself a precedent, and forms a rule of law for future cases, under like circumstances.[9]

Thus, though the common law was founded on general principles, its "expansive and comprehensive character" permitted usage and precedent to render it practical for the daily business of an active community. Moreover, when in consequence of new situations, courses of business, or combinations of fact, novel cases

[6] Fitchburg and Worcester RR. v. Hanna, 6 Gray 539, 541 (1856). In Langley v. Boston and Maine RR., 10 Gray 103 (1857), where goods were destroyed by fire in the railroad's depot before carriage had begun, it was held, *per curiam,* that a common carrier cannot exempt itself from its liability for those goods, although they had been accepted for transportation over a branch line which had been leased to another railroad. On commencement of common-carrier liability, see Angell, *Law of Carriers,* pp. 128–132, and Isaac F. Redfield, *A Practical Treatise upon the Law of Railways* (Boston, 1858, 2nd ed.), pp. 245–249.

[7] 10 Metc. 472 (1845).

[8] 1 Gray 263 (1854).

[9] *Ibid.,* at 267.

arise for which there is no precedent, "they must be governed by the general principle, applicable to cases most nearly analogous, but modified and adapted to new circumstances. . . ." As a result of this malleability, Shaw explained further, the common law possessed a perpetual vigor and vitality.

Therefore although steamboats and railroads are but of yesterday, yet the principles which govern the rights and duties of carriers of passengers, and also those which regulate the rights and duties of carriers of goods, and of the owners of goods carried, have a deep and established foundation in the common law, subject only to such modification as new circumstances may render necessary and beneficial.

Proceeding to the facts of this case, the Chief Justice noted that the railroad had transported goods to their destination and had placed them in its warehouse without having notified the plaintiffs, who were the consignees, of their arrival. Before the plaintiffs could possibly have removed the goods, they were destroyed by an accidental fire which burned down the warehouse. The fire was not caused by lightning, nor by any fault of the railroad. However, ruled Shaw, if the railroad was liable in its capacity as a common carrier, no argument could prevail that it was blameless for the fire; common carriers were bound as insurers to take the risk of fire not caused by an act of God.[10]

But was the railroad liable as a common carrier? For if the transit had come to an end, then the defendants possessed the goods as warehousemen and were responsible, under the more limited liability of bailees for hire, only for ordinary care;[11] and this liability would not extend to a loss by an accidental fire not caused by their default or negligence. "The question then is,"

[10] Apart from common-carrier liability for goods destroyed by fire, railroads were also liable for any damage to property, near and adjacent to the route of a train, communicated directly or indirectly by engine sparks. The decision on this point was given by Shaw in Hart v. Western RR., 13 Metc. 99 (1847), described by him as a case of "first impression" and of "great importance." This decision was based on a statutory modification of the common law rule which imposed liability for fire only in a case of proved negligence. Shaw construed the statute as throwing "the responsibility upon those who are thus authorized to use a somewhat dangerous apparatus, and who realize a profit from it" (Ibid., at 105). See also St. 1840, ch. 85, sec. 1; and Lyman v. Boston and Worcester RR., 4 Cush. 288 (1849).

[11] In the first announcement of this doctrine in Thomas v. Boston and Providence RR., 10 Metc. 472 (1845), the facts left no doubt that the goods remained in the warehouse under the railroad's liability as warehousemen, because the plaintiff, after the goods had been pointed out to him, neglected to remove them within a reasonable time. He sustained his loss after electing to keep them in storage at his convenience and at no extra charge.

stated the Chief Justice, "when and by what act the transit of the goods terminated." [12] The answer contended by the plaintiffs was that the goods were held in transit by the railroad as common carriers until delivered; that delivery was completed only after the consignee had been given notice of their arrival and a reasonable time for their removal. Shaw rejected this argument.

He agreed that the old common-law rule of delivery still applied to goods transported by vehicles that were able to carry them directly to homes and places of business; he disagreed on the applicability of the rule to railroads, "whose line of movement and point of termination are locally fixed." A necessary condition of the railroad business, and one known to shippers, he insisted, was that goods on arrival must be safely stored in a warehouse without extra charges, to be held for the consignee, unless taken by him from the unloading platform. Adapting the old rule to new circumstances, the Court held that a delivery of the goods to the railroad's warehouse terminated the transit and discharged the railroad's common-carrier liability by transforming it into that of warehousemen.

The Chief Justice demonstrated a greater consideration for business expediency than for the legal argument that common-carrier liability continued until the railroad offered notice of the arrival of goods and an opportunity to remove them. In regard to notice, Shaw emphasized the intolerable burden to which railroads would be subjected if required to inform each consignee of the arrival of his particular shipment; to do so "would be nearly impossible" in the face of the volume and variety of business. But hardly as persuasive was his outright rejection of a right by the consignee to a reasonable time for removal, for the whole of Shaw's reasoning consisted of two points: first, that a railroad did not guarantee a specific arrival time; second, that arrivals were frequently at night or at some other time when at a railroad's convenience it kept the doors of its warehouse closed.

This reasoning is subject to criticism. If it were the business of the consignee, in the absence of notice, to gauge the arrival time of his goods, then it was the duty of the Court to explain why he should not be given a practical opportunity to take them out of the warehouse after they did arrive and whenever the warehouse was opened. Perhaps an objection of this nature was silently considered and meant to be rejected by Shaw's statement

[12] 1 Gray 263, 270 (1854).

that a contrary decision "would greatly mar the simplicity and efficacy of the rule, that delivery from the cars into the depot terminates the transit." [13]

Chief Justice Redfield of Vermont, while acknowledging Shaw as one "who has perhaps no superior upon this continent, as a wise and just expositor of the law, as a living and advancing study," questioned this decision on the grounds that the plaintiffs were given no opportunity to remove their property before the liability of warehousemen supervened.[14] In the New Hampshire case of *Moses v. Boston and Maine Railroad,* decided in 1855,[15] the high court of that state disapproved of Shaw's departure from "the rigorous principles of the common law," rejected the doctrine of his decision, and stated: ". . . We cannot but think that by it the salutary and approved principles of the common law are sacrificed to considerations of convenience and expediency, in the simplicity and precise and practical character of the rule which it establishes." [16] What became known as the "Massachusetts doctrine" on the termination of common-carrier liability has prevailed only in Georgia, Illinois, Indiana, Iowa, Massachusetts, and Pennsylvania; the courts in the rest of the Union have adopted the New Hampshire doctrine that common-carrier liability continues after goods have been transported to their destination, at least until the consignee has had a reasonable time to remove them.

Shaw's new view of the common law, with its "rigorous principles" relaxed for railroads, was excessively harsh on shippers. Either they must arrange to be on hand to take their goods directly off the unloading platform whenever the trains arrived, day or night, or they chanced an unrecoverable loss of the goods in the warehouse through theft or accidental fire. Stated crudely, the Shaw Court favored railroads over shippers. In the only two cases during the period under study in which shippers won suits, the facts pointed to unusual situations.[17] The general tenor of the Court's decisions is more evident from other cases where the determination that the railroad was clothed with the limited

---

[13] *Ibid.,* at 276.

[14] Redfield, *Railway Law,* pp. 253–256.

[15] 32 N.H. 523 (1855).

[16] *Ibid.,* at 540.

[17] Stevens v. Boston and Maine RR., 1 Gray 274 (1854); Kimball v. Western RR., 6 Gray 542 (1856).

liability of warehousemen shifted the whole burden of the loss upon the shippers.[18]

The Court favored railroads over shippers in still another new construction of the common law. In England, a railroad's acceptance of goods for shipment to a destination beyond its own termination, even beyond the realm, was held prima facie evidence of an undertaking to carry the goods to the place directed; and for any damage or loss to the goods while they were in the possession of successive carriers by which they were trans-shipped, the original carrier was liable.[19] This rule was not followed by the Shaw Court. In *Nutting v. Connecticut River Railroad*,[20] it was held that in the absence of a special contract, a railroad receiving goods consigned to a place beyond its terminus and paid only for their transportation over its own line is not liable for any losses after the goods have been delivered to the connecting railroad. This was the first American case in which a railroad was a party where the point was directly decided on a question involving loss of freight, English decisions notwithstanding. The doctrine is as important today in the age of worldwide commerce as it was the time of its announcement, when, because there were few great through-roads, goods were trans-shipped over many small, connecting roads.

III

As might be expected, railroads sought to restrict and even to extinguish their liability for freight and baggage under the common law.[21] Railroads, which were said "to exercise a public employment" and "to owe special duties to the public in consideration of the special privileges they have received,"[22] were bound to accept everything offered for carriage under the onerous liability of safe delivery. A successful attempt to diminish this liability would have an obvious impact upon law and business. Emulating earlier common carriers, railroads announced by way of notices, both general and special, that in certain cases they did not consider themselves responsible at all, and in others, only on

---

[18] Lewis v. Western RR., 11 Metc. 509 (1846); Lichtenheim v. Boston and Providence RR., 11 Cush. 70 (1853); Denny v. New York Central RR., 13 Gray 481 (1859).

[19] E. L. Pierce, *A Treatise on American Railroad Law* (New York, 1857), pp. 457–458; Redfield, *Railway Law*, p. 282.

[20] 1 Gray 502 (1854).

[21] On liability for baggage and its definition, see Jordan v. Fall River RR., 5 Cush. 69 (1849) and Collins v. Boston & Me. RR., 10 Cush. 506 (1852).

[22] Pierce, *Railroad Law*, pp. 415–416.

prescribed terms. From the time of the first and leading cases, which were decided by the courts of New York against the right of a railroad to limit its liability by notice, the early tendency in other jurisdictions was to follow suit.[23]

Oddly, this issue, which was so important and assumed many forms, was not the subject of a great deal of litigation before the Shaw Court. In *Thomas v. Boston and Providence Railroad,* argued directly on the question of notices but decided on other grounds, the New York decisions were more or less endorsed; and the remark was made that in construing the "doctrine of the common law, as applied to carriers . . . we are neither disposed to relax its requisitions nor give countenance to ingenious devices by which its provisions may be evaded." [24]

Not until 1853, in *Brown v. Eastern Railroad,*[25] did the Court decide an issue relating to notice, and then only by an opinion allegedly confined to as narrow a question as the facts would permit. The Court specifically disclaimed consideration of the "vexed question of the right of common carriers to limit their common law liabilities, by notice to the public to the effect that they will not be responsible for the baggage of passengers, or for merchandise transported by them as public carriers." [26] But this disclaimer was not sound, for the "vexed question" was in fact considered, at least to the extent of conceding in principle the very right claimed by railroads; and the concession was made without questioning that right. Indeed, what the Court had not considered was the right of the public in general, and of passengers and shippers in particular, to have railroads held strictly accountable for their common-law obligations.

Only eight years had passed since the dictum in the Thomas case on "ingenious devices" had been coupled with the approving reference to the New York decisions discountenancing even special contracts as an expedient for limiting carrier liabilities.[27] But now these same New York decisions were qualified in the Brown case:

The doctrine is nevertheless gradually being incorporated into the jurisprudence of the times, that such limitations may under proper

[23] Hollister v. Nowlen, 19 Wend. (New York) 234 (1838), and Cole v. Goodwin 19 Wend. 251 (1838). See also Angell, *Law of Carriers,* pp. 236 ff.

[24] 10 Metc. 472, 479–480 (1845).

[25] 11 Cush. 97 (1853).

[26] *Ibid.,* at 99.

[27] Thomas v. Boston and Providence RR., 10 Metc. 472, 479, 480 (1845); and see *supra,* note 23.

qualifications and safeguards, for securing due notice to the traveller, or the party for whom goods are to be transported, be held operative and binding upon the parties. [Citations omitted]

Without questioning the right of common carriers to make reasonable limitations as to the extent of their liabilities for baggage or merchandise to be transported by them, and *conceding the decisions to that effect to be sound* . . .[28]

Thus, in the United States as in England, where at first the courts sternly held railroads answerable as common carriers, concessions were made which relaxed their general liability.[29]

In the Brown case, the rule was announced that a railroad might limit its common-law obligations for baggage as well as for merchandise, on condition that notice must be "specific and certain," that is, "must be brought home" to the party; and the burden of proof was on the railroad.[30] No doubt this rule clearly defined what the Court considered to be "proper qualifications and safeguards"; however, the Court was grossly remiss in making the unwarranted assumption, *sub silentio,* that the passenger or shipper, without any positive act beyond reading a notice, and without recompense, relinquished a valuable right heretofore protected at common law. On the contrary, the presumption should have been that parties would insist upon their rights, rather than agree to their limitation by inference.[31] Yet the

[28] 11 Cush. 97, 99 (1853). Italics added.

[29] Redfield, *Railway Law*, pp. 267–270, 276–282. The English decisions went so far to the other extreme that Parliament was obliged to interfere to restore some semblance of common carrier responsibility.

[30] In the case at bar the Court ruled that notice had not been "brought home" to the party. The specific holding was that a notice, printed separately on the back of a passenger's ticket and alleging that the company would not be responsible for baggage exceeding $50.00 in value, was invalid as raising no legal presumption that the passenger had knowledge of it. See also Sanford v. Housatonic RR., 11 Cush. 155, 157 (1853), and Malone v. Boston and Worcester RR., 12 Gray 388 (1858).

[31] Consider the language of Nelson, J., in delivering the opinion of the U.S. Supreme Court: The carrier "should not be permitted to exonerate himself without the assent of the parties concerned. And this is not to be implied or inferred from a general notice . . . if any implication is to be indulged from the delivery of the goods under the general notice, it is as strong that the owner intended to insist upon his rights, and the duties of the carrier, as it is that he assented to their qualification. The burden of proof lies on the carrier, and nothing short of an express stipulation by parol or in writing should be permitted to discharge him from duties which the law has annexed to his employment" (New Jersey Steam Navigation Co. v. Merchant's Bank, 6 How. 344, 383, 1848). See also Pierce, *Railroad Law,* p. 417, and an able essay, "The Law of Carriers' Notices," in *Law Reporter,* 15:241–264 (1852), which concludes that the "doctrine that a carrier may limit his responsibility by a notice . . . is contrary to public policy and good morals. . . ."

Court nullified those rights by treating a general notice as a special contract.

IV

The law of evidence relating to the competency of witnesses, like so many branches of law, was also affected by the advent of railroads. A contrast between two cases[32] suggests the difficulty in assessing the influence of "taught tradition" on the decision of particular questions. In the one case, an old rule excluding parties as witnesses was followed; in the other, the Court made an exception to an old rule excluding the testimony of agents on behalf of their principals.[33] It may have been no more than coincidence that the immediate gainor of both decisions was a railroad corporation.

In the Snow case, the railroad had negligently lost the plaintiff's trunk. The only question, one of "much practical importance to the community," was whether he was a competent witness to testify as to the contents and value of the trunk. Although no one else could offer such testimony, the Court refused to modify a common-law rule of evidence that no person shall be a witness in his own cause in a civil court. This was an "ancient" rule which had "existed for ages," justified by the Court on the grounds that the witness's interest might tempt him to fraud or perjury.

The Court did not evaluate this justification, however, and so did not consider whether the witness's interest was a valid objection to the weight of his evidence rather than to his competency. Nor did it consider the implications of the fact that fraud and perjury might be criminally punished. The Court also chose to avoid consideration of the precedent pointed out to it that in Pennsylvania, passengers had been admitted as witnesses on ground of necessity in similar cases of lost baggage.[34] The Court must have felt that the case of a passenger could not validly be distinguished from that of other parties as witnesses, and so shrank from a decision which would have radically altered the law of evidence.

[32] Snow v. Eastern RR., 12 Metc. 44 (1846), and Draper v. Worcester & Norwich RR., 11 Metc. 505 (1846).

[33] See John H. Wigmore, *A Treatise on the Anglo-American System of Evidence* (Boston, 1923, 2nd ed., 5 vols.), I, sec. 575.

[34] Snow v. Eastern RR., 12 Metc. 44, 45 (1846), where Whitesell v. Crane, 8 Watts & Serg. (Pa.) 369 was cited. See also Redfield, *Railway Law,* p. 311, and other cases there cited to the same point.

The Draper case provides an interesting counterpoint since it relates to the competency of an agent of the defendant railroad. As in the Snow case, however, the fact that a railroad was a party did not from a legal standpoint alter the issue. Whereas the Snow case involved the competency of any party as a witness, the Draper case was on the competency of the agents of corporations generally.

The plaintiff in the latter case, seeking damages for the non-delivery of merchandise, alleged that the testimony of a freight-house worker, whose duty it was to deliver the goods, should not be admitted because he was directly interested in the outcome. But the Court upheld his competency on ground that only the liability of the corporation was called into question. "It is difficult to perceive the interest which the witness has in the present suit," Shaw stated.[35]

The fact is, of course, that whatever the lack of legal liability on the part of this employee, he was in a practical sense liable to his employers for his job if they had to pay for his non-delivery of the goods. He was as likely to commit perjury as was the passenger in the Snow case, for his interest was at least as great.

What is even more striking in the contrast between these two decisions of the same year is that the Draper case was frankly settled on considerations of business welfare and not on a common-law rule of evidence which had "existed for ages." Here an exception was made to the old rule that an agent or employee cannot testify in behalf of his principal. The exception, declared Shaw,

is founded on those considerations of general expediency, growing out of the usual order and course of business; and without such modification of the general rule, business would be greatly impeded. A different rule would operate as a great obstruction to the transactions of merchants, ship owners, carriers and other dealers; but it would nearly prevent the operations of corporate companies, who must act entirely through various classes of officers and agents.[36]

The exception was well-founded, and the Draper decision made good law. But the Snow decision worked an injustice to passengers and left the common law stiff and unyielding in a situation that needed freer play. The legislature was forced to

[35] Draper v. Worcester & Norwich RR., 11 Metc. 505, 508 (1846).
[36] *Ibid.*

intervene with a statute permitting a passenger to put in evidence his own descriptive statement of the contents of lost baggage.[37]

V

Under common law, because of the obvious distinction between persons and goods, public carriers incurred a responsibility for the safety of passengers materially different from the responsibility incurred for their baggage or for freight. Carriers were not liable to passengers for accidents that no skill or care could prevent. The theory was that passengers were capable of taking care of themselves and of exercising their vigilance and foresight in the maintenance of their rights, whereas the owners of goods, who had entrusted them to the carrier, were not; nor were persons transported under the same custody as bales of goods. These principles were announced by Chief Justice Shaw in the earliest cases tried in his Court arising out of injuries to railroad passengers.[38]

In the first of these cases, *Gerry v. Boston and Providence Railroad,* 1836, the jury, guided by Shaw's instructions, found against the passenger who negligently contributed to his own injury — frozen fingers — by walking two miles in icy weather to the nearest inn, rather than choosing to wait in the stalled train with the rest of the passengers for a rescue sleigh. This case illustrates that the passenger was responsible for ordinary care on his own part. Theophilus Parsons, commending the Chief Justice for his charge in "Gerry v. the Ry Co.," thought it to be "full and clear on the rights, duties, and liabilities of common carriers of all classes, particularly passengers; — and this is a subject growing more interesting to the community every day. There are few legal questions more frequently presenting themselves and of which so little is known." [39]

[37] St. 1851, ch. 147, sec. 5. Upheld in Harlow v. Fitchburg RR., 8 Gray 237 (1857), *per* Shaw, C.J., where the statute was construed so broadly as to lend its protection to passengers even when their property had been lost by the railroad as warehousemen.

[38] Gerry v. Boston and Providence RR., *Daily Evening Transcript* (Boston), Dec. 29, 1836; Thompson *et al.* v. Boston and Providence RR., *ibid.,* Jan. 6, 1837, and the *Boston Morning Post,* Jan. 6, 1837. In an 1845 case, the Court noted that the carriage of passengers in public conveyances for hire "is comparatively a modern practice." According to the Court's research, the very first case of a passenger's suit to recover damages for personal injuries sustained in an accident, was tried in 1791 before Lord Kenyon. Defendant was the proprietor of a horse-coach company. See Ingalls v. Bills, 9 Metc. 1, 7–8 (1845).

[39] Parsons to Shaw, Dec. 30, 1836, Shaw Papers.

Early in 1837, in a group of cases that were tried together and were the first to involve passenger injuries from the collision of trains,[40] Shaw summed up the law as follows. Railroads could not insure the safety of passengers in any event, but were responsible for the strictest care. Not the utmost precaution against all possible danger, but reasonable and proper precaution necessary to the occasion was required. Thus, a railroad would be liable for passenger injuries if an accident happened because of its failure to provide roads, engines, or cars built with the highest skill that science and the experience of time would permit, or because of its failure to provide employees with the same skill. The passenger, however, took the risk of an accident which might occur in spite of the precaution that skill, care, and experience could give.

Quite probably, the *Massachusetts Reports* do not include a single case on the simple question of railroad liability for accidents to passengers because the Chief Justice so lucidly explained the appropriate legal principles in the above trial cases. Not a case was reported until *McElroy v. Nashua and Lowell Railroad,* in 1849,[41] and then on a complication of the question. The plaintiff, a passenger, had been injured in consequence of the careless management of a switch at the junction point where another railroad connected with the tracks of the defendant company; the switch had been constructed and attended by an employee of the other railroad. Speaking for the Court, Shaw held that these circumstances in no way excused the defendants from liability. The law required the most exact care of trains, track, and of "all the subsidiary arrangements necessary to the safety of passengers." Consequently, "it was within the scope of [defendant's] duty to see that the switch was rightly constructed, attended and managed, before they were justified in carrying passengers over it." [42]

The Court was not disposed to construe the common law with a similar strictness when the person injured on the train was not a passenger. The leading case of this nature arose when a woman, who had entered the cars of a train to assist an aged relative to take a seat as a passenger, went onto the platform after the train had begun to move without notice, and either jumped or was

---

[40] Thompson *et al.* v. Boston and Providence RR., *loc. cit., supra,* note 38. See also F. H. Chase, *Lemuel Shaw* (Boston, 1918), pp. 224–226.

[41] 4 Cush. 400 (1849).

[42] *Ibid.,* at 402–403. See also Schopman v. Boston and Worcester RR., 9 Cush. 24 (1851).

thrown off by its subsequent violent jerks.[43] The decision that no damages were recoverable for her crippling injuries was the first one reported in Massachusetts wherein the doctrine of contributory negligence was applied in a railroad accident. If the plaintiff had contributed "in any degree" to the cause of the injury by attempting to leave after the train started, then the company was not liable even though it was also guilty of negligence in having started the train with violent jerks. A second notable point of law featured in the decision was that merely "ordinary" care, as contrasted with "extraordinary" care, was all that was required of railroads when the character of a passenger carrier was not assumed toward persons on their cars or premises. On this ground, the Court ruled that the railroad was not obligated to give "special" notice of the train's departure, that is, notice beyond the printed time-table, as would have been required in the case of a passenger. This rule disregarded the safety of non-passengers in and about the cars; for it was based on the unconsidered assumption that the habitual notices of train departure — the ringing of bells and the conductor's cry — were designed only as admonitions to passengers. Yet railroads usually permitted passengers' friends to crowd the station and board the trains.

Suits brought by travellers, afoot or in vehicles, because of non-fatal injuries suffered in collision at railroad crossings, were the occasions of still other important developments in the law. A railroad crossing at a level with a highway was a point of danger, and the degree of care and caution required by both the traveller and the railroad was a matter of consequence to human safety. The Chief Justice addressed himself to this problem in *Bradley v. Boston and Maine,* an 1848 case,[44] the first in which a party to a suit was a non-passenger who had sustained non-fatal injuries.[45] The defendants contended that they were bound to

[43] Lucas v. New Bedford & Taunton RR., 6 Gray 64 (1856).
[44] 2 Cush. 539 (1848).
[45] A very early case grew out of an accident in 1832, even before the earliest road was in operation. A traveller had fallen into an open highway excavation made in the construction of the railroad, but brought his suit against the town in which the highway was located (Currier v. Inhabitants of Lowell, 16 Pick. 170, 1834). When the town in turn brought an action for indemnity against the railroad, the railroad sought to evade responsibility for taking safety precautions on the grounds that none had been prescribed by its charter. The Court, *per* Wilde, J., quickly fastened upon railroads the principle of common-law liability, *sic utere tuo, ut alienum non laedus,* which bound corporations as well as individuals. This was the first tort case against a railroad (Inhabitants of Lowell v. Boston and Lowell RR., 23 Pick. 24 (1839). The Court also observed that the railroad would have been held liable if it, instead of the town, had been made a party to the original suit.

exercise only ordinary care, that is, the care usually exercised in passing crossings. Shaw replied for the Court that the care ordinarily observed would be the test of "due care" only if railroads had existed so long that a standard had been established by usage. But, "in consideration of the recent introduction of the use of railroads," he promulgated the important safety doctrine that compliance with the provisions of a statute requiring certain specified signals would not exempt a railroad from the obligation of using reasonable diligence in other respects, if the circumstances of the case — the exigency of crossing a highway — rendered the use of other precautions reasonable.[46]

The Chief Justice clarified this rule in *Shaw v. Boston and Worcester Railroad,* in 1857,[47] a case of "much interest and importance" to the community and to the growth of the law. A battery of distinguished legal talents were engaged: Ebenezer Hoar, Benjamin F. Butler, Charles G. Loring, and George Bemis for the railroad company, and Rufus Choate and H. F. Durant for the plaintiff. Each party alleged negligence on the part of the other. The company denied that its train gave no notice of its approach to the crossing; the plaintiff denied the accusation of careless driving. In three successive trials, the jury awarded damages in favor of the plaintiff, in the amounts of $15,000, $18,000 and $22,500 respectively (the last amount was the highest ever awarded in a like case up to that time). After each verdict, the defendants carried the case to the full bench of the Supreme Judicial Court on exceptions to the rules of law announced at the trial sessions of the Court. On the third and final argument of this complex case, judgment was awarded on the verdict.

The Chief Justice was the spokesman for the full bench. He practically settled the basic law of due care and negligence in actions of this nature, by his analysis and statement of the legal principles governing them, which may be summarized as follows. A railroad is bound to guard against all accidents "likely" to occur, which may be reasonably anticipated from the time, place, and circumstances. A railroad is also bound to take "extraordinary and unusual precautions" as may be useful to the safety of travellers, should an "unusual" situation arise; for example, a violent storm, which can be anticipated. But the failure to take such precautions at any particular occasion of an extraordinary character, which

---

[46] See also Linfield v. Old Colony RR., 10 Cush. 562 (1852), and Whittaker v. Boston and Maine RR., 7 Gray 98 (1856).

[47] 8 Gray 45 (1857).

cannot be foreseen, will not render the railroad responsible for negligence.

A second principle, Shaw asserted, was that the burden of proof is on the plaintiff: first, to show on his part that he was not guilty of contributory negligence; and second, to show that the defendant railroad did not use such precaution and care as men of ordinary skill, prudence, and experience would have used, by means of which the collision might have been averted.[48] The same degree of care and caution is incumbent upon both the railroad and the driver of the vehicle. If it appears from the whole evidence that both parties used all due care and caution, notwithstanding which an accident occurs, then, declared Shaw, "it is one of those cases of pure accident, to which all human beings are constantly exposed, for which no person is at fault" for the damage sustained by the other.

VI

Cases involving fatal injuries were governed by still other rules of law. *Carey v. Berkshire Railroad* and *Skinner v. Housatonic Railroad,* decided together in 1848,[49] were cases of first impression. The actions were to recover damages for the loss of relatives killed as a result of the defendants' negligence. In the Carey case, the victim was a day laborer, the husband of the plaintiff "who was poor . . . and by his death, was left to provide for herself and the support of three small children." In the Skinner case, the victim was the plaintiff's eleven-year-old son.

Here were potentially great cases. They were the first resulting from fatal injuries caused by railroad accidents. The question they presented was on the liability of a railroad for negligently killing a human being. Because railroads so endangered life the question was important enough, but it extended generally to any tortfeasor's liability for causing death. Surprisingly, this major question had never before been decided by an American court. Moreover, the cases were tragic in the extreme; the economic stakes were high; and a basic matter of public safety was involved. No "taught tradition" existed to control the outcome. It was, therefore, the perfect occasion for one of Shaw's treatise-like opinions which would explore the whole law of the subject, analyze the principle governing the decision, and explain its social benefits. Instead, Shaw assigned the opinion to Theron Metcalf, a new

---

[48] See also Robinson v. Fitchburg and Worcester RR., 7 Gray 92 (1856).
[49] 1 Cush. 475 (1848).

appointee, who speaking for the unanimous bench mechanically followed an English precedent which had the effect of exempting tortfeasors from liability for the deaths they caused.

Metcalf, after noting that the "actions raise a new question in our jurisprudence," stated that they could be maintained only upon "some established principle of common law." [50] No such principle was found in "the English books"; on the contrary, in 1808 Lord Ellenborough, in *Baker v. Bolton*,[51] ruled that the death of a human being is no ground for an action for damages. "Such, then, we cannot doubt, is the doctrine of the common law," stated Metcalf, "and it is decisive against the maintenance of these actions." [52]

A decision based on authority is plausible enough, particularly if opposing authority is absent. But this decision seemed especially plausible because of the existence of certain statutes enacted before the cases arose. These statutes, although strangely not here relied upon by plaintiffs, indicated that the legislature had been aware that the common law was either uncertain or inhumane and had sought to remedy the situation. One statute made common carriers liable to a fine, recoverable by indictment, for the benefit of the survivors of persons killed by the carriers' wrongful acts.[53] The other statute made tortfeasors liable to any suit which an accident victim would have been entitled to bring had he lived.[54]

Given those statutes and the fact that they were not the basis of the Carey-Skinner suits, there is no doubting the Court's view that the common law must prevail. The real question, which warrants full discussion, is whether the common law, or the Court's interpretation of it, was sound.

That Lord Ellenborough's ruling in *Baker v. Bolton* should have been invoked is understandable; that he should have been blindly followed, without full and independent consideration of the question, was most unworthy of the Shaw Court, if not of less able judges. It is not just that Ellenborough himself had cited no authority and had spoken merely at nisi prius. More important, he, like Metcalf who emulated him, did not give a reasoned judgment. To say as Metcalf did, relying on his lordship, that "the

[50] *Ibid.*, at 477 and 478.
[51] 1 Campb. 493 (1808).
[52] 1 Cush. 475, 478 (1848).
[53] St. 1840, ch. 80. Carriers could not be indicted for killing non-passengers until St. 1874, ch. 372, sec. 163 was passed.
[54] St. 1842, ch. 89, sec. 1.

death of a human being is not the ground of an action for damages," because "in a civil court, the death of a human being cannot be complained of as an injury," is an explanation which invites comparison with the one offered by the judge in W. H. Auden's "Law Like Love":

> Law, says the judge as he looks down his nose,
> Speaking clearly and most severely,
> Law is as I've told you before,
> Law is as you know I suppose,
> Law is but let me explain it once more,
> Law is The Law.

What is the explanation of these decisions? What principle underlay them, and what was its origin and validity? The answers to these questions are imbedded in the history of England's criminal law.

At an early time, retributive justice was very much a matter of personal vengeance. Gradually the claims of public justice superseded many private claims, and felonies came to be considered as offenses against the state. As a result all civil remedies in favor of the parties injured by felony were held to merge in the felony.[55] Homicide *per infortunium,* or accidental killing in the course of a lawful act, though technically not a felony, was also criminally prosecuted. The penalty, as in the case of felony, was forfeiture to the Crown of all the property of the guilty party. Forfeiture, of course, rendered wholly futile any civil actions for damages. As a result, even though the death by wrongful act injured the family by depriving its members of their common-law rights to the services of the deceased, the injury to the family could not legally be the basis of an action for damages. In short, death, by converting a private wrong into a public one redressable by forfeiture, had the effect of barring civil redress for the tort that caused the death.[56]

This, then, was the origin and purpose of the principle underlying the rulings more than two centuries later in *Baker v. Bolton*

[55] Huggins v. Butcher, Yelv. 89 (1607).

[56] For the history of this matter, see William S. Holdsworth, *A History of English Law* (London, 1893 ff., 14 vols.), III, 310–313 and 331–336; Holdsworth, "The Origin of the Rule in *Baker v. Bolton,*" *Law Quarterly Review,* 32:431–437 (Oct. 1916); James F. Stephen, *A History of the Criminal Law of England* (London, 1883, 3 vols.), III, 23, 26, 49–50, and 64–65; Gustavus Hay, Jr., "Death as a Civil Cause of Action in Massachusetts," *Harvard Law Review,* 7:170–176 (Oct. 1893); Percy H. Winfield, "Death as Affecting Liability in Tort," *Columbia Law Review,* 29:239–254 (March 1929).

and the Carey-Skinner cases. But by the time of Ellenborough, criminal prosecution of homicide *per infortunium* and the penalty of forfeiture for conviction had long ended.[57] Therefore no longer was there any reason to disallow a civil suit for such damages as one might prove he had sustained from the loss of a person killed by tortious act. But Ellenborough seems to have remembered only that death, even if accidentally caused in the course of a lawful act, could not render the killer civilly liable.[58] As Sir William S. Holdsworth pointed out, the "dictum" of *Baker v. Bolton* was based on a "misreading of legal history" and "even on technical grounds" was illogical and unsound, as well as unjust.[59]

The Shaw Court at least recognized a connection between the question in the Carey-Skinner cases and "the maxim, that trespass is merged in a felony," as Metcalf put it. Yet he expressly ruled that the maxim "has no application to the cases now before us. In neither of them was the killing felonious, and there is, therefore, no felony, in which a private injury can merge." [60] From this fact only one conclusion was justifiable: the private injury may be civilly redressed, there being no rationale for a contrary holding; or to put it as a legal proposition, a tort is actionable if there is no felony in which it may merge.[61]

That homicide *per infortunium* was no longer criminal was not the only fact robbing the Carey-Skinner opinion of a rationale. Contributing even more heavily toward the same end was the fact that the common law of Massachusetts never recognized the English rule that civil remedies in favor of an injured party merge in a felony.[62] Moreover, the penalty of forfeiture, which in England had made compensation to the injured party an impossibility, was "rarely, if ever, exacted here." [63]

[57] Hay, p. 173, and Stephen, pp. 76–77, both citing Sir Michael Foster's *Crown Pleas* (1762).

[58] There was no precedent whatever for such a ruling. Between the 1607 decision in Huggins v. Butcher, Yelv., 89, and Baker v. Bolton, 1808, there were no analogous cases, and these two were distinguishable. In the first, death was the result of a brutal beating; in the second, death was the result not of felony but of an accident in the course of a lawful act.

[59] Holdsworth, III, 334–336.

[60] Carey v. Berkshire RR., 1 Cush. 475, 478 (1848).

[61] Holdsworth, discussing Baker v. Bolton, argued that the right to a civil action which merged in felony was merely suspended until prosecution of the felony. "*A fortiori* he ought to be able to sue if the tortious act causing death does not amount to a felony" (*History of English Law*, III, 334).

[62] Boston & Worcester RR. v. Dana, 1 Gray 83, 97 (1854).

[63] *Ibid.*, at 98. In 1641 the Tenth Liberty of the Massachusetts Body of Liberties abolished forfeiture. See Richard B. Morris, *Studies in the History of American Law* (New York, 1930), pp. 109, 249–250.

These facts were elaborately stated by the Shaw Court, six years after the Carey-Skinner decision, in connection with a different matter. At that later time the Court undertook the kind of inquiry it ought to have adopted earlier, instead of slavishly following Ellenborough. Speaking of the English rule that civil remedies merge in a felony, the Court said: ". . . We feel at liberty to regard its adoption or rejection as an open question, to be determined, not so much by authority, as by a consideration of the origin of the rule, the reasons on which it is founded, and its adaptation to our system of jurisprudence." [64]

Lack of precedent to hold otherwise added no more merit to the Carey-Skinner decision than the uncritical acceptance of discreditable English authority. As a matter of fact, however, there were American precedents not in accord with *Baker v. Bolton*. One, known to the Shaw Court, was a New York decision of 1838 which sustained the right of a father to recover damages for the death of his son caused by a negligent driver.[65] The facts of this case and the ground of damage — loss of the child's services until the time he would have been twenty-one — identically matched those of the Skinner case. Yet Metcalf distinguished away the precedent on the grounds that the question, on the right to maintain the action, had been assumed and passed *sub silentio* without being decided.

In neighboring Connecticut, however, there was a 1794 case, not mentioned by the Shaw Court, in which the decision was directly on the point that there was a right to maintain an action for death by wrongful act.[66] Indeed, Professor Richard B. Morris has noted the existence of New England precedents of the colonial period, in which the courts awarded damages to the relatives of deceased in both civil and criminal actions.[67] It was a reflection on the Shaw Court, and on nineteenth-century American courts generally, that their colonial predecessors should have been more advanced in affording a remedy at common law to the survivors in cases of death by wrongful act. Perhaps the colonial courts lacked the judicial sophistication which cares more for procedure than for substance. In any event, they seemed more concerned

[64] Boston & Worcester RR. v. Dana, 1 Gray 83, 97 (1854).
[65] Ford v. Monroe, 20 Wend. (N.Y.) 210 (1838). See Francis B. Tiffany, *Death by Wrongful Act* (Kansas City, Mo., 1913, 2nd ed.), p. 8.
[66] Cross v. Guthery, 2 Root (Conn.), 90 (1794).
[67] *Studies in the History of American Law*, pp. 250–256. Morris points out, however, that the precedents for maintaining a civil action were rare.

with the problem of the tortfeasor's liability than with the injured plaintiff's technical right to maintain an action.

The injured plaintiffs in the Carey-Skinner cases were seeking to prove damages sustained by them as a result of the deaths of relatives. A wholly different question would have been presented if the plaintiffs had been acting as the legal representatives of the deceased seeking damages sustained by the deceased, instead of by his survivors. In such a case the governing rule would have been that actions for personal injury do not survive, but die with the party. This rule of obscure origin[68] has never been satisfactorily justified, particularly since death does not terminate actions based on contract or on torts affecting personal property.

Because of judicial confusion, as Holdsworth suggests, this rule very likely had a shadowy influence upon the outcome of *Baker v. Bolton* and consequently upon the Carey-Skinner cases.[69] But at common law, where distinctions count heavily, there was a wide theoretical difference between the suit of a survivor in his own right and that of a representative on behalf of deceased.

Massachusetts, unlike England and many of the states, did not supersede the common law by making wrongful death a civil cause of action for injury to the family. The Commonwealth's "survival statute" of 1842,[70] however, provided that the right of bringing an action of trespass on the case for personal injuries should survive the death of the person entitled to bring such an action by vesting in his executor or administrator. As Shaw stated, "It was the obvious purpose of the statute to reverse this rule of law (that death terminates the right of action); to provide that the right of action should survive, as in cases of damage to property." [71]

[68] See Holdsworth, III, 576–583, and H. Goudy, "Two Ancient Brocards," in Paul Vinogradoff, ed., *Essays in Legal History* (London, 1913), 215–229. Goudy, p. 227, concluded that the rule that a personal right of action comes to an end with the death of the party "came into our law owing to a misunderstanding by Bracton of the Roman Law, his inaccurate use of its language, and the consequently erroneous doctrine adopted by Fitzherbert and others."

[69] See Holdsworth, III, 333–335. Parliament was the victim of the same confusion in the very Act which reversed the rule of Baker v. Bolton. The Act, which created a new cause of action in wrongful death cases, recognized that death injures the family and that the injury is the basis of a cause of action in their behalf. Yet the same Act required that the death must be caused by a tort entitling the deceased to bring the action had he lived and vested the cause of action in the deceased's executor or administrator, for the benefit of family, instead of vesting it in the family themselves. The confusion is apparent: deceased's cause of action vested in his representative who sued for a cause of action belonging to the survivors (Fatal Injuries, or, Lord Campbell's Act, 9 & 10 Vict. ch. 93, 1846).

[70] St. 1842, ch. 89, sec. 1.

[71] Hollenbeck, Adm. v. Berkshire RR., 9 Cush. 478, 480 (1852).

Thanks to Shaw, however, many tortfeasors still escaped liability for causing death, for in the Kearney-Mann cases, decided together in 1851, he narrowed this statutory right to sue.[72] He could do this only because the cases showed that death, from railroad collision, was instantaneous. The dispositive words in Shaw's opinion were: "The cause of action must accrue during the lifetime of the party injured. Here there was no time, during the life of the intestate, at which a cause of action could accrue, because the life closed with the accident, from which the cause of action would have otherwise accrued." [73]

That instantaneous death aborts the right to sue was an innovation on the old common-law rule relating to the non-survival of the cause of action. Before Shaw's decision there had never been any need to consider the time lapse between injury and death. Indeed the old common-law rule did not require a causal relation between the injury and the death. Whenever it happened and from whatever cause, it ended the right to sue. Though Shaw could not find support in prior authority for his rule on instantaneous death, it was logically reasonable. But so would have been a decision that there is always a fleeting moment of life between injury and death, during which time the cause of action accrues. Certainly such a decision would have been more in accord with the general purpose of the statute. "Life or death, that is the test," he broadly declared. At least that test sustained a cause of action in a case where the accident victim lingered several hours, though unconscious.[74]

The Kearney-Mann decision, as well as the Carey-Skinner decision, in which he concurred, reveal Shaw as less the conservator of the common law, tempering it to serve a growing community's requirements of justice, than the conservative rigidly following what he believed to be the old law. Yet he once remarked that in novel accident cases — he was speaking specifically about railroad accidents — decision should be upon "the fullest deliberation" and upon principles that avoid the "danger of working injustice." [75]

Shaw might claim that "law," slight though it was, supported these decisions, but he could make no claim for their justice. There was "danger of working injustice" when the common law

[72] Kearney, Adm. v. Boston & Worcester RR., 9 Cush. 108 (1852), and Mann, Adm. v. Boston & Worcester RR., *ibid.*

[73] *Ibid.*, at 110.

[74] Hollenbeck, Adm. v. Berkshire RR., 9 Cush. 478 (1852).

[75] Shaw v. Boston & Worcester RR., 8 Gray 45, 65 (1857).

was construed to disallow the compensation of the immediate survivors of persons killed as a result of negligence, whether by common carriers or anyone else. There was something anomalous, to say the least, in rules which guaranteed a person damages for the death of a horse carelessly lost by a carrier in an accident,[76] but which prevented him from recovering for the loss of a loved one in the same accident. Moreover it was an absurdity of the common law, and dangerous public policy as well, that there should be liability imposed for causing non-fatal accidents, but as a result of these decisions, no liability for causing fatal ones. The common law as construed by the Shaw Court made it costly for carriers to scratch but cheap to kill, particularly if the killing were instantaneous.

VII

In the memoir of his late "Chief," Justice Thomas made this arresting statement:

The first puff of the engine on the iron road announced a revolution in the law of bailments and of common carriers. . . . How much his wisdom, foresight, and that clear comprehension of the principles of the common law which enabled him to separate the rule from its old embodiments and to mould it to new exigencies, contributed to build up this law, to give it system and harmony, and a substratum of solid sense, is well known to the profession.[77]

The revolution in the common law was, however, a limited and uneven one. On certain fronts, bold innovations were made by configuring the law anew, precedent notwithstanding — as in the decision permitting a railroad employee to give evidence on behalf of his principal, the corporation; or that exempting a railroad from common-carrier liability for goods delivered to a connecting carrier for trans-shipment.[78] On other fronts, the impact of new experience upon hoary legal maxims resulted in important doctrinal modifications — as in the decision converting carrier lia-

---

[76] In the case of a horse (see White v. Winnisimmet Co., 7 Cush. 155, 156 (1851), liability was imposed without regard to the question whether death was instantaneous or lingering, for the owner, not the horse, sustained both the legal damage and the right of action. The common law did not consider whether human beings should be entitled to the same rights to life as to property.

[77] "Sketch of the Life and Judicial Labors of Chief Justice Shaw," *Proceedings*, Massachusetts Historical Society, 10:67 (1867).

[78] Draper v. Worcester and Norwich RR., 11 Metc. 505 (1846); Nutting v. Connecticut River RR., 1 Gray 502 (1854).

bility into the less rigorous liability of warehousemen; or that allowing the limitation of liability by notice.[79] On yet other fronts, the revolution halted, and the roar of the railroad signaled only that the rules of the common law were not of a fleeting character — as in the decision excluding the testimony of a passenger regarding the contents of his lost baggage; or that preventing an action from being maintained for the death of a human being.[80]

Generally speaking, the Shaw Court was more given than not to change or modification. Fresh circumstances or new combinations of fact were frequently the occasion of varying degrees of accommodation in the common law. Where the law kept progress with the pressure of events, such accommodation was understandable. Yet there were cases in which the Court arbitrarily accepted the old and inflexible rules. That the law cannot remain static in a dynamic society is of course no recommendation of doctrinal change for its own sake. Certainty and stability in law have their own legitimate claims. But why did the Court provide for growth in the law in some decisions and stifle the possibility of growth in others?

Justice Holmes wrote of Shaw that "few have lived who were his equals in their understanding of the grounds of public policy to which all laws must ultimately be referred." [81] Shaw himself remarked: "In considering the rights and obligations arising out of particular relations, it is competent for courts of justice to regard considerations of policy and public convenience . . ." [82] It is suggestive that this statement was made in the context of an opinion that established for American jurisprudence the conservative fellow-servant doctrine. The relevant point, in regard to the question above, is that the Shaw Court expounded law as an active and conscious participant in the concerns of the legislative halls and the market-place.

This point takes on meaning when added to the fact that in the very great majority of cases to which railroads were parties, decisions were favorable to their claims. Moreover, a correlation of the disposition of cases with construction of the common law reveals that whenever the law was modified, the effect of the modification was favorable to railroad development or the railroad

---

[79] Norway Plains Co. v. Boston and Maine RR., 1 Gray 236 (1854); Brown v. Eastern RR., 11 Cush. 97 (1853).

[80] Snow v. Eastern RR., 12 Metc. 44 (1846); Carey v. Berkshire RR., 1 Cush. 475 (1848).

[81] *The Common Law* (Boston, 1881), p. 106.

[82] Farwell v. Boston and Worcester RR., 4 Metc. 49, 58 (1842).

business;[83] whenever the law was held stationary, these same ends were served.[84] In the numerous and varied cases touching railroads in their exercise of eminent domain, the railroads came off best in Court on the theory that they acted in the name of the public or served its interest. This was true of cases involving chartered rights and powers; public contracts; tax-exemption; general depreciation in the value of real estate; and land damage occasioned by an impediment in the use of a public right.[85] Railroads also came off best in cases bearing on rules of evidence; fatal accident; injury to non-passengers; discriminatory rate practices; and termination of common-carrier liability by notice, by trans-shipment, or by supervention of warehouseman liability.[86]

The evidence drawn from case law thus indicates that the Shaw Court was biased in favor of railroads. The Chief Justice, like so many of his time, linked that which was beneficial to railroads with industrial expansion, which in turn was linked with the grand march of the Commonwealth toward a more prosperous life.[87] The new mode of transportation held forth the promise, and the fulfillment as well, of rescuing Boston from economic

[83] The only exception to this generalization, which omits decisions governed by statutory changes of the common law, was a holding that a railroad which received goods from a wrongdoer however innocently, without the consent of the owner, has no lien on them for their carriage. The ground of decision was that the doctrine of *caveat emptor* applied with the same force to carriers as to private persons. The practical effect of this change of the common law was merely to induce railroads, at the Court's suggestion, to protect themselves from loss by looking to the title of goods and by demanding prepayment. See Robinson v. Baker, 5 Cush. 137 (1849); Stevens v. Boston and Western RR., 8 Gray 262 (1857); and Clark v. Lowell and Lawrence RR., 9 Gray 231 (1857).

[84] Excluded, of course, from this generalization are such very elementary principles of *res judicata* as common-carrier liability for negligent injury to passengers or freight, or corporate liability for the acts of agents — principles which no Court could be expected to flout.

[85] Newburyport Turnpike Corp. v. Eastern RR., 23 Pick. 326 (1839), Brainard v. Clapp, 10 Cush. 6 (1852); Boston Water Power Co. v. Boston and Worcester RR., 23 Pick. 360 (1839); Inhabitants of Worcester v. Western RR., 4 Metc. 564 (1842); Proprietor of Locks and Canals v. Nashua and Lowell RR., 10 Cush. 385 (1852); Davidson v. Boston and Maine RR., 3 Cush. 91 (1849). Citations in this and the next note are illustrative, not exhaustive.

[86] Draper v. Worcester and Norwich RR., 11 Metc. 505 (1846), Snow v. Eastern RR., 12 Metc. 44 (1846); Carey v. Berkshire RR., 1 Cush. 475 (1848); Kearney, Administratrix v. Boston and Worcester RR., 9 Cush. 108 (1853); Lucas v. New Bedford and Taunton RR., 6 Gray 64 (1856); Shaw v. Boston and Worcester RR., 8 Gray 45 (1857); Fitchburg RR. v. Gage, 12 Gray 393 (1859); Brown v. Eastern RR., 11 Cush. 97 (1853); Nutting v. Connecticut River RR., 1 Gray 502 (1854); Norway Plains Co. v. Boston and Maine RR., 1 Gray 263 (1854).

[87] It cannot be determined from the manuscript Shaw collections nor from the published records of the Massachusetts railroad companies whether the Chief Justice was himself a railroad stockholder.

disaster. As a growing infant industry and public improvement, the railroad had its claims upon a public-spirited Court, and as a corporate business, upon a conservative Court.

In short, the factor of judicial paternalism provides an answer to the question why some decisions but not others allowed for growth in the law. Growth in the law took place where it contributed to railroad growth; *stare decisis* governed where it too contributed to railroad growth. To paraphrase Justice Thomas, the first puff of the engine on the iron road announced a capitalist revolution in the common law. Strictly private interests were invariably forced to yield to the larger interests of the railroad, symbol of corporate enterprise, industrial expansion, and the public interest. On rare occasions, for instance where human life was concerned or where the legislature had not intervened to regulate rates, the common law was made to sacrifice even the public interest. Clearly, Chief Justice Shaw made the railroad the beneficiary of legal doctrine.

1 0

LABOR LAW

The Fellow-Servant Rule

I

The leading American opinion on the fellow-servant rule was given in 1842 by Chief Justice Shaw in the case of *Farwell v. Boston and Worcester Railroad*.[1] Stripped of qualifications, the rule was that a servant, or employee, injured through no fault of his own by the negligence of a fellow servant, could not maintain a claim for damages against his master, or employer. By this rule American capitalism, at a critical stage in its development, was relieved of an enormous financial burden for industrial accidents which it would otherwise have incurred. The losses from injury on the job were sustained by the workers themselves.

Shaw did not actually originate the fellow-servant rule. He had two recent precedents for his decision in the Farwell case, one an English decision of 1837, the other an 1841 decision by the South Carolina Court of Errors.[2] But neither of these precedents were sufficiently strong or clear enough to establish the rule. In both, the issue was obscured by the extraneous question of whether the employee, when injured on his employer's vehicle, could recover damages in the capacity of a passenger. The English case involved a non-industrial situation: a butcher's boy fell off a delivery van. The opinion by Lord Abinger was very weakly reasoned and founded upon no discernible principle. By its illustrations it was chiefly applicable to the case of domestic servants.[3] The American

[1] 4 Metc. 49 (1842).

[2] Priestly v. Fowler, 3 Meeson & Welsby 1 (1837); Murray v. S. Car. R.R., 1 MacMillan (S. Car.) 385 (1841).

[3] The decisions establishing the fellow-servant rule "are founded one upon another, until we reach Priestly v. Fowler, which is usually cited as the original authority for the doctrine. Yet that case, it will be found, did not raise the question for decision, and is no authority for the rule" (Thomas G. Shearman and Amasa

case did not involve employees of equal rank, so that the issue was additionally obscured by the question whether the superior servant acted as the representative of his principal toward the inferior servant injured by his negligence. Moreover, the majority opinion occasioned a scathing dissent by three judges.

It remained for the great Shaw, with his gift for clarifying imperfectly understood principles, to establish the fellow-servant rule in a position of near impregnability. Justice Field, speaking for the Supreme Court of the United States in 1884, said that Shaw's opinion in the Farwell case "exerted a great influence in controlling the course of decisions in this country." [4] Cited and followed perhaps hundreds of times by the courts of a great majority of the states, and in England as well, it was almost everywhere commended in the highest terms for the soundness of its reasoning. Professor Chafee has estimated that Shaw's remarkable skill in expounding the fellow-servant rule in the Farwell case considerably delayed its replacement by workmen's compensation acts.[5]

Yet legal historians have long differed as to whether the rule, when announced, conformed with common-law principles. Professor Edward Berman, for example, has viewed it as a departure from the ancient maxim of *respondeat superior,* which holds a master liable to third persons for injuries caused by the negligent acts of a servant committed in the regular course of his employment.[6] Dean Roscoe Pound, however, has maintained that the fellow-servant rule was not an exception to any principle of law that expressed a universal idea of justice. On the contrary, he considers the rule to be a refusal to establish an exception to the general principle that liability for tort must flow from fault.[7]

A. Redfield, *A Treatise on the Law of Negligence,* New York, 1869, sec. 86, p. 102). All citations from Shearman and Redfield refer to this first edition. See also Augustine Birrell, *Four Lectures on the Law of Employers' Liability at Home and Abroad* (London, 1897), pp. 25–27.

[4] Chicago, Milwaukee, & St. Paul RR. v. Ross, 112 U.S. 377, 385–386 (1884).

[5] Zechariah Chafee, Jr., "Lemuel Shaw," *D.A.B.* New York, in 1910, was the first state to enact a workmen's compensation law.

[6] Berman, "Employers' Liability," *Encyclopedia of Social Sciences,* V, 514–515. See also Marland C. Hobbs, "Statutory Changes in Employers' Liability," *Harvard Law Review,* 2:212–230 (1888); Francis H. Bohlen, "Voluntary Assumption of Risk," *Harvard Law Review,* 20:14–34 (1906), p. 32; and Charles F. Beach, *Treatise on the Law of Contributory Negligence* (New York, 1885), sec. 98, p. 315.

[7] Pound, "The Economic Interpretation and the Law of Torts," *Harvard Law Review,* 53:365, 375 ff. (1940). See also Francis M. Burdick, "Is the Law the Expression of Class Selfishness?" *Harvard Law Review,* 25:349–359 (1912); and William L. Prosser, *Handbook of the Law of Torts* (St. Paul, 1941) p. 515.

Aside from this conflict over the conformity of the fellow-servant rule with older common-law principles, no historian has analyzed critically the one opinion, Shaw's, which all concede to have established the rule.

II

Nicholas Farwell was a railroad engineer employed for two dollars a day. One day he drove over a track whose switch had been improperly left open by a switchman employed by the same railroad. The engine was derailed, and Farwell was thrown to the ground; his right hand was crushed by the wheels of the train. In his claim that the railroad company was liable to him for damages because of the switchman's negligence, he distinguished his case from the precedents. His argument was that he and the switchman were not fellow servants because they were engaged in distinctly independent jobs and were not jointly employed for a common purpose.

Shaw, commencing his opinion for a unanimous Court, noted that the action was one of new impression in Massachusetts and involved a principle of great importance. "The question is," he declared, "whether, for damages sustained by one of the persons so employed, by means of the carelessness and negligence of another, the party injured has a remedy against the common employer." [8] This was the first comprehensive definition of the question, uncomplicated by the issue of passengership. Shaw's answer to the question contained substantially all the arguments used by courts in succeeding years to uphold the fellow-servant rule.

He first rejected the applicability of the principle which rendered an employer liable for the acts of his servants. The principle "presupposes that the parties stand to each other in the relation of strangers, between whom there is no privity, and the action, in such case, is an action sounding in tort." [9] Therefore the maxim *respondeat superior* was limited to the case of "strangers," and did not extend to the case of an employee bringing an action against his employer to recover for an injury arising in the course of employment.

If the employee's claim could be maintained at all, Shaw added, it must be placed on the ground of contract. Since there was no express contract between the parties on the point at issue,

---

[8] Farwell v. B. & W. RR., 4 Metc. 49, 55 (1842).
[9] *Ibid.*, at 56.

the claim must be placed on an *implied* contract arising out of the relation of master and servant.

Shaw then proceeded to go beyond the precedents and to expound the doctrine of assumption of risk, which provided the first ground of decision.[10] Considerations of "justice," he averred, required that one who engaged in the employment of another for pay "takes upon himself the natural and ordinary risks and perils" incident to the performance of his service. Shaw was "not aware of any principle" which should except these perils arising from the negligence of a fellow servant.[11] In legal presumption, an employee's pay was adjusted to the risks of the job, risks as likely to be known and guarded against by him as by his employer.

The Chief Justice rested the second ground of decision on considerations of "policy" that promoted the benefit of all the parties concerned — "the basis on which implied promises are raised." [12] Accordingly he set forth the following doctrine, which he said was drawn from policy:

Where several persons are employed in the conduct of one common enterprise or undertaking, and the safety of each depends much on the care and skill with which each other shall perform his appropriate duty, each is an observer of the conduct of the others, can give notice of any misconduct, incapacity or neglect of duty, and leave the service, if the common employer will not take such precautions and employ such agents as the safety of the whole party may require. By these means, the safety of each will be much more effectually secured, than could be done by a resort to the common employer for indemnity in case of loss by the negligence of each other.[13]

Regarded in this light, it was the ordinary case of one sustaining an injury in the course of his own employment, voluntarily undertaken with full knowledge of the attendant risks. The injury must be deemed the result of "pure accident," and the loss must rest where it fell, unless there was a remedy against the actual wrongdoer — a matter on which the Court gave no opinion.[14]

The final ground of the decision presented the doctrine of

[10] "The defense of assumption of risk as recognized was first declared in this country as a principle involved in the application of the law of master and servant, by the Massachusetts court in 1842" (W. F. Bailey, *Treatise on the Law of Personal Injuries, Including Employer's Liability, Master and Servant and Workmen's Compensation Acts*, Chicago, 1912), vol. II, sec. 353, p. 939.

[11] 4 Metc. 49, 57.

[12] *Ibid.*, at 58.

[13] *Ibid.*, at 59.

[14] See *infra*, p. 175.

common employment. The plaintiff had pressed the argument that where two servants were jointly employed in the same department, one might not maintain a claim against the master for the negligence of the other; but this rule did not apply where the servants were employed in different departments, at a distance from each other, and unable to influence or control the conduct of each other. The Chief Justice merely replied that it would be extremely difficult to establish a practical rule based on this "supposed distinction," when the servants were commonly employed.

In an effort to clarify further the principle of the case, Shaw explained it in greater detail. The plaintiff's argument rested upon an assumed principle of responsibility that did not exist. The master was not exempt from liability merely because the servant could better provide for his own safety when employed in immediacy with those whose negligence might injure him; "but because the *implied contract* of the master does not extend to indemnify the servant against the negligence of any one but himself; and he is not liable in tort, as for the negligence of his servant, because the person suffering does not stand towards him in the relation of a stranger, but is one whose rights are regulated by contract . . . Hence the separation of the employment into different departments cannot create that liability . . ." [15]

Shaw concluded his opinion with a word of caution. He did not mean, he said, that there were no implied warranties and undertakings in the relation of master and servant. It was still an undecided question whether the claim might be maintained on the grounds that train, track, switches, and any of the subsidiary arrangements, and equipment were improperly constructed,[16] or on the grounds that persons of unsuitable skill and experience were employed.[17]

[15] *Ibid.*, at 60–61.

[16] But see King v. B. and W. RR., 9 Cush. 112 (1851), where the Court held *per* Fletcher, J., counsel for the same defendant in the Farwell case, that a locomotive fireman could not recover against the railroad for an accident occasioned by an improperly constructed switch. In Seaver v. B. and M. RR., 14 Gray 466 (1860), the employee was again without a remedy in the case of an accident resulting from a defect in an axle. In neither of these cases could plaintiffs possibly know about the latent risks which eventuated in their injuries; the conclusion must be that employees assumed the extraordinary risks of their jobs. On this point see Shearman and Redfield, *Negligence*, sec. 87, pp. 103–104, and Bailey, *Personal Injuries*, vol. II, sec. 356. For a contrast between the protection offered to passengers and employees, respectively, see McElroy v. N. and L. RR., 4 Cush. 400 (1849), where it was held, *per* Shaw C.J., that a railroad is liable to an injured passenger for a carelessly managed switch.

[17] See Cayzer v. Taylor, 10 Gray 274 (1857).

III

The Chief Justice's opinion is not above criticism, in spite of the marked deference with which it was received by almost all American courts.[18] A mass of concurring cases no doubt lends weight to its persuasiveness, but an opinion must be judged on its own merits. Shaw's opinion was unsoundly reasoned: his construction of the maxim *respondeat superior* may be doubted; his contract theory was neither good law nor just law; and his argument from policy conflicted with the public interest.

It is difficult to regard the Chief Justice's decision as anything less than an exception to a general principle. That a master is liable for the acts of his servant is an ancient rule of common law, based on the reason that every man must conduct his own affairs, whether by himself or by agents, without causing injury to others. Accordingly, an injury caused by a servant, "in the course of his employment, and acting within the scope of his authority," is considered, in contemplation of law, an act of the master for which he is answerable.[19] Shaw departed from this principle when he excluded employees from the protection given to the rest of the world, an exclusion made on the assumption that employees are not third parties or "strangers." [20]

[18] The remark of the New York Court of Appeals was fairly typical: "To the elaborate opinion by Chief Justice Shaw nothing can be added without danger of impairing the force of his reasoning" (Coon v. S. and U. RR., 5 N.Y. 492, 1842). The House of Lords did Shaw the signal honor of reprinting his opinion in a volume of its reports: 3 Macq. 316 (1858). Cranworth, Lord Chancellor, adopted Shaw's reasoning in Bartenshill Coal Co. v. Reid, 3 Macq. 266 (1858). Beach stated that the fellow-servant rule as laid down by Shaw "is expounded and enforced with such learning and ability, and with such cogency of logic, that this opinion has ever since been regarded one of the most profound and masterly to be found in any of our law reports" (*Contributory Negligence*, sec. 98, p. 315).

[19] Farwell v. B. and W. RR., 4 Metc. 49, 56.

[20] 1 Bl. *Comm.*, sec. 429. Shaw relied upon Blackstone, yet the latter stated the principle without qualifications. Pound has written that the maxim *respondeat superior* is not of universal application, nor broad enough to support the employer's liability for the torts of his employee contrary to the intent of the employment ("The Economic Interpretation and the Law of Torts," p. 375). However, the U.S. Supreme Court has said: "The rule of 'respondeat superior,' or that the master shall be civilly liable for the tortious acts of his servant, is of universal application, whether the act be one of omission or commission, whether negligent, fraudulent or deceitful. If it be done in the course of his employment the master is liable; and it makes no difference that the master did not authorize, or even know of the servant's act or neglect, or even if he disapproved or forbade it, he is equally liable, if the act be done in the course of employment" (Philadelphia and Reading RR. v. Derby, 14 How. 468, 486, 1852). See also, Joseph Story, *Commentaries on the Law of Agency* (Boston, 1846, 3rd ed.), sec. 452; and Shearman and Redfield, *Negligence*, sec. 59, p. 65, and sec. 65, pp. 72–73.

But there was no good reason why employees of the same company should not have been regarded as strangers to each other, in standpoint of law, because they were not privy to each other's contract with their employer. Indeed, the Shaw Court so ruled thirteen years later.[21] Thus the fact that two persons happen to be fellow servants is irrelevant when one is injured by the second acting in the "course of his employment" and "in the scope of his authority." In such case the liability of the employer should have remained the same as it would have been in the case of an innocent passerby who might have been injured by the very act of negligence which derailed the train and crippled Farwell. In the case of the passerby, the negligent switchman would have been considered the agent of the railroad, and for his act the road would have been liable. Yet Shaw made a distinction because of the fact that Farwell and the switchman, though legally strangers, happened to have been fellow servants — as if that ambiguous relationship could have metamorphosed an act of negligence from one committed in the course of agency to one not in the course of agency.

Shaw's flat assertion that the employee could not recover in tort, under the maxim *respondeat superior,* because his rights were regulated by contract, is also questionable. First, the unanimous opinion of the Supreme Court of the United States is that "the maxim of 'respondeat superior,' which, by legal imputation, makes the master liable for the acts of his servants, is *wholly irrespective of any contract,* express or implied, or any other relation between the injured party and the master." [22] Second, there are causes of action with a remedy in both tort and contract. For example, the rights of a passenger may be regulated by a contract of safe carriage, yet for an injury received on the journey by the negligence of the carrier's agent or servant, the passenger may bring an action either for tort or for breach of contract.

By excluding the applicability of the maxim *respondeat superior,* Shaw could decide the case on the theory that the law implies a contract of non-liability on the master's part, which in turn is placed on the ground that employees assume the "ordinary" risks incident to their employment. Shaw reasoned that the work was voluntarily undertaken with "full knowledge of the risks" that were "as likely" to be foreseen and guarded against

---

[21] Albro v. Jaquith, 4 Gray 99 (1855), discussed *infra*, pp. 175–176.
[22] Philadelphia & Reading RR. v. Derby, 14 How. (U.S.) 468, 485 (1852). Italics added. See also note 20, *supra*.

by employees as by their employer. This is the doctrine of "assumption of risk." It is dubiously grounded because it includes all the risks arising from the negligence of others.

Unlike the situation in the 1837 English case,[23] where the employee was literally in a position to know that the van was overloaded, since his own weight contributed to the overloading, Farwell could not possibly have known whether the switch had been left open at some intermediary point on the track over which he drove his engine between Boston and Worcester. The law does not require prescience as a constituent of due care. Farwell, an innocent victim of someone else's negligence, could not possibly have guarded against the unknowable. Moreover it is not clear why he should have assumed the risks of a fellow servant's negligence when he did not assume the risks of his master's.[24]

What is an "ordinary risk"? It is one necessarily incident to the particular work and which may be prevented by ordinary or due care. No risk, however, should be regarded as ordinary which cannot be prevented by the utmost and extraordinary care on the part of the injured person. The Court's promiscuous usage of "ordinary" risk made possible its later decision that the risks assumed by an employee included even those which resulted from the *gross* negligence of another employee.[25]

Shaw comforted employees with the thought that their wages were adjusted to the risks which they assumed. The thought was unrealistic. As Charles Warren has commented, "Students of political economy know that as a matter of fact wages of a particular workman are not regulated in this way." [26] Inequality of bargaining power between employees and employers gave the latter "the power to make a harsh bargain." [27] In short, this "most unsatisfying" [28] doctrine of assumption of risk, from any standpoint, was an untenable assumption by Shaw.

So too was the doctrine of common employment, another

[23] Priestly v. Fowler, 3 Mees. & Wel. 1 (1837).

[24] "The assumption of risk," wrote Morris R. Cohen, "is purely the judicial invention of Lord Abinger, C. J. Shaw, and Baron Alderson. Yet so powerfully do legal fictions work and so short is the legal memory of men that a doctrine of which there was no trace before 1837 is in 1911 treated as a law of nature and courts doubt whether a legislature has the right to abolish it" ("The Process of Judicial Legislation," *American Law Review,* 48:176, 1914).

[25] Albro v. Agawam Canal Co., 6 Cush. 75 (1850).

[26] Warren, *"Volenti Non Fit Injuria* in Actions of Negligence," *Harvard Law Review,* 8:457, 466 (1895).

[27] Bohlen, p. 22.

[28] *Ibid.,* p. 31, note 1.

corollary of Shaw's contract theory in the Farwell case. According to this doctrine, where two men work for a common employer, there can be no exceptions to the latter's non-liability for their injuries on the job. Thus did Shaw reply to Farwell's argument that workers in different departments, in no way associated together and unable to guard against mutual negligence, are not fellow servants.

Shaw asserted that "it would be extremely difficult to establish a practical rule" on the basis of departmental distinctions; moreover, that "it would be extremely difficult to distinguish, what constitutes one department and what a distinct department of duty." [29] This was tantamount to a refusal to do justice in a court of justice because of the difficulty of making the attempt. Difficulties might have been imagined in hypothetical cases, but the facts of the case at bar presented an engineer who made the run between Boston and Worcester, and a switchman who tended the switch at Newton, a point in between.[30] Shaw treated the two as if they worked at the same bench and knew each other's habits. His reasoning in support of the doctrine of common employment, as Professor Prosser says of the fellow-servant rule generally, "had little validity in the case of large industries where the plaintiff might be injured by the negligence of a fellow servant he had never seen." [31]

Shaw phrased the doctrine of common employment so indiscriminately that he lumped together as fellow servants all persons serving the same employer, irrespective of their grade, as well as of their department.[32] To state a case that was decided by the

[29] 4 Metc. 49, 60 (1842).

[30] In Priestly v. Fowler, 3 Mees. & Wel. 1 (1837), the fellow servants worked together on the same van; in Murray v. South Car. RR., 1 MacMillan 385 (1841), they were an engineer and a fireman on the same locomotive. The distinction between these cases and the Farwell case is obvious.

[31] *Torts*, p. 515.

[32] Shearman and Redfield, *Negligence*, sec. 102, pp. 118–119, state that in Massachusetts "the courts have had a tendency to narrow the remedies for negligence by technical and unsound decisions, and especially to favor corporations at the expense of servants. If the Massachusetts doctrine [of common employment] should be adopted, it would afford complete immunity to a large class of employers, such as railroad companies, owners of large factories, foundries, mines, &c., who are accustomed, and indeed often compelled, to intrust the selection of almost all their servants to one or more superintendents. It would be almost impossible to prove that a superintendent had a reputation for selecting incapable subordinates, and that his employer was aware of it; yet, upon the theory which holds a general superintendent to be only a fellow-servant with those whom he employs, such proof would be necessary in order to maintain an action by one of the servants against the common employer on account of the negligence of another servant."

Shaw Court eight years after the definition of the doctrine is to reveal its full significance. In the first *Albro* case, it was held that a spinner in a large textile mill could not recover against her employers for the gross negligence of their vice-principal, a general superintendent in charge of production and personnel. The Court stated: "This case cannot be distinguished in principle from the case of *Farwell v. Boston and Worcester Railroad*. . . . The plaintiff and the superintendent must be considered as fellow servants . . ."[33]

That Shaw had clearly departed from the rule which he once had affirmed — "In law, for every wrong there is a remedy" — is evident from the decision in the second *Albro* case.[34] The same spinner who had been nonsuited in an action against her *employers* was told that she had no legal remedy against the very mill *superintendent* whose gross negligence had caused her injuries. The opinion of the Court is perplexing because the ground of decision is placed on the fact that the superintendent, at the time of his negligence, *was* acting in the course of employment as an agent of the common employer. The Court reasoned that for his negligence, an agent is responsible *only* to his employer with whom alone he has a contract requiring his diligence. To this contract, fellow servants are strangers or "third persons."

And because this [contract] is the sole origin and foundation of his duty, he is responsible only to the party to whom it was due for the injurious consequences of neglecting it. It is not pretended that he

[33] Albro v. Agawam Canal Co., 6 Cush. 75, 76, 77 (1850). The doctrine in this case was rejected in several states. In Ohio, Illinois, Louisiana, Nebraska, Tennessee, Texas, and Utah, the courts held employers liable where the servant was injured by another who was superior in authority, and the same qualification of the fellow-servant rule was adopted with modifications in Arkansas, Kansas, Kentucky, Missouri, and North Carolina (Bailey, *Personal Injuries,* vol. II, sec. 544, p. 1515, and cases cited therein under the heads of the respective states). In Indiana, Illinois, Kentucky, Louisiana, Missouri, Nebraska, Utah, and Tennessee, the courts held employers liable where the servant injured and the one who injured him were not associated together in their work, or were in different departments (Bailey, vol. II, sec. 561, p. 1551). In all these states, the principle of the fellow-servant rule was accepted; however its rigors were lessened by the operation of the qualifications in the superior servant and departmental rules. Wisconsin was the only state in which the fellow-servant rule, for a short time, was repudiated altogether (Chamberlain v. M. and M. RR., 11 Wis. 238, 1860; but see Moseley v. Chamberlain, 18 Wis. 700, 1861). In the U.S. Supreme Court, the superior-servant rule was sustained as an exception to the fellow-servant rule (Hough v. RR. Co., 100 U.S. 213, 1879; C. and M. RR. v. Ross, 112 U.S. 377, 1884; and B. and O. RR. v. Baugh, 149 U.S. 368, 1892).

[34] Albro v. Jaquith, 4 Gray 99 (1855), *per* Merrick, J., in whose opinion Shaw concurred.

had entered into any stipulation, or made any positive engagement with the plaintiff, in relation to the service which he had agreed to render to their common employer. She therefore can have no legal right to complain of his carelessness or unfaithfulness; for he had made himself, by no act or contract, accountable to her.[35]

Glaring inconsistencies are patently discernible between this opinion and the one in the Farwell case. Indeed, if fellow servants are "third persons" or strangers to each other from a legal standpoint, because no privity of contract exists between them, then no basis exists for the fellow-servant rule: the maxim *respondeat superior* should apply as it does in all cases of negligence by an employee toward third persons.

The fellow-servant rule was spun out of judicial implications from a contractual relationship — "as sheer invention as the Original Contract between kings and their subjects."[36] The implications were based, said Shaw, upon "considerations of policy," namely, the promotion of the "safety and security of all." Shaw reasoned that this end was best achieved if employees know that they cannot recover against their common employer, but must themselves bear the burden of injury from each other's negligence. Thus the law induces all to exercise the greatest skill and care, since all are interdependent for their safety. A careful employee can "leave the service" if his employer will not act upon a notice regarding the incapacity or carelessness of a fellow servant.

Shaw's "considerations of policy" were misconceived, leaving the employer's implied contract of non-liability without a policy rationale. In the first place, reasons already existed for the exercise of great care by each employee, reasons so compelling that the inability to recover against the common employer added nothing to the general safety. A man is prompted to caution and vigilance on the job not because he has no right to an action for injury, but because he fears mutilation and pain. Most men prefer to remain able-bodied, and to work to provide for their families. Against the few who prefer disability compensation, the law of contributory negligence presents almost insuperable difficulties.

In the second place, throwing the burden of loss upon injured employees, by exempting the employer from liability, detracted from the general safety. When an employer is not liable to his

[35] *Ibid.*, at 100, 101. Shearman and Redfield comment that the second Albro decision is "one of a class which greatly diminishes our respect" for the Massachusetts courts (*Negligence*, sec. 102, p. 120). See also note 32, *supra*.

[36] Birrell, p. 20.

workers for the negligence of anyone but himself, his inducements to hire persons of the greatest skill and care are diminished. As Professor Seavey pointed out, "One who is responsible for all the consequences is more apt to take precautions to prevent injurious consequences from arising . . . *respondeat superior* results in greater care in the selection and instruction of servants than would be used otherwise. . . . The history of the Employers' Liability Acts and of the Workmen's Compensation Acts, showing a decreasing mortality in an increasingly dangerous environment, indicates that the proper place to apply pressure is on the employer." [37] Judge Walton of Maine expressed the point more bluntly: "There is but one vulnerable point about these ideal existences, called corporations; and that is, the pocket of the moneyed power that is concealed behind them; and if that is reached they will wince. When it is thoroughly understood that it is not profitable to employ careless and indifferent agents, or reckless and insolent servants, better men will take their places, and not before." [38]

Policy required the most stringent liabilities upon railroads in particular, since the public, as well as workers, were exposed to increased chances of accident when the most diligent persons were not employed. Indeed, if Shaw's advice had been acted upon, and the best employees left the service of the railroads because careless men were hired, the public would have had to depend for their safety upon the less able employees remaining. Railroads owed special duties and liabilities to the public, particularly since they were both "public works" and common carriers possessing special privileges and powers.

But of course, railroad employees, like factory workers, were not free agents, as Shaw assumed, able to leave their jobs at will. Poverty is blind to risks, and Shaw was blind to that fact. "The cornerstone of the common law edifice," as Professor Prosser says,

was the economic theory that there was complete mobility of labor, that the supply of work was unlimited, and that the workman was an entirely free agent, under no compulsion to enter into the employment. He was expected therefore to accept and take upon himself all the usual risks of his trade, together with any unusual risks of which he had knowledge, and to relieve his employer of any duty to protect

[37] Warren Abner Seavey, "Speculations as to 'Respondeat Superior,' " *Harvard Legal Essays* (Cambridge, 1934), pp. 447, 448, and 449.
[38] Goddard v. G. T. RR. of Canada, 57 Me. 202 (1869), quoted in Prosser, pp. 28–29, note 43.

him. The economic compulsion which left him no choice except starvation, or equally dangerous employment elsewhere, was entirely disregarded.[39]

These economic theories of complete mobility of labor and an unlimited supply of work, so foreign to reality, were written into the law "with an appalling record of inhumanity on the part of employers in the way of working conditions." [40]

Consideration of the public safety is not the only basis for the view that policy required employers' liability at common law for employee injuries innocently sustained on the job. There is also the consideration that employers, who were tending to become ever larger corporations, could best afford to foot the bill for industrial accident; indeed, that the cost was part of the costs of production and should have been passed on to consumers. Finally, there is the consideration that the community in general suffered when the loss fell upon the disabled worker. But perhaps judges of more than a century ago could not have appreciated such considerations, which underlay the modern workmen's compensation acts.

IV

Why did Shaw decide as he did? Any informed guess must proceed upon the assumption that he expounded and configured the common law conscientiously, to the best of his understanding and without overt bias. It cannot be maintained that he was an "anti-labor" judge, because in little more than a week after the *Farwell* decision he gave his celebrated opinion in favor of trade-unions, in the case of *Commonwealth v. Hunt*.[41] There is, however, a revealing economic interpretation of the decision, particularly if attention is focussed upon the fact that the defendant was a railroad corporation, rather than upon the fact that plaintiff was a worker.

Not many years had passed since the railroad had been ridiculed as a useless absurdity. The first railroad was opened for travel in Massachusetts only a mere eight years before the Farwell case. Government aid, together with the grant of special privileges and powers, played a prominent role in the establishment of the railroad, but its economic feasibility at the time of the case was not yet assured. As late as 1854, Shaw's desire to maintain the

[39] Prosser, p. 506.
[40] *Ibid.*, p. 392.
[41] 4 Metc. 111 (1842), discussed in Chapter 11, *infra*.

"confidence of moneyed men in these enterprises" was, in part, a factor in his decision that a railroad charter granting exclusive privileges was an irrepealable contract.[42] Charles Warren, commenting on the Farwell case, wrote: "Undoubtedly, the fact that a contrary decision would have imposed a great burden on these struggling institutions had a great effect in influencing the decision reached in this case." John M. Shirley, writing in 1883 for the *American Law Review,* noted that the "rule first laid down in Farwell's case was established by a great and wise legislator as a species of protective tariff for the encouragement of infant railway industries." [43]

The Shaw Court, as has been shown, made the railroad the beneficiary of the common law. With rare exception, railroad interests were paternally promoted. In accident cases where passengers, highway travellers, and other individuals were pitted against a railroad, they were given a kind of rough justice like that meted out to railroad employees.[44]

As such cases indicate, Shaw was particularly conservative in the field of tort law, and it is significant, in understanding his Farwell opinion, that tort was involved. "Perhaps more than any other branch of law," remarks Prosser, "the law of torts is a battleground of social theory" and of "the conflict between capital and labor . . ." [45] Shaw, by generally giving preferential treatment to industrial interests over strictly personal ones, tended to insulate the former from tort liability. His Farwell opinion fitted this pattern of pro-railroad and conservative tort law decisions, without conflicting with his opinion in *Commonwealth v. Hunt.* Shaw's great admirer, Justice Holmes, although the author of many an opinion that in effect was pro-labor, also wrote opinions

[42] Boston & Lowell RR. v. Salem & Lowell RR., 2 Gray 1 (1854).

[43] Warren, *A History of the American Bar* (Boston, 1911), 486. Shirley is quoted by Warren at p. 487.

[44] See Carey v. Berkshire RR., 1 Cush. 475 (1848); Kearney v. B. & W. RR., 9 Cush. 108 (1851); Lucas v. N.B. & T. RR., 6 Gray 64 (1856); Robinson v. F. & W. RR., 7 Gray 92 (1856).

[45] Prosser, pp. 15, 33. Of course, Shaw decided the Farwell case on a theory of contract law as well as tort law. The employer's non-liability was an implication Shaw drew from the contract of employment. Yet, Prosser's remark about tort law can be equally applied to contract law. As Holmes put it: "You always can imply a condition in a contract. But why do you imply it? It is because of some belief as to the practice of the community or of a class, or because of some opinion as to policy. . . . Such matters really are battle grounds where the means do not exist for determinations that shall be good for all time, and where the decision can do no more than embody the preference of a given body in a given time and place" (Oliver Wendell Holmes, "The Path of the Law," in Max Lerner, *The Mind and Faith of Justice Holmes,* Boston, 1943, p. 80).

representing a "retrogression in the humanization of the law of torts." [46]

Of course, the fellow-servant rule benefited industry generally, not just railroads. Although Shaw was especially partial to railroad interests, which were involved in the case of first impression, his opinion would probably have been no different had the defendant been a textile concern. It was only a few years after the Farwell case that the fellow-servant rule and its corollary doctrines, assumption of risk and common employment, were applied by the Shaw Court against a factory worker.[47] Thus the rule is probably best interpreted by Professor Bohlen when he says that it was a limitation of the vicarious liability of employers for the purpose of avoiding a "burden upon the development of business and manufacture . . . commercial necessity required it . . ." [48]

That Shaw himself based the fellow-servant rule largely upon extra-legal "considerations of policy" warrants this interpretation in kind. But he also presented "considerations of justice," strictly legal in character, that make possible an interpretation in the light of legal theory. Here he relied most heavily upon the doctrine of assumption of risk, based on a legal theory of consent and expressed in the old common-law maxim, *volenti non fit injuria:* to one who consents no injury is done.[49] The relevance of this theory of consent is found in Pound's striking phrase, "the free contract of a free man," [50] an insight into the common law's individualistic spirit which suffuses Shaw's opinion.

A free man is an individual who is free to master his own destiny, pursue the calling of his choice, care for himself, and bind himself by contract. If he undertakes a dangerous occupation he assumes the risks to which he has exposed himself, because as Shaw stressed, he acts voluntarily and with full knowledge that harm may befall him from the negligence of those with whom he works. The common law does not protect him from the consequences of his own choice and action. Thus, by his voluntary conduct he in effect consents to assume his loss, thereby relieving his employer of it. Since a free man cannot be bound except by his

---

[46] *Harvard Law Review,* 36:113 (1922). For Holmes' conservatism in tort law, see U.S. Zinc Co. v. Britt, 258 U.S. 268 (1922), and Baltimore & Ohio RR. Co. v. Goodman, 275 U.S. 66 (1927); see also the comment of Max Lerner, pp. 201–207.

[47] Albro v. Agawam Canal Co., 6 Cush. 75 (1850).

[48] Bohlen, p. 31.

[49] *Ibid.,* 14, 22, 30–32; Warren, *"Volenti Non Fit Injuria," Harvard Law Review,* 3:466; and Prosser, pp. 117, 377, 383–387.

[50] Pound, *The Spirit of the Common Law* (Boston, 1921), p. 49.

consent, that is, by a contract of his own making, Shaw felt the necessity of referring the master's non-liability to the worker's contract of employment.

Viewed from this standpoint, a risk which is unknown, or even unknowable, can be "assumed" by a worker because it is his consent to take the risk and not his knowledge of it that is determinative. Moreover, his consent converts what would otherwise be a tortious act into a neutral one, that is, one not wrongful in law and for which there is no remedy. Thus, for the fellow-servant rule and for the doctrine of assumption of risk, there is a semblance of a juristic rationale that permits some degree of respect even for the worst elements in the line of decisions beginning with the Farwell case. Yet the rationale rests upon a legal fiction which has little relation to economic reality, because the worker whose consent was judicially implied had no real choice or freedom of contract. As an English judge tersely declared, it was "his poverty and not his will which consented." [51]

A final legal consideration helps explain why Shaw decided as he did. He was adhering to the rule that there shall be no liability without personal fault. The difficulty here, however, is that he was simultaneously making an exception to the maxim *respondeat superior* as expressed in the rule that the principal is liable for the torts of his agents.[52] Both these rules can be maintained by persuasive considerations of justice, and both were

[51] Hawkins, J., in Thrussell v. Handyside, 20 Q.B.D. 359 (1888), quoted in Prosser, p. 514.

[52] See Harold J. Laski, "The Basis of Vicarious Liability," *Yale Law Journal,* 26:105–135 (Dec. 1916), and T. Baty, *Vicarious Liability* (Oxford, 1916). Pound insists that the fellow-servant rule must be considered as a refusal to extend vicarious liability. The rule, he claims, is understandable as part of the "strong tendency" or "movement" of the nineteenth century common law to restrict liability to fault. For American judges, acting in the light of their common law training, to arrive at any other conclusion than that of Shaw's in the Farwell case, Pound adds, "would have been quite impossible." See Pound's *Formative Era of American Law* (Boston, 1938), p. 87; *Interpretations of Legal History* (New York, 1923), pp. 104, 109–110; and "The Economic Interpretation and the Law of Torts," pp. 373–385. As a matter of fact, Baty's *Vicarious Liability* elaborately documents the process by which the courts, with increasing tempo, extended vicarious liability down through the course of the nineteenth century. Thus the fellow-servant rule was an exception to and not a part of the common law trend. It will not do to say that it was impossible for an American court to have decided other than Shaw did, or that the maxim *respondeat superior* could not have been held applicable; for the courts of more than a dozen states adopted the superior servant and departmental rules which made vital exceptions to the fellow-servant rule, rejecting it at least in part on ground of the maxim. See note 33, *supra.* But for his comments in *The Spirit of the Common Law* on individualism in the fellow-servant rule, Pound has obscured understanding of the rule.

equally applicable to the case. Shaw's choice of the one with the harsher consequences was in keeping with the strict individualism which pervaded his whole opinion, as well as the common law and American philosophy. If the theory of implied consent and the rule of no liability without fault were the taught law, influencing Shaw's thinking, then Maitland's aphorism that "taught law is tough law" [53] takes on new meaning: it was tough on accident victims, particularly of the working class.[54]

[53] Maitland, *English Law and the Renaissance*, p. 18, quoted in Pound, *Formative Era of American Law*, p. 144.

[54] "Assumption of risk is a judicially created rule which was developed in response to the general impulse of common law courts . . . to insulate the employer as much as possible from bearing the 'human overhead' which is an inevitable part of the cost — to someone — of the doing of industrialized business. The general purpose behind this development in the common law seems to have been to give maximum freedom to expanding industry" (Tiller v. Atlantic Coast Line RR., 318 U.S. 54, 1943).

11

LABOR LAW

Trade Unions and Criminal Conspiracy

In the same term that he formulated the fellow-servant rule, Shaw handed down another opinion which had as great an impact upon the fortunes of labor. *Commonwealth v. Hunt*,[1] his best known and most widely praised opinion, is the Magna Charta of American trade-unionism, for it removed the stigma of criminality from labor organizations.

For five centuries, ever since the English Statute of Labourers of 1349, Anglo-American criminal law had periodically attempted to suppress the collective efforts of workers to improve their conditions of employment. In a leading case decided in 1721, for example, a union that sought wage increases was held to constitute a criminal conspiracy.[2] By the Anti-Combinations Act of 1800, Parliament perpetuated the sanctions of the criminal law against every worker who "enters any combination to obtain an advance of wages, or to lessen or alter the hours of work." Trade-unionism was straitjacketed for decades after.[3]

Underlying this policy of English legislation was the common-law doctrine of criminal conspiracy which the American courts, beginning with the Philadelphia Shoemakers' Case in 1806, also conscripted to do battle against unions.[4] The vague crime of con-

---

[1] 4 Metc. 111 (1842).

[2] Rex v. Journeymen Tailors of Cambridge, 8 Modern 10 (K.B., 1721). Although poorly reasoned and reported, this case played an influential role as a precedent in both England and America.

[3] William S. Holdsworth, *A History of English Law* (London), 1903 ff., 14 vols.), XI, 496–498, and XIII, 339–346; James F. Stephen, *A History of the Criminal Law of England* (London, 1883, 3 vols.), III, 202–227.

[4] R. S. Wright, *The Law of Criminal Conspiracies and Agreements* (American ed., Philadelphia, 1887); Francis B. Sayre, "Criminal Conspiracy," *Harvard Law Review*, 35:393–427 (Feb., 1922); "The Trial of the Boot and Shoemakers of Philadelphia," 1806, in John R. Commons *et al.*, eds., *Documentary History of American Industrial Society* (Cleveland, 1910–1911, 11 vols.), III, 59 ff. See Walter

spiracy — no other so eludes exact definition — served employers in the early nineteenth century in much the same way as the labor injunction did at a later date. Collective action by employees, the only effective means to realize their demands, could be proscribed and punished under the rubric of criminal conspiracy when all else failed.

Law, in some respects, is only a thing of wax shaped to serve dominant institutional interests. But the official reporter of the labor-conspiracy trial of the Pittsburgh cordwainers in 1815 was overly blunt in making the point. "The verdict of the jury," he said, "is most important to the manufacturing interests of the community for it puts an end to these associations which have been so prejudicial to the successful enterprise of the capitalist . . ." [5] The rationale of the labor-conspiracy doctrine was usually expressed in a more public-spirited manner and seemed reasonable enough from the viewpoint of prevailing economic theory. When workers organized and attempted to impose union standards, they interfered with the natural operations of the free market. Collective rather than individual bargaining, by throttling the law of supply and demand, artificially raised wages and prices. That could ruin honest employers and extort the community. A general price hike, provoked by a series of strikes, might even drive out local trade and perhaps damage America's competitive position in world markets. The interests of the public, as well as profits, must be considered.

Then too, the wage-fund theory predicated that there was only a fixed part of the national income available for wages. The selfish efforts of any single group of workers to aggrandize its natural share robbed the rest. Anyway, labor was merely another commodity to the upper orders of society who, finding the theories of Malthus congenial, cynically pointed out that efforts to ameliorate the workers' lot would increase the population in a world of limited food supply.

Not the least of the menace of unions was the inherently coercive character of their activities. Employers, forced to yield to union demands, were denied their liberty: the right to contract freely, by hiring men of their own choosing, and by paying only what a good balance sheet would permit. The employees them-

Nelles, "The First American Labor Case," *Yale Law Journal*, 41:165–200 (Dec. 1931). See generally Hampton L. Carson, *The Law of Criminal Conspiracies and Agreements as Found in the American Cases* (Philadelphia, 1887).

[5] "Report of the Trial of the Journeymen Cordwainers of the Borough of Pittsburg," Commonwealth v. Morrow, 1815, in Commons, IV, 16.

selves lost their liberty by the compulsion to join a journeymen's society and to abide by its dictates and exactions.

American judges generously larded their opinions in labor-conspiracy cases with this social philosophy. To an age which placed much faith in the beneficences of self-reliance, nothing but good could come from the atomistic efforts of individual employees. The evil so "pregnant with public mischief and private injury" [6] lay in combinations and in united action, the very basis of conspiracy; indictments for that crime periodically plagued American workers. At least a dozen cases ended in convictions between 1806 and 1842,[7] the date of Shaw's decision in *Commonwealth v. Hunt.*

II

That great case was instigated, in 1840, not by an employer but by a disgruntled employee, one Jeremiah Horne, a member of the Boston Journeymen Bootmakers' Society. The union fined Horne for having done some extra work without pay, an infraction of union rules. The fine was removed after Horne's employer recompensed him, but he seems to have borne a grudge. Soon fined again for another infraction, he refused to pay despite the advice of his employer who even offered to give him the money. The union countered by expelling Horne, requiring that he sign its rules and pay fines totaling seven dollars as a condition of his reinstatement. When he stubbornly persisted in his defiance, again rejecting his employer's advice to become a member in good standing, the union insisted that he be fired. The employer, probably anxious to avoid a strike, complied; he knew the union's rule that its members would not work for anyone employing a non-member whose discharge had been demanded. Horne then complained to the District Attorney, Samuel D. Parker, who seems to have mustered a loathing for workers' organizations second only to that he had displayed against Abner Kneeland whom he had prosecuted for blasphemy several years earlier.

The indictment charged luridly that the Boston Journeymen Bootmakers' Society was a criminal conspiracy to maintain what

---

[6] Recorder Moses Levy in the Philadelphia Shoemakers' Case, 1806, in Commons, III, 230.

[7] For a list of American labor cases before 1842, see Appendix to Walter Nelles, "Commonwealth v. Hunt," *Columbia Law Review*, 32:1128 ff., at 1166–1169 (Nov. 1932). Although I cannot accept Nelles' interpretation of Shaw's decision, I am indebted to him for his superbly researched and massive article covering all stages of this case.

a later age called a closed shop; to compel Horne to be fired; and to oppress and impoverish him, his employer, and others who did not acquiesce in union regulations. At the trial in Boston Municipal Court before Judge Peter O. Thacher, prosecutor Parker called a number of shoe manufacturers and master cordwainers to testify in support of the indictment, but interestingly enough, none of them shared his views that the union was tyrannical, its rules enslaving, its dues extortionary, its methods oppressive. For example, Horne's employer, Isaac Wait, testified that while he did not feel free to employ any but union members, he had not been injured by the union and believed that it fixed reasonable wages and provided good workmen.[8]

The defendants, seven journeymen shoemakers who worked for Wait, were represented by young Robert Rantoul, Jr., already a distinguished reformer and a brilliant leader of Democratic politics in the Bay State.[9] He turned the employers' testimony to his own advantage in an effort to prove that the union was lawful and constructive, and he showed an analogy between it and such respected organizations as the Boston Bar and the Boston Medical Association: they too fixed prices, charged dues, and imposed disciplinary measures for infractions of prescribed rules. Rantoul's point, that combinations are not per se conspiracies, was supplemented by the contention that the common-law crime of labor conspiracy — "part of the English tyranny from which we fled" — was repugnant to freedom and should not be accepted in America. But his argument was for the most part too learned and detailed; he addressed the jury for two full days as if they were appellate judges.

The unrestrained remarks by Judge Thacher, charging the jury, practically directed a verdict of guilty. Eight years earlier, he had gratuitously informed another jury that the doctrine of criminal conspiracy applied to "combinations, amongst journeymen mechanics and laborers, to raise their wages, and regulate the hours of work," even if such objectives were not a whit implemented by any act.[10] Now, in 1840, he told the jury trying the journeymen shoemakers that if unions became widespread,

[8] The report of the trial in Thacher's *Criminal Cases*, 609 (1840) is supplemented by the generous excerpts from the manuscript notes of Robert Rantoul, Jr., defense counsel, reprinted in Nelles, "Commonwealth v. Hunt," *passim*.

[9] See Merle E. Curti, "Robert Rantoul, Jr., The Reformer in Politics," *New England Quarterly*, 5:264–280 (1932).

[10] Quoted in Arthur M. Schlesinger, Jr., *The Age of Jackson* (Boston, 1945), p. 166.

all industry and enterprise would be suspended, and all property would become insecure. It would involve in one common, fatal ruin, both laborer and employer, and the rich as well as the poor. It would tend directly to array them against each other, and to convulse the social system to its centre. A frightful despotism would soon be erected on the ruins of this free and happy commonwealth.

Properly instructing the jury to take the law from the court rather than from counsel, Thacher concluded: "It is my duty to instruct you, as a matter of law, that this society of journeymen boot-makers, thus organized for the purposes described in the indict-ment, is an unlawful conspiracy against the laws of this common-wealth." [11]

The jury, taking only twenty minutes, obliged with a verdict of guilty. Noting such speed and the fact that the trial had created "political feelings," a Whig paper commented with satisfaction that "it may be proper to remark that the jury was composed of gentlemen of both political parties." [12] It was probably of no con-sequence, therefore, that Rantoul and the only Boston paper sym-pathetic to the union were Jacksonian, while the prosecutor, trial judge, and other city papers were Whig.

III

On Rantoul's exceptions to Thacher's charge, mainly to the point that the indictment described a conspiracy, the case came before Chief Justice Shaw and his associates. At the appeal, the Commonwealth was represented by its attorney general, James T. Austin, who relied heavily upon the standing law of England and America. Rantoul, with the precedents against him, resorted to technical deficiencies in the indictment and sought to distinguish his case. But these conventional legalisms were merely insurance against the failure of his primary position, namely that "the Eng-lish common law of conspiracies is not in force in this State." [13]

A conservative bench of the taught legal tradition would not be likely to find such an audacious claim convincing. But Lemuel Shaw, a teacher of law and a creator of its traditions, could imbue its letter with fresh spirit. With consummate craftsmanship he hewed closely to the old doctrine, yet liberated trade-unionism from its oppressive touch. This was no little achievement because he bluntly declared at the outset of his opinion that "the common

[11] Thacher's *Criminal Cases*, pp. 654, 653.
[12] *Boston Advertiser*, Oct. 23, 1840.
[13] Commonwealth v. Hunt, 4 Metc. 111, 115 (1842).

law in regard to conspiracy in this Commonwealth is in force." [14] Intending neither to blacken nor to whitewash workers' organizations, he colored them with legality, leaving them viable but subject to prosecution for conduct of a truly criminal character. In so doing, he reconciled the standing law with the needs of a free society.

Shaw's strategy was to establish a case for reversal of the conviction within the path of received doctrine, insofar as it was adaptable to the conditions of Massachusetts. Great judges, those who keep the law advancing, notch pioneer trails from the main travelled ones, partly because the custom of the craft commands deference to the old landmarks and partly because those who follow will search for the familiar ways. So Shaw began by mapping the crime of conspiracy, with its irregular contours and unsettled boundaries. Culling cases and commentators, he found decisions that resisted classification, rules not always consistent, and a wide variety of conduct deemed unlawful; the activities of unions constituted only one class of conspiracy. Of the few established rules, the most important was that unlawful agreement is the gist of the offense and is completed by the mere act of combination without any step towards execution of the agreement.

But an accurate description of the crime itself was wanting. Never was Shaw's gift for restatement of law more needed; never was he confronted by such "great difficulty" in "framing any definition . . . which shall specifically identify this offense." He provided an ends-means formula that virtually codified the doctrine in language as specific as an inherently vague crime would allow. A conspiracy, he said in words to be commonly accepted as definitive, "must be a combination of two or more persons, by some concerted action, to accomplish some criminal or unlawful *purpose,* or to accomplish some purpose, not in itself criminal or unlawful, by criminal or unlawful *means.*" [15] Conscious of imprecision, he added the important procedural point that an indictment must state whether the criminality of a conspiracy consists in its purpose or means, and must "fully and clearly" particularize on the character and facts of the crime.

The Chief Justice then turned to the merits of the case. As was usual in labor conspiracy cases, the indictment had been clothed in prejudicial supposition, namely, that the defendants had conspired "perniciously and deceitfully . . . wickedly . . .

[14] *Ibid.,* at 121.
[15] *Ibid.,* at 123 (italics added).

unjustly and corruptly." "Stripped . . . of the qualifying epithets," the principal charge was stated objectively by Shaw: the
defendant workers had formed a union for the purpose of induc-
ing "all those engaged in the same occupation to become members
of it," in other words, to establish a closed shop.[16] Shaw's next six
words provided the legal foundation of trade-unionism. "Such a
purpose is not unlawful."

The reasoning here was that the organized power of workers
might be used for "useful and honorable purposes" or abused for
"dangerous and pernicious ones." The latter, if "real and actual,"
must be specially charged, because the Court would not assume a
crime neither averred nor proved. From the facts of the case one
might as likely assume that the purpose of the union was to provide assistance to its members in times of misfortune, or to raise
their intellectual and social condition, or to improve their craftsmanship. They might even have combined to raise their wages.
Although no such purpose had been averred in the indictment, it
would be "perfectly justifiable," said Shaw, even in England since
a statute of 1825.[17]

Having upheld the lawfulness of a trade union whose purpose
was to establish a closed shop, and having asserted by dictum the
lawfulness of a purpose to raise wages, Shaw next ruled that the
means employed to achieve the purpose were also lawful in this
case. The men would not work for a person who after due notice

[16] *Ibid.*, at 129. Article 14 of the constitution of the Boston Journeymen
Bootmakers' Society, founded in 1835, stated: "Any member working for a Society
shop, and knowing a journeyman to be at work for the same who is not a member
of this society, shall immediately give notice to the other journeymen, who on
receiving such information, shall quit work for that shop; provided, such shop
shall have a majority of society men on work, but if their number be less, they
may continue until work can be obtained elsewhere." Quoted in Nelles, "Commonwealth v. Hunt," *Columbia Law Review*, 32:1134.

[17] St. 6 Geo. IV, ch. 129, 1825. This act, inspired by the reform efforts of
Francis Place and Joseph Hume, recognized the right of workers to agree upon the
wages and hours for which they would work, but imposed criminal penalties upon
almost any trade union activity by which the right could be exercised. That Shaw
read the act too generously in favor of unions is evident from the fact that in
Reg. v. Rowlands, 2 Den. *Crim. Cases*, 364 (1851), Erle, J., summing up, ruled that
it was an indictable conspiracy for leaders of a trade union to demand certain
wage increases and to compel the employer's agreement by organizing a strike. Sir
James F. Stephen concluded from this case that "at common law all combinations of
workmen to affect the rate of wages," even after the statute, "were illegal" (*A
History of the Criminal Law of England*, III, 217-218). It was not until 1875 that
Parliament freed trade union activity by providing that combinations to do "any
act in . . . furtherance of trade disputes between employers and workmen shall
not be indictable as a conspiracy if such act committed by one person would not
be punishable as a crime." 38 & 39 Vic., ch. 86, quoted in Stephen, pp. 225-226.

employed a journeyman not a member of their union. "Are these means criminal?" Shaw asked. "The case supposes that these persons are not bound by contract, but free to work for whom they please, or not to work, if they so prefer. In this state of things, we cannot perceive, that it is criminal for men to agree together to exercise their own acknowledged rights, in such a manner as best to subserve their own interests." [18]

The indictment had also charged a conspiracy "to compel one Wait to turn out of his employ one Jeremiah Horne." Shaw dismissed this count on ground that it too involved no criminality in purpose or means. Had the union used force or fraud, or induced the employer to breach a contract for service with Horne,[19] "compel" might convey the sense of unlawful coercion. But, reiterated Shaw, the compulsion was by lawful means: "It was the agreement not to work for him, by which they compelled Wait to decline employing Horne longer." [20]

Other judges had a considerably lower threshold of tolerance for organized pressure by labor aimed at controlling the hiring and firing process. Chief Justice Beasley of New Jersey, for example, easily found unlawful coercion in an effort "to dictate to this employer who he should discharge from his employ. This was an unwarrantable interference with the conduct of his business . . ." [21] By contrast, Shaw was sufficiently objective to take into account what any realist must understand, that in the normal relations between employers and employees, bargaining inevitably involves restraints and pressures of a sort, as did competition it-

[18] Commonwealth v. Hunt, 4 Metc. 111, 130 (1842).

[19] Inducement to breach of contract was not clearly recognized to be even a tort until 1853, yet Shaw took for granted that a combination for that purpose would be a criminal conspiracy. Lumley v. Gye, 2 El. & Bl. (1853); Holdsworth, IV, 384–385, and XIII, 347. Nelles suggested that Shaw was informing textile interests that if labor were put on a contractual basis, there would be little to fear from unions. *Columbia Law Review*, 32:1162.

[20] 4 Metc. 111, 133 (1842).

[21] State v. Donaldson, 3 Vroom. (N.J.) 151 (1867). This is one of the few cases, after Commonwealth v. Hunt, in which an American court arrived at a different conclusion from Shaw. Probably out of deference to Shaw's reputation, Beasley alleged his entire concurrence in the principles and result of Commonwealth v. Hunt which he deluded himself into believing was "clearly distinguishable" from his own case. It is said of Beasley that for some years after his admittance to the bar, "he was more noted as a billiard player and wing shot than for legal acumen" (Dayton Voorhees, "Mercer Beasley," *D.A.B.*). Beasley's views were really in line with those of the early nineteenth-century judges who believed that an agreement for a closed shop is inherently and unlawfully coercive. See, for example, the remarks of Recorder Levy in the Philadelphia Shoemakers' Case of 1806 in Commons, III, 235, and Judge Roberts in the Pittsburgh Cordwainers' Case of 1815, in Commons, IV, 81–82.

self, the force which all respectable men believed responsible for progress in industry.

A similar spirit characterized Shaw's disposal of the charges of conspiracy to "impoverish" Horne, his boss, and other employers. These charges had been framed to conform with the old doctrine of Serjeant Hawkins that a combination to impoverish a third person by indirect means is a criminal conspiracy.[22] Without repudiating Hawkins' doctrine, Shaw tempered its absolutism because he had a hard-headed insight into the workings of a competitive economy. In a passage which the business community might appreciate, he put the hypothetical case of a group of merchants who sold their product so cheaply that their rivals were ruined. This consequence would earn the successful competitors an indictment for conspiracy if Hawkins' doctrine were mechanistically applied.[23] "Yet it is through competition," Shaw declared, "that the best interests of trade and industry are promoted." He would not choke off that competition, depriving the public of its benefits. It followed that a combination which tends to impoverish another "may be highly meritorious and public spirited." [24] Criminality would depend upon the means; none used by the union were illegal despite their alleged injurious effects upon others.

This conclusion resulted from a line of reasoning built upon unstated implications. From the unquestioned and unquestionable premise that competition among businessmen benefits the public, although some persons may suffer, Shaw had implied that competition among employers and employees, and among employees themselves, also benefits the public, although some may suffer. Thus he believed that a worker might be forced from his trade, without legal redress, for refusing to belong to a union which welcomed him. He apparently also believed that among the journeymen bootmakers of Boston, union membership had become a condition of employment, one of the many which must be accepted by those who would ply their craft or risk the consequences.

[22] William Hawkins was the author of *A Treatise of the Pleas of the Crown* (London, 1716). His formulation of the conspiracy doctrine, one of the earliest and most influential, was: "That all confederacies wrongfully to prejudice a third person are criminal at common law; as a confederacy by indirect means to impoverish a third person . . ." *Pleas of the Crown*, vol. I, ch. 72, sec. 2. See Francis B. Sayre, "Criminal Conspiracy," *Harvard Law Review*, 35:393-427 (Feb. 1922).

[23] Chief Justice Gibson of Pennsylvania, in Commonwealth v. Carlisle, Brightly's Rep. (Pa.) 36 (1821), had developed a similar point in an interesting case which saw a combination of employers prosecuted for a conspiracy to depress wages. This case was not cited by court or counsel in Commonwealth v. Hunt.

[24] 4 Metc. 111, 134 (1842).

IV

Had the decision gone the other way, buttressing the conspiracy doctrine against labor unions, some historians would have construed the case as another example of law made to serve capitalist interests; others would have seen it as an example of the tenacity of the taught legal tradition. But it is less easy to explain the actual decision — so favorable to workers — which came from a bench composed exclusively of Federalist-Whigs, presided over by Lemuel Shaw, all of whom shared the outlook of the propertied classes and were trained in the crusty conservatism of the common law. The decision is even more perplexing because it followed on the heels of *Farwell v. Boston and Worcester Railroad*,[25] which forced workers to bear the cost of injuries caused by the negligence of fellow servants, and correspondingly reduced industry's overhead expenses. As Professor Walter Nelles wrote, Shaw "overthrew the sub-structure upon which a Tory criminal law against labor organizations could respectably have been established," but he was "no sentimental friend of the poor workingman."[26]

Nelles' explanation of Shaw's motivation in *Commonwealth v. Hunt* has been widely adopted by historians of labor law.[27] He regards the decision as a strategic judicial maneuver to gain an objective far removed from the legal arena. A pro-labor decision was the price of warding off a radical movement in politics that would capitalize upon workers' grievances and jeopardize the protective tariff on Massachusetts textiles. As Nelles put it:

In 1842 . . . tariff protection, then the absorbing concern of textile interests, required workingmen's support. Any excitement of resentment among even a small group of workingmen might jeopardize the prospect of securing the desired legislation. . . . Great efforts were being made to win everyone possible, especially workingmen, to the "American System" of protection; in the first half of 1842 there was scarcely an issue of a Whig newspaper that did not contain tariff propaganda. . . . it would be dangerous to throw out among workingmen any fresh bone of contention; demagogues and reformers might win enough votes to sway the balance of power. I am convinced that Shaw was subconsciously if not consciously influenced by such a thought when he decided *Commonwealth v. Hunt*.[28]

[25] 4 Metc. 49 (1842); see Chapter 10, *supra*.
[26] "Commonwealth v. Hunt," p. 1151.
[27] E.g., Charles O. Gregory, *Labor and the Law* (New York, 1946), p. 28; Elias Lieberman, *Unions before the Bar* (New York, 1950), p. 24.
[28] "Commonwealth v. Hunt," pp. 1158–1159.

As evidence that a decision against labor would have had terrible consequences for Whiggery and protectionism, Professor Nelles notes the political repercussions of two New York cases in the mid-1830's. In one, the workers of Geneva, striking to maintain union wage-rates, forced the discharge of an employee who had worked for less and had refused to pay the union fine. The strikers were indicted under a New York statute which prohibited conspiracy to commit "any act injurious . . . to trade or commerce." Chief Justice Savage of the New York Supreme Court, purportedly construing the vague statute by common-law standards, held against the workers. He reasoned that higher wages raised prices and so injured local trade. "It is important to the best interests of society," concluded Savage, "that the price of labor be left to regulate itself." [29] On the strength of this decision, the tailors of New York City who had struck against a wage cut were arrested and convicted for criminal conspiracy at a trial presided over by Judge Edwards who believed unions to be un-American.[30]

Labor greeted these cases with a response that startled conservatives. It so happened that for a variety of reasons — high prices, extension of the suffrage, the Jacksonian war on "monopolies" — workers were becoming more organizationally and politically conscious. The two conspiracy prosecutions catalyzed this growing consciousness. A week after Judge Edwards heavily fined the leaders of the tailors' union, he and Chief Justice Savage were burned in effigy at a mass protest rally attended by 27,000 people, described by the organ of the New York General Trades' Union as "the greatest meeting of working men ever held in the United States." [31] Resolutions called for a "separate and distinct party, around which the laboring classes and their friends can rally with confidence," and a state convention was summoned. Its program called for the repeal of all anti-union laws and for popular election of judges for short terms. An "Equal Rights Party" was organized and shortly fused with the Locofocos. The fall elections of 1836 showed that the balance of power between

[29] People v. Fisher, 14 Wend. (N.Y.) 1 (1835).

[30] The Twenty Journeymen Tailors Case, 1836, in Commons, IV, 315. "Every American," said Edwards, "knows that . . . he has no better friend than the laws and that he needs no artificial combination for his protection. They are of foreign origin . . ."

[31] John R. Commons *et al., History of Labour in the United States* (New York, 1918, 2 vols.), I, 409–411; Philip S. Foner, *History of the Labor Movement in the United States* (New York, 1947), pp. 156–157.

the Whigs and Democrats was controlled by the radicals; three
of the four candidates for Congress endorsed by them were
elected.[32]

In 1842, these events were very recent history. Savage's decision was urged upon Shaw as the latest authority, but he distinguished it on ground that it had been founded upon a statute
having no counterpart in Massachusetts. Professor Nelles comments that Shaw "doubtless knew a better reason" and finds it in
the political aftermath of Savage's opinion and in agitator's
abuse. Summarizing his thesis, Nelles stated:

> In 1842 the air of depression was charged with intimations of
> what might become formidable radical movements. . . . If such a
> man as Rantoul, whose basic tenet was the class struggle . . . were
> given the bootmakers' case to take into politics, the repercussions
> upon the campaign for tariff protection might be disastrous. The
> result expected from protection, prosperity, could be trusted to dis-
> solve radicalism. During depression it would not have been sensible
> to risk further excitement of uneasy minds and consciences by de-
> claring the criminality of an actually inoffensive labor union in a case
> with which no important interest was in fact deeply concerned. . . .
> Shaw, sure that he knew better the best interests of the textile industry
> than mill stockholders themselves, was not the man to invite trouble
> for the sake of a sterile rag of principle. . . . What has preceded sug-
> gests that the campaign for tariff protection may have had a larger
> share of responsibility for the decision of *Commonwealth v. Hunt*
> than the reasons stated in the opinion.[33]

It is no doubt comforting to have one's preconceptions and
sense of consistency fortified. A case which by all expectations
should have gone the other way is demonstrated to have played
its proper economic role: capitalism and conservatism are the
intended beneficiaries of an apparent labor victory. Even the
"inconsistency" of this decision cheek-by-jowl with the fellow-
servant decision is dissolved if the former is rightly understood
as a strategic blow for business interests. The tariff, *deus ex
machina,* accounts for everything. It even permits a consistent
image of Shaw: his "conscience" remains "tory"; the "constituency
to which his sense of obligation was keenest" continues to be
"State Street and Beacon Hill, the bankers, the textile manufacturers, the railroad builders." [34]

But like the theory that was spoiled by the facts, Nelles'

[32] Foner, pp. 157–158; Schlesinger, *Age of Jackson,* pp. 194–199.
[33] "Commonwealth v. Hunt," pp. 1161–1162.
[34] *Ibid.,* p. 1152.

explanation has its infirmities. There is not the slightest evidence to suggest that Lemuel Shaw believed in protective tariffs. Of course, he should have, given his "conscience" and "constituency." But by the same reasoning he should have allowed damages for tide-mill owners whose property was flooded by the authority of the legislature; should have invalidated legislative control of private banks and of railroad rates; indeed, should have found illegality in the closed shop. Yet he did none of these things, and insofar as is known did not support high duties on textiles.

Unfortunately Shaw's tariff views after 1829 are unknown. As of that year, when Webster had already gone over to protectionism for the sake of Massachusetts' industry, Shaw championed free trade. Appointed the chairman of a Boston committee to oppose the Tariff Act of 1828, he wrote a remonstrance to Congress which *The Free Trade Advocate* of Philadelphia applauded.[35] Years later, Senator George F. Hoar declared, "No more powerful statement of the argument against high protection can be found. I have been surprised that the modern free traders have not long ago discovered it, and brought it to light." [36] According to his biographer, "Shaw never came to take any other view of this question, but held to his free-trade principles." [37]

Therefore, if we may assume with Professor Nelles (1) that Shaw's decision was governed by his tariff views (free trade); (2) that he "knew better the best interests of the textile industry than the mill stockholders themselves"; and (3) that a decision against labor would jeopardize the cause of high protection — the conclusion must follow that Shaw would have decided *against* labor. But whatever its conclusion, this whole line of reasoning

[35] *Memorial to Congress against the Tariff Law of 1828, by Citizens of Boston* (Boston, 1829). A pamphlet, 16 pp. The committee was heavily weighted with merchants and shippers, including Henry Lee and Thomas Ward. Samuel S. Shaw, "Lemuel Shaw, Early and Domestic Life," *Memorial Biographies of the New England Historic and Genealogical Society* (Boston, 1885, 9 vols.), IV, 217.

[36] George F. Hoar, *Autobiography of Seventy Years* (New York, 1903, 2 vols.), II, 387. Shaw's argument was against protection generally, not just against the Tariff of Abominations. His thesis was: "That the imposition of high duties upon important commodities without regard to revenue, but with a principal view permanently to support any particular manufacture, or other branch of domestic industry, by the exclusion of a rival commodity or great increase of its price, is unjust in principle, erroneous in policy, and calculated to impose a heavy burthen upon the community, without any adequate advantage." *Memorial to Congress*, p. 3.

[37] F. H. Chase, *Lemuel Shaw*, p. 311. Chase submits no evidence in support of this point.

based upon the tariff implies a crude theory of judicial decision in which considerations of law are completely ignored.

Shaw's judicial character should not be misunderstood. Contrary to Professor Nelles, his decisions most definitely could not be dictated nor influenced by the fear of political consequences or of criticism, no matter how radical. He was the very man who would invite trouble for the sake of principle. His whole judicial career is evidence of supreme integrity built upon devotion to, even obsession with, principle. If there was ever a time when he would buckle under abuse, or shape his decisions to avoid political radicalism, or compromise his principles, that time was during the tense days of the fugitive slave cases. He did not succumb then or ever to any course of conduct which he regarded as inconsistent with his understanding of the law or his obligations as a judge.

V

The Chief Justice's opinion may very well have been influenced by subtle considerations of strategy, though not for purely extra-legal purposes. Professor Mark DeWolfe Howe has implied that the decision represents Shaw's answer to the movement for codification of the common law.[38] By extending the protection of that law to labor unions, Shaw sought to show that the old English doctrines, purged of their inequitous effects, could be adapted to American conditions for the common good. His opinion by helping to systematize and liberalize the common law was meant to deflate the codification movement.

This movement, according to Charles Warren, was the result of five related factors:

first, the old, underlying antagonism of the American public towards the Common Law, as being of English origin; second, the ever-active jealousy, entertained by laymen in a democracy, towards lawyers, as a privileged class and a monopoly, and the consequent desire to make the law a layman's law; third, the increase in the number of law reports deemed, even then, to be "vast and unwieldy"; fourth, the success of the *Code Napoléon* in Europe; fifth, the influence of Jeremy Bentham.[39]

The "desire to make the law a layman's law" was part of a larger popular desire to democratize the law through legislation, rather

[38] Professor Howe has implied as much by his arrangement of the materials in his *Readings in American Legal History* (Cambridge, 1949). In Chapter Five, "The Nineteenth Century Movement for Codification," Shaw's opinion in Commonwealth v. Hunt follows pro-codification statements.

[39] Charles Warren, *A History of the American Bar* (Cambridge, 1912), p. 508.

than keep it a thing of mystery in the control of conservative courts. To single out that desire as the most important force behind codification, or to assert that parties sharply split on codification, would be partially misleading. Nevertheless the ultra-codificationists were the Jacksonians like Frederick Robinson of the Massachusetts legislature, "a leader of the Democratic left-wing," whose "career was based on a clear conviction of the class basis of politics." [40]

In a speech before the Central Trades' Union of Boston, Robinson scathingly indicted the whole common-law system as an enemy of the people. "The judiciary in this State," he declared, "is the headquarters of the aristocracy. And every plan to humble and subdue the people originates there." His most blistering comments were reserved for the conspiracy doctrine as applied to labor. As he saw it, the answer to the wicked, cumbrous, and obscure system of foreign, that is, English, origin was to be found in "republican laws, enacted in codes, written with the greatest simplicity and conciseness, alphabetically arranged in a single book, so that every one could read and understand them for himself.[41]

The foremost advocate of thoroughgoing codification in Massachusetts — and this may be of significance in understanding Shaw's decision on labor conspiracy — was Robert Rantoul, Jr. Rantoul shared Robinson's distempered opinion of the common law, that "ambiguous, base-born, purblind, perishable common law," which had its origin in "folly, barbarism, and feudality." Double-distilled by judicial reasoning until it became "rank poison," the common law was judge-made law, legislative in nature and "essentially aristocratical." Judges not only usurped legislative power, but they made the law at their "will or whim." One could not know what the law is before or after the judges laid it down. If the great storehouse of precedents would not yield a plausible one, a precedent could be extorted to mean what it did not contain. The result was that almost any case could be decided either way, only to be distinguished later by ingenious expedients.

The democratic solution, in Rantoul's opinion, was for the legislature to reduce the common law to a written and unbending

---

[40] Schlesinger, p. 168.

[41] Frederick Robinson, "On Reform of Law and the Judiciary, in an oration delivered before the Trades' Union of Boston and Vicinity, July 4, 1834," reprinted in Howe, pp. 455–460.

code that would eliminate the arbitrary discretion of judges and make the law knowable. "Statutes," said Rantoul with a Jacksonian confidence in strong legislatures, "speak the public voice" — this by way of contrast to the law made by judges "out of the reach of popular influence." The common law "is subversive of the fundamental principles of free government." The lesson was clear: "All American law must be statute law." [42]

Rantoul expressed these views in a speech of 1836, within a month after the notorious conviction of the journeymen tailors in New York City. In 1840 at the trial of the journeymen bootmakers in Boston Municipal Court, he reread parts of this speech to the jury.[43] On the appeal before the Supreme Judicial Court he had the good sense to restrain himself. The published digest of his argument shows only the single heresy that "the English common law of conspiracy is not in force in this State." But his well-publicized sentiments on the common law and on the need for codification were unhappily familiar to the Chief Justice.

Shaw cherished the traditional system. To him the common law was a science, founded upon pure reason and natural justice adapted to the conditions of society. Trial by jury, habeas corpus, and free government itself were mothered by the common law. Life, liberty, and property were insured by it; stability and progress too. Its fixed principles, so intrinsically perfect and comprehensive, allowed for modifications in public policy and habit, yet maintained the necessary ingredients of duration and certainty. Pacific resolution of social conflict, exact and equal justice, and ordered liberty: these were the harvest of the common law as administered by an independent judiciary.

To these views Shaw was totally committed, and from time to time gave them explicit expression from the bench. He did not have to invent a pretext to reaffirm his faith when delivering his opinion in *Commonwealth v. Hunt,* because the case necessitated discussion of the reception of the common law in America. But with the exception of a passing reference to it as "wise and humane," Shaw ignored the charges of the ultra-codificationists. If he meant to disprove them, he could not have been more subtle. He let the judgment speak for itself.

It said, in effect, that not even the conspiracy doctrine of the

[42] Robert Rantoul, Jr., "Oration at Scituate, Massachusetts, 4 July, 1836," reprinted in Howe, pp. 472–478. Professor Howe places Rantoul's speech immediately before Shaw's decision in Commonwealth v. Hunt.

[43] Nelles, "Commonwealth v. Hunt," p. 1143, note 46.

common law was class-oriented or "aristocratical." It said too that harshness, unfairness, and ambiguity in the common law as received in America would not be endured. Shaw made the point by noting that the same doctrine might be in force in both England and America, yet might operate differently. The criminality of a combination's means or purpose

must depend upon the local laws . . . All those laws of the parent country, whether rules of the common law, or early English statutes, which were made for the purpose of regulating the wages of laborers, the settlement of paupers, and making it penal for anyone to use a trade or handicraft to which he had not served a full apprenticeship — not being adapted to the circumstances of our colonial condition — were not adopted, used or approved. . . .[44]

To be sure, in New York as in England to combine in order to raise wages, strike, or maintain a closed shop seemed to be an indictable conspiracy, but Shaw pointed out that the crime was a statutory one. Codificationists could read the implied moral: legislatures might be reactionary, but in Massachusetts, at least, the common law was liberalism itself. It was the Supreme Judicial Court, not the General Court, which recognized the legality of trade-union activities.

This interpretation of Shaw's decision as a check upon the forces of codification must be cautiously advanced. In the first place, *Commonwealth v. Hunt* was decided in the same term of the Court as the case that gave life to the fellow-servant rule.[45] That rule was not calculated to earn the gratitude of the workers or to disarm the legal reformers. It gave them fresh evidence of the harshness and upper-class favoritism of the "judge-made" law. If Shaw's opinions were given with half an eye on the codification movement, he seemed to be operating at sixes and sevens, for his two labor decisions tended to cancel each other out, the one a boon and the other, almost simultaneously, a bane. On the other hand, the immediate impact of the decisions upon the codification movement tended to be unequal. The fellow-servant rule, representing as it did the creation of new law, did not aggravate an historic sense of injustice like that associated with the conspiracy doctrine. By contrast, codificationists like Rantoul and Robinson lost their chief arguing point when Shaw handed down his opinion in *Commonwealth v. Hunt.*

[44] Commonwealth v. Hunt, 4 Metc. 111, 122 (1842).
[45] Farwell v. B. & W. RR., 4 Metc. 49 (1842).

But this anti-codification theory of the decision has a second possible flaw. By 1842 the codification movement in Massachusetts had nearly spent itself. No case of that year could have vitally affected it one way or the other. At best, a spectacularly unpopular decision might have invited only a statute aimed at superseding the common law on the one disputed point. But the main body of the common law would still have been safe from the codifier's ambitions. Indeed those who wanted sweeping reform never controlled the movement in Massachusetts. They could provoke the appointment of commissions, as Rantoul did, but the commissions were staffed with men of sound views — mere revisers of statutes, or at best, partial codifiers.

The commission which prepared the first general revision of the Massachusetts statutes restricted itself to statutory simplification and systematization, although New York had earlier blazed the way for a statutory revision incorporating considerable codification of some common-law areas.[46] Led by Charles Jackson, formerly of the Supreme Judicial Court, the Massachusetts commissioners declared in their report of 1835 that it would be of "questionable utility" to reduce the common law to a "positive and unbending text . . ." They strongly urged retention of the traditional legal system.[47] As the *American Jurist* commented in 1835: "A few years ago, codification had a direful import to the conservative party in jurisprudence; and not wholly without reason; since some of its early champions were sturdy radicals in legal reform. In this view codification was another name for juridical revolution." [48] But, as the magazine indicated, the alarm subsided when statutory revision was substituted for codification.

In the following year, however, Governor Everett recommended that settled common-law principles be incorporated with the new *Revised Statutes* as a uniform code. Justice Joseph Story headed the new commission "to take into consideration the practicability and expediency of reducing in a written and systematic code the Common Law of Massachusetts or any part thereof." [49] Story's early enthusiasm for codification had cooled down by the mid-1830's. In 1836 he could say, when writing to a friend on the progress of his commission, "We shall report favorably to the

[46] Warren, *History of American Bar*, pp. 524–535; Howe, pp. 472–473.
[47] Howe, p. 473.
[48] "Revision of the Laws of Massachusetts," *American Jurist*, 13:344–345 (April 1835).
[49] Charles Warren, *History of Harvard Law School* (New York, 1908, 2 vols.), I, 503.

codification of some branches of the commercial law. But the
report will be very qualified and limited in its objects. We have
not yet become votaries to the notions of Jeremy Bentham. But
the present state of popular opinion here makes it necessary to
do something on the subject." [50]

The report of the Story Commission recommended codification of the common law on crimes, criminal procedure, and
evidence, as well as in several areas of commercial law. The
legislature, in response, appointed another commission in 1837
to codify only the criminal law. A sample code on murder was
submitted to the legislature in 1839, and by 1844 the work of the
commission was completed. But after 1837 the legislature showed
only a monumental lack of interest in the subject of codification;
it rejected the proffered criminal code of 1844. Nothing further
was done except for certain procedural reforms, even after David
Dudley Field revitalized the campaign for codification in New
York.[51] Massachusetts seemed to be immune to the contagion.

There is little in the listless history of codification in Massachusetts to suggest that Shaw needed to pacify the reformers. To
be sure, the legislature had not yet taken conclusive action as of
1842, and no one could know that the criminal code, at that very
time still in the drafting stage, would fail of adoption two years
later. But it is not likely that the controlling factor in Shaw's
mind was the relation of his decision to the fortunes of the codification movement. If Justice Story, of all people, received little
legislative encouragement because he was too radical on the
issue, Rantoul would find it easier to codify the laws of China
than the common law of Massachusetts. In the last analysis, men
like Joseph Story, Charles Jackson, Willard Phillips, and Luther
Cushing, who composed the Massachusetts commissions on codification, posed no real threat to Shaw's mistress, the common
law.

In a larger sense, Shaw's opinion in *Commonwealth v. Hunt,*
together with scores of earlier opinions by him, did tend to defeat
the codification movement. That movement thrived on the confusion, complexity, and contradictions that characterized the common law. Shaw, however, was a systematizer.[52] His opinions ranged

[50] *Ibid.,* 504.
[51] Warren, *History of American Bar.* p. 531; Howe, pp. 471–472.
[52] The editors of a contemporary legal journal, praising Shaw's opinion in
Commonwealth v. Hunt for its "uncommon learning and power," said significantly:
"This decision must remain of great and permanent value as chiefly defining and
settling the law upon an important subject in regard to which the law was before
a good deal complicated, confused, and uncertain" (*Law Reporter* 7:13, 1844).

over a subject, giving reasoned explanation of underlying principles. At the same time he did not antagonize the legislature by
defeating its enactments. The result was that his opinions helped
correct the conditions which had stimulated the code mania without provoking the legislature to self-assertion. The work of the
treatise writers and of other eminent state judges also helped put
the common law in reasoned order. Ironically it was Story, an
advocate of codification, whose influence was greatest in saving
the common-law system from legislative restatement. His series
of commentaries, like Shaw's opinions to a lesser degree, securely
established the common law during the critical, formative period
in our legal history.[53] *Commonwealth v. Hunt* was not a stake
through the heart of codification. It was only another nail in the
coffin that these sons of Massachusetts had long been constructing,
by chance or design.

VI

Dean Pound offers an explanation of Shaw's opinion differing
radically from those based on the tariff or codification. "When
one studies the history of the law as to conspiracy and the relation of Hawkins's doctrine (relied upon by those who prosecuted
labor unions as conspiracies) to received professional ideals of the
social order in America, it is perfectly possible to understand
[*Commonwealth v. Hunt*] . . ."[54]

Pound's point, of course, is that the taught legal tradition, as
transmitted through precedents, doctrines, and precepts on the
subject of conspiracy, determined Shaw's judgment. It would be
a valid point if the conviction of the workers had been sustained. Granted Shaw worked with the old materials. But what
makes his opinion different from all its predecessors is that he
distinguished or ignored the precedents others held as controlling; he greatly restricted Hawkins' doctrine which others applied
and even expanded;[55] and above all, he found only lawfulness
where others found criminality. Not Shaw's but the views of
Recorder Levy, Chief Justice Savage, and Judge Thacher are
explicable in terms of the received notions of law and the social
order. The striking thing about Shaw's opinion is its nonconformist character.

[53] See Francis R. Aumann, *The Changing American Legal System* (Columbus,
1940), pp. 125–131 and 142–153.

[54] Roscoe Pound, *The Formative Era of American Law* (Boston, 1938), p. 88.

[55] Sayre, "Criminal Conspiracy," pp. 402–409 and 414, best explains the judicial
interpretation of Hawkins' doctrine.

VII

The most plausible if not a watertight explanation of *Commonwealth v. Hunt* is suggested partly by the language of the opinion itself. Shaw regarded combinations, whether by entrepreneurs or workers, as inherent in a free, competitive society, and he saw a social gain in the competition between interests. Here are premises from which the judgment might reasonably follow. But as Justice Frankfurter said in another connection, "We must be on our guard against over-sophistication, and not find luminous, deeply conceived, rational processes where there is only tentative, groping, obscure empiricism . . ."[56] That advice is appropriate here because Shaw did not, as in other opinions, assert that the case turned upon considerations of public policy or community expediency; nor did he fully state the policy upon which his decision ultimately rested. All he offered were tantalizing hints.

On an earlier occasion, when cautioning a grand jury against all forms of partisanship, he had noted that it was "the general tendency of society in our times, to combine men into bodies and associations, having some object of deep interest common to themselves, but distinct from those of the rest of the community. . . . It not unfrequently happens, that these objects are opposed by other bodies and associations . . ."[57] As if it were an axiom of liberty itself, he stated in *Commonwealth v. Hunt* his belief in the right of free men "to work for whom they please, or not to work, if they so prefer." Therefore they could "agree," that is, combine to form a union, "to exercise their own acknowledged rights in such a manner as best to subserve their own interests."[58] Here was an extension to special interest groups of the social-contract theory that was part of his thinking.[59]

But the interests of one group "not infrequently . . . are opposed by other bodies." Attainment by one must be at the expense of another. Shaw recognized that rugged competition claimed its victims, might even impoverish a man by taking his profits or his job. Toughminded enough to realize also that competitors played to win, he acknowledged that the rules of the game sanc-

[56] Felix Frankfurter, *The Commerce Clause* (Chapel Hill, 1937), p. 9.
[57] Lemuel Shaw, C. J., *A Charge Delivered to the Grand Jury for the County of Essex . . . May Term, 1832* (Boston, 1832), pp. 7–8.
[58] Commonwealth v. Hunt, 4 Metc. 111, 130 (1842).
[59] Shaw, *A Charge Delivered to the Grand Jury*, p. 4.

tioned peaceable compulsion and other methods that stopped short of force, fraud, or breach of contract.

The whole process was justified by the supposition that when men freely pursued their own interests, individually or in combination, society generally stood to gain. Thus a group may compel others to do its bidding and may even succeed in ruining them; yet its actions may be "highly meritorious and public spirited," as Shaw put it, because of the ultimate social gain: ". . . it is through that competition, that the best interests of trade and industry are promoted." [60] Unless his analogy, drawn from the competition between businessmen, did not mean what in its context it implied, Shaw was willing to believe that society might benefit from unions, provided of course that they played within the rules of the game. He expressly noted that the "power" which derived from a closed shop could be exercised for "useful" purposes.[61]

To use Justice Frankfurter's phrase, the "tentative, groping, obscure empiricism" in Shaw's thinking was expressed in finished form by Justice Holmes, who started with the premise that "free competition means combination." [62] When the journeymen boot-makers were charged with conspiracy to compel and impoverish third persons, Shaw, having the wit to see that the doctrine could cut both ways, disposed of the charge by analogizing from business competition. Holmes, on a question whether peaceful picketing could be enjoined, made explicit an implication which he found in Shaw: conflict between employers and employed is also a form of competition. "If," said Holmes, "the policy on which our law is founded is too narrowly expressed in the term free competition, we may substitute free struggle for life. Certainly, the policy is not limited to struggles between persons of the same class, competing for the same end. It applies to all conflicts of temporal interests." That it was lawful for a union to benefit itself at the expense of injuring its antagonists was "decided as long ago as 1842 by the good sense of Chief Justice Shaw, in *Com. v. Hunt,* 4 Metc. (Mass.) 111." [63]

In sum, Shaw founded his decision on the belief that benefits to the public might accrue from the contest between unions and

[60] 4 Metc. 111, 134 (1842).
[61] The way to so advanced an insight was eased by the fact that the union before the bar had a fine record and was commended by many employers. See *supra*, p. 186.
[62] Vegelahn v. Guntner, 167 Mass. 92, 108 (1896).
[63] *Ibid.*, at 107, 109.

employers. Holmes also held this view of the case. He explained its ultimate ground by the proposition that "free competition is worth more to society than it costs, and that on this ground the infliction of the damage is privileged. *Commonwealth v. Hunt*, 4 Met. 111, 134." [64]

Shaw's tolerance of trade-unionism extended well beyond approval of the right of workers to organize. It was the legality of the union's activities, its methods and purposes, not just the lawfulness of its existence, which constituted the issue in the case. The express holding was that a combination of workers to establish and maintain a closed shop by the employment of peaceable coercion is not an indictable conspiracy. Even after the passage of more than a century, this still implies a latitudinarian attitude toward trade-unions. Moreover, though the indictment did not charge a conspiracy to raise wages, Shaw indicated that a combination for that purpose would not constitute a crime, nor would a cession of work for that purpose or for the purpose of gaining and keeping a closed shop.

The Chief Justice did not restrict his opinion to a narrowly defined issue. His holding and his dicta demonstrated his belief that the common law should not penalize normal union activity. He made it possible, so far as he could, for unions to operate and grow. In effect he had ruled that workers might do collectively anything that they might do individually. Without repudiating the conspiracy doctrine, he narrowed its applicability in labor cases, though he left it available for future use. A single worker could not lawfully engage in violence, for example; it would be criminal conspiracy for a group to do so. A single worker would be civilly liable for breach of contract; breach of contract by a combination of workers would be criminally liable. Justly applied, the common law, in the absence of statutory regulation on the subject, retained its legitimate function, by threatening punishment for conduct by workers truly destructive of the public interest.

But even as clarified by Shaw's definitive formulation, the conspiracy doctrine was sufficiently nebulous for courts to discover criminality in some labor activity that was merely personally repugnant to the judges sitting. The letter of the formula could be satisfied, if not the spirit with which Shaw infused it, by naming ends or means as illegal. Picketing, for instance, may be

[64] *Ibid.*, at 106.

regarded as an act of violence, or the purpose of a strike as an unwarrantable interference with private enterprise.

Yet it was forty years after *Commonwealth v. Hunt* before the conspiracy doctrine was again a prominent feature of efforts to crush trade-unionism. In the interim, the law of labor combinations was governed by Shaw's opinion. Professor Edwin E. Witte, after patiently searching through newspapers, discovered three conspiracy prosecutions against workers between 1842 and 1863 and another seven before 1880.[65] That none of these cases was fought to a finish in the appellate courts is evidence of the influence of Shaw's reputation. Chief Justice Beasley's opinion of 1867 for the New Jersey Supreme Court is the exception, and he was forced to contrive a distinction from *Commonwealth v. Hunt* that was no distinction at all.[66]

The conspiracy doctrine flourished again in the 1880's, and only a few states responded to labor's protests by enacting statutes half-heartedly intended to nullify this common-law crime.[67] Nevertheless the doctrine was shortly eclipsed by the injunctive remedy. The character of the action changed but not its anti-labor animus. After the passing of the Sherman Act of 1890, with its prohibition on combinations and conspiracies in restraint of trade, the courts, during the high noon of American capitalism, were quick to find in this "anti-trust" legislation an effective weapon against unions. Almost any union activity could be proscribed as "restraint of trade" and be speedily enjoined. The criminal suit, with its requirement of a jury, was slower, costlier, and much less safe; and so the common law conspiracy doctrine faded away before its streamlined counterpart.

But no counterpart of Lemuel Shaw — dispassionate and beholden to no special interests; concerned for the integrity of the law and of the judicial process; and towering in stature and influence — was on the scene to check the process. When in 1896 Justice Oliver Wendell Holmes of the Massachusetts Supreme Judicial Court invoked Shaw's name and decried the use of the injunction against peaceful picketing, he spoke in dissent.[68]

[65] Witte, "Early American Labor Cases," *Yale Law Journal,* 35:825, 829 (May 1926).
[66] State v. Donaldson, 3 Vroom. (N.J.) 151 (1867). See *supra,* note 21.
[67] Witte, pp. 830–832.
[68] Vegelahn v. Guntner, 167 Mass. 92, 104 (1896).

12

CRIMINAL LAW

Murder, Madness, and Malice

I

While Shaw was Chief Justice, the Supreme Judicial Court still possessed exclusive jurisdiction over all capital crimes: capital cases were tried by a jury presided over by the Chief Justice attended by his associate judges. At such a trial all points of law were argued fully by counsel and settled on the spot by decisions as "final and conclusive" as those of the highest appellate court on a bill of exceptions. This practice of having the court of last resort act as the trial court in capital cases was rooted in the consideration that both the defendant and the public had a unique interest in avoiding repeated trials and securing in the first instance a verdict based on correct and authoritative rulings.[1] Members of the Supreme Judicial Court also sat singly at nisi prius sessions. Thus for three decades Shaw was concurrently a trial judge and an appellate judge, an experience denied to his modern colleagues. He knew the penal law and left his mark on it.

He had an exalted regard for criminal jurisprudence. It was more than just a system of retributive justice to him. Its object "in a free government," he told a grand jury in 1832, "is the preservation of the public peace," a matter which he took to mean "much, very much":

[1] Webster v. Commonwealth, 5 Cush. 386, 394–395 (1850), *per* Shaw, C. J. In case of a conviction the Court at its discretion might entertain a motion for a new trial when a mistake in point of law was alleged, but such motions were of "rare occurrence" and allowable, "if allowable at all," said Shaw, "only on occasions of real difficulty and importance." Commonwealth v. York, 9 Metc. 93, 100 (1845).

It implies not only a state of tranquillity and repose, but the triumph of law and justice over all violence and fraud, and the security of personal and civil liberty against the usurpation of all lawless and ungoverned will. It implies, on the part of the citizen, a feeling of security in the enjoyment of all his personal and political, civil and social rights.

These are among the dearest and most valuable objects, for which men unite in civil society, and are justly regarded as the ultimate aim of every well ordered community, and the attainment of which, the founders of our Commonwealth hoped to secure, by a Government of laws.[2]

Shaw was one of the foremost expositors of the substantive criminal law during his time. Although his rulings signalized a new departure in the law of both criminal conspiracy and the criminal responsibility of the insane,[3] generally it was his talent for restatement rather than his originality which distinguished his criminal law utterances. The necessity of instructing twelve laymen good and true sharpened his concern for elementary principles and their lucid explanation.

His jury charges reflect the premises of an ancient jurisprudence. The "lawless and ungoverned will," to use a phrase from his grand jury charge of 1832, is the object of the criminal law's sanctions. Blackstone had called it the "vicious will"; others, earlier, the "guilty will." From time beyond legal memory English jurists had regarded individuals as free moral agents possessing a will to act lawfully or unlawfully by choosing between right and wrong. Thus only free moral agents could justly be held criminally responsible for their acts, because only the exercise of a free and rational will could cause a crime.

The will was inseparably related to purpose or intent as an indispensable mental element of crime. Six centuries before Shaw, Bracton spoke of *"voluntas nocendi,"* the guilty will or intention without which the law imputed no criminality to an act. Coke, using the more familiar phrase *"mens rea,"* put it as a maxim, traceable to the early twelfth century, that an act does not make its doer guilty unless his mind is also guilty.[4] Hale, who in 1682

[2] Lemuel Shaw, C. J., *A Charge Delivered to the Grand Jury for the County of Essex . . . May Term, 1832* (Boston, 1832), p. 9.

[3] Commonwealth v. Hunt, 4 Metc. 111 (1842); Commonwealth v. Rogers, 7 Metc. 500 (1844).

[4] James F. Stephen, *A History of the Criminal Law of England* (London, 1883, 3 vols.), II, 94, fn. 1; Jerome Hall, *General Principles of Criminal Law* (Indianapolis, 1947), ch. 5, "Mens Rea and Moral Culpability"; and Francis Sayre, *"Mens Rea,"* Harvard Law Review, 45:974–1026 (1932).

provided the first systematic treatment of *mens rea,* also placed the criminal will at the center of criminality. "The consent of the will," he declared, "is that, which renders human actions either commendable or culpable . . . where there is no will to commit an offense, there can be no . . . just reason to incur the penalty . . ." [5]

The will to commit an offense implies, as Shaw put it, "a sane man, a voluntary agent, acting upon motives" who must be presumed to contemplate and intend the consequences of his own acts.[6] Thus the theory of the criminal law holds that no act, however reprehensible or even fatal its consequences, is punishable unless the doer, exercising his will and understanding, voluntarily and knowingly intends a criminal deed. The legal shorthand for this is "criminal intent" *(mens rea),* which in the case of murder is described as "malice aforethought." [7] Shaw's own rulings on malice aforethought were crucial and controversial turning points in the American history of the law of homicide.[8] The same may be said of his rulings on insanity as a defense against the charge of murder.[9]

Given the theory of the criminal law on *mens rea,* it follows that an insane person is not criminally responsible for what he cannot help doing. If he commits an injury as a consequence of his mental disease, he is not guilty of crime, although the same act if done by a sane man would be a crime. One cannot be considered a free moral agent with the mental capacity to possess the requisite criminal intent or malice aforethought, if insanity deranges the will or understanding, or provokes compulsive behavior. This would seem a simple proposition, but it was imperfectly understood for centuries before Shaw's time; moreover, as a legal rule it was applied with the most extraordinary confusion, which still persists.[10]

Before Lord Hale, English jurists considered the law of insanity "only in the most casual and fragmentary manner." [11] Hale

---

[5] Quoted in S. Sheldon Glueck, *Mental Disorder and the Criminal Law* (Boston, 1927), p. 132.

[6] Commonwealth v. York, 9 Metc. 93, 103 (1845).

[7] Courtney S. Kenny, *Outlines of Criminal Law* (American ed., New York, 1907), ch. 3, "The Mental Element in Crime"; Stephen, II, ch. 18, "Criminal Responsibility."

[8] Commonwealth v. York, 9 Metc. 93 (1845); Commonwealth v. Webster, 5 Cush. 295 (1850); Commonwealth v. Hawkins, 3 Gray 463 (1855).

[9] Commonwealth v. Rogers, 7 Metc. 500 (1844).

[10] Henry Weihofen, *Mental Disorder as a Criminal Defense* (Buffalo, 1954), pp. 1–2.

[11] Stephen, II, 150.

himself got little beyond the fleeting insight of Bracton who in the thirteenth century provided the germ of both the "knowledge" and the "wild beast" tests of insanity.[12] Bracton had defined an insane person as one who does not know what he is doing, who lacks in mind and reason, "and who is not far removed from the brutes." [13] The great English jurist and historian of the criminal law, Sir James Stephen, said that Hale's chapter on the law of insanity is "marked by the ignorance of the age in which it was written." [14] Yet, though Hale believed in diabolic possession and thought that "the moon hath a great influence in all diseases of the brain," [15] he had the surest perception of the relationship between the criminal irresponsibility of the insane and the *mens rea*. He was also the first to distinguish between insanity that excuses at the criminal law and insanity that does not. But if judges looked to Hale for a test which they could give to juries on the responsibility of the "partially insane," they would find this statement: "The best measure I can think of is this; such a person as labouring under melancholy distempers hath yet ordinarily as great understanding as ordinarily a child of fourteen years hath, is such a person as may be guilty of treason or felony." [16]

From Hale's time to Shaw's a century and a half later, no legal writer of authority discussed the matter on its merits. Nor, as Stephen has pointed out, were the circumstances such that there was ever an opportunity "for a solemn judgment laying down the principles of law by which the relation of insanity to crime might be determined." [17] As a matter of fact, the first such judgment in England or America by a court of last resort was *Commonwealth v. Rogers*, in which the opinion of the Supreme Judicial Court was given by Chief Justice Shaw in February of 1844.[18] But this

---

[12] The knowledge test is the test of knowing right from wrong. Weihofen (p. 55) claims that it derives from the test of knowing good from evil, found in Hawkins, *Pleas of the Crown*, of 1716.

[13] Quoted by Glueck, p. 126. Bracton did not treat insanity as a defense to crime; he was concerned only with civil liability.

[14] Stephen, II, 150.

[15] Quoted by Glueck, p. 135.

[16] *Ibid.* Glueck's fifth chapter is an excellent historical survey of the legal tests of the criminal responsibility of the insane.

[17] Stephen, II, 151. He adds (p. 152): "I know of no single instance in which the Court for Crown Cases Reserved, or any other court sitting in banc, has delivered a considered written judgment on the relation of insanity to criminal responsibility . . ."

[18] 7 Metc. 500 (1844). There were, however, a number of earlier cases tried before inferior courts in which nisi prius judges charged on the criminal law of insanity. The English cases generally followed Hale, while the early American cases followed the English ones. See Glueck, pp. 139–156.

is first only in the technical sense. In June of the preceding year, the Lords Justices of England, responding to questions put by the House of Lords, *but not before them judicially,* gave a brief opinion which embodies what became known as the "McNaghten Rules." [19]

These rules, although in some respects grievously erroneous and deficient from the standpoint of psychiatry, are the basis of the modern law of insanity in criminal cases and have been followed in "thousands of English and American decisions." [20] The rules are as follows. The legal presumption of sanity must be disproved to the satisfaction of the jury. To establish a defense on the ground of insanity, it must be proved that the accused "was labouring under such a defect of reason, from disease of the mind, as not to know the nature and quality of the act he was doing, or if he did know it, that he did not know he was doing what was wrong." He must not know "the difference between right and wrong." But if the accused was "conscious that the act was one which he ought not to do" and which violates the law, he is punishable. If the act is committed under an insane delusion, his criminal responsibility is to be determined by the question whether the facts with respect to which the deluison exists are as he imagines them to be.

II

As mentioned, Shaw gave the first opinion for a court of last resort on the criminal responsibility of the insane. The case, *Commonwealth v. Rogers,*[21] was also the first to receive the Mc-

[19] Answers of the Judges to the House of Lords, *re* Reg. v. McNaghten, 10 Clark & Finnelly 200 (1843). McNaghten, a paranoiac, killed Sir Robert Peel's secretary, mistaking him for Peel. His acquittal, on ground of insanity, occasioned the debate in the House of Lords which resulted in the House propounding their questions to the Judges.

[20] Glueck, p. 161. Prof. Glueck, who writes with the authority of one who knows both the legal and psychiatric literature, has a valuable critical analysis of the McNaghten Rules at pp. 161–186. Stephen, II, ch. 19, "The Relation of Madness to Crime," also offers a penetrating discussion. See also Weihofen, pp. 55 ff., and Hall, pp. 479 ff.

[21] 7 Metc. 500 (1844). This official report of "the opinion on the law of the case," given by Shaw in his charge to the jury, was excerpted by the Court Reporter from the *Report of the Trial of Abners Rogers, Jr.* (Boston, 1844), edited by George T. Bigelow and George Bemis, who brilliantly defended Rogers against a charge of murder for the admitted slaying of the warden of the Massachusetts State Prison. Rogers' first trial in July, 1843, ended in a hung jury; the second trial began on Jan. 30, 1844. Shaw presided at both trials, attended by two associates. Bigelow was later elevated to the Supreme Judicial Court and became Chief Justice on Shaw's retirement. Bemis became renowned as a penal reformer. The

Naghten Rules for America. Without mentioning the rules by name,[22] Shaw embodied their substance in his opinion — not, however, without first providing them with the theoretical basis which they lacked; and not without considerably improving them by adding a new dimension: the test of irresistible impulse.[23]

Just as Lord Hale's had been the most meaningful approach to the problem that had been made by a legal commentator, so Shaw's was the most meaningful approach by a judge. That is, both Hale and Shaw recognized at the outset what others, including the Lords Justices of England had been only dimly aware of, that the mental requirement of *mens rea* must be the basis of any test of insanity as a defense to a criminal charge. In his first sentence Shaw considered the *mens rea* of a "responsible agent" and declared that "to constitute a crime, a person must have . . . a criminal intent and purpose . . ." This he defined in terms of "will" as well as "intellectual power" and "knowledge." Later in his opinion he discussed "impulse" as a force negativing the will. The point is that the McNaghten Rules, based upon a narrow faculty psychology, stress only the cognitive or intellectual elements of both the *mens rea* and mental life. By contrast Shaw

---

defendant in the case, shortly after his acquittal "by reason of insanity," committed suicide on an "irresistible impulse."

[22] Shaw cited no precedents whatever in his charge to the jury. Theron Metcalf, the Court Reporter, added a footnote referring to the "opinion of the judges given to the House of Lords" and to a few early trials and treatises (Commonwealth v. Rogers, 7 Metc. 500, 502, 1844). At the trial of Rogers, counsel on both sides referred to the McNaghten Rules (*Trial of Abner Rogers, Jr.*, pp. 20, 59–60).

[23] Weihofen, p. 85, says the irresistible impulse test is of American origin and traces it to an Ohio nisi prius judge in State v. Thompson, Wright's Ohio Rep. 617, 622 (1834). But the case shows that the judge spoke only of the power to do or to forbear the act; this was a recognition of the volitionary element in the *mens rea* but not of irresistible impulse. The only legal authority called upon by Rogers' counsel to support this test was English: Lord Denman, charging in Reg. v. Oxford, 9 Car. & P. 525, 546–547 (1840), said ". . . if some controlling disease was, in truth, the acting power within him, which he could not resist, then he will not be responsible." Yet Denman's opinion as a whole shows that he did not subscribe to the test; moreover, he was one of the Lords Justices who promulgated the McNaghten Rules which made no suggestion of it. Rogers' counsel also cited the *Seventh Report of the English Criminal Law Commissioners*, pp. 18–19, where the irresistible impulse test is unmistakably stated: "This capacity to distinguish [right from wrong] does not exist, where a delusive or diseased impulse hurries one away at the moment of the action, so that no time is afforded for deliberation, though the mind could discriminate correctly, if such time were afforded. In other words: morbid irresistible impulse, though accompanied with consciousness, is as adequate an exemption, as total unconsciousness" (*Trial of Abner Rogers, Jr.*, pp. 102–103).

was equally concerned with the volitional elements, from the psychological and legal standpoints.[24]

Although he inconsistently adopted the knowledge test of the McNaghten Rules, with its truncated concept of *mens rea,* he deepened it. The knowledge test required that, to be criminally responsible, a man must know the nature of his act or know that it was wrong under the law. Shaw further individualized this knowledge by requiring also that the accused must rationally understand "the relation in which he stands to others, and in which others stand to him" and must be able to apply "to his own case" an otherwise abstract understanding of the nature of his act. Lack of such understanding made good a plea of insanity; by implication, possession of such understanding invalidated the plea.[25]

Thus far, by following the English authority, Shaw had ignored his earlier recognition of the will or volition, without which the *mens rea* would be incomplete. Yet he perceived that a mentally deranged person may know the criminal character of his deed in relation to his own case without being responsible.[26] Therefore he compensated for the deficiency of the knowledge test by making his great contribution, the test, as he called it, of "irresistible and uncontrollable impulse." Without it, he would have been at a loss to account for the evidence of the trial that showed Rogers knew right from wrong, knew what he was doing, and acted rationally most of the time. As Shaw stated the test:

If then it is proved, to the satisfaction of the jury, that the mind of the accused was in a diseased and unsound state, the question will be, whether the disease existed to so high a degree, that for the time being it overwhelmed the reason, conscience, and judgment, and whether

[24] Dean Wigmore, speaking of volition, says: "This distinct element in criminal intent consists not alone in the voluntary movement of the muscles (*i.e.* in action), nor yet in a knowledge of the nature of the act, but in a combination of the two, — *the specific will to act, i.e.* the volition exercised with conscious reference to *whatever knowledge the actor has* on the subject of the act." John H. Wigmore, *A Treatise on the Anglo-American System of Evidence* (Boston, 1923, 2nd ed., 5 vols.), II, sec. 242. Italics added.

[25] 7 Metc. 500, 502 (1844).

[26] Prof. Keedy stated that Commonwealth v. Rogers seemed to make the plea of irresistible impulse a good defense per se, despite capacity to distinguish right from wrong. Keedy also criticized Shaw's opinion for its inconsistencies, mainly semantic, but in my opinion has not noted the important substantive inconsistencies which derived from Shaw's attempt to follow the McNaghten Rules while attempting, simultaneously, to account for the volitionary element of the *mens rea.* Edwin R. Keedy, "Insanity and Criminal Responsibility," Part 2, *Harvard Law Review,* 30:724–729 (May 1917).

the prisoner, in committing the homicide, acted from an irresistible and uncontrollable impulse: If so, then the act was not the act of a voluntary agent, but the involuntary act of the body, without the concurrence of a mind directing it.[27]

The psychiatric validity of the irresistible impulse test has been accepted in cases of mental disease which strikes at the volitional-inhibitory system.[28]

From 1800 to 1843 the legal trend, climaxed in the Mc-Naghten Rules, had been to reduce the concept of mental disease to merely a symptom called "delusions," just as the *mens rea* had been reduced to merely its cognitive elements.[29] Postulating the case of a man who labors under "partial delusion only, and is not in other respects insane" — a condition which is unknown to psychiatry — the McNaghten Rules laid down a test of criminal responsibility that virtually ignored the fact of insanity itself; for the Lords Justices said that the so-called partially deluded "must be considered in the same situation as to responsibility as if the facts with respect to which the delusions exist were real." [30] Shaw followed this test when he ruled that proof of delusion will rebut a charge of murder if the delusion "is such that the person under its influence has a real and firm belief of some fact, not true in itself, but which, if it were true, would excuse his act." [31] But what if the mistaken belief, *even if true*, would *not* legally excuse the act?

Shaw used a legal test for the insane which is the same as that for the normal individual who acts upon a sincere but mistaken belief. If, for example, a man killed in the belief that he was defending himself against an imminent attack on his life, his act is excusable; but it is not if he were defending himself against

[27] 7 Metc. 500, 502 (1844). Notwithstanding this and similar statements by Shaw, Dean Pound declared that "Judge Shaw did nothing except what was done in M'Naghten's case" (*Journal of Criminal Law and Criminology*, 2:544, Nov. 1911). Prof. Hall, who apparently shares with Pound a singular and mysterious idea as to what constitutes the test of irresistible impulse, says of Shaw that "though his language is ambiguous, it is clear enough to indicate definitely that he did not adopt the irresistible impulse test" (p. 508). Hall, a champion of the McNaghten Rules, criticizes that test at length (pp. 508–526).

[28] Glueck, pp. 304–312, 378–379, 385–388; Weihofen, pp. 20–21, 82–85; Keedy, "Insanity and Criminal Responsibility," Part 1, *Harvard Law Review*, 30:535, 550–551 (April 1917); Benjamin Karpman, "Criminality, Insanity, and the Law," *Journal of Criminal Law and Criminology*, 30:597, 605 (Jan.–Feb. 1949).

[29] Glueck, pp. 159, 175, 425. The trend began with Erskine's argument in Hadfield's case, 27 How. *St. Tr.* 1282 (1843).

[30] 10 Clark & Fin. 200 (1843).

[31] 7 Metc. 500, 503 (1844).

an injury to his dignity, real or delusory. This test of mistaken fact,[32] when applied to the case of a paranoiac, is inadequate, even shocking. Contrary to the assumptions of the test, delusions, however striking, are only external manifestations of a disease that affects the whole mind and personality, rendering its victims unable to reason or control their conduct in the manner of normal persons. Moreover, the very disease that may lead to irresistible homicide may also make it impossible for the accused to show motives and circumstances that would prove the connection, required by law, between the delusion and the homicide. A sane man may prove why he thought he was acting in self defense; but the distorted mind of the "madman" may so color his experience as to make the connection incommunicable to a rational judge and jury, except perhaps through the medium of a psychiatrist.

Although Shaw erred in following the test laid down by the Lords Justices in relation to delusion, he did not wholly adopt their faulty psychological position that one may suffer from "partial delusions" and be otherwise mentally sound. He profited from the expert testimony at the trial.[33] Indeed, his high regard for expert opinion resulted in one of his notable rulings in the Rogers case. Against the objections of the prosecution, he held that the testimony of those who are professionally experienced in the treatment of the insane is admissible in evidence and entitled to "great weight" even if they have not examined the accused.[34] It was this testimony which probably accounts for the fact that he did not mistake the delusion for the disease. Instead of regarding persons as sane except for their delusions, he spoke of "partial

[32] Stephen, II, 159–168; Glueck, pp. 171–173, 300–304, 367; Keedy, pp. 536, 554–559, 736; Weihofen, pp. 103–113. Prof. Weihofen states (p. 108) that only ten states, not including Massachusetts, still follow this test.

[33] Three distinguished physicians, all superintendents of institutions for the care of the mentally diseased, testified. One was the noted Dr. Isaac Ray, author of the treatise, *Medical Jurisprudence of Insanity* (1838). Ray and others influenced the course of the criminal law of insanity when they testified before Shaw on the validity of the theory that certain types of mental diseases provoke irresistible or uncontrollable impulses for which the actors cannot be held mentally responsible. *Trial of Abner Rogers, Jr.,* pp. 157, 162, 163.

[34] 7 Metc. 500, 505 (1844). Unfortunately, modern judges too frequently display a shocking disregard for expert psychiatric evidence. Compare Shaw's attitude with that of his successors in 1926 who said that the trial judge, having seen the witness testify, could form a commonsense judgment on his responsibility "more reliable as a practical guide to accomplishment of justice than the refined distinctions and technical niceties of alienists and experts on psychopathic inferiority" (Commonwealth v. Devereaux, 257 Mass. 391, 1926).

insanity . . . accompanied by delusion," the delusions being "symptoms" indicating "that the mind is in a diseased state."[35]

This understanding on Shaw's part, together with his concern for the volitional element in the *mens rea,* led him to recognize that when a case involved delusion, the traditional test for determining responsibility in cases of mistaken belief of fact was deficient. To this traditional test, which he had adopted, he added an *alternative* one. It was the test of irresistible impulse, the same he had earlier added to the test of knowing right from wrong.

Shaw ruled that when the delusion indicates to an experienced person a disease of the mind whose "known tendency . . . is to break out into sudden paroxysms of violence," the killing, even if without any precedent of violence in the personal history of the accused, when connected to the previous symptoms, shows "that the outbreak [of the disease] was of such a character, that for the time being it must have overborne memory and reason; that the act was the result of the disease and not of a mind capable of choosing; in short, that it was the result of uncontrollable impulse, and not of a person acted upon by motives, and governed by the will."[36]

Professor Glueck comments that Shaw showed "a more open-minded attitude towards the defense of insanity . . . than many of his successors in various States have shown up to the present."[37] This is sheer understatement, given the judicial disregard sometimes shown for psychiatric evidence and given the fact that a large majority of the state courts have not adopted some form of the irresistible impulse test.[38] Consequently, in these jurisdictions, persons suffering from mental diseases which attack the volitional-inhibitory system and render them psychologically and morally

[35] 7 Metc. 500, 503 (1844).

[36] *Ibid.,* at 503.

[37] Glueck, p. 247, f.n. 2.

[38] Weihofen, p. 4, reports that a recent study shows that only in the legal profession is there a relatively large distrust of psychiatry. See also footnote 34, *supra.*

At various times twenty-four states have subscribed to the irresistible impulse test; at present there are only fourteen, plus three others partially, and the federal courts. The U.S. Supreme Court followed Commonwealth v. Rogers in Davis v. U.S., 160 U.S. 469, 485 (1895). See Weihofen, pp. 51–52 and 101–102. Weihofen presents (pp. 129–173) a valuable digest of the tests of irresponsibility of every jurisdiction, as of 1954. In England, the irresistible impulse test was never adopted. Reg. v. Stokes, 3 Car. & K. 185 (1848); Reg. v. Barton, 3 Cox. C.C. 275 (1848); Reg. v. Thomas, 7 Crim. App. 36 (1911). In 1953 a British Royal Commission on Capital Punishment concluded that the McNaghten Rules were so defective that they ought to be changed. The proposed change consists of an additional test: "at the time of committing the act, the accused, as a result of disease of the mind . . . was incapable of preventing himself from committing it" (quoted in Weihofen, p. 67).

irresponsible for their conduct, are held criminally responsible if their cases will not fall within the narrow McNaghten Rules. That a sympathetic jury might return a verdict of not guilty in such a case would show that the charge of the court on the law had been ignored; but the verdict of guilty punishes the sick who cannot control their behavior and, lacking volition, lack also the *mens rea* of the crime.

If Shaw, like the Lords Justices, labored under an intellectualistic psychology, unconcerned with the emotional drives which are the mainsprings of crime, at least he interconnected impulse, volition, and the *mens rea*. The ambiguities and inconsistencies in his opinion derive from the fact that he was under the spell of the Lords Justices, yet tried to profit from the most enlightened medical opinion of his day. The result was a hotch-potch of the worst and the best. That the substantive rules of criminal law governing insanity are today so confused, inadequate, and subject to interminable criticism from psychiatrists, is attributable to the fact that contemporary judges, unlike Shaw, generally resist the opinions of medical science. Given the state of law and psychology in 1844, Shaw did all that could be done.

But it was not enough, because he did not realize that an irresistible impulse need not be temporary and sudden. It may be the subject of long and reflective brooding before it is acted upon. Free will or volition may be absent even where there is no irresistible impulse in Shaw's sense of the term. His test did not therefore encompass the majority of the mentally ill who not only can intellectually differentiate right from wrong, but who act deliberatively even as they are irresistibly driven by emotional forces toward the wrong. Their behavior, when the result of their illness, is not morally culpable and should not be criminally punishable.

The first judicial recognition of this came in New Hampshire,[39] but the test there adopted, largely as a result of the influence of Dr. Isaac Ray[40] whose earlier ideas had also influenced Shaw, was universally repudiated by other courts until 1954. At that time "a great event in law"[41] took place. The United States Court of Appeals for the District of Columbia, in *Durham v. United States,* stated: "The rule we now hold must be applied

[39] State v. Pike, 49 N.H. 399 (1869).

[40] See note 33, *supra,* and Louis E. Reik, "The Doe-Ray Correspondence," *Yale Law Journal,* 63:183 (1953).

[41] Harry Kalven, Jr., in "Insanity and the Criminal Law," Symposium in *University of Chicago Law Review,* 22:317 (Winter 1955).

. . . is not unlike that followed by the New Hampshire Court since 1870. It is simply that an accused is not criminally responsible if his unlawful act was the product of mental disease or mental defect." [42] In time the state courts will undoubtedly accept this new federal test. Shaw deserves some credit for it, because his was the first opinion to recognize even partially that an act is the product of mental illness if it cannot be controlled.

III

Although he was more sympathetic to a defense of insanity than most of his contemporaries, Shaw was accused of being a "bloody Jeffries" for his rulings on the *mens rea* when sane men were charged with murder. A New York newspaper informed its readers that Shaw "will be the first of American judges associated in position and character with the band of cruel and corrupt English judges of whom Jeffries is foremost." [43] In Philadelphia a story comparing Shaw to the "witchburners" of Salem was headlined, "Judicial Murder in Boston." [44] An anonymous lawyer published a pamphlet which accused Shaw of making "a farce and a mockery" of trial by jury, of dictating prejudiced, incorrect law, and of "unscrupulous prostitution" of the judiciary.[45]

More responsible sources used temperate language but were equally critical. Boston's respected and conservative law journal declared that "the whole community shudders at the law of malicious homicide as expounded by the learned Chief Justice"; the editors raised the question whether he had allowed a "fair trial." [46] Joel Parker, a professor at Harvard Law School and formerly Chief Justice of New Hampshire, published in America's most influential magazine a long critique of Shaw's rulings on homicide.[47] A century later a distinguished legal historian reiterated the "unfair trial" theme — "a hanging charge if ever there was one" — and concluded that Shaw "violated a cherished tradition of Anglo-American criminal justice: every man is presumed to be innocent until he is proved guilty." [48]

[42] 214 F. 2d 862, 874–875 (App. D.C., 1954).

[43] Quoted in F. H. Chase, *Lemuel Shaw* (Boston, 1918), p. 207.

[44] Richard B. Morris, *Fair Trial* (New York, 1952), p. 196.

[45] *A Statement of Reasons Showing the Illegality of That Verdict upon Which Sentence of Death Has Been Pronounced against John W. Webster.* By a Member of the Legal Profession (New York, 1850), pp. 22–23.

[46] "The Webster Case," *Monthly Law Reporter*, 13:1, 13, 16 (1850).

[47] Joel Parker, "The Law of Homicide," *North American Review* (Boston), **72**: 178–204 (Jan. 1851).

[48] Richard B. Morris, pp. 156, 194.

All this critical fire was directed at Shaw because of his part in the Webster-Parkman murder case.[49] Edmund Pearson, the historian of homicide, entitles his account of the crime "America's Classic Murder" and adds that it is the "most celebrated murder, and the one which lives longest in books . . ." [50] It was the grisly character of the crime and the prominence of the participants which made for "the most sensational murder trial in American history up to that time." [51] A century later writers are still intrigued by the crime.[52] The story by now is so familiar that only a brief account is necessary.

Dr. John W. Webster, editor of the *Boston Journal of Philosophy and the Arts,* a member of American and international scientific academies, and Erving Professor of Chemistry at Harvard, was in debt. His principal creditor was Dr. George Parkman, a wealthy eccentric who financed Harvard's new medical school. Parkman, reputedly the best-known man in Boston, became "perhaps the most socially distinguished victim in the annals of American crime." [53] On learning that Webster had borrowed from others on property already mortgaged to him, Parkman demanded his money. Webster, who had run through his large inheritance and lived beyond his means, was desperate. Though he did not have the money, he invited Parkman to his laboratory in the medical school on the promise that the debt would be settled.

According to Webster's subsequent confession,[54] which was not made until after a plea of innocence had ended in a sentence of death, there was a stormy scene at the showdown meeting. Parkman, in a rage upon learning that he was not to be paid, shouted, "Scoundrel . . . liar!" and promised to get Webster fired. Unable to endure the torrent of "threats and invectives," Webster seized a heavy stump of wood and killed his tormentor

[49] George Bemis, ed., *Report of the Case of John W. Webster* (Boston, 1850); Commonwealth v. Webster, 5 Cush. 295 (1850).

[50] Edmund Pearson, *Murder at Smutty Nose and Other Murders* (New York, 1926), pp. 94, 113.

[51] Morris, p. 166.

[52] Professor Morris presents the latest, fullest, and best account in his *Fair Trial* (1952), pp. 156–203; Cleveland Amory's bestseller, *The Proper Bostonians* (New York, 1947), also devotes a chapter to the crime, pp. 207–227. See also Stewart Holbrook, "Murder at Harvard," *The American Scholar,* 14:425–435 (Autumn 1945); Pearson, pp. 94–114; H. B. Irving, *A Book of Remarkable Criminals* (London, 1918), pp. 189–213; and Chase, pp. 189–210.

[53] Amory, p. 220.

[54] "Prof. Webster's Confessional Statement," in Bemis, ed. *Trial of Webster,* pp. 564–579.

with a single blow. "I saw nothing," he confessed, "but the alternative of a successful removal and concealment of the body, on the one hand, and of infamy and destruction on the other." So he dragged the body to a sink and butchered it; the head, viscera, and some limbs were burned in a furnace, the thorax and upper part of one thigh jammed into a trunk, and the pelvis, a leg, and the other thigh thrown down a laboratory privy connected below with a sealed vault.

When the janitor's discoveries revealed the crime, the *Evening Transcript,* genteel newspaper of the proper Bostonians, noting that the prisoner was "a gentleman connected by marriage with some of our most distinguished families," invoked Hamlet's "O, horrible! O, horrible! most horrible!" [55] The trial before the Supreme Judicial Court lasted eleven days, beginning January 26, 1850. It was "a cause of intense excitement, extending through the whole length and breadth of the land, and reaching even into foreign countries." [56] The device of changing the court-room audience every ten minutes permitted sixty thousand people to glimpse the proceedings. Jared Sparks, historian-president of Harvard, one of a long parade of eminent character witnesses for Webster, commented, "Our professors do not often commit murder." But the evidence showed that the Erving Professor of Chemistry indubitably had. The verdict of guilty was reached by the jury after a couple of hours of prayer and a few minutes of deliberation. Yet the case stands, according to an authority, "as a classic example of how a jury can reach a sound verdict despite an unfair trial." [57]

IV

What was there about Shaw's conduct of the trial that brought such criticism down upon his head? His defamers unanimously single out one crucial point in his three-hour charge to the jury. That point involves proof of malice;[58] it therefore strikes to the

---

[55] Quoted in Amory, p. 220.
[56] Parker, p. 179.
[57] Morris, p. 156.
[58] Technically, in discussing the law of homicide, malice should be rendered as "malice aforethought." But "aforethought" is really superfluous since it does not mean deliberation, premeditation, or considerable lapse of time; it denotes purpose in contradistinction to chance. A malicious intent formed only an instant before the execution of that intent is malice "aforethought." Commonwealth v. Webster, 5 Cush. 295, 306 (1850); Kenny, *Criminal Law*, p. 123.

heart of the criminal law, because it deals with the character of the *mens rea* and the test of its existence. The accusation is that Shaw implied the existence of malice as a matter of law and, by so doing, shifted the burden of proof from the prosecution to the accused. He ruled, so it is said, that the burden is on the accused to disprove the Court's implication of malice rather than upon the prosecution to prove its existence. By so ruling he allegedly violated a maxim that a man is to be presumed innocent, innocent of the *mens rea* as well as of the deed, until proved guilty.

Here is no small matter, particularly to the accused whose life is at stake. The existence of malice distinguishes murder from manslaughter, and manslaughter, the unlawful killing of a human being without malice, does not carry the death penalty.

Precision in stating what Shaw actually ruled is important for evaluating his opinion fairly. The true rule of the Webster case was this: in a case where it has been proved to the jury beyond reasonable doubt that the accused committed the homicide intentionally, and where no evidence is adduced showing extenuating circumstances, the law will imply malice.[59] In such a case, that is, the Court will instruct the jury that malice has been established as a matter of law, whereas it is normally left to the jury to determine the existence of malice from all the evidence.

Shaw had actually decided the identical point in an elaborate opinion five years earlier, oddly enough without attracting any criticism whatever. That earlier and leading case was *Commonwealth v. York*.[60] A drunken Irishman had solicited a colored girl in the Negro section of town, provoking a fight which ended with a knife in his heart. Probably because it was a run-of-the-mill homicide involving the unwashed orders of society, no special public attention was given to the trial or to the opinion on the law, the same law that in Webster's case touched off a century of animadversion.

In legal circles, however, the York case was immediately recognized for its importance. The *Monthly Law Reporter,* then the nation's foremost legal journal, commented in March, 1845:

The point finally passed upon by the court has not been exceeded in interest and importance by any decision in criminal cases in this country for many years; and it is not a little remarkable that so many capital cases should have passed off in England and America during

[59] 5 Cush. 295, 305 (1850).
[60] 9 Metc. 93 (1845).

the last hundred years, without the necessity of deciding, in full bench, this question which is so wrought into the texture of criminal jurisprudence.[61]

It is also "not a little remarkable" that the same journal, five years later, should have "shuddered" [62] at the law of malicious homicide "so wrought into the texture of criminal jurisprudence."

The fact is that Shaw made no new law in either the York or Webster cases. Nor did he apply old principles in any novel way. Rather, he restated and explained the old law *in its most liberal light*, in effect, codifying it that way.

On the question of malice, the York case deserves the attention which has been lavished on the Webster case, although the latter is preëminent as an exposition of the character and use of circumstantial evidence. Interestingly, York's case was decided by the Supreme Judicial Court in its purely appellate capacity. At the trial the jury had returned a verdict of guilty, on an indictment of murder, after the Chief Justice's instructions on the rule of implied malice. Counsel for defense, Richard Henry Dana, Jr., moved for a new trial on ground that the jury had been misdirected; in effect he was asking the court of last resort, which had sat as the trial court, to reverse itself. No doubt the motion was granted — a rare occurrence — only because, as the *Law Reporter* noted, the point at issue had not been decided "in full bench" in England or America for a century.

Equally doubtless, the fact that Judge Wilde dissented sharply accounts for the unusual armor of authority in which the Chief Justice clad his opinion. He rarely resorted to citation of precedents piled like Ossa upon Pelion; but his court was rarely split, and Wilde was his oldest and most respected associate. No less than twenty pages of Shaw's opinion are wholly devoted to stating and quoting authorities, mostly English nisi prius cases and treatise writers. The roll-call of names reads like a "who's who" of English jurisprudence. That fact is significant. When Joel Parker, the former Chief Justice of New Hampshire, wrote his critique of Shaw's charge on malicious homicide in Webster's case, he was forced to acknowledge what other critics have ignored: ". . . the legal doctrines he promulgated are but those which are found in English books generally received as learned treatises, and even as authorities; which had previously been recognized to some extent . . . and which, at a former time, upon the occasion of the trial of York, had the concurrence and sanction of a majority of his brethren." [63]

These generally received doctrines which Shaw conscientiously explained deal with the proof of malice. To laymen malice means ill-will, but in law it denotes the *mens rea,* a state of mind manifested by an intent to do an unlawful act. Since the devil himself, as the old saying goes, knoweth not the mind of man, how can the malicious state of mind be proved? The answer is that malice can be implied from the facts proved by the whole evidence.

Shaw produced sound reasons for that implication. As he put it, "A sane man, a voluntary agent, acting upon motives, must be presumed to contemplate and intend the necessary, natural, and probable consequences of his own acts." [64] Moreover, "The wilful and voluntary act of destroying the life of another is an act wrong and unlawful in itself, injurious in the highest degree to the rights of another, being the greatest wrong which can be done to him . . ." [65] Therefore, since malice "characterizes . . . the wilful doing of an injurious act without lawful excuse," [66] it is imputed to a killing done intentionally and without excuse, and particularly so when a deadly weapon is used, a condition specified again and again by Shaw for the rule of implied malice.

The striking thing about Shaw's explanation of the law is the careful way he restricted the cases in which malice should be judicially implied. Cases of unintentional homicide he set aside to be governed by other rules. "But the case, to which the rule

[63] Parker, p. 182. The list of Shaw's authorities includes, among others, Foster, Coke, Hale, Hawkins, Blackstone, East, Russell, Bacon, Chitty, Roscoe, Starkie, Coleridge, and Tindal. That the law which Shaw laid down was received in America is evident from his quotation from the recently published treatise on evidence by Prof. Greenleaf of Harvard: "Thus, on a charge of murder, malice is presumed from the fact of killing, unaccompanied with circumstances of extenuation; and the burden of disproving the fact is thrown upon the accused" (Simon Greenleaf, *A Treatise on the Law of Evidence,* Boston, 1842–1843, 3 vols., I, sec. 34). So too, the work of the Massachusetts Commission on Codification of the Common Law, not cited by Shaw, stated: "Malice aforethought is presumed in respect to homicide, and the burthen is on the party who does a homicide to show a legal justification or extenuation." (Willard Phillips and Samuel B. Walcott, eds., *Report of the Penal Code of Massachusetts, Prepared [by the] . . . Commissioners 'to Reduce . . . the Common Law as Relates to Crimes . . . to a Written and Systematic Code.'* Boston, 1844, ch. on "Homicide," sec. 27). The commissioners added in a footnote that, "The presumption of malice aforethought, where the fact of homicide is proved, is a familiar doctrine in the law of homicide."

[64] Commonwealth v. York, 9 Metc. 93, 103 (1845).

[65] *Ibid.,* at 105.

[66] *Ibid.,* at 104.

we are now considering applies," he said, "is one where the life of the deceased has been taken by the accused, by a voluntary act, a wound inflicted with great violence, with a deadly weapon, and upon a vital part." [67] He reiterated that rule in one form or another perhaps a dozen times in the course of his opinion, always characterizing the homicide he was discussing by the words "intentionally," "wilfully," or "voluntarily."

But even if it were proved beyond reasonable doubt that the homicide was intentional, the implication of malice would not be conclusive. It would constitute merely a prima facie case of malice, that is, a rebuttable one. If, however, guilt of intentional homicide has been proved beyond reasonable doubt, and if nothing else is shown, that is, if no excuse or justification is apparent, no extenuating circumstances known, then *and only then* would a verdict of murder instead of manslaughter be justified.

This rule fitted the situation in the Webster case. The prisoner had pleaded innocence, insisting that Parkman had left his laboratory alive and without there having been any altercation. Yet the intentional homicide was overwhelmingly proved and no excuse or justification was apparent. Nor were the circumstances attending the homicide known. Not until after the trial did Webster, under sentence of death, confess; and the events leading immediately to the crime and the identity of the murder weapon were revealed only then.

Significantly, had the confession come during the trial, Webster would have proved himself guilty of murder despite the fact that his confession was "a carefully calculated effort to rebut the inference of premeditation and malice." [68] His story, if believed, would have rebutted the inference of premeditation, but not of malice, because he had killed on the provocation of mere words. "It is a settled rule of law," said Shaw, "that no provocation by words only, however opprobrious, will mitigate an intentional homicide, so as to reduce it to manslaughter." [69]

[67] *Ibid.*, at 102.

[68] Morris, p. 201.

[69] Commonwealth v. Webster, 5 Cush. 295, 305 (1850). This case was decided according to common law rules. Murder was not legislatively defined and divided into degrees until 1858. The statute of that year, fixing death as punishment for first degree murder, defined that degree as murder committed with premeditation, or committed in an attempt to commit any felony punishable with life imprisonment, or committed with "extreme atrocity and cruelty" (St. 1858, ch. 154). Had the statute been on the books at the time of Webster's trial, the law would probably have demanded his life anyway.

Related to the question of malice is the even more complex and equally controversial question of the burden of proof. It is misleading to allege simply that Shaw shifted to the defense the burden of disproving malice. To be sure, he did so, if it were a case of intentional and unexcused homicide that had been proved by the prosecution beyond reasonable doubt.[70] But the burden of proof, as York's counsel admitted, "was indeed lightened by requiring him to produce only a preponderance of belief, or an equilibrium, in favor of his defense." [71] That is, Shaw ruled that the accused could disprove malice by something less than proof beyond reasonable doubt.[72]

What this means, for all practical purposes, is that the burden of proof actually does not shift from the prosecution. For if the intentional homicide is established, malice cannot be disproved except by showing through extenuating circumstances that the killing was justifiable or excusable. But in such a case the rule of judicially implied malice would not even operate. It would be for the jury, not the Court, to determine the existence of malice from the whole of the evidence. And by Shaw's own reasoning in the York case, reasoning which he clarified in a case ten years later,[73] the fact of malice must be proved beyond reasonable doubt by the prosecution.

Take, for example, a case where the defense concedes the homicide and attempts to show that it was provoked by more than mere words, which the prosecution denies. According to the rule laid down by Shaw in York's case, the crime would be reducible to manslaughter on a mere preponderance of defense's evidence, or evidence equal in weight to the prosecution's, yet leaving reasonable doubt. The only possible effect that this rule can have, when the circumstances attending the crime are introduced in evidence, is to force the prosecution to prove malice beyond reasonable doubt.

v

Shaw explicitly held so in 1855 in the little-known Hawkins case.[74] There he also restricted the rule of implied malice even

---

[70] Commonwealth v. York, 9 Metc. 93, 119–122 (1845), adducing overwhelming authority for the rule even in cases where only the act of killing had been proved.

[71] *Ibid.*, at 95.

[72] *Ibid.*, at 94, 115–117. The leading definition of "reasonable doubt" is Shaw's in the Webster case, 5 Cush. 295, 320 (1850). It has been quoted "innumerable times" (Wigmore, *A Treatise on Evidence*, V, sect. 2497, p. 465).

[73] Commonwealth v. Hawkins, 3 Gray 463 (1855).

[74] *Ibid.*, at 465–466.

more severely than before, stating that it applied only when nothing is shown beyond proof of intentional homicide. Of course, that qualification had been made in the York and Webster cases. But in those cases it seemed to mean that the rule applied only when there was no apparent excuse or justification for the crime. In the Hawkins case Shaw insisted that he had meant the rule would not apply even then. He construed the words, "and nothing further is shown," to mean that the facts and circumstances surrounding the crime are not known, *in addition to* lack of extenuation.

The rule of the Hawkins case was:

The murder charged must be proved; the burden of proof is on the Commonwealth to prove the case; all the evidence on both sides, which the jury find true, is to be taken into consideration; and if, the homicide being conceded, no excuse or justification is shown, it is either murder or manslaughter; and if the jury, upon all the circumstances, are satisfied, beyond a reasonable doubt, that it was done with malice, they will return a verdict of murder; otherwise, they will find the defendant guilty of manslaughter.[75]

Whether this statement represents, as Shaw would have it, a mere clarification of the rule of the earlier cases, or a retreat from that rule, or an additional qualification on its applicability is not important.

What is very important is that Shaw actually liberalized in favor of accused persons the ancient rules of evidence on malice and burden of proof. It is interesting to note a fact, in regard to the Webster case, which no critic of the Chief Justice has pointed out. Webster's counsel, "a master of the criminal law," [76] agreed completely with the rule of malice expounded by Shaw. That agreement was expressed voluntarily when the jury were lectured on the law of homicide which they must apply to the facts of the case.[77] If the law as laid down in the then recent York case had been cruel law, bad law, or unfair law, it would hardly have been urged upon the jury by counsel for defense at his own initiative.

More significant is the fact that many of the English authorities of the highest repute had stated that malice would be implied

[75] *Ibid.*
[76] Claude Fuess, "Pliny Merrick," *D.A.B.* Merrick also served on the Court of Common Pleas from 1843–1848, and in 1853 was appointed to the Supreme Judicial Court. E. D. Sohier was associated with him as Webster's counsel.
[77] Bemis, ed. *Trial of Webster*, pp. 216–218, 221–222, 308.

as a matter of law from the mere fact of killing;[78] whereas Shaw annexed a number of vital qualifications: intentional killing, deadly weapon, nothing else shown, and so on. No critic since Joel Parker in 1851 has noted this. As Parker put it, "The principle, as stated in the conclusion of the Chief Justice is more favorable for the prisoner than that stated generally in the books he cites, — more favorable than the previous rulings in this State, founded on those books." [79]

Thus it is quite erroneous to say that Shaw violated a cherished maxim of Anglo-American criminal justice. At no point did he infringe upon the presumption of innocence.[80] It would be closer to the truth to say that the particular maxims which were involved in these cases, on implied malice and the burden of proof, were not very cherishable, but that Shaw made them more so, or at least more fair. The longest part of his opinion in the Webster case is an exposition of the character and use of circumstantial evidence. The exacting rules which he laid down to control such evidence are a model of fairness and have been followed ever since by jurisdictions across the nation. Several of Shaw's greatest opinions were reaffirmations of the ideal of criminal justice and fair trial.[81] His charge to the jury in the Webster case deservingly belongs among them as another liberalization of the criminal law.[82]

[78] See Shaw's citations in Commonwealth v. York, 9 Metc. 93, *passim*. Wilde's dissenting opinion (pp. 125–134), is chiefly based upon an inexplicable and inexcusable misconstruction of Shaw's opinion for the majority, which Wilde treated as having implied malice from the mere fact of the killing. Most of what Wilde said did not conflict with what Shaw said on the question of malice. Their differences on the matter of burden of proof were also more apparent than real, although Wilde, who oversimplied the question, avoided the theoretical traps which Shaw set for himself. Shaw's opinion in the Webster case spoke for a unanimous Court, which included Wilde.

[79] Parker, p. 186. Parker's article, correctly read, is less a criticism of Shaw than of the standing law. Parker argued on the basis of what the law should be, not what it was; his was an appeal to the state legislatures to reform the law of homicide.

[80] On the presumption of innocence, see Wigmore, V, sec. 2511, and Francis Wharton, *A Treatise on the Law of Homicide* (Philadelphia, 1875), secs. 30, 646–647.

[81] *E.g.*, Commonwealth v. Rogers, 7 Metc. 500 (1844); Fisher v. McGirr, 1 Gray 1 (1854), discussed *infra*, pp. 262, 283–289, Commonwealth v. Anthes, 5 Gray 185 (1855), pp. 290–295, and Jones v. Robbins, 8 Gray 329 (1857), pp. 295–301.

[82] The law as laid down in the Webster case has met with general concurrence. American courts agree that the prosecution can sustain its burden of proof in the first instance by proving only that the defendant killed intentionally; they agree too that such proof requires the defendant to come forward with some evidence

proving excuse or justification. Beyond this there is some disagreement. If the defendant fails to come forward with proof mitigating the intentional homicide, according to most courts the jury may, and according to other courts, should convict for murder. On the burden of proof, most courts now agree with the rule as last stated by Shaw, that is, as stated in Hawkins' case; a few courts still follow the rule as he stated it in York's case. See Jerome Michael and Herbert Wechsler, *Criminal Law and its Administration* (Chicago, 1940), pp. 39–40. The rules of the York case were the same or more liberal than those of England until 1935 when the phraseology akin to that of Hawkins' case seems to have been adopted. Kenny, pp. 36, 129, 139; Michael and Wechsler, p. 39.

13

THE POLICE POWER

State Regulation and Judicial Self-Restraint

I

Lemuel Shaw was the greatest state judge expounding constitutional law before the Civil War. Before his accession to the bench, he once remarked that under the head of constitutional law, "a title hardly known in any other system of jurisprudence," Americans daily witnessed profound and original discussions on the "science of political philosophy." [1] Shaw's own opinions on federalism, the commerce power, eminent domain, the contract clause, and due process of law bore out the truth of his statement. His most distinguished contribution, however, was to the concept of the police power, which he defined in classic terms as the power to legislate for the common welfare. [2]

Shaw's period constituted the formative years in the growth of the police power. By the eve of the Civil War, the most prominent feature of constitutional law, as Professor Corwin has pointed out, was "the practical approximation of the police power of the states to the sovereignty of the state legislatures." [3] Nevertheless, obstructions to the free play of legislatures were spelled out by written constitutions, bills of rights, and the federal system. As

---

[1] Lemuel Shaw, "Profession of the Law in the United States. Influence of the Form of Government and Political Institutions upon the Law and Its Professors." Extract from an Address Delivered before the Suffolk Bar, May, 1827. *American Jurist and Law Magazine,* 7:64 (Boston, Jan. 1832).

[2] Commonwealth v. Alger, 7 Cush. 53, 85 (1851). Mott says that this was probably the first case in the state courts to speak of the "police power" (Rodney L. Mott, *Due Process of Law,* Indianapolis, 1926, sec. 113, p. 302, note 13). As a matter of fact, Shaw used the term as early as 1837 in Commonwealth v. Kimball, 24 Pick 359, 363. For an example of the general acceptance of Shaw's definition in the Alger case, see Thomas M. Cooley, *A Treatise on Constitutional Limitations* (Boston, 1903, 7th ed.), p. 830.

[3] Edward S. Corwin, "The Doctrine of Due Process of Law before the Civil War," *Selected Essays on Constitutional Law* (Chicago, 1938, 5 vols.), I, 234.

the police power grew, so did the power of the courts over legislative enactments, for judicial review was intended to preserve proper limits on government. To the task of defining the rights and powers of the state versus the national government or private citizens, Chief Justice Shaw brought talents of a high order.

Shaw complemented his legal learning with extensive experience in the world of affairs. Eight years' service in both branches of the state legislature had given him an intimate understanding of legislative problems. He also appreciated the needs of business: for seventeen years he had been a director of the New England Bank, and held valuable properties in other banks and insurance companies. His connections were with the men of enterprise — the new railway builders and mill entrepreneurs. The rights of property were as sacred to him as to any other conservative, but his qualities of statesmanship, both political and judicial, enabled him to place the requirements of the community before strictly private interests. Although Shaw devoted his judicial office to enlarging the state police power, he was scarcely a petty advocate of state's rights and a narrow interpretation of national powers. On the contrary, he was a vigorous Union man, a member of the Webster-Story nationalist wing of the Whig party. His opinions, moreover, make clear his understanding that judicial review shaped public policy. He knew, too, that the application of constitutional law to a given case was often an adjustment of colliding economic and political forces between supposedly rival governments in a federal system, or between individuals and the state legislature. Such a man was superbly qualified for the difficult job of expounding the police power.

II

In 1832, two years after his appointment to the Court, Shaw delivered an opinion memorable for inaugurating the near supremacy of the legislature during his incumbency.[4] This opinion was occasioned by the refusal of the county commissioners of Hampshire to give effect to a special statute which required the county to bear equally with the town of Norwich the cost of a new bridge in the town. But for this statute, the cost would have been borne wholly by the town. Shaw rejected the claim of unconstitutionality with the observation that the judicial power was not to be exercised lightly, nor in any case where it cannot be made to appear plainly that the legislature had exceeded its au-

[4] Norwich v. County Commissioners of Hampshire, 13 Pick. 60 (1832).

thority. "It is always presumed," he declared, "that any act passed by the legislature is conformable to the constitution and has the force of law, until the contrary is clearly shown." [5] Moreover, if the legislature had exercised a power confided to it by the state constitution, "it is to be presumed, in just deference to the authority of a coordinate branch of the government, that in any particular case, it was done discreetly, and with a just regard to the relative rights and interests of different portions of the community." [6] The Court, continued Shaw, would look to the existence of the power, not the mere forms in which it was exercised. Extreme cases of the possible abuse of a power would not test the existence of the power itself.

To be sure, the Chief Justice assumed the right of the Court to judge the constitutionality of legislative enactments. But the significance of the opinion lies in its tone of judicial restraint and in its express confidence in the legislature. Many a judge — Marshall comes to mind [7] — has voiced similar sentiments, and in the next breath has proceeded to consign to the judicial wastebasket the statute before him. Shaw, however, converted the presumption-of-constitutionality theme into a cardinal rule that he honored by observance.

His philosophy of judicial review, which made possible the expansion of the police power, was most fully expressed in 1834 in Wellington's case. [8] Here Shaw wrote a thousand-word exposition on the now classic theory of judicial review. This opinion was clearly intended to settle for all time the right of the Court to void an act of the legislature, but the point was made with a consummate tact which disarmed any fears of judicial encroachments. The Chief Justice spoke of the respect and deference due the legislature. When called upon to review the constitutionality of a statute, he asserted, the Court would "approach the question with great caution, examine it in every possible aspect, and ponder upon it as long as deliberation and patient attention can throw any new light on the subject, and never declare a statute void, unless the nullity and invalidity of the act are placed, in their judgment, beyond reasonable doubt." Presumption was always in favor of the statute's validity. Even when invalidity was clearly shown, an act would be void only in respect to those par-

[5] *Ibid.*, at 61.
[6] *Ibid.*, at 62.
[7] Fletcher v. Peck, 6 Cranch 87, 128 (1810).
[8] Wellington *et al.* Petitioners, 16 Pick. 87 (1834).

ticulars and as against those parties whose rights were affected.[9] In other words, the Court would decide the case before it and nothing else.

These views were coupled to words of deep respect for the legislature — words which carried conviction. There was no better way to inspire confidence in the decisions of the judiciary, on questions of public law, than to cement relations of reciprocal regard between Court House and State House.

III

The first general law whose constitutionality the Chief Justice had occasion to sustain was one intended to restrict the practice of medicine to properly qualified persons.[10] The state legislature carried out this intention by the curious but effective device of denying the benefit of law to any person, seeking to recover fees for professional medical service, who did not possess a license from the Massachusetts Medical Society or a degree in medicine from Harvard University. Shaw swept aside the argument of Franklin Dexter, in *Hewitt v. Charier,* that the statute violated the "equal privileges" clause of the state constitution.[11] The legislature, thinking of the lives and health of the citizens, had wisely acted upon the maxim that prevention is better than cure. "It appears to us," Shaw said for the Court, "that the leading and sole purpose of this act was to guard the public against ignorance, negligence and carelessness in the members of one of the most useful professions, and that the means were intended to be adapted to that object." [12] Justification of legislation in the name of the public welfare was to become the outstanding feature of police-power decisions.

IV

1837 was a banner year in the history of the police power. In the Miln, Briscoe, and Charles River Bridge cases[13] before the supreme national tribunal, state acts which the Marshall Court would probably have brought within the prohibitions of the federal Constitution were validated by the Taney Court. And in

[9] *Ibid.,* at 95–97.

[10] St. 1818, ch. 113, sec. 1.

[11] 16 Pick. 353 (1835); Art VI, Declaration of Rights.

[12] 16 Pick. 353, 356.

[13] Mayor of New York v. Miln, 11 Pet. 102 (1837); Briscoe v. Bank of Kentucky, 11 Pet. 257 (1837); Charles River Bridge v. Warren Bridge, 11 Pet. 420 (1837).

Massachusetts, Chief Justice Shaw handed down two opinions which further extended the scope of the police power.[14]

Both opinions developed out of efforts on the part of the enemies of temperance reform to break government regulation of the liquor trade. Temperance reform in Massachusetts was a strongly organized movement which counted among its leaders many of the most notable politicians, clergymen, and educators of the day.[15] They had by 1832 succeeded in combining legal coercion with moral suasion. An act of that year[16] prohibited the retail sale of spiritous liquors in quantities under twenty-eight gallons. While this was not in terms a prohibition law, it certainly diminished convivial consumption at neighborhood grog-shops. Moreover, no dealer might sell without a license, and the law left it to the discretion of the county commissioners of each county to license as many applicants as they should decide "the public good may require." Consequently many counties promptly became dry at the election of dry commissioners. One writer estimated that in about five years after the Act of 1832, "fully three-fourths of Massachusetts found itself under prohibition." [17] It was this legislation that was contested before the Shaw Court.

The case of *Commonwealth v. Blackington*[18] was confined to state constitutional issues. The defendant had been arrested for violating the liquor law. His counsel, Robert Rantoul, argued that the law unconstitutionally invaded property rights and violated the "equal privileges" clause because it made possible the licensing of only one or a few dealers, who would then possess exclusive privileges.

In rejecting these contentions, Shaw explained the theory of state legislative powers. The Massachusetts constitution fixed a few fundamental principles for general guidance, but it did not detail a system of practical rules for the daily regulation of government or people. It had, instead, invested the legislature with a full power and authority to make all laws for the good and

[14] Commonwealth v. Blackington, 24 Pick. 352 (1837), and Commonwealth v. Kimball, *ibid.*, at 359.

[15] John A. Krout, *The Origins of Prohibition* (New York, 1925), pp. 90–92, 108–110.

[16] St. 1832, ch. 166, sec. 2, as amended by Rev. Sts. 1835, ch. 47, sec. 3.

[17] Wendell D. Howie, "One Hundred Years of the Liquor Problem in Massachusetts," Appendix "B" to the Report of the Special Commission on the Regulation of the Liquor Traffic in Massachusetts. House Doc. No. 1300. Reprinted in *Massachusetts Law Quarterly*, 18:76–284 (March 1933). Quoted remark at p. 128.

[18] 24 Pick. 352 (1837).

welfare of the Commonwealth. "A large discretion is thus given to the legislature to judge what the welfare of the Commonwealth may require; and this power is restrained only so far, as not to be expressly or by necessary implication, repugnant to the constitution. The power is the general rule: the restraint of it the specific exception." [19] Such theory has long been common in state constitutional law, but it was hardly taken for granted in Shaw's time.

Proceeding to the arguments in the case, the Chief Justice agreed that individuals had a right to possess and enjoy property. But this, he said, was simply a "general truth . . . by no means repugnant to any salutary laws designed to regulate the means of acquiring property . . ." [20] The liquor traffic was undoubtedly a means of acquiring property, and as such, was entitled to protection "under due regulation." There were many laws affecting property and imposing regulations upon trade — witness the inspection and marketing laws; the laws made with a view to revenue, health, peace and good morals; those regulating professions in which the public have an interest, and those regulating vessels and railroads. These laws have never been deemed unconstitutional, added the Chief Justice.

To the argument that the liquor law granted exclusive privileges to licensed persons, Shaw replied that the real object of the law was to promote the public good. If privileges accompanied the grant of a license, they were wholly incidental to this object as a means of achieving it; they were not granted to the dealer for his own sake.

The second liquor case of 1837, *Commonwealth v. Kimball*,[21] involved federal issues. For the first time, the Court had to determine the extent to which the exercise of the police power was limited by the national Constitution. The case arose on a conviction for selling without a license. This time Rantoul, again counsel for the defendant, had the makings of a stronger argument. On the basis of his contentions, Shaw defined the question before the Court: was the liquor law,[22] insofar as it prohibited the sale of intoxicants without the required dollar license, repugnant either to the clause of the Constitution which prohibited States from

[19] *Ibid.*, at 357.
[20] *Ibid.*
[21] 24 Pick. 359 (1837).
[22] Rev. Sts., 1835, ch. 47.

laying duties or imposts on imports, or to the clause which empowered Congress to regulate foreign commerce?[23]

Great questions must be greatly resolved. Shaw rose to the
occasion. Characteristically, he began with first principles. Recognizing the "complexity" of the federal system, he explained that
in their respective areas of jurisdiction, the state and national
governments were supreme. To the latter the Constitution had
confided a few great subjects of administration in which the
states were commonly interested, together with full "collateral,
incidental and implied powers" requisite to govern in all details.
"All other powers of sovereign government," declared the Chief
Justice, "necessary and proper, to provide for the peace, safety,
health, morals and general welfare of the community, remain
entire and uncontrolled, to the State government; and in the exercise of them, they have the right and power to resort to all adequate and appropriate means, for carrying these powers into effect,
unless they happen, in any particular instance, to come directly
in conflict with the *operation* of some law of the United States
made in pursuance of its enumerated powers." [24] To the extent
of such conflict, Shaw added, the state law must yield, "and to
that extent and no further," it is invalidated.

Turning to the regulatory power that had been challenged before the Court, he said: "It is not to be presumed, that the constitution was intended to inhibit or restrain the exercise of so
useful and necessary a power," unless particular provisions denied
the power, or it interfered with the accomplishment of national
purposes. The burden of proof lay upon those "who would set up
and enforce the restraint." [25] The liquor law, however, neither
in its terms nor in its operation prohibited the sale of spirits by
the importer; nor did it profess to raise a revenue by the charge
of one dollar for a license.

The defendant, relying on *Brown v. Maryland* [26] had argued
against the law on ground that it did not distinguish sales by the
importer in original packages from sales of liquor not imported,
not sold by the importer, or not in the original packages. But
Shaw was not to be misled by an irrelevancy, for the defense had
not made out that the sales had been by the importer in the origi-

[23] Art. I, secs. 8 and 10.
[24] 24 Pick. 359, 360–361. Italics added.
[25] *Ibid.*, at 361.
[26] 12 Wheaton 419 (1827).

nal package. On the contrary, the case involved the retail sale of liquor that had been bought from the importer and had become "mixed up with the general mass of that class of merchandise offered for sale in small quantities by the retailer." [27] Moreover, in *Brown v. Maryland,* the liquor license had cost $50, which amounted to a tax or impost on foreign commerce for the purpose of raising a state revenue.

Shaw was not content to rest the decision on a mere distinction of the case from the one decided by Marshall. He was eager to dispose of the issue "on broader grounds." The liquor law, he declared redundantly, fell within "that large class of powers necessary to the regulation of the police, morals, health, internal commerce, and general prosperity of the community, which are fully subject to State regulation; and . . . which do not interfere with the *exercise* of any power vested in the general government." [28]

Shaw's opinion in *Commonwealth v. Kimball* was notable for several reasons. Although he was protecting the partial sovereignty which the United States Constitution reserved for the states, his point of departure — the doctrines of implied powers and supremacy of Congressional law — was nationalistic, and made his advocacy of the police power all the more persuasive. His opinion also manifested his familiar restraint in exercising judicial review — limits were imposed on the extent to which a law would be voided. Most significant, these limits depended upon the extent to which the state law conflicted with the *operation* of a national law. The conflict did not depend upon theoretical repugnance, which usually rests upon deduction from a priori concepts; it depended upon empirical grounds. While deeply conceived standards cannot be extracted from Shaw's opinion, its suggestion of an empirical test enrichened constitutional theory in a day of absolutist legal formulas. This empirical test was to be amplified in an opinion by Shaw given five years later in the famous Passenger case. [29]

Finally, Shaw's approach was distinguished for a willingness to tolerate energetic state action. He required more than the mere

[27] 24 Pick. 359, 362.
[28] *Ibid.,* at 363. Italics added.
[29] Norris v. City of Boston, 4 Metc. 282 (1842). James Kent deserves credit for having been the first to advance an empirical test to resolve questions of conflict between state and federal commerce acts. Kent said that state power could be exercised concurrently "until it comes practically in collision with the actual exercise of some congressional power" (Livingston v. Van Ingen, 9 Johnson's R. (N.Y.) 507, 578, 1812).

existence of dormant national powers — in this case the commerce power — to impose necessary limitations on the police power. Unless particular provisions of the Constitution spelled out prohibitions, state legislation could be drawn into question only in the presence of a positive exercise of federal power. Here there is an emphasis different from Marshall's approach. While Marshall was concerned with the defense of the national Constitution against state encroachments, Shaw was concerned with preserving the residual powers of the states against their erosion by dogmatic construction.

In all this, there is some similarity between Shaw's views and Taney's, although Shaw's lack Taney's explicit proposal of concurrent powers over commerce. Still, when the liquor interests in Massachusetts vainly carried their appeal from Shaw's decision to the Supreme Court, much that was in Taney's opinion resembled Shaw's[30] — a resemblance that becomes clearer when the opinions of the two Chief Justices are compared in the Passenger case: *Norris v. City of Boston.*[31]

v

The question in the Passenger case was whether there was anything repugnant to the Constitution and laws of the United States in a state act[32] that prohibited the landing of alien passengers in any Massachusetts port until the master or agent of the vessel should pay to the state boarding officer the sum of two dollars for each passenger. Several objections to this act were proposed by Rufus Choate, who pitched his argument principally on the themes of an unconstitutional regulation of foreign commerce and a levying of an impost on imports. The purpose of the act, as explained by Chief Justice Shaw, was to help provide for the support of foreign paupers. By the poor laws of Massachusetts, every pauper was cared for; one need be only a human being requiring relief. The law in regard to alien passengers was a branch of the poor laws designed to "secure the State and its citizens from unreasonable burdens, whilst providing for the exercise

[30] License Cases: Thurlow v. Massachusetts, 5 How. 504 (1847). The Kimball case, 24 Pick. 359 (1837), was not appealed. Commonwealth v. Thurlow, decided at the same time, 24 Pick. 374 (1837), was on an improperly drawn indictment for violation of the liquor law. Shaw set aside the conviction and ordered a new trial at which time defendant was properly convicted. Then, in face of the Kimball decision, defendant brought the case to the Supreme Court.

[31] 4 Metc. 282 (1842); 7 How. 238 (1849).

[32] St. 1837, ch. 238, sec. 3.

of a duty of humanity towards those, who in the ordinary course of life are placed within its borders." [33]

In upholding this act, Shaw delivered a powerfully reasoned opinion. First establishing beyond doubt the competency of the state to legislate on the subject of paupers,[34] Shaw showed that the means adopted to accomplish the object of the act were suitable, appropriate, and within the powers of the State. Then he reached the central issue of the case: did the act conflict with Article I, section 8, of the United States Constitution, which vests Congress with the power to regulate foreign commerce?

To answer this question, declared the Chief Justice, it was not necessary to decide whether Congress' power over commerce was exclusive, so that the "mere existence of the power prevents the State from making any law on the subject"; or whether it is a "concurrent power, which the States may use until congress has acted upon the subject." "Supposing," however, that the power was exclusive, yet the states might tap their reserved powers of police to legislate on subjects such as health and inspection, which "essentially affect commerce." If, in testing the competency of a state to pass a particular law, one looks at "the ends to be achieved," it cannot be inferred that the state is powerless to act simply because Congress has an affirmative grant to legislate on the same subject. The power of Congress was exclusive only in this sense: a state can pass no law whose real purpose is to regulate interstate or foreign commerce, or on any subject which by the Constitution is to be generally administered by the national government.[35]

Shaw was realist enough to know, however, that a regulation of commerce on the one hand, and on the other, legislation necessary for the promotion of the health, welfare, and safety of the citizens of the states, might relate — as he put it — to "subjects so intimately connected with each other, that in accomplishing their respective objects, the same species of means may, and often necessarily must, be resorted to." [36] And both state and federal

---

[33] 4 Metc. 282, 285 (1842).

[34] See on this point Mayor of New York v. Miln, where even Story, J., said in his dissent: "I admit that they [the states] have a right to pass poor laws, and laws to prevent the introduction of paupers into the state, under like qualifications" (11 Pet. 102, 156, 1837). Story's dissent was based on his belief that the New York statute, which required ship captains to provide certain data about their passengers from foreign ports, was an unconstitutional regulation of commerce.

[35] 4 Metc. 282, 292–293 (1842).

[36] *Ibid.*, at 293–294.

laws might operate directly upon the same "instruments of commerce." Both, for example, might require the boarding and examination of ships, the examination of ships' papers, the mustering of crew and passengers, the detention of ships and persons, and the inspection of cargoes. How were the two laws, in such case, to be reconciled?

For answer to this question, Shaw proposed a rule so simple yet sagacious that it is astonishing that it did not appeal immediately to the good sense of American judges. Test the two laws experimentally, said Shaw, and see if they actually conflict in operation: "the State law will be constitutional or not, according as congress has or has not adopted and exclusively appropriated the same means, so that the operation of the one is inconsistent with, and necessarily excludes the other. . . . But if the specific means do not conflict with each other, both may stand and operate together, upon the same subjects." [37] At another point he said:

If therefore it should at any time be found, that the health and quarantine laws, the pilot laws, the poor laws, or any other laws of the States, or either of them, made in pursuance of their powers, become oppressive, or tend to obstruct our legitimate intercourse with foreign nations, it would remain for congress, in the exercise of its acknowledged powers to regulate commerce, to provide a system of uniform and equal laws, to remove such impediments . . . and by force of these laws, those of the several States, in conflict with them, would be annulled.[38]

The implication is that while Congressional power is not exclusive — its mere existence is not a prohibition on the power of the states to pass laws "affecting" commerce — yet Congress may act upon ordinarily local situations by passing a single, uniform law to remove "impediments" and to supersede all otherwise legitimate police regulations.

Here is a philosophy of constructive nationalism which dignifies the free formulation of state policy in the realm of political economy. Instead of a conception of the nation and the states as competing sovereignties, there is a vision of cooperative federalism; in the place of abstract theorizing, there is flexible "doctrine" of judging by experience. "Doctrine," however, may be an infelicitous word when the attention of a court is directed to the

[37] He found no Congressional law whose operation was burdened by the state law.

[38] 4 Metc. 282, 296 (1842).

question: can the state and national law stand and operate together? What Shaw contributed to the solution of the intricate problem of the relationship of the police power to the commerce power, was more a usable method than a rigid formula.

Still another problem had to be solved in the Passenger case. Was the required payment of two dollars per passenger a violation of Article I, section 10, which prohibited state imposts on imports? Shaw's decision here was not marked by the same originality which thus far had distinguished his opinion. He limited the compass of the commerce clause by accepting uncritically the proposal, which had originated with Justice Barbour,[39] that persons are not the subject of commerce. The effect of such an argument would have permitted the states to establish their own immigration barriers in the absence of national law. The Chief Justice was on better ground when he refused to regard the two-dollar requirement on an impost, which was, he said (referring to Marshall's definition[40]) a tax levied on imported articles. If the state act, under the color of carrying into effect a police regulation, had as its purpose the raising of a revenue on foreign commerce, it would be unconstitutional. But its purpose was to defray the cost of administering the poor law system that provided relief for "every suffering member of the human family . . . including the foreigner," within state limits.

In the Supreme Court of the United States, a bare majority reversed Shaw's decision and held the Massachusetts Passenger Act, together with a similar one of New York, unconstitutional.[41] Each member of the majority wrote a separate opinion. All five apparently considered that Congress' power over commerce was exclusive, thereby converting a mere affirmative grant into an implied prohibition on the states without considering whether the state legislation in question actually interfered with the effective working out of national policy. The majority created a sharp and artificial distinction between police and commerce without realizing, as had Shaw — and Taney and Woodbury dissenting — that the different labels often stood for the same things, or for things intimately related in the economy.

Not until 1852, in the Pilot case,[42] did the Supreme Court arrive at some agreement on the commerce power. Then Justice

---

[39] Mayor of New York v. Miln, 11 Pet. 102, 136 (1837).
[40] Brown v. Maryland, 12 Wheat. 419, 437 (1827).
[41] Passenger Cases, 7 How. 238 (1849).
[42] Cooley v. Board of Wardens, 12 How. 299 (1852).

Curtis, speaking for the Court, advanced a compromise view: commerce embraced many unlike subjects, some demanding a uniform national rule, others demanding diverse local rules to meet local situations; only in the former case was exclusive regulation by Congress required, and by implication, state legislation forbidden. This test lacked the more practical character of Shaw's, for his was less a formula difficult to apply.[43] He would uphold the state legislation if it did not conflict with operation of a national act, or, if in the absence of Congressional action, it did not violate an exclusively national purpose. If there was a weakness in Shaw's test, it lay in his failure to define the almost undefinable: what was a national purpose? Curtis, in the Pilot case, also left this question unanswered. Shaw preferred to have Congress, by positive legislation, determine whether state action conflicted with a national purpose.

In sum, the difference between Shaw and the Supreme Court was that Shaw, in the absence of Congressional action, would tend to uphold the state act; the Supreme Court would tend to presume that Congressional inaction signified that no power was to be exercised over a subject of commerce involving a national purpose. Thus, the Pilot formula permitted the voiding of state regulations on ground that they acted upon a subject requiring national legislation. As business more and more crossed state boundaries, state powers were curbed, and many a business went unregulated until Congress acted.

VI

Another notable year in the history of the police power was 1839. In two cases, the power of the state to regulate banking corporations was assailed before the Shaw Court; in both, unanimous decisions sweepingly sustained the state.[44] These decisions take on added meaning when it is noted that the regulations in question were intended to control the over-expansion of credit, excessive issuance of bank notes, and the loose financial practices generally, all of which contributed to the Panic of 1837. That Massachusetts' banks came out of the panic in better condition than those of any other state is attributable in the main to her

---

[43] For an illustration of Shaw's application of his test, see Dunham v. Lamphere, 3 Gray 268 (1855).

[44] Commonwealth v. Farmers and Mechanics Bank, 21 Pick. 542 (1839); Crease v. Babcock, 23 Pick. 334 (1839).

model banking legislation.[45] The decisions of 1839 upheld the right of the legislature to shape private banking practices in the public interest.

In both cases, the existence of the contract in the charter of incorporation was called upon to defeat the contested statutes. In the Charles River Bridge case, Taney had narrowly construed a charter against the corporation, reasoning that all ambiguities in the charter operate in favor of the public. This decision substantially modified the Dartmouth College rule which threatened to put corporations beyond the pale of state intervention. Yet the intervention sustained in the Charles River Bridge case consisted simply in the chartering of a competing corporation. In the bank cases before the Shaw Court, the intervention was direct and thoroughgoing.

Commonwealth v. Farmers and Mechanics Bank involved the validity of a statute[46] that provided for the appointment of bank commissioners, by the governor, to determine the condition and ability of the banks to fulfill obligations, and to inquire into violations of chartered duties. The commissioners were empowered to visit all banks with free access to their vaults and records, and to require the sworn testimony of bank officials and agents, under pain of strict penalties. The statute further provided that the findings of the commissioners were to be prima facie evidence; and that upon application to the Supreme Judicial Court, an injunction would issue forthwith to suspend the operation of the bank until full hearings — at which time the Court might make the injunction perpetual. Under this statute, the state commissioners sued for an injunction against the Farmers and Mechanics Bank because, among other specified malpractices, it had gone into operation before at least half of its capital stock had been paid in specie and because it had made improper loans.

Rufus Choate, arguing for the bank against the injunction, attacked every provision of the statute in a vain effort to prove that the legislature had no authority to pass it. His most important contention was that the charter was a grant "of power to do business, not while the corporation proceeds legally or with safety to the public, but so long as the grant remains in force." [47]

[45] See Fred Shannon, *America's Economic Growth* (New York, 1940), p. 299. For the history of bank legislation in Massachusetts through the period of the Panic of 1837, see Edwin Merrick Dodd, *American Business Corporations until 1860* (Cambridge, 1954), pp. 201–218 and 273–277.

[46] St. 1838, ch. 14.

[47] Commonwealth v. Farmers and Mechanics Bank, 21 Pick. 542, 546 (1839).

Chief Justice Shaw, however, was of another mind. Speaking for his Court, he explained that the legislature's object in passing the statute was to prevent banks from "becoming dangerous to the public" by their mismanagement. He said:

When it is considered how important it is to all the great interests of the community, that banks should be managed uprightly and with integrity, and according to the rules of law prescribed for their regulation, in their charters and by general laws, and how important it is that they should enjoy the confidence of the community, there seems to be no doubt that the objects proposed are proper subjects for the exercise of legislative power.[48]

Reviewing the statute, provision by provision, Shaw upheld the legislature.[49] He invoked considerations of the public interest to justify the rule that chartered privileges and immunities could not exempt corporations from the operation of laws made for "general regulation and government." In this case, the Chief Justice's most enduring contribution to the police-power concept was contained in the remark that a suit, such as the present one, might "to a certain extent interfere with the liberty of action, and even with the right of property . . . but this cannot be considered as going beyond the limits which justice requires . . ."[50]

Here, in 1839, Shaw revealed an almost precocious understanding of the central premise of the police power — the right of the legislature to "interfere" with "liberty" or "property" for the sake of the common welfare. Though Shaw had not yet formulated a systematic concept of the police power, its scope, and, what is perhaps even more important, its limits, neither had anyone else. Indeed, no judge would ever clearly perform this feat, for the police power was by nature vague and comprehensive. From the beginning, it was closely identified with the whole mass of a state's residual powers of sovereignty. Marshall was thinking of the police power when he spoke of a state's power "to regulate its police, its domestic trade, and to govern its citizens."[51] Taney, as

[48] *Ibid.*, at 551.
[49] St. 1838, ch. 14 remained in force for five years, during which time the bank commissioners obtained injunctions against seven banks. The board of commissioners was reestablished in 1851 with the same powers as formerly. Davis R. Dewey, *State Banking before the Civil War* (Washington, 1910), p. 129.
[50] 21 Pick. 542, 551 (1839).
[51] Gibbons v. Ogden, 9 Wheat. 1, 208 (1824). The term itself was not used until 1827 by Marshall in Brown v. Maryland, 12 Wheat. 419, 443. Not until 1837 was the term used again, by Shaw in Commonwealth v. Kimball, 24 Pick. 359, 363, and by Barbour and Thompson in Mayor of New York v. Miln, 11 Pet. 102, 139, 148.

late as 1847, used promiscuously broad language when he declared: "What are the police powers of a State? They are nothing more or less than the powers of government inherent in every sovereignty to the extent of its dominions." [52] Only Shaw at this early date recognized that the objective of the police power is the promotion of the public welfare, that it was to be accomplished by regulation, and that the regulation must trench upon private rights.[53]

The second bank case of 1839, *Crease v. Babcock*,[54] arose out of the refusal of the Chelsea Bank to honor its notes. The legislature, in answer to this refusal, repealed the bank's charter.[55] Four prominent lawyers of the Suffolk bar insisted before the Court that the repeal act was unconstitutional as a violation of the state's contract with the bank. But they did not rest their claim merely on the protection of the contract clause of the United States Constitution. They contended that when the legislature reserves a right of repeal, the adjudication must be by a court of law and not by a mere legislative proceeding. In other words, they proposed that the right of repeal, under the police power, could not be exercised except with judicial consent. This was somewhat analogous to the argument of a later day that property had been deprived without due process of law.

That the Chief Justice and his Whig brethren selected as their spokesman Justice Marcus Morton, the only Jacksonian on the bench, suggests the extent to which the Court was prepared to sustain legislative control of banks.[56] Morton pointed out that the bank, incorporated in 1836, had accepted its charter under the provisions of a general law "intended to regulate the banking operations of the Commonwealth, and [which] virtually consti-

---

References to the "police power" did not become common in the U.S. Supreme Court until the 1840's. The first judge to use the term after Shaw was Trumball in Jones v. People, 14 Ill., 196 (1852). See W. G. Hastings, "The Development of Law as Illustrated by the Decisions Relating to the Police Power of the State," *Proceedings of the American Philosophical Society*, 39:359 ff., at 414 and *passim* (Sept. 1900).

[52] License Cases, 5 How. 504, 583 (1847).

[53] This generalization is based upon Shaw's opinions in Commonwealth v. Blackington, 24 Pick. 352 (1837) and Commonwealth v. Kimball, *ibid.*, at 359, as well as upon his opinion in Commonwealth v. Farmers and Mechanics Bank, 21 Pick. 542 (1839).

[54] 23 Pick. 334 (1839).

[55] St. 1837, ch. 225.

[56] Morton became governor in 1840, and in his address to the legislature on Jan. 22, he coupled private banks with the old Bank of the United States as being based upon the privilege of "monopoly." See Arthur B. Darling, *Political Changes in Massachusetts, 1824–1848*. (New Haven, 1925), p. 252.

tutes the charters of all banks." [57] Violation of this law subjected
the bank to the penalties of another law, also incorporated into
the bank's charter.[58] By the latter law, all acts of incorporation
might be amended, altered, or repealed, on account of charter
violation, "at the pleasure of the legislature . . ." These statutes
governed the construction of the contract in the case.

What of the argument that the bank could not be dissolved
without a judicial proceeding? "The effect of this argument," said
Morton, "is to raise banks above the control of the legislature . . ." [59] As charters were granted "with a view to the public
welfare, as well as to promote private interest and individual enterprise," the legislature would not repeal capriciously nor without due inquiry. The legislature had in fact exercised the power
of repeal, "and therefore," continued Morton, "by the courtesy
and confidence, which is due from one department of the government to another, we are bound to presume that the contingency,
upon which the right to exercise it depended, has happened."
Neither the inquiry nor the repeal would be a judicial act, for
the power to make or revoke grants was legislative in nature. "It
is indispensable that this inquiry should, in the first instance, be
made by the legislature. No other body can do it for them. They
have restricted themselves from exercising the power of repeal,
until a certain event happens . . . and the corporators confide in
the wisdom and justice of the legislature not to exercise the power
unless facts clearly authorize and require them to do it. This is
not an unreasonable confidence." [60]

In short, one might almost sum up the doctrine of the Court
in 1839 as the legislature giveth, the legislature taketh away
— praised be the name of the legislature. It should be clear, however, from the fact that the legislature was exercising reserved
rights, that this doctrine, which was later modified by Shaw,[61]
represented no radical departure from the Dartmouth College
rule.[62]

VII

Taken together, the cases that had thus far come before the
Shaw Court had developed no clear limitations on the police

[57] Rev. Sts., 1835, ch. 36.
[58] Rev. Sts. 1835, ch. 44, sec. 23.
[59] 23 Pick. 334, 343 (1839).
[60] *Ibid.*, at 344-345.
[61] Commonwealth v. Essex Co., 13 Gray 239 (1859), discussed *infra*, pp. 277-279.
[62] Dartmouth College v. Woodward, 4 Wheaton 518 (1819).

power. The mere announcement by Shaw of the general incapacity of the legislature to controvert the constitutions of Massachusetts or the United States, was not a definition of a doctrine of
law narrowing regulatory powers. Specific limitations were not to
be defined until the 1850's. Until then, the police power concept
appeared capable of continued expansion.

Commonwealth v. Tewksbury is a case in point.[63] It is significant not merely as an example of the supremacy of the police
power over property rights, but also for its strides toward a definition of that power. The case seemingly presented a trivial issue:
the legality of a $20 fine on one William Tewksbury for having
removed sand and gravel from his own beach. Shaw, however,
turned the trivial into the important.

He saw in this case a contest between the right of property
and the rights of the public. The defendant had been fined for
having violated a statute[64] that sought to protect Boston harbor
by conserving the natural embankment of its beaches, and he had
argued that the statute was unconstitutional because it amounted
to an appropriation of his property for public uses without compensation.[65] In an opinion that cited no precedents, Shaw denied
the argument and explained the principle of regulation involved.

In Shaw's view, the challenged law had not taken private property for public uses. Rather, it was "a just and legitimate exercise
of the power of the legislature to regulate and restrain such particular use of the property as would be inconsistent with, or injurious to, the rights of the public." [66] The rights of property, as
he showed, were not absolute. Under the maxim, *sic utere tuo ut
alienum non laedas,* all property was held subject to the condition
that its use should not injure the equal rights of others or impair
"the public rights and interests of the community." Such use or
abuse of property might be abated as a nuisance at common law.[67]

[63] 11 Metc. 55 (1846).

[64] St. 1845, ch. 117.

[65] By Article X of the Massachusetts Declaration of Rights, "Whenever the
public exigencies require, that the property of any individual should be appropriated to public uses, he shall receive a reasonable compensation."

[66] 11 Metc. 55, 57 (1846).

[67] Shaw gave as an example the case of a building, located in an inhabited area,
used for storing explosives. Baker v. Boston, 12 Pick. 183 (1831) was the case of a
nuisance important for developing the municipal police power. The city had filled
in a watercourse which had become foul with sewage. Plaintiff alleged that this
act injured the value of his property and obstructed a right he had long enjoyed
of using the creek for navigation. The Court held, *per* Wilde, J., that it was the
right and duty of the City to remove all nuisances which may endanger the life of
the citizens. "Police regulations," said Wilde, "to direct the use of private property

The defendant's case, however, was not an action at common law; he had been indicted for violating a statute. Could the legislature interfere with his use of his own property *before* he became amenable to the provisions of the common law? Shaw explained that the common law did not adequately protect the public. What might be dangerous under one set of circumstances might in another be harmless, but the safety, health, and comfort of the community could not be left to the restraint of a nuisance already committed. It was, therefore, competent for the legislature, said Shaw, "to interpose, and by positive enactment to prohibit a use of property which would be injurious to the public, under particular circumstances." [68] In other words, by showing that the general welfare might require the anticipation and prevention of prospective wrongs, Shaw established for the police power a broader base than the conventional restraints of the common law normally permitted.

Trained in the common law, Shaw was not quick to break away from it. Consequently he cautioned that state control constituted a "high power, and is to be exercised with the strictest circumspection, and with the most sacred regard to the rights of property, and only in cases amounting to an obvious public exigency." But because the Court permitted the legislature to judge the case of "an obvious public exigency," no specific limits were put upon this "high power," nor was a rule evolved that would make clear when compensation would be required in such a case. The Court was certain only that a law forbidding an owner to remove the soil composing a natural embankment to navigable water did not take the property from him for public benefit, by eminent domain. Instead, that law prevented a particular use of the land from becoming a public nuisance.

VIII

If *Commonwealth v. Tewksbury* was a preliminary excursion into the sources of the police power, *Commonwealth v. Alger*, in 1851, was an elaborate exploration.[69] Here Chief Justice Shaw

---

so as to prevent its proving pernicious . . . are not void, although they may in some measure interfere with private rights without providing for compensation . . . and if by such regulations an individual receives some damage, it is considered as *damnum absque injuria*. The law presumes he is compensated by sharing in the advantages arising from such beneficial regulations" (p. 193).

[68] 11 Metc. 55, 57. See *infra*, notes 89–90.

[69] 7 Cush. 53–104 (1851). The case is reported for the March session of 1851. Actually it was argued a year earlier, but was not decided until 1853.

delivered his great disquisition on the police power in an opinion that is one of the most influential and frequently cited in constitutional law.[70] In a broad sense, Shaw established the authority of the legislature to control the use of private property in the interests of the general welfare.

The case was brought on an indictment against the defendant for having breached a statute that prohibited the erection of a wharf beyond boundary lines established by authority of the legislature in Boston harbor.[71] Shaw's achievement and the extent of the public regulation involved can best be appreciated when matched against the formidable argument of Benjamin R. Curtis for the defendant.[72] Curtis showed that the defendant had built the wharf on his own property, flats which were held in fee under a grant dating back to the colonial ordinance of 1641. Since the object of the grant was to enable riparian proprietors to build wharves, he alleged that the statute was inconsistent with contract rights.[73] Though this was a plausible contention, Curtis recognized its inadequacy to sway the court which had delivered the Tewksbury opinion, upon which the government rested its case. He therefore tried to narrow the scope of police-power control over property.

The chief point upon which his efforts hinged was that the defendant's wharf did not interfere with public rights. Even the government admitted that the wharf did not in fact obstruct navigation. How then, Curtis argued, could the police power reach such property? "The state cannot interfere with vested rights, for the purpose of protecting the harbor or any other public interest, without compensation." [74] The legislature might restrain certain uses of property without making compensation only in cases where the particular thing done or prohibited was a violation of public rights or of a right granted. This distinction, Cur-

[70] See Cooley, *Constitutional Limitations*, p. 830, and Hastings, "Development of Law," *Proceedings*, American Philosophical Society, 39:422. See also Owners of the Brig. James Gray v. The Ship John Fraser, 21 How. 187 (1858). In Commonwealth v. Bearse, 132 Mass. 542, 546 (1882) the Court said: "No exposition has been given of this power more thorough and satisfactory, or more often quoted with approval, than that of Chief Justice Shaw."

[71] St. 1837, ch. 229, as amended by Sts. 1840, ch. 35; 1841, ch. 60; and, 1847, ch. 278.

[72] Only a year after his argument in the Alger case, Curtis was appointed to the U.S. Supreme Court where he won enduring fame in Cooley v. Board of Wardens, 12 How. 299 (1852) and Scott v. Sandford, 19 How. 393 (1857).

[73] A grant is a contract, etc. Fletcher v. Peck, 6 Cranch 87 (1810).

[74] 7 Cush. 53, 59 (1851).

tis insisted, was important: there was no case of a nuisance or violation of rights as in the Tewksbury case. There, carrying away the soil was a right not granted; here, there was a right to build wharves. The "police power," concluded Curtis, is a power "to prohibit a particular use . . . a power to regulate, and not a power to destroy. And this cannot be done if the grant from the public, either expressly or by a necessary implication, authorizes that particular use. . . . If there is any doubt in this case the Court ought to lean in favor of private rights." [75]

Shaw, however, had no doubts in the case, although he was "deeply impressed with the importance of the principles which it involves, and the magnitude and extent of the great public interests, and the importance of the private rights, directly or indirectly to be affected by it." [76] He saw before him two questions: (1) what are the rights of riparian proprietors to the flats over which the tide ebbs and flows? and (2) what are the powers of the legislature to limit, control, or regulate the exercise and enjoyment of these rights? On the first question Shaw wrote the definitive opinion in support of the rights of riparian proprietors, under the old colonial ordinances, to hold tide land in fee, with the power to build wharves, provided that the public right of navigation not be obstructed. But the real issue was joined in the second question.

Shaw's point of departure was a majestic statement on the paramountcy of public over property rights:

We think it a settled principle, growing out of the very nature of well ordered civil society, that every holder of property, however absolute and unqualified may be his title, holds it under the implied liability that his use of it may be so regulated, that it shall not be injurious to the equal enjoyment of others having an equal right to the enjoyment of their property, nor injurious to the rights of the community. All property in this commonwealth, as well that in the interior as that bordering on tide waters, is derived directly or indirectly from the government, and held subject to those general regulations, which are necessary to the common good and general welfare. Rights of property, like all other social and conventional rights, are subject to such reasonable limitations in their enjoyment, as shall prevent them from being injurious, and to such reasonable restraints and regulations established by law, as the legislature, under the governing and controlling power vested in them by the constitution, may think necessary and expedient.[77]

[75] *Ibid.,* at 62–63.
[76] *Ibid.,* at 64.
[77] *Ibid.,* at 84–85.

What he had in mind, said the Chief Justice, was not the right of eminent domain by which the government can appropriate private property to public use on payment of compensation. "The power we allude to," he explained, "is rather the police power, the power vested in the legislature by the constitution, to make . . . all manner of wholesome and reasonable laws . . . not repugnant to the constitution, as they shall judge to be for the good and welfare of the commonwealth, and of the subjects of the same." [78] He added, too, that it was much easier to perceive the existence and sources of the police power than to "mark its boundaries, or prescribe limits to its exercise." But he copiously illustrated its principle and application in a variety of cases.

Only after his discussion had ranged comprehensively over first principles — Shaw could not confine himself to a mere judgment on the facts of a case — was the concrete question reached. Did the statute in question legitimately restrain the defendant from building his wharf beyond the harbor lines? The statute, Shaw affirmed, came within the principle of the police power, though it "trench[ed] somewhat largely on the profitable use of individual property." What of the arguments that the wharf was not in fact a nuisance and was not an obstruction to navigation? On what ground was legislative restraint justified?

Shaw answered clearly and definitely,[79] exhibiting once again his respect for the authority of the legislature. He took the position that because the common law of nuisances imperfectly protected public rights, indeed, left even private rights unsettled, the state was impelled to establish by specific legislation authoritative and precise rules for the benefit and obedience of all.

This was no pontification on Shaw's part; he reached his conclusion after patient analysis and full explanation. The problem as he saw it lay not so much in judging whether a particular use of property was harmless or injurious. More important, who was to judge? Injurious use might, of course, be abated as a nuisance. Whether injurious or not, however, the necessity of restraints was to be judged "by those to whom all legislative power is intrusted by the sovereign authority." The power of the legislature to regulate the erection of wharves sprang from (1) the original right of

---

[78] *Ibid.*, at 85.

[79] Compare Ernest Freund, *The Police Power* (Chicago, 1904). Freund mystifyingly stated: "If the court in this case found any justification for the exercise of the police power, beside the public right of navigation, it failed to point out with clearness such additional ground" (Sec. 405, p. 425).

government to regulate property in general, since all property is held subject to some restraint for the common good; (2) the reserved right of the government, under the colonial ordinances, to guard against hindrances to navigation; (3) the general right of government to promote public rights by acting upon riparian property, which is especially affected with "great public interests." [80]

If, continued the Chief Justice, it was the right of the government, in the absence of any positive enactment, to abate a public nuisance, and it was the duty of individuals to refrain from injurious use of their property, then the legislature could "interpose" by statutory action. It could define and secure the public right, declare what shall be deemed injurious, and regulate the use of property. "Things done may or may not be wrong in themselves, or necessarily injurious and punishable as such at common law," he said; "but laws are passed declaring them offenses, and making them punishable, because they *tend* to injurious consequences; *but more especially for the sake of having a definite, known and authoritative rule which all can understand and obey.*" [81]

A slaughterhouse, for example, might be punishable as a nuisance if erected too close to a town, but "who shall say, who can know, what distance shall be too near or otherwise?" Yet the public, tradesmen and residents alike, need to know. Certainty and precision can be obtained, said Shaw, by positive enactment that fixes and enforces a rule. He showed by analysis that the principle of the police power for which he contended, although imperfectly understood in the past, had been applied in a number of early, analogous cases.[82] In these cases the legislature had declared and enforced the public right, although by so doing had regulated private rights and superseded the common law by statute.

By this line of reasoning, Shaw reached the case of the statute in question. It did not effect a public appropriation of the defendant's property; nor did it operate retroactively or, in a discriminatory manner, solely against him. Its prohibitions applied to all and were intended to fix boundaries in a case where the public interest required them. "But of this," Shaw declared, "the legislature must judge." [83] That the defendant's wharf did not

[80] 7 Cush. 53, 95 (1851).
[81] *Ibid.*, at 96. Italics added.
[82] See especially Stoughton v. Baker, 4 Mass. 522 (1808) and Commonwealth v. Chapin, 5 Pick. 199 (1827).
[83] 7 Cush. 53, 102 (1851).

impede navigation afforded him no relief, because public need required a law, and it must be obeyed:

A consideration of this fact illustrates the principles we have been discussing. The reason why it is necessary to have a certain and authoritative law, is shown by the difficulty, not to say impracticability, of inquiring and deciding as a fact, in each particular case, whether a certain erection in tide water is a nuisance at common law or not; and when ascertained and adjudged, it affords no rule for any other case, and can have little effect in maintaining and protecting the acknowledged public right. It is this consideration, (the expediency and necessity of defining and securing the rights of the public,) which creates the exigency, and furnishes the legislature with the authority to make a general and precise law; but when made, because it was just and expedient, and because it is law, it becomes the duty of every person to obey it and comply with it. The question under the statute therefore is, not whether any wharf, built after the statute was made and promulgated, was an actual obstruction to navigation, but whether it was within the prohibited limit.[84]

The principal features of this long opinion have been followed here in some detail because of the importance of the case in constitutional law and in Shaw's career. Though courts and commentators have acclaimed the opinion, the fact that its one critic is Ernst Freund must give pause — long enough to ascertain that his objections are not fastidiously grounded. Freund alleged that Shaw's "definition of the police power ('sic utere tuo ut alienum non laedas,' etc.) is very vague, and its application to the case in hand . . . is based on no intelligible principle." He is also critical because Shaw did not define the conditions by which property rights may be subordinated to the public welfare, and adds that Shaw "failed to point out with clearness" the justification for the exercise of the police power besides the public right of navigation.[85]

It is true that Shaw formally defined the police power in vague terms as the power to legislate for the common good, but his understanding of the power surpassed his definition. Elsewhere in this opinion he spoke of the power of the legislature, on behalf of the public, to "trench somewhat largely on the profitable use of individual property." [86] Indeed, as early as 1839 he referred to

---

[84] *Ibid.*, at 104.

[85] Freund, *The Police Power*, sec. 405, p. 425. The parenthesis and enclosed words — "('sic utere tuo ut alienum non laedas')" — are Freund's. Note that he claims Shaw defined the police power in terms of the *sic utere* maxim.

[86] 7 Cush. 53, 88 (1851).

the power to "interfere with the liberty of action, and even with the right of property . . ." [87] He understood too that the real meaning of the police power was to be found in its operation as an instrument of government. His use and understanding of the police-power concept, as well as his formal definition of it, should be considered. Not expressly but in effect he defined it as "the power of promoting the public welfare by restraining and regulating the use of liberty and property." This is Freund's definition;[88] it too is vague, as indeed all definitions must be because of the nature of the power itself. Freund wrote after the police power had been debated and analyzed for half a century; Shaw discussed the concept when it was still novel. The seminal thinker rarely turns out a finished product, but Shaw was more than merely suggestive.

To say, as do Freund and Edward S. Corwin, that Shaw defined the police power in terms of the common-law maxim *sic utere tuo ut alienum non laedas* is to miss a vital point: he was abandoning the maxim as too narrow a ground to justify legislative action in a case such as the one at bar.[89] As a matter of fact, in the whole of his long opinion, Shaw referred to the maxim only once, and then only to illustrate an analogous point he was making.[90] Nowhere did he equate the police power with the maxim. As for Shaw's alleged failure to justify the exercise of that power, it should be obvious that he did, repeatedly. Justification lay in "the

[87] Commonwealth v. Farmers and Mechanics Bank, 21 Pick. 542, 551 (1839).

[88] Freund, *The Police Power*, p. iii.

[89] See Commonwealth v. Alger, 7 Cush. 53, 104 (1851), quoted *supra* at p. 252. Note Corwin's misleading characterization of the Alger case: "Here also Chief Justice Shaw for the first time associated the police power with the Cokian maxim, 'sic utere tuo ut alienum non laedas,' whereby the power was later put into leading strings to the common law, more particularly the law of nuisance." (Edward S. Corwin, *The Twilight of the Supreme Court*, New Haven, 1934, p. 68). This statement ignores the Tewksbury case, 11 Metc. 46 (1846); implies a definition in terms of the *sic utere* maxim; and fails to point out Shaw's effort to escape from putting the police power into the leading strings of the common law of nuisances which would have made legislation merely declaratory of the common law.

[90] See Commonwealth v. Alger, 7 Cush. 53, 86. Those who see the police power as having been defined by Shaw in terms of the *sic utere* maxim refer to his general introductory statement, at 84–85, on the implied liabilities under which property is held. They fail to see that in this same statement Shaw asserted not only that property shall be held subject to restraints on its injurious use—the *sic utere* maxim being implied; apart from this and in *addition* to it, Shaw said that property was also held subject to such "regulations established by law, as the legislature . . . may think necessary and expedient." The ground of this assertion lay in the theory that property "is derived from the government, and held subject to those general regulations, which are necessary to the common good and general welfare" (*ibid.*, at 85).

254   *Chief Justice Shaw*

expediency and necessity of defining and securing the rights of the public" by an authoritative and exact law.[91]

[91] Freund himself is the authority for the following statement, which is scarcely more than a rephrasing of Shaw: "The common law of nuisance deals with nearly all the more serious or flagrant violations of the interests which the police power protects, but it deals with evils only after they have come into existence, and it leaves the determination of what is evil very largely to the particular circumstances of each case. The police power endeavors to prevent evil by checking the tendency toward it, and it seeks to place a margin of safety between that which is permitted and that which is sure to lead to injury or less. This can be accomplished to some extent by establishing positive standards and limitations which must be observed, although to step beyond them would not necessarily create a nuisance at common law" (*Police Power,* sec. 29, pp. 25–26).

To be sure, Freund admitted that Shaw's opinion "recognises" that the police power may justify reasonable restraints upon that which would not be a common law nuisance. Freund added, however, that the opinion did not "recognise that in its judgment as to what is reasonable the legislature is controllable by the courts" (*ibid.,* sec. 406, p. 425). Here then is the gravamen of Freund's criticism. When he speaks of a failure to define the "conditions" which justify a subordination of property rights, he means a failure to assert a requirement of judicial approval. Yet the undesirability of judicial supremacy over the legislature is too familiar a tenet of modern constitutional thought to require comment here. Freund cannot mean a failure to propose specific restraints upon the police power, because here, in the Alger case, for the first time, Shaw did that very thing. He intimated that if the legislature had singled out defendant so to deprive him of his particular rights, the failure to compensate him might impair the validity of the statute (7 Cush. 53, 102). In addition, Shaw declared that if the statute had not been prospective in its terms, if it had operated to punish a use of property which would not have been a public nuisance before its passage, it "would be *ex post facto,* contrary to the constitution and to the plainest principles of justice, and of course inoperative and void" (*ibid.,* at 103–104). In these statements is the germ of the doctrines of discriminatory classification and retroactive prohibition which later courts have converted into major limitations on the police power. See Cooley, *Constitutional Limitations,* pp. 554–563; Freund, *Police Power,* sec. 538, p. 567 and sec. 685, p. 707; and Mott, *Due Process,* sec. 222, pp. 563–564.

Note, finally, the curious contrast between Freund's criticism of Shaw for not recognizing that the reasonableness of police legislation is to be controlled by the courts, and Corwin's eagerness to see in Shaw's use of the word "reasonable" a door held wide open to judicial review. "The Doctrine of Due Process of Law before the Civil War," *Selected Essays,* I, 235. But it is obvious that the door was forced open by later courts. Shaw intended that reasonableness be judged by the legislature, not by the judiciary. He said: "Having once come to the conclusion that a case exists, in which it is competent for the legislature to make a law on the subject, it is for them . . . to make such reasonable regulations *as they may judge necessary* to protect public and private rights, and to impose no larger restraints upon the use and enjoyment of private property, than are in *their judgment* strictly necessary to preserve and protect the rights of others" (7 Cush. 53, 102–103, 1851; italics added). In 1855, the same Court rejected a direct plea that reasonableness is to be determined by the judiciary and not the legislature (Commonwealth v. Hitchings, 5 Gray 482). In this connection, note the error in Mott, *Due Process of Law,* p. 568, where Cooley, in 1868, is said to have been the first to support the right of the legislature to decide the scope of the police power.

IX

No chapter in the post-Civil War history of the police power is more familiar than that of state regulation of businesses affected with a public interest. "The doctrine of property affected with a public interest," wrote Freund, "was definitely formulated in this country in the (1877) case of Munn v. Illinois." [92] The origins of that doctrine, however, may be traced back at least several decades to the earliest Massachusetts decisions upholding the exercise of eminent domain by turnpike, bridge, canal, mill, and railroad companies.

The legal theory which embraced all such enterprises has been explained in connection with the development of early railroad law.[93] Although privately financed and operated for private gain, these enterprises were all characterized by Shaw as "public works" because they were established by public authority on consideration that the public would benefit from them. This was the sole justification of their chartered powers to impair or appropriate private property at a compensation. If, as Shaw said in 1831,[94] "the public interest in such a case coincides with that of the mill owner," then, regulation of that mill owner — or turnpike or canal company, as the case might be — was but a step away. For if a business was public in nature, or at least was devoted to a public use, the public had a right under the police power to protect its "interest" by regulation. The point might be put in the form of an axiom: where eminent domain entered, the police power could follow.

In one way or another the police power may undoubtedly reach every species of property. Although the burden of proof as to the unconstitutionality of its exercise is upon the party, courts frequently set forth a legal justification of the regulation when giving grounds of decision. For this reason, any case in which Shaw associated a particular business with the public interest, in order to extenuate a "taking" under eminent domain, provided the *ratio decidendi* for a future case involving the constitutionality of government control of that business. The Shaw Court, for example, had no hesitancy in sustaining regulation of rates,

[92] *Police Power*, sec. 372, p. 380. Munn v. Illinois, 94 U.S. 113 (1877).
[93] See Chapter 8, *supra*.
[94] Fiske v. Framingham Mfg. Co., 12 Pick. 67, 70 (1831).

profits, and services, in the railroad cases that have been discussed in an earlier chapter.[95]

In Shaw's day there was no comparable legislation in the case of factories. Factory legislation was promotional rather than regulatory; he never had the opportunity of deciding the constitutionality of legislative fixing of maximum prices and minimum standards for labor or manufactures. Yet there is reason for believing that he would have sustained such legislation, given the opportunity.

To be sure, it is not immediately apparent that mills and factories are public utilities or public works like railroads, which though privately owned were considered "public highways" built to serve all comers. The cotton or iron mill would seem to lack those characteristics justifying a grant of eminent domain on their behalf or making them more amenable to the police power. But in Massachusetts the legislature, sustained by the courts, fostered such infant industries by authorizing them, in the name of the public interest, to damage private property if necessary to create water power.[96] The mill acts (as legislation of this kind was called) originated in colonial days when waterpowered gristmills were so essential to the economic welfare of an agrarian community. By custom and statute, the mills were recognized as a kind of public works, obligated to serve everyone and to charge reasonable rates. So long as water remained the principal source of power, Massachusetts continued its mill acts, authorizing mill owners to flood private property for the purpose of building a head and fall of water with which to power their mills.

Although the duty of interpreting the mill acts devolved primarily upon Shaw,[97] the work of his predecessors provided im-

---

[95] See Inhabitants of Worcester v. Western R.R., 4 Metc. 564, 566 (1842); Vermont & Mass. R.R. v. Fitchburg R.R., 9 Cush. 369 (1852); Boston & Worcester R.R. v. Western R.R., 14 Gray 253 (1859); and Lexington & West Cambridge R.R. v. Fitchburg R.R., 14 Gray 266 (1859).

[96] The decisions on this point were adopted in many states, although some, including New York and Michigan, ruled otherwise. See Cooley, *Constitutional Limitations*, 7th ed., pp. 771–773 and cases there cited. In the U.S. Supreme Court, Shaw's decisions, cited in note 97, *infra*, were followed. See Head v. Amoskeag Mfg. Co., 113 U.S. 9, 19, 24–26 (1884).

[97] See Fiske v. Framingham Mfg. Co., 12 Pick. 67 (1831); Palmer Co. v. Ferrill, 17 Pick. 58 (1835); Williams v. Nelson, 23 Pick. 141 (1839); French v. Braintree Mfg. Co., 23 Pick. 216 (1839); Cary v. Daniels, 8 Metc. 466 (1844); Chase v. Sutton Mfg. Co., 4 Cush. 152 (1849); Murdock v. Stickney, 8 Cush. 113 (1851); Hazen v. Essex Co., 12 Cush. 475 (1853); Gould v. Boston Duck Co., 13 Gray 442 (1859). See also the opinion *per* Putnam, J., in Boston & Roxbury Mill Co. v. Newman, 12 Pick. 407 (1832).

portant precedents. However, the Court under Chief Justice Parker had accepted extensions of the mill acts with considerable reluctance. Those acts, which were in derogation of the common law,[98] were intended at first to aid the building of gristmills on small streams for the benefit of the very farms whose meadows were flooded. When the rights of flooding were later vested in textile and iron factories built on the rivers, many people believed that farm lands were being "sacrificed to the speculating spirit of manufacturers."[99] Shaw's immediate predecessor believed that the new mill acts were "incautiously copied from the ancient colonial and provincial acts which were passed when the use of mills, from the scarcity of them, bore a much greater value compared to the land used for the purposes of agriculture than at present."[100] In 1827, in a case involving a woolen manufacturer, the Parker Court remarked that the reasons for legislative "encouragement of mills . . . may have ceased."[101]

The government's grant of special privileges and powers to mill owners was, of course, strongly resisted by the private interests that were injuriously affected. In 1832 Richard Fletcher, later one of Shaw's associates, argued against the constitutionality of a mill act on ground that the creation of water power for manufacturing purposes "was not a matter of public convenience and necessity, but of private speculation."[102] The argument was vainly made, yet it was repeated again before Shaw — and rejected — as late as 1853 when counsel argued that the grant of eminent domain to a mill corporation was unconstitutional because "manufacturing purposes" allegedly did not serve a "public use."[103]

The doubts expressed by counsel and by Chief Justice Parker in regard to the mill acts were not unreasonable. The considerations which justify a holding that the gristmiller exercises a "public employment" or that the railroads are "public works," do not seem to apply to the case of an "iron works" or a "textile manufactory." It is important, however, that the legislature thought so and that Shaw, unlike Parker, agreed.

[98] At common law the flooding of another's property might bring an action for damages; the mill dam itself might be abated as a nuisance.

[99] *American Jurist* (1829), quoted by Charles Warren, *History of the Harvard Law School* (New York, 1908, 2 vols.), II, 237.

[100] Stowell v. Flagg, 11 Mass. 364, 368 (1814).

[101] Wolcott Woolen Mfg. Co. v. Upham, 22 Mass. 292, 294 (1827).

[102] Boston & Roxbury Mill Corp. v. Newman, 12 Pick. 467, 472 (1832). The case provides a brief legal history of mills.

[103] Hazen v. Essex Co., 12 Cush. 475, 477 (1853).

Shaw envisioned great public benefits accruing from industrialization, and on the theory that the benefits outweighed the purely private costs, he invariably sustained the legislature. He believed that factories, like railroads, brought increases in population and in real estate values, as well as jobs, stores, schools, "and all the usual incidents to the establishment of a manufacturing village in a district which was before exclusively or essentially agricultural." [104] It was on the basis of this policy consideration, prosperity and progress, that Shaw declared:

The establishment of a great mill-power for manufacturing purposes, as an object of great public interest, especially since manufacturing has come to be one of the great public industrial pursuits of the commonwealth, seems to have been regarded by the legislature and sanctioned by the jurisprudence of the commonwealth, and, in our judgment, rightly so, in determining what is a public use, justifying the exercise of the right of eminent domain.[105]

Shaw's identification of manufacturing with public purposes and uses provided a generously broad base for the emerging doctrine of business "affected with a public interest." Although the legislature favored only waterpowered mills with the right of eminent domain, Shaw saw quite clearly that the same public benefits "would ensue, from the establishment of steam manufactories, without any head of water." [106] He saw, in other words, that a manufacturing business, regardless of its source of power, was, for economic reasons clothed with a public character. The conclusion, then, is that Shaw was outlining a legal doctrine, founded upon considerations of public policy, which could serve as the basis of future decisions sustaining police-power regulations of any industrial enterprise.[107]

It was certainly consistent with this doctrine that the Chief Justice should have considered the business of water-supply a public function. His opinion on this point in the 1849 case of *Lumbard v. Stearns*[108] was the first of its kind in this country. Professor Beale, referring to the state of the law on public utilities, at the time of Shaw's decision, wrote, "We had emerged from the later middle ages into the nineteenth century with the

[104] Palmer Co. v. Ferrill, 17 Pick. 58, 63–64 (1835); see also Boston & Roxbury Mill Corp. v. Newman, 12 Pick. 476, 477 (1832).

[105] Hazen v. Essex Co., 12 Cush. 475, 477–478 (1853).

[106] Palmer Co. v. Ferrill, 17 Pick. 58, 64 (1835).

[107] This general position was adopted by the U.S. Supreme Court in Nebbia v. New York, 291 U.S. 502, 536–537 (1934).

[108] 4 Cush. 60 (1849).

general belief, at least in America, that the only employments which could be called 'public' and restrained were the carriers and the innkeepers; and so late as 1862 the courts of three states held that a gas company was a mere private corporation, not subject to control by the state." [109]

Lumbard v. Stearns arose when a property owner contested the constitutionality of a statute[110] that incorporated and authorized an aqueduct company to divert the water from his private springs, at a compensation, for the purpose of supplying the town of Springfield. The charter of the company obligated it to provide free water to the town in the case of fire; imposed penalties for supplying impure water; and vested superintending powers in the town board of health and the county commissioners. These provisions Shaw found to be in conformity with the "public use" declared in the preamble. "The supply of a large number of inhabitants with pure water," he announced, "is a public purpose." The fact that there was no express provision which obligated the corporation to supply at reasonable terms any who should apply did not impair the validity of the statute. Any capricious or oppressive act by the corporation would be a plain abuse of its franchise, for by accepting its charter it undertook "to do all the public duties required by it." Otherwise, he threatened, the franchise might be annulled.[111]

"This doctrine," stated Professor Beale, "made its way slowly; but at last the courts accepted [it] on Judge Shaw's authority, and Lumbard v. Stearns became a leading case." [112] Together with his "public works" decisions on water power, mills and factories, and especially turnpikes and railroads, this decision upholding a publicly regulated water-supply business as public in use and purpose, established the foundation of the emerging law of public utilities.

x

The liquor problem plagued Massachusetts law and politics throughout the entire period under study. Regulatory schemes inevitably cast for the Court the duty of assessing the extent to which private rights were subject to the will of the majority. The

[109] Joseph H. Beale, "Lemuel Shaw," in W. D. Lewis, ed., *Great American Lawyers* (Philadelphia, 1907), III, 484.
[110] St. 1848, ch. 303.
[111] 4 Cush. 60, 62.
[112] Beale, "Lemuel Shaw," 484.

law of 1835,[113] which had been sustained in the Blackington and Kimball cases,[114] was replaced in 1838 with more stringent legislation.[115] The old law had permitted county commissioners to license as many innkeepers and retailers as they should decide the public good required. Accordingly, effective regulation varied from county to county, depending upon whether wet or dry commissioners were elected. The new legislation amounted in practice to state-wide prohibition because liquor could be retailed only in quantities of fifteen gallons or more on a cash-and-carry basis.

This has been called the first prohibition legislation in the United States. It was the subject of such furious opposition that the Whig governor, Edward Everett, who had signed the bill, was deposed in favor of Judge Morton, a moral suasionist.[116] Less than a year after the Act of 1838 had gone into operation, and before a single one of the scores of convictions obtained in the lower courts for violations had reached the high Court, the Act was repealed.[117] Although it had been condemned by the foes of restrictive legislation as a violation of property rights — even the new Jacksonian governor concurred here — there can be no doubt that the Shaw Court, given the chance, would have sustained it. An equivalent chance would come years later.[118] Meanwhile the Court, in an opinion by the Chief Justice, construed the repeal law as an automatic revival of the original Act of 1835,[119] and the foes and friends of temperance were temporarily stalemated in their respective efforts to extend or abolish legal coercion.

During the decade of the forties, however, evangelists of the Washington Temperance Society gave fresh impetus to the cause of prohibition. Converts by the thousands recruited under the banner of total abstinence, and a number of states experimented with the Massachusetts Fifteen Gallon Law. In 1847, Chief Justice Taney, in the course of his opinion upholding state licensing acts, off-handedly mentioned that he could see nothing in the Constitution to prevent a state from regulating the liquor traffic "or from prohibiting it altogether if it thinks proper." [120] Five years

---

[113] Rev. Sts. 1835, ch. 47.

[114] 24 Pick. 353 (1837), and 24 Pick. 359 (1837), discussed *supra*, pp. 233–237.

[115] St. 1838, ch. 157.

[116] Howie, *Liquor Problem in Massachusetts*, pp. 137, 139–153; Krout, *Origins of Prohibition*, pp. 264–272; Darling, *Political Changes in Massachusetts*, pp. 239–243.

[117] St. 1840, ch. 1.

[118] See Fisher v. McGirr, 1 Gray 1, 1854. Discussed *infra*, pp. 283–289.

[119] Commonwealth v. Churchill, 2 Metc. 1, 1854.

[120] License Cases, 5 How. 504, 577 (1847).

later, Maine, under the inspired extremism of Neal Dow, became the first state to pass an absolute prohibition law.[121] The following year, in 1852, Massachusetts outlawed the manufacture and sale of intoxicants.[122]

"Never since the doctrine of vested rights had been formulated," writes Professor Corwin, "had such reprehensible legislation, from the standpoint of that doctrine, been enrolled upon the statute books."[123] At bottom, the issue raised by such legislation was whether the police power could justify an uncompensated impairment in the value of private property which had not been taken for public use.[124] Shaw's position on this issue constituted a decided endorsement of the police power.[125] Indeed, Shaw quite took for granted that property might be virtually destroyed in the name of public health and morals. That he sustained the power of the legislature, in such a case, is not at all remarkable. In the 1850's, state courts everywhere sustained prohibition laws, or intimated that they would do so if the legislation were properly drawn with procedural safeguards.[126]

The single noteworthy exception was the notorious Wynehammer case,[127] in which the New York Court of Appeals converted a due process clause into a substantive limitation on the police power. This case instituted a novel point of departure in the history of due process of law through its doctrine that not even procedural safeguards could remove the taint of unconstitu-

[121] Chapter 9 in Krout's *Origins of Prohibition* deals with the Washingtonians, chapter 11 with the progress of legislation in various states, especially Maine.

[122] St. 1852, ch. 322.

[123] Corwin, "Doctrine of Due Process of Law Before the Civil War," *Selected Essays*, I, 225.

[124] "Perhaps there is no instance in which the power of the legislature to make such regulations as may destroy the value of property, without compensation to the owner, appears in a more striking light than in the case of these statutes. The trade in alcoholic drinks being lawful, and the capital employed in it being fully protected by law, the legislature then steps in, and by an enactment based on general reasons of public utility, annihilates the traffic, destroys altogether the employment, and reduces to a nominal value the property on hand. Even the keeping of that, for the purposes of sale, becomes a criminal offence; and, without any change whatever in his own conduct or employment, the merchant of yesterday becomes the criminal of to-day, and the very building in which he lives and conducts the business which to that moment was lawful becomes the subject of legal proceedings, if the statute shall so declare, and liable to be proceeded against for a forfeiture" (Cooley, *Constitutional Limitations*, 7th ed., p. 850).

[125] Fisher v. McGirr, 1 Gray 1, 27, 28, 41 (1854). See also Mugler v. Kansas, 123 U.S. 623 (1887).

[126] See Mott, *Due Process*, sec. 118, pp. 314–317; and Freund, *Standards of American Legislation* (Chicago, 1917), pp. 197–199 and cases cited.

[127] Wynehammer v. People, 13 N.Y. 378 (1856).

tionality from a statute violating existing property rights. The ruling was that the power of government could not go so far as to diminish the value of property in liquor by (1) prohibiting its possession for sale as a beverage; (2) declaring all such liquor a nuisance; and (3) in effect, subjecting all stock on hand to forfeiture. This could not be done "even by the forms which belong to 'due process of law.' " [128]

Although the Wynehammer doctrine of due process rode the wave of the future, the historic or orthodox meaning of due process of law may be found in *Fisher v. McGirr*.[129] In this case, in 1854, Chief Justice Shaw equated due process or the law of the land with those procedures which safeguard persons in their liberty and property, chiefly the methods and forms that appertain to trial by jury. Faced with a prohibition statute very similar to the one before the New York Court in the Wynehammer case, Shaw spoke in the following terms of the power of government:

> We have no doubt that it is competent for the legislature to declare the possession of certain articles of property, either absolutely, or when held in particular places, and under particular circumstances, to be unlawful, because they would be injurious, dangerous or noxious; and by due process of law, by proceedings *in rem,* to provide both for the abatement of nuisance and the punishment of the offender, by the seizure and confiscation of the property, by the removal, sale, or destruction of the noxious articles.[130]

Shaw added that to abate a nuisance, property might be declared forfeit and sold for public benefit or destroyed "as the wisdom of the legislature direct [sic]." He specifically stated that the legislature might enact a prohibition law and declare liquor to be a nuisance.[131] By no means, however, did Shaw regard these powers over property as absolute. They were to be exercised only according to what he called a "well guarded system of regulations." Since the particular prohibition statute, in *Fisher v. McGirr*[132] managed to violate many of the *forms* of due process, the Court unanimously voted "unconstitutional." [133]

[128] *Ibid.,* at 420.

[129] 1 Gray 1 (1854). See Mott, *Due Process,* pp. 123, 143–144, 175, 177, and 208; and Louis B. Boudin, *Government by Judiciary* (New York, 1932, 2 vols.), II, 374–385.

[130] 1 Gray 1, 27 (1854).

[131] *Ibid.,* at 28.

[132] St. 1852, ch. 322, sec. 14.

[133] For extended discussion of this case, see *infra*, pp. 283–289.

Shaw's opinion was a constructive check on the extravagances of the legislature, as well as a source of energy for the police power. Chastened, the legislature reënated a prohibition law for the most part with unobjectionable enforcement procedures.[134]
The constitutionality of the new law was upheld in a series of cases which drew the Court's inspection to one provision after another.[135] One of these cases, *Commonwealth v. Clap,* decided in 1855, was notable for the Court's abrupt rejection of the argument, supported by the Wynehammer doctrine,[136] that prohibition unconstitutionally impaired property rights. A month later, in 1855, another *per curiam* opinion denied the argument that the reasonableness of the penal sections of the same act "is a question to be determined by the judiciary, and not by the legislature." [137]

In the following year, in *Calder v. Kurby,* the liquor interests pressed the Wynehammer doctrine again,[138] as well as the contract clause of the national Constitution, in an effort to have the act invalidated for its annulment of a license to retail spirits. Bigelow for the Court said, "The whole argument of the counsel for the plaintiff is founded on a fallacy." The license, unlike a charter, was not a contract. Its only effect, under the statute authorizing its issuance,[139] was to permit authorized persons to carry on regulated trade in articles "injurious to the welfare of the community." A police regulation of this kind, concluded Bigelow, might be repealed at the will of the legislature. The doctrine in this case repudiated dicta to the contrary in Ohio and New Hampshire,[140] and eventually became accepted in all the states. "The doctrine," comments Freund, "represents an extreme application of the

---

[134] St. 1855, ch. 215. Section 32 of this act, dealing with appellate procedures, was promptly invalidated in an opinion *per* Shaw, C.J., as impairing the right of jury trial. Sullivan v. Adams, 3 Gray 476 (1855).

[135] Commonwealth v. Lafontaine, 3 Gray 497 (1855); Commonwealth v. Edwards, 4 Gray 1 (1855); Commonwealth v. Clap, 5 Gray 98 (1855); Commonwealth v. Hitchings, 5 Gray 482 (1855); Calder v. Kurby, 5 Gray 597 (1856); Commonwealth v. Williams, 6 Gray 1 (1856); Jones v. Root, 6 Gray 435 (1856); Allen v. Staples, 6 Gray 491 (1856); Mason v. Lathrop, 7 Gray 354 (1856); and Commonwealth v. Murphy, 10 Gray 1 (1857).

[136] People v. Toynbee, 20 Barb. (N.Y.) 168 (1855). In this companion case to Wynehammer v. People, 20 Barb. 567 (1855), 13 N.Y. 378 (1856), the New York Supreme Court voided a prohibition law effecting a deprivation of property.

[137] St. 1855, ch. 215, secs. 15 & 34; and Commonwealth v. Hitchings, 5 Gray 482 (1855).

[138] See note 136, *supra;* and Calder v. Kurby, 5 Gray 597 (1855).

[139] Rev. Sts. 1835, ch. 47.

[140] Hirn v. State, 1 Oh. St. 15 (1852); Adams v. Hackett, 27 N.H. 289 (1853).

theory that the state cannot by any act of its own hamper or burden the future exercise of the police power." [141]

In 1857, in one final attempt to get the prohibition law overturned, the argument was urged, on the authority of *Wynehammer v. People,* that an act which prohibited the sale of liquor owned before its passage was unconstitutional. Chief Justice Shaw, no doubt considering that his opinion in *Fisher v. McGirr* was the correct exposition, trenchantly dismissed the Wynehammer decision with the remark that that case was "of no force here." [142] In 1858, *Commonwealth v. Logan* was directly to the point that liquors "owned by a person when the statute went into operation are . . . included within the prohibition." [143]

A year later, in 1859, the Court again rejected arguments based on *Wynehammer v. People.* The case was *Commonwealth v. Howe,*[144] in which was drawn into question the constitutionality of a police power enactment[145] declaring as nuisances, "to be regarded and treated as such," all buildings used for purposes of prostitution or illegal gambling,[146] or for the illegal holding or sale of liquor. This statute was not necessarily as severe as it sounded or as the defendant's counsel made it out to be. It did not require the summary abatement and destruction of buildings put to noxious use. As construed by Shaw in an earlier case,[147] property owners were afforded every procedural safeguard and were protected against abatement by individuals whose own rights were not injured.[148] The abatement, moreover, commonly consisted

[141] *Police Power,* sec. 564, p. 591.

[142] Commonwealth v. Murphy, 10 Gray 1, 3 (1857).

[143] 12 Gray 168 (1859).

[144] 13 Gray 26 (1859).

[145] St. 1855, ch. 405.

[146] Gaming as well as gambling had long been regulated in public houses — inns, taverns, and the like (St. 1798, ch. 20; Rev. Sts. 1835, ch. 47, sec. 9 and ch. 50, sec. 17). In 1841, the Court, *per* Shaw, C.J., upheld an indictment brought on the provisions against bowling; the question of constitutionality was not at issue (Commonwealth v. Goding, 44 Mass. 130, 1841). In 1857, it was held *per curiam* that St. 1855, ch. 429, which prohibited billiards or bowling after certain hours, was constitutional: "It is clearly within the power of the legislature to make police regulation as to the hours and modes of occupying places of amusement, so as to make their use consistent with the peace of the community. The reasons which induced the legislature to make it penal to suffer any persons to play after certain hours in the evening are not for us to inquire into" (Commonwealth v. Colton, 74 Mass. 488, 1857).

[147] Brown v. Perkins, 12 Gray 89 (1858). Action of tort for the breaking and entry of plaintiff's grocery in Rockport by three hundred women — all in town "who could walk or move on crutches," some armed with hatchets.

[148] See also Fisher v. McGirr, 1 Gray 1 (1854).

in putting a stop to the immoral use of the building. However, the fact that the building and not its use was declared a nuisance made the statute potentially the most destructive of vested rights in state constitutional history; for the statute authorized by implication the actual razing of the property. No compensation was due the owner in such a case, because, by a principle announced by Shaw[149] if the legislature declared property to be a nuisance and it became forfeited by process of law, the title was divested by the judgment. Thus the upholding of the statute by the Court as a valid exercise of the police power represented the peak of legislative control over property rights.[150]

[149] *Ibid.,* at 27, 28, and 41.

[150] Freund's massive treatise on *The Police Power* neglects this important case (Commonwealth v. Howe, 13 Gray 26, 1859). Note, however, that Freund's section on "Property unlawfully used, and forfeiture," is confined to cases of summary abatement — abatement without the procedural safeguards guaranteed in Fisher v. McGirr, including trial by jury and judicial process in forfeiture proceedings. Accordingly, the decision in Commonwealth v. Howe does not conflict with the rule in Freund that neither a house of ill-fame, nor a building where liquor is illegally kept, may be torn down summarily (*Police Power*, sec. 525, pp. 557–558).

14

CONSTITUTIONAL LIMITATIONS

Judicial Review and the Contract Clause

I

Judicial review implies restraints upon the legislature. In Massachusetts the Supreme Judicial Court apparently took for granted its power to nullify legislation. The earliest recorded decision of any state court by which a state act was voided as a violation of the United States Constitution was in the Massachusetts case of *Derby v. Blake,* in 1799.[1] The Court anticipated by ten years Marshall's decision in *Fletcher v. Peck,*[2] by invoking the contract clause against the validity of the act of the Georgia legislature repealing the Yazoo land grants.

Fifteen years passed before the judicial power was turned against the Massachusetts legislature. Then, in 1814, a special resolution which suspended the statute of limitations in favor of a particular creditor was declared unconstitutional as repugnant to the "standing laws."[3] The legislature had no authority, declared the Court through Justice Jackson, to set aside the operation of a general law so that one citizen might enjoy privileges denied to all others. In 1817, Chief Justice Parker pronounced the unconstitutionality of a Congressional enactment which provided for the removal of certain customs cases to federal courts after final judgment by a state tribunal.[4] The statute was of

[1] *Columbian Centinel* (Boston), Oct. 9, 1799, reprinted in 226 Mass. 618–625, Supplement (1927). The *Massachusetts Reports* begin with 1804. This case appears to have been forgotten by that date. It was rediscovered and first cited by Charles Warren, *A History of the American Bar* (Boston, 1909), p. 269 note.
[2] 6 Cranch 87 (1810).
[3] Holden v. James, 11 Mass. 396 (1814).
[4] Wetherbee v. Johnson, 14 Mass. 412 (1817).

minor importance and had already expired; more important was the state judiciary's assertion of a superintending power over the lawfulness of even national legislation. These three cases of 1799, 1814, and 1817, respectively, were all the Massachusetts precedents before Shaw's accession to the bench — and the first, the unreported *Derby v. Blake,* was a "lost" precedent.

Under Shaw, the Court discharged its duties confident in its right to enforce constitutional limitations, though unwilling to encroach upon the province of the legislature. Respect for the legislature, even deference to it, was a maxim with the Court, as we have seen. In the definitive exposition on judicial review to be found in the *Massachusetts Reports,* Shaw laid down the following limitations on the exercise of the judicial power: (1) prima facie and upon its face, an act is valid; (2) an issue of constitutionality will be considered only in a real case, where parties are adversely affected by the operation of an act; (3) the Court will construe an act in its most favorable light; (4) any circumstance necessary to lend an act validity will be presumed until the contrary is clearly shown; (5) the burden of proof lies with the parties alleging unconstitutionality; (6) only those provisions that exceed the limits of legislative power will be deemed void.[5]

But Shaw never questioned the right of the Court to declare an act unconstitutional. In the same case he summed up the theory of judicial review in one rambling sentence:

Still however it cannot be doubted, and I believe it nowhere denied, that in a limited government like ours, acting under a written constitution with numerous and detailed provisions, a constitution which is in itself perpetual and irrepealable except by the people themselves, and which imposes many restraints upon the power of the legislature by express provisions and many others by necessary implication, and where the same constitution has provided for the establishment of a judiciary as a coordinate department of the government, with power in all cases to expound the laws, to declare what has and what has not the force of law, and to apply them to the investigations and adjustment of the rights, duties, and obligations of citizens, in the actual administration of justice, it is clearly within the power, and sometimes the imperative duty of courts, to declare that a particular enactment is not warranted by the power vested in the legislature, and therefore to the extent, to which it thus exceeds the power of the legislature, it is without efficacy, inoperative, and void.[6]

[5] Wellington *et al.* Petitioners, 16 Pick. 87 (1834).
[6] *Ibid.,* at 95–96.

Four days after this opinion, and less than two months after a mob had burned down a convent in Charlestown,[7] the Court held void a Charlestown by-law that discriminated against Catholics.[8] Under the by-law, the town required licensed approval from its selectmen before it permitted a corpse to be brought within its limits for burial. Persistently and without assigning reasons, the selectmen had refused to license the Catholic authorities of Boston to bury their dead in the Catholic cemetery in Charlestown. This fact was accepted by the Court as indication that the by-law, under the guise of a public-health regulation, was an absolute prohibition against an unpopular minority. It was therefore void because, having been enacted in bad faith, it imposed unreasonable restraints and directly infringed upon the right of property in the cemetery, without public advantage.[9]

In an unreported case in 1842, Shaw, sitting alone, for the first time struck down a general statute of the Massachusetts legislature. The case was *Commonwealth v. Coolidge*,[10] brought in 1842 on a writ of habeas corpus to secure the freedom of the fugitive slave George Latimer. The Abolitionist counsel based their argument on the provisions of the Massachusetts Personal Liberty Law of 1837 intended to guarantee fugitive slaves a jury trial. Shaw ruled that insofar as the state act concerned fugitive slaves, it conflicted with the constitutional provision for the return of runaways, the Fugitive Slave Law of 1793, and *Prigg v. Pennsylvania*,[11] and was therefore void.

The next exercise of the judicial power was in 1849, when the

---

[7] The literature on this subject is extensive. For a lively article which cites the important sources, see Ray A. Billington, "Burning of Charlestown Convent," *New England Quarterly*, 10:3–24 (March 1937). At the trial of the rioters, Shaw's conduct was scrupulously fair in the face of virulent religious prejudice. One of several important rulings was that "witnesses of all religious persuasions are placed on the same footing, and each is to stand on his own individual character" (Commonwealth v. Buzzell, 16 Pick. 154, 156, 1834).

[8] Austin v. Murray, 16 Pick. 121 (1834).

[9] For other cases in which municipal by-laws were voided, see City of Boston v. Jesse Shaw, 1 Metc. 130 (1840) and Coffin v. Nantucket, 5 Cush. 269 (1850). Worcester v. Western R.R., 4 Metc. 564 (1842) was on the illegality of a town tax on railroad property within the limits set aside for a public use.

[10] See *Law Reporter*, 5:482 (March 1843); *The Liberator*, Oct. 28, Nov. 5, and Nov. 24, 1842; *Boston Post*, Oct. 21, Oct. 24, and Nov. 1, 1842; and letter of City Attorney E. G. Austin, "To the Public," *The Emancipator and Free American* (Boston), Dec. 1, 1842. For a fuller discussion of this case, see *supra*, pp. 78–85.

Fisher v. McGirr, 1 Gray 1 (1854) was the first *reported* case in Massachusetts history in which the full bench of the Supreme Judicial Court declared unconstitutional a general statute of the state legislature of Massachusetts.

[11] 16 Peters 539, 617–618 (1842).

Court invalidated a private legislative resolve.[12] A party who held
lands only for his lifetime sold them in fee without providing for
the interests of persons who were entitled to them after his death.
The Court deemed the legislature's confirmation of the sales an
unconstitutional interference with vested rights, on ground that
the heirs had been deprived of their property without compensation "by a special act of legislation." "The court is bound to
presume," said Justice Fletcher tactfully, "that the effect and
operation of this part of the resolve escaped the notice of the legislature, and that it could not have been their intention to do what
in fact is done by this portion of the resolve, in its present form." [13]

During fifty years of *reported* decisions, with the exception
of two private resolves, the acts of the Massachusetts legislature
passed the gauntlet of the Supreme Judicial Court unscathed.
Then, in the six years from 1854 to 1860, the Court felled eight
statutes (three in 1854 alone) and construed another in such a
way as to defeat the intentions of the legislature.[14] Only the nature of these particular cases, which fortuitous circumstances had
brought up for review within a short span of years, accounts for
the frequent exercise of a judicial power long dormant. With the
exception of *Warren v. Mayor and Alderman of Charlestown*,[15]

[12] Sohier v. Massachusetts General Hospital, 3 Cush. 483 (1849).

[13] *Ibid.*, at 493.

[14] Fisher v. McGirr, 1 Gray 1 (1854); Commonwealth v. Proprietors of New
Bedford Bridge, 2 Gray 339 (1854); Warren v. Mayor & Alderman of Charlestown,
3 Gray 84 (1854); Sullivan v. Adams, 3 Gray 476 (1855); Jones v. Robbins, 8 Gray
329 (1857); Commonwealth v. Essex, 13 Gray 239 (1859); Robinson v. Richardson,
13 Gray 454 (1859); Central Bridge Corp. v. City of Lowell, 15 Gray 106 (1860).
The case in which the Court defeated the legislature's intention was Commonwealth
v. Anthes, 5 Gray 185 (1855).

[15] 3 Gray 84 (1854). In this case, St. 1854, ch. 433, by which Charlestown was
annexed to Boston, was voided for failing to provide the citizens of Charlestown
with representative districts and an opportunity to vote for members of the
General Court and Congress. The act was "hastily drawn" and could be properly
reenacted under the Court's instructions.
The case was important for the amendment, announced by the Chief Justice,
to his old rule of construction, that if a statute is unconstitutional in part, only
that part will be voided. This, Shaw now declared, is true only if the parts are
wholly independent of each other; but if mutually connected and dependent upon
each other, as in this case, so that the parts could not be carried into effect separately, then the whole act is void. This new rule of constitutional construction was
adopted by the U.S. Supreme Court in People v. Commissioners of Taxes &
Assessors, 94 U.S. 418 (1876), and thereafter was frequently cited and followed.
Two great, or rather, notorious cases deserve notice. In Pollock v. Farmers' Loan
& Trust Co., 158 U.S. 601, 635–636 (1895), Shaw's rule was quoted at length as a
justification for holding unconstitutional the entire income tax written into the
Tariff of 1894. But never was Shaw put to a more disreputable use than in
Carter v. Carter Coal Co., 298 U.S. 238, 316 (1935), when he was cited as an

which dealt with the right to vote, all the cases involved some violations of procedural due process or the sanctity of contracts.

II

Article I, section 10 of the United States Constitution, which forbids any state from impairing the obligation of a contract, was the principal weapon employed by the United States Supreme Court for the protection of vested rights during most of the nineteenth century. Beginning with *Fletcher v. Peck* in 1810,[16] there were a score of cases by 1860 in which state acts were held unconstitutional on ground of repugnance to the contract clause.[17] But in Massachusetts, the precedents of the national tribunal notwithstanding, not until 1854 did an act of the General Court fall victim to the contract clause; by 1860 there were only two more such cases.[18]

It was surely not from lack of opportunity that the Supreme Judicial Court refrained from resorting to the contract clause before 1854. Perhaps the most celebrated opportunity came in 1829, when Lemuel Shaw, of counsel for the plaintiff in the Charles River Bridge case, urged that the prohibition of that clause be applied to defendants' act of incorporation; but his views did not muster a Court majority.[19] As Chief Justice, Shaw rejected many an argument, based on the contract clause, that questioned the constitutionality of legislation. In 1839 alone, six cases raised the contract clause issue; in each the legislation was sustained.[20] In one of these cases the Court upheld a general law by which every act of incorporation passed after 1831 was subject "to amendment, alteration, or repeal, at the pleasure of the legislature; provided, that no act of incorporation shall be re-

authority for invalidating the New Deal's Bituminous Coal Act of 1935; although the Act twice declared that its price-fixing and labor provisions were separable, the Court held that the unconstitutionality of the one brought about the fall of the other.

[16] 6 Cranch 87 (1810).

[17] Benjamin F. Wright, *The Contract Clause of the Constitution* (Cambridge, 1938), pp. 63 ff.

[18] Commonwealth v. Proprietors of New Bedford Bridge, 2 Gray 339 (1854); Commonwealth v. Essex Co., 13 Gray 239 (1859); and Central Bridge Corp. v. City of Lowell, 15 Gray 106 (1860).

[19] Charles River Bridge Co. v. Warren Bridge Co., 7 Pick. 344 (1829).

[20] Bigelow v. Pritchard, 21 Pick. 169; Commonwealth v. Farmers & Mechanics Bank, 21 Pick. 542; Smith v. Morrison, 22 Pick. 430; Newburyport Turnpike Co. v. Eastern R.R., 23 Pick. 326; Crease v. Babcock, 23 Pick. 334; Boston Water Power Co. v. Boston & Worcester R.R. Co., 23 Pick. 360 — all 1839.

pealed, unless for some violation of its charter, or other default . . ." [21]

On the whole, strict construction of chartered rights, resolution of conflicts in favor of the public, and a generous interpretation of the legislature's powers, explain why the contract clause remained only an idle threat for so long. Only when the legislature attempted to increase the previously incurred obligations of public-service corporations, did the conservatism of the Court make itself felt on the subject of the sanctity of contracts.

In 1854, immediately preceding the first reported Massachusetts case in which an act was voided for violation of the contract clause, Shaw delivered an opinion intended to illuminate the views of the Court, although as many questions were raised as settled. The case was *Boston and Lowell Railroad v. Salem and Lowell et al.*[22] Construing a statute which by necessary implication granted exclusive rights to a public-service corporation, Shaw sustained the authority of the legislature to enter into any contract in pursuance of its unlimited powers to regulate the public rights and interests. A contract once made, Shaw declared, was binding and irrepealable; it vested rights which, even though exclusive, could not be divested.[23]

What then became of the unlimited powers to regulate? Could the legislature diminish, or even cede away, by contract, any of the sovereign powers of government? If a charter was irrepealable, except of course, for violation or other default, could the legislature covenant to disable itself from a future exercise of the powers entrusted to it for the regulation of the public good? There was no doubt that the power of eminent domain could not be contracted away; on this point Shaw himself had given the leading opinion, which was confirmed by the United States Supreme Court.[24] It was also settled, by decisions of that Court, that a contract of tax exemption is protected by the contract clause; that is, that the power to tax — surely an attribute

[21] Crease v. Babcock, 40 Mass. 334 (1839); Rev. Sts. 1835, ch. 44, sec. 23.

[22] 2 Gray 1 (1854). See also *supra.* pp. 124–126.

[23] On the point that a grant of exclusive rights will be held irrevocable, see The Binghampton Bridge, 3 Wallace 51 (1866); New Orleans Gas Co. v. Louisiana Light Co., 115 U.S. 650 (1885); Pearsall v. Great Northern R.R., 161 U.S. 646, 663 (1895).

[24] Boston Water Power Co. v. Boston & Worcester R.R. Co., 23 Pick. 360 (1839), discussed *supra,* pp. 123–124; and West River Bridge Co. v. Dix, 6 How. 507 (1848). See also Pennsylvania Hospital v. Philadelphia, 245 U.S. 20 (1917).

of sovereignty — could be alienated.[25] But the United States Supreme Court had by the 1850's given no opinion on the issue regarding the police power.

Shaw's position must be implied from his 1854 opinion in *Boston and Lowell Railroad v. Salem and Lowell Railroad et al.* Wisely advising the legislature to act considerately and make special reservations when chartering a public service corporation, he said:

> In making such grants and stipulations, no doubt great caution and foresight are requisite on the part of the legislature, a just estimate of the public benefit to be procured, and the cost at which it is to be obtained; and as great changes in the state of things may take place in the progress of time, a great increase of travel, for instance, on a given line, which changes cannot be specifically foreseen, it is the part of wisdom to provide for this, either by limitation of time, reservation of a power to reduce tolls, should they so increase, at the rates first fixed, as to become excessive, or of a right to repurchase the franchise, upon equitable terms, so that the contract shall not only be just and equal in the outset, but within reasonable limits continue to be so.[26]

In sum, Shaw may be said to have stood for the protection of public regulatory powers on condition that the regulation preserved inviolable whatever rights had been vested by contract. In other words, the contract clause did not remove from state control private rights and properties that depended upon charters for their existence or enforcement; but while those rights and properties might be regulated, in conformity with specific charter provisions or a general reservation[27] of the power to alter or amend, they could not be impaired.

The inference is clear: the police power, being limited by the contract clause, might indeed be contracted away in some respects. Subsequent cases made the inference concrete and answered two questions which had not yet been settled. (1) By general law the legislature had restricted its power of *repeal* to the case of a violation or default of a corporate charter enacted *after* March 11, 1831; but the restrictive condition of violation or default did not expressly apply to the powers of *amendment* or *alteration;*

[25] New Jersey v. Wilson, 7 Cranch 164 (1812); Piqua Branch of the State Bank v. Knoop, 16 How. 369 (1853). For a list of the later cases in which it was held that the powers of taxation may be surrendered, see Wright, *Contract Clause,* p. 74, note 44; 93, n. 8; 94, n. 10; 96, n. 20; and 97, n. 28; and on the subject in general, see Wright, pp. 179–194.

[26] 2 Gray 1, 33–34 (1854).

[27] Rev. Sts. 1835, ch. 44, sec. 23.

to what extent therefore were these powers limited by the contract clause? (2) To what extent were the powers of amendment or alteration limited by the contract clause in respect to corporate charters enacted *before* March 11, 1831? Moreover, both questions ask: could a charter be modified if the public good demanded?

Commonwealth v. Proprietors of New Bedford Bridge, decided in 1854,[28] provided an answer to the last question: regardless of the public good, a charter could not be modified by any act of the legislature materially changing the obligation of the contract. The defendants' original act of incorporation, dated 1796, authorized a toll bridge "with two suitable draws, which shall be at least thirty feet wide." [29] This had been amended in 1851 to specify draws of at least sixty feet, in order to relieve the congestion of river traffic.[30] When the defendants defied the legislature, an indictment was brought for a nuisance occasioned by obstruction of navigation.

For the Commonwealth, it was argued that the word "suitable" in the charter meant adequate to all the purposes of navigation: "What was suitable sixty years ago, when the bridge was built, may not be suitable for the much larger vessels and steamboats now used." [31] It was also contended on the same side that the legislature cannot, by a grant, deprive itself of authority to regulate the same public matter by subsequent acts. The defendants countered by arguing that their charter did not provide for an enlargement of the draws in any contingency, and that the amendment of 1851 was unconstitutional because it imposed additional duties that in effect divested rights without compensation.[32]

[28] 2 Gray 339 (1854).
[29] St. 1796, ch. 19, sec. 6.
[30] St. 1851, ch. 318, sec. 1.
[31] 2 Gray 339, 342–343.
[32] The case also settled a fundamental point in corporation law. Defendants argued that an indictment for nuisance could not be maintained against them, because a corporation, although liable to indictment for non-feasance, or an omission to perform a legal duty, is not amenable by this form of prosecution for a misfeasance, or the doing of any act unlawful in itself and injurious to the rights of others. It was said by the Court, in reply: "There are *dicta* in some of the early cases which sanction this broad doctrine, and it has thence been copied into text writers, and adopted to its fullest extent in a few modern decisions. But if it ever had any foundation, it had its origin at a time when corporations were few in number, and limited in their powers, and in the purposes for which they were created. Experience has shown the necessity of essentially modifying it; and the tendency of the more recent cases . . . has been to extend the application of all legal remedies to corporations, and assimilate them, as far as possible, in their legal duties and responsibilities, to individuals. . . . there is no good reason for

The Court, speaking through Justice Bigelow, decided that the indictment, based on the amendment to the charter, could not be maintained. The legislature had no authority "without the assent of the defendants, in any way [to] affect or impair the original terms of the charter, by annexing new conditions, or imposing additional duties, onerous in their nature, or inconsistent with a reasonable construction of the compact."[33] Since no power to amend or change the charter had been reserved, the act of 1851 was unconstitutional for establishing a burden not contemplated by the contract.[34]

But was it not a "reasonable" construction of the contract to hold that the provision for "suitable" draws implied that the legislature reserved a power to regulate the draws from time to time? No, because:

The Commonwealth has no more power or authority to construe the charter, than the corporation. By becoming a party to a contract with its citizens, *the government divests itself of its sovereignty* with respect to the terms and conditions of the compact, and its construction and interpretation, and stands in the same position as a private individual. If it were otherwise, the rights of parties contracting with the government would be held at the caprice of the sovereign, and exposed to all the risks arising from the corrupt or ill judged use of misguided power. The interpretation and construction of contracts, when drawn in question between parties, belongs exclusively to the judicial department of the government.[35]

These words do not compel admiration for the Court. The action of the legislature was surely neither capricious, corrupt, nor misguided; the Court's language to this effect was gratuitous. More important, the new doctrine that the police power could be "divested" by contract was a pernicious abstraction, for no doctrine of constitutional law that cripples simultaneously the power of government and the progress of commerce is practical or toler-

---

their exemption from the consequences of unlawful and wrongful acts committed by their agents in pursuance of authority derived from them. Such a rule would, in many cases, preclude all adequate remedy, and render reparation for an injury, committed by a corporation, impossible. . . . There is no principle of law which would thus furnish immunity to a corporation" (Commonwealth v. New Bedford Bridge, 2 Gray 339, 345–346, 1854).

[33] *Ibid.*, at 348.

[34] This decision is not easily reconcilable with an earlier decision which extended to railroads chartered *before* St. 1840, ch. 85, the liabilities imposed by that act for damage occasioned by fire communicated by locomotive engines. See Lyman v. Boston & Worcester R.R., 4 Cush. 288 (1849).

[35] 2 Gray 339, 350 (1854). Italics added.

able. But no judges appreciated this fact better than the bench presided over by Chief Justice Shaw.

Having declared the 1851 amendment to the original charter unconstitutional, Bigelow observed that the maintenance of draws suitable to the river traffic "at the time of their construction" did not constitute compliance with the charter itself. "We think the scope and purpose of the act were much broader, and that it was framed with a wise forecast to meet future exigencies." Adopting the Commonwealth's position, he explained that the legislature had intended to provide permanently against any impediments to navigation. The requirement that the draws be "suitable" imposed an obligation of adapting them to changing needs. If the draws were not suitable, defendants "violate the duty imposed on them by the terms of their charter, and thereby cause an unlawful obstruction to a navigable stream." [36]

What appeared to be discordant parts within the same opinion was, on the contrary, a harmonious scheme. Resolution came with this announcement: "Whether the defendants have in fact complied with the terms of their charter, by constructing their draws in a suitable manner . . . is to be adjusted and settled in the regular tribunals . . ." [37] Thus, judicial review enabled the Court to eat its cake and have it too: having ruled that the police power might be at least partially surrendered, it decided that the corporation might still be regulated — under judicial supervision. That is, although the legislature could not amend the original charter in the way it sought to, the corporation might be indicted for maintaining a nuisance by not providing suitable draws. Indeed the Commonwealth might conceivably sue for revocation of the charter on ground of default.

In the end, then, the Court insured the free flow of river commerce even as it set limits on the power of the legislature to increase the obligations of a contract. Of course, at common law, questions of nuisance, as in the present case, were customarily adjudicated by the courts. But from the standpoint of constitu-

[36] *Ibid.*, at 351–352 (1854).

[37] *Ibid.*, at 352–353. This decision on the sole right of the courts to construe a contract and determine whether its obligations have been complied with, was put to an unusual use in the U.S. Supreme Court by Field, J., dissenting, in an effort to expand judicial review by enforcing the contract clause against Congress. See Sinking Fund Cases, 99 U.S. 700, 760 (1878) and Bridge Co. v. U.S., 105 U.S. 470, 504 (1881). The decision of the Shaw Court in the New Bedford Bridge case was also cited by the Supreme Court as an authority for the irrevocability of an express contract. See St. Louis v. Western Union Telegraph Co., 148 U.S. 92, 103 (1892).

tional law, the case constituted an early precedent in which the judiciary assumed responsibility for determining issues of fact and policy better left to an informed legislature.[38]

The doctrine that the police power could be "divested" by contract was substantially modified only a year after it had been promulgated by the Court, though the modification was not expressly stated. In *Calder v. Kurby,* in 1855,[39] it was held that a liquor license, though granted for a valuable consideration, was not a contract within the meaning of the Constitution and consequently could be annulled at the pleasure of the legislature. A contrary rule would have brought within the ambit of the contract clause the whole field of community health and morals, with the result that regulatory powers over even these subjects of domestic police might also be surrendered by contract.[40] But by distinguishing a license to sell from an act of incorporation, the Court could rule that in the absence of such an act, the legislature "might regulate trade, prevent injurious practices, and promote the good order and welfare of the community," as well as modify or annul at will any privilege not protected by the contract clause.[41] Professor Freund characterized this decision as "an extreme application of the theory that the state cannot by any act of its own hamper or burden the future exercise of the police power." [42]

Later decisions of the United States Supreme Court expressly declared the police power to be inalienable in respect to the public health, safety, or morals.[43] It seems, however, by the doc-

[38] Cf. Crease v. Babcock, 23 Pick. 334 (1839).

[39] 5 Gray 597 (1855).

[40] No court ever endorsed such a doctrine. See Stone v. Mississippi, 101 U.S. 814 (1880).

[41] 5 Gray 597, 598 (1855).

[42] Ernst Freund, *The Police Power* (Chicago, 1904), sec. 564, p. 591. See also Thomas M. Cooley, *A Treatise on Constitutional Limitations* (Boston, 1903, 7th ed.), p. 400 and note thereto.

[43] Beer Co. v. Massachusetts, 97 U.S. 25 (1878); Fertilizing Co. v. Hyde Park, 97 U.S. 33 (1878); Stone v. Mississippi, 101 U.S. 814 (1880); Butchers' Union Co. v. Crescent City Co., 111 U.S. 746 (1884). In the latter case, the Court declared, *per* Miller, J.: "While we are not prepared to say that the legislature can make valid contracts on no subject embraced in the largest definition of the police power, we think that in regard to two subjects so embraced, it cannot, by any contract, limit the exercise of those powers to the prejudice of the general welfare. These are the *public health* and *public morals*" (111 U.S. 746, 750). Benjamin F. Wright stated that the post-Civil War development of the concept of the inalienable police power — which was countered by the growth of the due process clause as a limitation — did not represent an attempt to expand the scope of the police power, "but a means of restricting that scope in its application to certain varieties of legislation believed to be of especial importance to the health, morals, or safety of the community" (*Contract Clause*, p. 91).

trine of still other decisions, that in respect to controls over corporate enterprise, the police power might indeed be contracted away,[44] although in a case where the legislature has explicitly reserved the right of regulation and no exclusive grant has been made, modification or revocation of grants to public utility and private corporations of all kinds has been sustained.[45] Freund, who concluded that the police power "in the narrower sense of the term" was inalienable, asserted that the extent to which the contract clause "restricts the operation of the police power has never been precisely formulated."[46]

III

The decision of the Shaw Court in the New Bedford Bridge case had turned on the fact that the corporation had been chartered before the act reserving to the legislature the power to amend all charters granted after 1831. But what if the corporation had been chartered *after* that date? To what extent were the reserved powers of amendment or alteration limited by the contract clause? This question was decided in a leading opinion by Shaw in the 1859 case of *Commonwealth v. Essex Co.*[47]

The case presented these facts. The corporation, in erecting a dam for the creation of water power, had complied with the provisions of its charter of 1845 by building sluices or fishways across the dam, in a mode prescribed by public commissioners, to permit the passage of migratory fish. The fishways, however, soon proved to be insufficient. When the corporation requested authorization to increase its capital stock, the legislature, in 1848, seized an opportunity by granting permission only on condition that liability be assumed for damage to the fishing rights of riparian owners above the dam. Upon its acceptance of the act of 1848,

---

[44] New Orleans Gas Co. v. La. Light Co., 115 U.S. 650 (1885); New Orleans Water Works Co. v. Rivers, 115 U.S. 674 (1885); Louisville Gas Co. v. Citizens Gas Co. 115 U.S. 683 (1885). Railroad Commissioners Cases, 116 U.S. 335 (1886), holding that the state, by positive grant, can divest itself of the power to regulate railroad charges; Stone v. Farmers' Loan and Trust Co. 116 U.S. 307, 325 (1886); see also, among some of the later cases, City Ry. Co. v. Citizens St. R.R. Co., 166 U.S. 557 (1897); Walla Walla v. Walla Walla Water Co., 172 U.S. 1 (1898); Louisville v. Cumberland Tel. & Tel. Co., 224 U.S. 649 (1912); Grand Trunk Western Ry. v. South Bend, 263 U.S. 125 (1923). On decisions to the point that municipal rate controls over public utilities may be contracted away, see Wright, *Contract Clause*, pp. 137–138, 174–175. On the alienability of the police power in general, see *ibid.*, pp. 141–148, 170–177; Robert L. Hale, "The Contract Clause: II," *Harvard Law Review*, 57:654–663, May 1944); Freund, *Police Power*, secs. 362–363, pp. 361–368.

[45] Wright, *Contract Clause*, pp. 141–142, 211.

[46] Freund, *Police Power*, sec. 362, p. 362; sec. 555, p. 582.

[47] 13 Gray 239 (1859).

the corporation paid out damages to riparian owners roughly equivalent to what the costs would have been to perfect the old fishways. Eight years later, in 1856, the legislature required the corporation to perfect the fishways.[48] The question before the Court, then, was whether the act of 1856 was a valid exercise of the reserved power to alter or amend, or an unconstitutional impairment of the contract expressed in the act of 1848.

The decision went against the constitutionality of the act of 1856. Shaw did not rule whether, in the absence of the intervening act of 1848, the requirement of 1856 might have been a valid amendment of the original charter of 1845; yet he intimated as much.[49] He explained that although the obstruction of the passage of fish was not a common-law offense, to have such unobstructed passage was a public right; accordingly, private rights, incident to the public right, were subject to regulation by the legislature.

But the legislature might exercise, "diminish," or "release" its regulatory powers as in its judgment the public good might require. By the act of 1848, a choice had been made, as Shaw put it,

to substitute, for the public right intended to be provided for by the fishways required, a provision for the payment of damages by the company to every riparian owner of fishing rights along the river above said dam, giving them a remedy against the company where none existed before, for all damages occasioned by the stopping or impeding the passage of fish up and down the Merrimac River by the said dam.[50]

In other words, instead of requiring the better performance of a preëxisting duty, the act of 1848 imposed a different and new liability upon the corporation — exempting it, in effect, from making suitable fishways. The act of 1856 was unconstitutional for annulling the exemption and increasing the obligations of the contract.

Could the act of 1856 be justified as coming within "the power of the legislature to amend or alter"? "It seems to us," declared Shaw, "that this power must have some limit, though it

[48] St. 1845, ch. 163; St. 1848, ch. 295; St. 1856, ch. 289.
[49] See Commissioners of Inland Fisheries v. Holyoke Water Power Co., 104 Mass. 451 (1870), where the legislature was sustained in requiring new and better fisheries. The exercise of the reserved powers to alter and amend bore directly on the original charter of the corporation, without any intervening contract complicating the question.
[50] 13 Gray 239, 251 (1859).

is difficult to define it." After posing several hypothetical cases, he "extracted" from them a rule by which reserved powers might be reconciled with the limitation of the contract clause: "where, under power in a charter, rights have been acquired and become vested, no amendment or alteration of the charter can take away the property rights which have become vested under a legitimate exercise of the powers granted." [51]

This rule wanted precision, but its import seems clear. A reasonable exercise of the reserved powers to carry into effect the original purpose of a grant would be judicially tolerated;[52] but no exercise of the reserved powers would justify defeating the object of the grant or substantially impairing vested rights.[53] The compromise position between regulation and property, together with the comprehensiveness of the rule, recommended itself to the Supreme Court of the United States. In 1873, in one of the earliest cases involving the same question which Shaw had decided, his rule was adopted by the high court as a useful guide.[54] Thereafter it was quoted with approval in several cases, and still survives as a limitation on the exercise of the police power.[55]

IV

When the work of the Shaw Court in relation to the contract clause is considered as a whole, the fact that astonishes is the limited serviceability of that clause as a bulwark to vested rights.

[51] *Ibid.*, at 253.

[52] See City of Roxbury v. Boston & Providence R.R. Corp., 6 Cush. 424, 431–432 (1850), where it was held, *per* Shaw, C.J., that the reserved power must be exercised "reasonably"; Massachusetts General Hospital v. State Mutual Life Assoc., 4 Gray 227, 232, 234 (1855) where it was held, *per* Dewey, J., that a regulation of corporate profits under the reserved power was reasonable; Commonwealth v. Fitchburg R.R. Co., 12 Gray 180, 188 (1858), for the dictum, *per* Thomas, J., that the legislature, under the reserved powers, may revoke the charter of a public service corporation which neglects its duties to the public; Commissioner of Inland Fisheries v. Holyoke Water Power Co., 104 Mass. 451 (1870) (see note 49, *supra*), sustained in Holyoke Co. v. Lyman, 82 U.S. 500 (1873).

[53] In the third and last case in which the Shaw Court voided a statute as repugnant to the contract clause, Central Bridge Corp. v. City of Lowell, 15 Gray 106 (1860), the corporation was rechartered, by St. 1843, ch. 50, with authorization to reconstruct its bridge and to include, in the reissuance of its capital stock, an extra $10,000 to represent the amount not yet reimbursed for the original cost. It was held, *per* Shaw, C.J., that St. 1857, ch. 205, which repealed the $10,000 provision of the earlier act, was unconstitutional for altering the contract.

[54] Miller v. State 82 U.S. 478, 498 (1873). See also Holyoke Co. v. Lyman, 82 U.S. 500, 516–518 (1873); Sinking Fund Cases, 99 U.S. 700, 741, 758 (1878); Lake Shore & Mich. S. R.R. Co. v. Smith, 173 U.S. 684, 690 (1898).

[55] Superior Water, Light & Power Co. v. City of Superior, 263 U.S. 125, 136–137 (1923).

If there was a link between capitalism and constitutionalism, it was the contract clause as construed by the Supreme Court, whether under Marshall or Taney. Brooks Adams once commented that the "capitalist . . . regards the constitutional form of government which exists in the United States, as a convenient method of obtaining his own way against a majority . . ." [56] Before the substantive interpretation of due process of law — an interpretation rejected by Shaw[57] — the contract clause was the chief repository of doctrines of constitutional limitations upon the majority's power to regulate the economy. Constitutional law at the federal-court level in the antebellum years was littered with the corpses of state enactments impaled on the contract clause. But not in Massachusetts. So far as the Shaw Court is concerned, the "basic doctrine of American constitutional law," contrary to Professor Corwin,[58] was not the doctrine of vested rights. It was the doctrine of plenary police power.

Not only were there merely three cases in which the Shaw Court voided legislative alterations of chartered rights, but in each the essential regulatory powers of the state were undiminished. In the New Bedford Bridge case, the corporation could take little comfort in the abstract doctrine that the police power might in some respects be contracted away. From the standpoint of the corporation the decision meant that unless it enlarged the draws of its bridge to accommodate river traffic, it stood guilty of maintaining a public nuisance; and for violation of its charter it stood in jeopardy of having its franchise revoked. The case was a Pyrrhic victory for vested rights, because the beneficiary of the decision was the public right to unclogged navigation.[59]

In the other two contract clause cases, the reserved power to alter or amend was defeated, but only as to the particularly faithless and arbitrary ways in which it was being exercised. The power of the legislature to force an improvement in the fishways of the Essex Bridge Company was actually sustained; what the Court objected to was the increasing of the obligations of the charter in this way *after* the legislature had already exercised its reserved power to make the company pay to riparian owners an

[56] Brooks Adams, *The Theory of Social Revolutions* (New York, 1914), p. 214.
[57] Discussed *supra*, pp. 261–265.
[58] Edward S. Corwin, "The Basic Doctrine of American Constitutional Law," *Selected Essays on Constitutional Law* (Chicago, 1938, 5 vols.), I, 101.
[59] Commonwealth v. New Bedford Bridge, 2 Gray 339 (1854).

amount in damages that would have been sufficient to improve the fishways.[60]

In the case of the Central Bridge Company, the legislature's power to regulate tolls and profits and to provide that a privately built bridge should eventually become the property of the public was unquestioned. Moreover, the Court ruled that the value of the bridge as a structure need not be paid for by the public, upon appropriating it, since the company had been reimbursed in tolls for the cost. The Court simply refused to permit the legislature to renege on its side of a bargain made in the public interest.[61]

In each of these cases, the Court protected the public interest, even when invoking the contract clause as a limitation on the power of the legislature. This generalization certainly does not describe the contract-clause decisions of the Supreme Court of the United States. The fact is that the Shaw Court was oriented toward the public interest, not vested interests — and this explains dozens of cases in which the legislature was sustained in the face of an argument derived from the contract clause.

[60] Commonwealth v. Essex Co., 13 Gray 239 (1850).
[61] Central Bridge Corp. v. City of Lowell, 15 Gray 106 (1860). See note 53, *supra*.

1 5

CONSTITUTIONAL LIMITATIONS

Criminal Justice and the Rights of the Accused

I

Due process of law lies at the core of the idea of justice. Vicious and ad hoc procedures, always used by tyrannies to victimize nonconformists and those who resisted oppression, have left their wake of "mutilated bodies and shattered minds along the way to the cross, the guillotine, the stake and the hangman's noose." [1] The historic purpose of due process is to guarantee fair and regularized procedures by which to determine whether life can be snuffed out or liberty abridged. In a civilized society, respecting the dignity of all men, misuse of the law-enforcement process is vigilantly guarded against by insuring that every citizen, in the words of the Massachusetts Declaration of Rights, "be tried by judges as free, impartial and independent, as the lot of humanity will admit." [2] It is more important to a free society that guilt or innocence be fairly judged than that the guilty be punished. The price is that some offenses go unpunished, but it is a price well worth paying to avoid the dangers of a police state. As Justice Holmes once said, "it is a lesser evil that some criminals should escape than that the Government should play an ignoble part." [3]

The fact is that fair and regularized procedures are crucial to the survival of all our most treasured rights. A man's home cannot be his "castle," his property cannot be his own, his right to express his convictions or to worship his God is robbed of security, if for the exercise of any of these rights he can be searched, ar-

[1] Chambers v. Fla., 309 U.S. 227, 236 (1940), *per* Black, J.
[2] Mass. Declaration of Rights, Article XXIX.
[3] Olmstead v. U.S., 277 U.S. 438, 470 (1928).

rested, and imprisoned by unjust procedures and unfair evidence. In a nation whose history has not been drenched with the blood of martyrs to the cause of conscience, the dangers to liberty derive from overzealous rather than from tyrannical law-enforcement agencies pursuing criminals rather than heretics. Even so, "the history of American freedom," as Justice Frankfurter noted, "is, in no small measure, the history of procedure." [4] "Bitter experience," he added, "has sharpened our realization that a major test of true democracy is the fair administration of justice. . . . Mr. Justice Brandeis and Mr. Justice Holmes gave quiet warning when they observed that 'in the development of our liberty insistence upon procedural regularity has been a large factor.' It is not for nothing that most of the provisions of the Bill of Rights are concerned with matters of procedure." [5]

As long as Lemuel Shaw's name will be remembered, it will be associated with mankind's sense of justice and fair play. There is a story still current among members of the Massachusetts Bar of the two prizefighters who, called as witnesses in a case, stood in the back of the courtroom where Shaw presided. As they watched him, two "blue black jaws dropped in admiration, and one said, not so much to the other as to himself, 'Christ, what a referee!' " [6] During the thirty years of Shaw's Chief Justiceship, the rights of accused persons were exactingly and constantly observed.

II

Probably a chance fact, but one of symbolic significance, was that the first reported decision of the Supreme Judicial Court in which a general statute was held unconstitutional turned on ground that the criminal proceeding authorized by the legislature was, in Shaw's words, "subversive of the rights of the subject." [7] Shaw's opinion in this case, *Fisher v. McGirr,* decided in 1854, belongs in the select group of his greatest utterances. The case presented a clash between the police power and civil liberties, specifically the rights to be free from unreasonable searches and seizures, to have notice, to have a charge clearly described, to confront one's accusers and give evidence on one's own behalf, to be tried by jury, and to be presumed innocent until proved guilty

[4] Malinski v. N.Y., 324 U.S. 410, 419 (1945).
[5] Sachar v. U.S., 343 U.S. 1, 23 and 25 (1952). See Burdeau v. McDowell, 256 U.S. 465, 477 (1921) for the remark by Brandeis.
[6] Charles P. Curtis, *It's Your Law* (Cambridge, 1954), p. 2.
[7] Fisher v. McGirr, 1 Gray 1, 39 (1854).

by admissible evidence. In a classic construction of the "law of the land" clause, Shaw held a statute void for denying the principles of due process that protected citizens in their liberty and property; and at the same time, he supported the plenary powers of the state, by due process of law, to prohibit and destroy certain property illegally used.

Fisher v. McGirr was on the constitutionality of the state prohibition act of 1852, which outlawed the manufacture or keeping of liquor for sale.[8] The main target of attack was Section 14, which provided for enforcement proceedings. This section directed that if any three persons should swear out a complaint that in their belief liquors were being kept or intended for sale in a stated place, the magistrate must issue a warrant of search. The sheriff, upon searching the designated premises, would seize any intoxicants found and impound them as evidence. The owner of the liquor, if known to the officer, was to be "summoned forthwith" before the magistrate, and if he failed to appear, or if appearing, could not prove that the liquor was lawfully held (as for interstate trade), the property would be declared forfeit and destroyed. The guilty individual was subject to fine and imprisonment.[9]

Rufus Choate, attorney general, argued in favor of the power of the government to protect the public health and morals by destroying property whose illegal use had been declared a nuisance by the legislature. Choate's arguments on this point, rebutting the plaintiffs' contention that property had been unconstitutionally divested without compensation, were successful. But he argued in vain to defend the validity of the mode of proceedings set forth in Section 14. He strained the words of the statute to instruct the Court how it should be "properly construed"; and urged that the Court should resolve all doubts in favor of the statute, supply deficiencies, correct inadvertences, and "make the proceedings what they ought to have been made in terms." [10]

Speaking for the Court, Shaw sustained the power of the legislature to control property in such a case as this, and by "due process of law" to provide both for the punishment of the of-

---

[8] St. 1852, ch. 322, sec. 14. Exceptions were made for imported liquor still in the original package, liquor intended for export or for special uses, such as medicinal or sacramental.

[9] Section 15 of St. 1852, ch. 322, provided for a two-week public notice, before judgment, to enable the owner to appear, in case he was unknown to the sheriff.

[10] 1 Gray 1, 18 (1854).

fender and the uncompensated destruction of his noxious property.[11] But what was "due process of law"? Had the statute, by Section 14, provided for such process? The questions would be answered by reference to certain principles of justice, intended for the security of persons and their property, which had been written into the Declaration of Rights of the state constitution.

Shaw found that the section violated Article XIV of the Declaration of Rights, which secured citizens against unreasonable searches and seizures. Neither the search warrant, nor the sworn complaint upon which it issued, had to name the person allegedly in possession of liquor with intent to sell illegally. Such a warrant, Shaw ruled, was too general and did not restrict the searching officer's authority. Because he was empowered to make a general search, rather than for particularly described liquors, those lawfully, as well as unlawfully held, might be — indeed, would be — seized. Even property intended for export, or imported and still in the original packages, would be seized: here was an interference with commerce that was under national jurisdiction.

To this line of reasoning an objection intrudes, namely, that the statute provided for as much certainty and definition of authority as circumstances could admit. For how could there be certainty in distinguishing between lawfully and unlawfully held liquors, and in naming their owner, before the search? Shaw was ready with a good answer: ". . . if these modes of accomplishing a laudable purpose, and of carrying into effect a good and wholesome law, cannot be pursued without a violation of the constitution, they cannot be pursued at all, and other means must be devised not open to such objections." [12]

Shaw had only begun his analysis. He meant to examine every facet of Section 14 in the light of "immutable" principles of justice to expose all the unconstitutional impurities. The measure disregarded other safeguards for the security of persons and property, besides the guarantee against unreasonable searches and seizures. Article X of the Declaration of Rights declared, "Each individual has a right to be protected in the enjoyment of his property, according to the standing laws"; and Article XII was a bastion of civil liberty:

[11] See Chapter 9, *supra,* p. 262, for a discussion of this aspect of Shaw's opinion and the quotation on due process.

[12] 1 Gray 1, 31 (1854).

No subject shall be held to answer for any crime or offense, until the same is fully and plainly, substantially and formally, described to him; or be compelled to accuse, or furnish evidence against himself; and every subject shall have a right to produce all proofs that may be favorable to him; to meet the witnesses against him face to face, and to be fully heard in his defence by himself, or his counsel at his election; and no subject shall be arrested, imprisoned, despoiled or deprived of his property, immunities or privileges, put out of the protection of the law, exiled, or deprived of his life, liberty or estate; but by the judgment of his peers, or the law of the land.

With these guarantees in mind, Shaw reviewed the enforcement proceedings step by step.

The complaint, under which the warrant issued, was *ex parte;* there was no provision in the statute for reëxamining the complainants at a later stage of the proceedings, nor was the defendant given an opportunity to meet them face to face. Since the warrant did not designate the person whose property was being taken, he did not have to be summoned to defend it or answer the complaint unless he "shall be known to the officer," who must act upon hearsay. But should the officer find the right person, he was to be "summoned forthwith." If he did not appear forthwith, his property might be adjudged forfeit and sentence might be declared against him personally, without further notice or proof. No day in court was given, no allowance made for excusable absence, no provision that personal notice should be given. These measures, Shaw concluded, were wholly inconsistent with the right of defending one's self and one's property, and of finding a safe remedy in the laws. The enforcement of a penal statute, he added,

should be surrounded with all the safeguards necessary to the security of the innocent, having the full benefit of the maxim, that every person shall be presumed innocent until his guilt be established by proof. He should have notice of the charge of guilty purpose . . . a time and opportunity to prepare his defence, an opportunity to meet the witnesses against him face to face, and the benefit of the legal presumption of innocence.[13]

The infirmities of Section 14 would seem apparent. But Shaw was not satisfied. He had a still "more formidable" objection against its constitutionality: no provision was made for a trial. The law-of-the-land or due-process clause of Article XII of the

[13] *Ibid.,* at 35–36.

Declaration of Rights, declared Shaw, had been understood "from Magna Charta to the present time, to mean a trial by jury, in a regular course of legal and judicial proceedings." [14] But this statute expressly directed that if defendant failed to appear, his property was forfeit with no further ado. If he did appear, his confiscated stock, even if illegally seized, stood as mute presumption of his guilt, but it could not be evidence to convict, because it was uncorroborated by such additional legal proofs of intent to sell as sworn testimony by witnesses. Yet no such testimony was required. Proof against defendant could not be found in complainants' oath. It was *ex parte,* made only to obtain a warrant, and was mere opinion, not fact. But if the defendant could not prove himself innocent, judgment for forfeiture and sentence passed automatically by a justice of the peace or a judge of the police court, vested with jurisdiction over an unlimited amount of property. "This statute," asserted Shaw, "declares that a subject may be deprived of his property . . . in an unusual mode, not by the judgment of his peers, or the law of the land." [15]

Thus far Shaw had considered the enforcement measures of Section 14 primarily as a proceeding *in rem,* by which property was sequestered, forfeited, and destroyed. He was only half done. Still to be examined were the proceedings *in personam,* by which offenders were personally punished through fine and imprisonment. With the requirements of the law of the land, or due process of law, uppermost in his mind, Shaw retraced the statute point by point. The effect was equally devastating. The statute was "subversive" of personal rights on many of the same grounds for its invalidity as a proceeding *in rem.*

One of the most notable features of this opinion was the novel rule of construction Shaw announced for the guidance of the Court in cases bearing on the guarantees of the Declaration of Rights.

In a law directing a series of measures, which in their operation are in danger of encroaching upon private rights; vesting in subordinate officers large powers, which, when most carefully guarded, are liable to be mistaken or abused, and which are to direct, limit and regulate the judicial conduct of a large class of magistrates; it is highly important that the powers conferred, and the practical directions given,

---

[14] *Ibid.,* at 37. See also Thomas M. Cooley, *Constitutional Limitations* (Boston, 1903, 7th ed.), pp. 500–505.

[15] *Ibid.,* at 39.

be so clear and well defined, that they may serve as a safe guide to all such officers and magistrates, in their respective duties; and in these respects, the statute itself must, on its face, be conformable to the constitution. . . . Besides; the rights of parties ought not to be made to depend on a doubtful interpretation of various, and in some respects, incompatible and conflicting provisions.[16]

As Shaw asserted, the legislature had probably not intended to direct a proceeding subversive of personal rights; the magistrates would probably have acted in conformity to the law of the land. But the Court could not be governed by such presumptions. The guarantees of the Declaration of Rights were "absolutely necessary," admonished Shaw, "to preserve the advantages of liberty, and maintain a free government." Therefore, "the people have a right to require of their lawgivers and magistrates an exact and constant observance of them." [17] Indeed, so important were these rights and freedoms that in the case of a statute that on its face seemed to impair them, the normal presumption of constitutionality would not obtain; nor would the Court defer to the best intentions of the legislature by construing the statute in its most favorable light. It is interesting to note that ninety years after Shaw had suggested this rule, the United States Supreme Court adopted a similar position with respect to the freedoms secured by the First Amendment.[18] The Kneeland blasphemy case is evidence, however, that Shaw himself did not apply this rule when those freedoms were at stake. His defense of civil liberties was restricted to the procedural rights of accused persons.

Fisher v. McGirr was distinguished for more than its rule of construction by which the judiciary can protect procedural liberties. Shaw's opinion was an order that the power of government to act upon vested rights be carried into effect by the law of the land — or not at all. Voiding the statute meant that the legislature could not unilaterally make the law of the land, for not every proceeding authorized by the legislature was due process of law. As a general rule, such process comprehended the forms and methods which surrounded a regular course of legal and judicial proceedings, in conformity with the guarantees written into bills of rights. Shaw's use of due process of law as a procedural limi-

---

[16] *Ibid.*, at 40–41.

[17] *Ibid.*, at 33.

[18] Thomas v. Collins, 323 U.S. 516, 529–530 (1945). See Robert E. Cushman, "Ten Years of the Supreme Court: 1937–1947," Part V, "Civil Liberties," in *American Political Science Review*, 42:43 (Feb. 1948).

tation on the police power stands as an instructive contrast, historically, to the novel, if not spurious, Wynehammer doctrine,[19] which in the aftermath of the Fourteenth Amendment became lodged in American constitutional law.

Shortly after *Fisher v. McGirr,* the legislature enacted a new prohibition statute[20] which complied with the standards laid down by the Chief Justice — except in one respect. Section 32 provided that pending the appeal of a conviction by a justice of the peace, or police court, "appellant shall be committed to abide the sentence of the said justice or court," until he furnished certain sureties. One Betsey Sullivan, convicted for selling without a license, failed to provide the sureties and was committed to serve her time, while waiting for appeal to the court of common pleas. On a writ of habeas corpus she was brought before Shaw, who held Section 32 unconstitutional.[21] "This is a penal statute," he said, "and must be construed strictly." Ruling that Article XII of the Massachusetts Declaration of Rights could be satisfied only by "an unobstructed and unclogged right of appeal" to a court where a jury trial might be had *de novo,* he reasoned that that right had been "trammeled" by the conditions set forth in the statute.

Robinson v. Richardson[22] was important for clarifying and enforcing the doctrine that a search warrant can be used only for a public purpose. The Court, speaking through Justice Merrick, voided that part of a statute[23] which authorized the issuance of warrants, by judges of insolvency, to search for property of debtors. "Search warrants," declared Merrick, "were never recognized by the common law as processes which might be availed of by individuals in the course of civil proceedings, or for the maintenance of any mere private right; but their use was confined to cases of public prosecutions, instituted and pursued for the suppression of crime or the detection and punishment of criminals." [24] Any warrant not implementing a public purpose would violate the fundamental principle, protected by Article XIV of the Declaration of Rights, that every citizen is to be free from all unreasonable searches and seizures of his person and possessions.

[19] Wynehammer v. People, 13 N.Y. 378 (1856). See the discussion of this case, *supra,* pp. 261–262.

[20] St. 1855, ch. 215.

[21] Sullivan v. Adams, 3 Gray 476 (1855).

[22] 13 Gray 454 (1859).

[23] St. 1856, ch. 284, sec. 36.

[24] 13 Gray 454, 456.

III

One of Shaw's most influential opinions, handed down in 1855, was on the unconstitutionality of any statute authorizing a jury to judge the law as well as the facts in a criminal case. This decision in *Commonwealth v. Anthes*[24] defeated the legislature's intention to give effect to a popular belief that the right to be judged by one's peers meant the right of one's peers to decide issues of law against the instructions of the trial judge. This popular belief derived from three sources: the practice of juries in the colonial period when, in the absence of a skilled legal profession, jurors were apt to be as qualified as judges; the inheritance from a revolutionary generation which denounced the right of royal officials to enforce "tyrannical" acts against patriotic offenders; and the institution of the general verdict which gives the jury the power, if not the right, to determine the law.[25] Still, mid-nineteenth-century Massachusetts was concerned more with the right of twelve good men and true to decide for themselves whether liquor license laws were valid in a proceeding against the local tavern-owner, than with the sources of that right.

In 1845, in *Commonwealth v. Porter*,[26] Shaw held that the judge had the sole right in a criminal case to decide the law involved in the issue, and the jury were obligated to receive the law from him. The outcry against this decision expressed itself in the state constitutional convention of 1853, which voted for an amendment giving to juries the right denied them by the Shaw Court. Although this amendment failed of popular ratification, along with all the others proposed by the convention, the legislature in 1855 enacted the following statute: "In all trials for criminal offenses, it shall be the duty of the jury to try, according to established forms and principles of law, all causes which shall be committed to them and, after having received the instructions of the court, to decide at their discretion, by a general verdict, both the fact and law involved in the issue. . . ."[27] It was this statute

[24] 5 Gray 185–304 (1855).
[25] See Mark DeWolfe Howe, "Juries as Judges of Criminal Law," *Harvard Law Review*, 52:582–616 (Feb. 1939), for a comprehensive discussion of the subject.
[26] 10 Metc. 263 (1845).
[27] St. 1855, ch. 152. The statute continued: "but it shall be the duty of the court to superintend the course of the trials, to decide upon the admission and rejection of evidence, and upon all questions of law raised during the trials, and upon collateral and incidental proceedings, and also to charge the jury, and to all bills of exception; and the court may grant a new trial in cases of conviction."

which Shaw nullified in *Commonwealth v. Anthes* in 1855 by ruling that it merely declared the common law as he had laid it down ten years earlier in *Commonwealth v. Porter*.[28]

Shaw's treatise-like opinion in the Anthes case on the respective provinces of judge and jury was characterized by the United States Supreme Court, when adopting his views in 1894, as "the fullest examination of the question upon principle, as well as upon authority, to be found in the decisions of any state court . . ."[29] The views expressed by Shaw were as follows. There are two distinct inquiries in every criminal prosecution. First, if there is such a law as that on which the indictment is founded, does it comprehend the acts charged against the defendant? This

[28] Before the Porter case in 1845, there had been no decision on the question in Massachusetts, although there were many dicta at nisi prius and in the *Massachusetts Reports*. For example, Shaw himself had declared in 1838, "In criminal cases, by the form in which the issue is made up, the jury pass upon the whole matter of law and fact" (Commonwealth v. Kneeland, 20 Pick. 206, 222, 1838). See also Commonwealth v. Blanding, 3 Pick. 305 (1825); Commonwealth v. Knapp, 10 Pick. 477, 495 (1830). St. 1807, ch. 140, sec. 15, which was in force in the state until 1836, affirmed the right of the jury to decide, at their discretion, both the law and the fact; this statute was never tested in the courts.

Before the Porter case, where the question had arisen in other state courts, the right of the jury to judge the law was favored in People v. Croswell, 3 Johns Cas. (N.Y.) 337 (1804), *per* Kent, J., with Lewis, C.J. and Livingston, J., dissenting; Bartholemew v. Clark, 1 Conn. 472, 481 (1816); Townsend v. State, 2 Blackf. (Ind.) 150 (1828); State v. Wilkinson, 2 Vt. 480, 488 (1829); McGowan v. State, 9 Yerger (Tenn.) 184, 194–195 (1836); Bostwick v. Gasquet, 10 La. 80 (1836); State v. Snow, 18 Me. 346 (1841); State v. Jones, 5 Ala. 666 (1843).

Only the courts of Kentucky, Ohio, and New Hampshire opposed the right of the jury before 1845. Montee v. Commonwealth, 26 Kent. R. 132, 149–152 (1830); Montgomery v. State, 11 Ohio R. 424, 427 (1842); Pierce v. State, 13 N.H. 536, 554 (1843).

The earlier cases in the U.S. Circuit Courts were preponderantly in favor of the right of jury. Henfield's Case, Fed. Cas. No. 6,360 (C.C.D.Pa. 1793); Fries' Case, Fed. Cas. No. 5,126 (C.C.D.Pa. 1799); Virginia v. Zimmerman, Fed. Cas. No. 16,968 (C.C.D.C. 1802); U.S. v. Smith & Ogden, Fed. Cas. No. 16,342a (C.C.D.N.Y. 1806); U.S. v. Poyllon, Fed. Cas. No. 16,081 (C.C.D.N.Y. 1812); U.S. v. Hodges, Fed. Cas. No. 15,374 (C.C.D.Md. 1815); U.S. v. Wilson, Fed. Cas. No. 16,730 (C.C.E.D.Pa. 1830). The right of the jury to decide the law even in civil cases was favored in Georgia v. Brailsford, 3 Dallas 1 (1794); Van Horne v. Dorrance, 2 Dal. 304 (1795); Bingham v. Cabbot, 3 Dal. 19 (1795).

In the U.S. Circuit Courts, the turning point against the right of the jury began in U.S. v. Shive, Fed. Cas. No. 16,278 (C.C.E.D.Pa. 1832), where it was ruled, *per* Baldwin, J., that the right of the jury to decide the law did not apply to questions of constitutionality. However, the first federal case in which the right of the jury was denied outright was U.S. v. Battiste, Fed. Cas. No. 14,545 (C.C.D. Mass. 1835) (2 Sumner's R. 240, 243–244), in an opinion *per* Story, J. This was followed in Stettinius v. U.S., Fed. Cas. No. 13,387 (C.C.D.C. 1839).

On the question of the "precedents," see *infra*, note 34.

[29] Sparf and Hansen v. U.S., 156 U.S. 51, 80 (1894).

inquiry raises abstruse legal questions, e.g., the meaning of the statute and its constitutionality, which only judges who are especially trained, experienced, and skilled in the law, may rightfully answer. The second inquiry, to be determined conclusively by the jury, is factual: has the defendant done the acts as charged? It merely seems that the jury possess the power, and therefore the right, of deciding the law by a general verdict which embraces both law and fact: although the verdict declares the law, it is the law as adjudicated by the judge in his instructions.

Shaw was ready with an answer to the obvious question which arises at this point: how can it be known whether the jury followed the law as laid down by the judge, or decided for themselves against his instructions? Candidly, Shaw replied that there is no way of knowing, for the record shows only the verdict — "guilty" or "not guilty" — and the jury cannot be legally asked what rules of law they followed. But, he added, the law presumes that the jury will do their duty, and having understood the directions of the judge, conform to them. And this presumption is necessary to preserve the defendant's right to due process by allowing him an appeal to a court of review on questions of law. For in the case of a conviction, if exceptions have been taken to any of the rulings of the trial judge, and these are sustained by a higher court, the verdict will be set aside and a new trial granted.

But this procedure can obtain only by presuming that the jury, having taken the law from the court, came to their verdict incorrectly because the law was laid down incorrectly. If, on the other hand, the jury could rightly exercise their own judgment on matters of law and decide contrary to the court's instructions, no writ of error could lie, because whether or not the jury had been misled by incorrect directions could not be determined. Indeed, where a statute purportedly authorized the jury to decide the law for themselves, the presumption would be that they had done so; and no ground of law would exist for setting aside a wrong conviction, because the law incorporated in their verdict, not being the law taken from the court, was unknowable.

To Shaw the latter consequences were appalling. If a criminal prosecution drew into question the constitutionality of the statute on which the state's case rested, a jury in deciding the issues of law for themselves would exercise the highest powers of judicial review. Merely to state such a right of the jury was for Shaw sufficient demonstration of its infirmity. But there was another consideration of equal weight in his reasoning. The case seemed to have been argued as if juries might be relied upon, in their private determination of the law, to rescue accused parties from a natural propensity of judges to favor the prosecution. This idea Shaw doubly rejected, as reflecting on the impartiality of judges and the constitution that secured their independence, and as not taking into account the fact that juries, whether motivated by prejudice or mistaken zeal, might return a conviction by overriding instructions favorable to the rights of the accused. Again, since the law judged by the jury was not taken from the court and could not be known, there could be no appeal: the accused would be denied due process of law.

Still another consideration, Shaw argued, was that the meaning and application of the law, if decided by the jury, could fluctuate in different cases, in effect annulling the security to which every citizen is entitled by a uniform administration of justice. To the end that there should be a government of laws and not of men, the state constitution provided for a single court of last resort, under judges as free and unbiased as the lot of humanity admitted, with powers of review and authority to pronounce the meaning of the law; its decisions, unlike a jury's, constituted precedents for all lower courts in order to insure certainty, stability, and equal operation of the law. So in the case of a conviction upon incorrect instructions, the defendant is granted a new trial at which the law, as adjudicated by the court of last resort, will be correctly stated for the guidance of the jury. Uniformity in justice insists, said Shaw, "that it is better that nine guilty persons should escape, than that one innocent man should suffer." [30]

Turning to the statute in question, Shaw proceeded to demonstrate, somewhat speciously, that it did not mean what it apparently purported. The jury were to try criminal cases "according to established forms and principles of law." This meant, said Shaw, that their decision of the law was the law received from the court. The statute was merely a "declaratory act, making no substantial change in the law regulating the relative rights and functions of the court and of the jury, in the trial of criminal cases." [31] Shaw

---

[30] Commonwealth v. Anthes, 5 Gray 185, 230 (1855).

[31] *Ibid.*, at 187. "As no statute of any consequence dealing with any relation of private law can be anything but in derogation of the common law, the social reformer and the legal reformer, under such a doctrine, had always to face the situation that the legislative act which represented the fruit of their labors would find no sympathy in those who applied it, would be construed strictly and would be made to interfere with the *status quo* as little as possible" (Roscoe Pound, *The Spirit of the Common Law*, Boston, 1931, pp. 156–157).

admitted, however, that the statute could bear a construction which empowered juries to take the law into their hands. He would not give it such an interpretation, for he wished to avoid having to invalidate the statute; but he stated that any statute which explicitly gave to the jury the right claimed would be unconstitutional. His reasons were variations on the theme of violation of the principles underlying trial by jury: infringement of the rights of the judiciary; prevention of the right of appeal on grounds of law; and creation of uncertainty in the law and inequality in its operation. The statute did not commend itself to Shaw even though it empowered the trial judge to grant a new trial if in his opinion a verdict of guilty was not warranted. This, Shaw said, could only make for a fruitless multiplicity of litigation so long as the law in the case could not be adjudicated conclusively by a court.

This opinion was one of the very few delivered by Shaw that did not receive the unanimous concurrence of his brethren. Of the five associate justices, Dewey and Thomas dissented, each in a separate opinion. Both scorned the idea that the statute merely declared the common law. ". . . We cannot shut our eyes," said Dewey, "to the fact, that there had been recently promulgated the decision of this court in *Porter's case* . . . and that, to a certain extent, there was an opinion in the community, adverse to that decision." The purpose of the statute, he stated, "was to change the law as declared . . . in *Porter's case.*" If this was not so, added Thomas, "enactment was but the idlest of ceremonies." [32] One can agree with both justices on this point. Nevertheless, in the twenty-six thousand words of dissent there will not be found on the theoretical level a satisfying answer to Shaw's objections to the right claimed for the jury. There is, though, this to be said of Thomas' opinion: he tried to make of the statute a means to increase the chances of the innocent. He reasoned that the jury should have the right to disregard the instructions of the judge *only* in cases where these instructions construed the law unfavorably to the accused. His good intentions, however, did not excuse his egregious inconsistencies. Thomas' opinion stands as an example of reasoning at war with itself.

One might, however, agree with some part of Thomas' lamentations: ". . . if this doctrine as to the right of the jury be an error, it is, in this country at least, an old one, the error of many of our wisest and most conservative judges and statesmen."

[32] *Ibid.*, at 239 and at 254.

". . . I cannot but feel that, if I err in these views, I err with the fathers; that I am in the old and beaten path, standing *super antiquas vias.*"[33] If earlier judges had believed in the right of the jury — a fact by no means proved [34] — Shaw's reasoning revealed the error of their opinion. In any event, Thomas was correct in saying that he was beaten, for time has vindicated Shaw. After *Commonwealth v. Anthes,* the courts of almost every state gradually adopted Shaw's views.[35]

IV

In 1857, in the case of *Jones v. Robbins,*[36] Shaw held invalid a statute which subjected offenders to infamous punishment without benefit of grand jury proceedings. In this case, as in *Commonwealth v. Anthes,* Shaw was seeking to protect the institution of trial by jury as he understood it. Notwithstanding his good intentions, the future was to prove that in *Jones v. Robbins* it was Shaw's turn to travel the "old and beaten path, standing *super antiquas vias.*" The United States Supreme Court in the 1884 case of *Hurtado v. California*[37] rejected Shaw's reasoning and held that the Fourteenth Amendment's requirement of due process of law does not prevent a state from abolishing the grand jury system of trial by jury. That decision, however, was no doubt influenced by the principle of federalism, not present in *Jones v. Robbins.* But beginning with the Supreme Court of Wisconsin in 1872,[38] most of the state courts have similarly rejected *Jones v.*

---

[33] *Ibid.,* at 274 and at 302.

[34] A considerable part of the majority and minority opinions in Commonwealth v. Anthes was devoted to an examination of the precedents. The same was true of the opinions in Sparf and Hansen v. U.S., 156 U.S. 51–183 (1894), in which Harlan, J., relying chiefly on the authority of Chief Justice Shaw, ruled for a majority of seven against the right of the jury, and Gray, J., relying chiefly on the opinion by Justice Thomas, dissented for himself and Shiras, J. In each of these cases, both sides cited a great many of the same cases, and even quoted the same words, but arrived at exactly opposite conclusions as to their meaning. At best, one can say only that the "precedents" on this question were extremely ambiguous. See also J. B. Thayer, *A Preliminary Treatise of Evidence at the Common Law* (Boston, 1898), 169, 256; and Howe, at note 25, *supra.*

[35] Only in Maryland does the jury possess an unqualified right to decide questions of law and constitutionality — making the "jurymen judges, and judges ciphers." The presiding judge "preserves order, watches the ventilation, and controls the mechanics of the trial." This system "has embarrassed the Court of Appeals, the nisi prius courts, produced confusion and occasional injustice for nearly a century" (Samuel K. Dennis, "Maryland's Antique Constitutional Thorn," *Univ. of Pennsylvania Law Review,* 92:34 ff., Sept. 1943).

[36] 8 Gray 329 (1857).

[37] 110 U.S. 516 (1884).

[38] Rowan v. State, 30 Wisc. 129 (1872).

Robbins by holding that a felony may be prosecuted by information instead of by indictment or presentment by a grand jury.[39]

Jones v. Robbins arose on a petition for a writ of habeas corpus. The petitioner set forth that he was a prisoner in the city jail, convicted for a felony. Without a petit jury or the prior intervention of a grand jury, he had been tried in a police court by a single magistrate upon a complaint. These facts presented the question whether the statute of 1855,[40] which authorized such proceedings, conformed to Article XII of the Massachusetts Declaration of Rights. The guarantee therein was that no citizen should be imprisoned or deprived of his life, liberty, or property "but by the judgment of his peers or the law of the land," and the legislature was enjoined against subjecting any person to a capital or infamous punishment without trial by jury.

The Chief Justice, in his opinion for the Court, ruled that the requirement of a petit jury trial had not been violated by the statute, for it provided that the party should have an unqualified right of appeal where trial by jury might be obtained. Nevertheless, in Shaw's view, the statute contained one fatal infirmity: it failed to provide also for indictment or presentment by grand jury. On this ground the statute was declared unconstitutional as repugnant to Article XII.

As Justice Merrick pointed out, however, in a dissenting opinion, Article XII did not expressly guarantee the grand jury system of trial by jury, nor was that system provided for at any point in the state constitution. By way of answer to Merrick's point, Shaw declared that civil liberties are to be interpreted broadly: ". . . We are rather to regard [the provisions of the Declaration of Rights] as the annunciation of great and fundamental principles . . . than as precise and positive directions and rules of action; and therefore, in construing them, we are to look at the spirit and purpose of them as well as the letter. . . . Many of them," continued Shaw, "are so obviously dictated by natural justice," as to be "plainly obligatory upon the consciences of

[39] See Mott, *Due Process of Law*, sec. 96, pp. 246–252, and cases cited therein.

An information is filed at the mere discretion of the government, without the intervention or approval of a grand jury. An indictment, while commenced by the government is laid before a grand jury for approval or rejection; a presentment is an accusation returned by a grand jury, based upon their own knowledge of the facts or the evidence, without any bill laid before them at the suit of the government. Joseph Story, *Commentaries on the Constitution* (Boston, 1858, 2 vols. 3rd ed.), II, secs. 1784, 1786, pp. 591–593.

[40] St. 1855, ch. 448.

legislators and judges, without any express declaration . . ." [41]
Such was the case respecting the right to proceedings by a grand
jury before trial.

Not content to place the ground of decision upon the principles of "natural justice" only, Shaw proceeded to argue that the
"law of the land" or due process clause of Article XII embraced
the right contended for:

This clause, in its whole structure, is so manifestly conformable to
the words of *Magna Charta,* that we are not to consider it as a newly
invented phrase, first used by the makers of our constitution; but we
are to look at it as the adoption of one of the great securities of
private right, handed down to us as among the liberties and privileges
which our ancestors enjoyed at the time of their emigration, and
claimed to hold and retain as their birthright.[42]

The "law of the land," Shaw reasoned, was not literally the
law in force at any given time, else the legislature might impair
civil liberties by simple statutory enactment. As the clause was intended to be a limitation upon the legislature, he concluded, it
must signify the "ancient established law and course of legal proceedings, by an adherence to which our ancestors in England, before the settlement of this country, and the emigrants themselves
and their descendants, have found safety for their personal
rights." [43]

To document his assertion that the "law of the land" comprehended the grand jury system of trial by jury in all cases of
crimes carrying infamous penalties, Shaw drew upon the authority
of Coke, Blackstone, Dane, Kent, and Story. Coke, in commenting
on the law-of-the-land clause of the Magna Charta — *"nisi per
legem terrae"* — said that the words laid down a requirement of
"due process of law, that is, by indictment or presentment of good
and lawful men." [44] To this Blackstone and Dane had each added

[41] 8 Gray 329, 340 (1857).
[42] *Ibid.,* at 342.
[43] *Ibid.,* at 243.
[44] *Ibid.,* at 346. See also at 343. In Hurtado v. California, 110 U.S. 516, 524
(1884), this passage from Coke is given in full as: "For the true sense and exposition of these words see the Statute of 37 E. 3, cap. 8, where the words, by the
law of the land, are rendered, without due proces of the law, for there it is said,
though it be contained in the Great Charter, that no man be taken, imprisoned or
put out of his freehold without proces of the law, that is, by indictment of good
and lawfull men, where such deeds be done in due manner, or by writ originall
of the common law. Without being brought in to answere but by due proces of
the common law. No man be put to answer without presentment before justices,

that informations of every kind are confined by the constitutional laws to mere misdemeanors only.[45] Kent had written that no person should be held to answer for "a capital or otherwise infamous crime, or for any offense above the common law degree of petit larceny, unless he shall have been previously charged on the presentment or indictment of a grand jury." [46] Both Kent and Story had followed Coke in defining "by the law of the land" as "due process of law, that is, by indictment or presentment of good and lawful men." [47] Summing up the authorities with a peroration on bills of rights, Shaw asserted that the right to be free from an open accusation of crime and from the trouble, anxiety, and expense of trial, before the establishment of a cause by a grand jury in cases of high offenses, was an ancient security to the innocent against hasty or oppressive prosecutions.

It should be noted that throughout his opinion, with respect to his own reasoning and the statements from authority, Shaw consistently limited the requirement of indictment or presentment by grand jury to the cases of "high offenses," "infamous crimes," and "crimes of magnitude," as distinguished from minor crimes not above the common-law grade of petty larceny. In order to clarify his views, he further defined a crime which required grand jury proceedings before trial as a crime visited by infamous punishment. Such punishment in Massachusetts, since the penal reform act of 1812, meant confinement to the state penitentiary, and, of course, capital punishment. By limiting the requirement of indictment or presentment only to cases of infamous punishment, as defined, Shaw took care not to hamper those prosecutions before police courts or justices of the peace which were necessarily instituted by complaint or information, and resulted, upon conviction, in confinement to the county jail or house of correction — not the state penitentiary. This distinction appears to have escaped the notice of Justice Merrick, the lone dissenter.[48]

Merrick, like Thomas and Dewey in the earlier case of *Commonwealth v. Anthes,* criticized the majority for finding in the state Declaration of Rights a limitation on the power of the legislature when none existed in terms. Indeed, Merrick could not

---

or thing of record, or by due proces, or by writ originall, according to the old law of the land. Wherein it is to be observed that this chapter is but declaratory of the old law of England." See Mott, chs. 3 and 5.

[45] 8 Gray 329, 346, citing 4 Bl. *Comm.* 310 and 7 Dane *Ab.* 280.

[46] 2 Kent *Comm.* (6th ed.) 12.

[47] *Ibid.,* at 13; and Story, *Commentaries on the Constitution,* II, sec. 1789, p. 595.

[48] 8 Gray 329, 367–368 (1857).

even find the grand jury requirement by inference. He insisted that the authorities would not sustain the position of the majority. Coke, for example, had mentioned indictment merely as one illustration of the due process of law sanctioned by common-law usage. By inference, other modes of proceeding, such as by complaint or information, had also been sanctioned. As for Kent, he had given a larger definition of due process of law as "law in its regular course of administration, through courts of justice," thus, too, inferentially allowing for more than merely grand jury proceedings.[49]

Merrick's construction of Coke and Kent was expressly adopted by the United States Supreme Court in *Hurtado v. California* where it was said by Justice Matthews, over the anguished dissent of Justice Harlan, that the "great" Chief Justice Shaw had "misunderstood" the authorities. Nevertheless, the criticism by Merrick and Matthews was misdirected. Contrary to their allegations, Shaw did not constrict the law of the land, or due process of law, to mean only indictment by grand jury. He clearly said, as quoted above, that these clauses intended the "ancient established law and course of legal proceedings" by which personal rights are secured — a definition as broad as Kent's. But like Kent and all the other authorities, including Coke, Shaw restricted those clauses *in the case of a high crime carrying infamous punishment* to mean a requirement of grand jury proceedings.[50]

Merrick derived from Commonwealth history two points of interest, the first of which was based upon usage. The legislature, from the time of the adoption of the state constitution, had frequently provided for prosecution by complaint or information in cases of misdemeanor or those not infamously punished; and the validity of these procedures, Merrick noted, had never been questioned. Yet Shaw did not disagree with him on this point which did not meet the issue of the case at bar, for the crime there was a felony punishable by imprisonment in the state penitentiary.

The second point of interest in the dissent consisted of persuasive, though non-judicial, opinions that the state constitution did not guarantee the grand jury system of trial by jury. The Massachusetts Constitutional Convention of 1820 and the later commission on the revision of state law had each held this opinion. But both of these bodies had recommended the adoption of a

---

[49] *Ibid.*, at 357–361.
[50] On this point see the lucid explanation *per* Harlan, J., in Hurtado v. Cal., 110 U.S. 516, 552–553 (1884).

specific guarantee of grand jury proceedings in the very cases for which Shaw contended.

The convention's proposal of an amendment was not ratified, as Merrick admitted, because it had been joined with another amendment, on a different subject, which proved objectionable to the people. And the commission's recommendation was disapproved by the legislature.[51] In other words, the conclusion to be drawn from Merrick's dissent is that Shaw and the majority of the Court were guilty of having accomplished a legal reform, earlier approved by a convention and a commission, which secured for the citizens of Massachusetts a right guaranteed to the citizens of the United States by the federal Bill of Rights.[52]

Shaw's opinion in *Jones v. Robbins* succeeded in freezing the old English common law and reading the frozen version into the state constitution; to this date his opinion continues in Massachusetts as the authoritative exposition of the meaning of due process of law in those criminal prosecutions which can result in infamous punishment.[53] Shaw's greatest achievement as a jurist, it will be recalled, lay in his adaptation of the common law to changing circumstances. This fact makes ironic the boast of Justice Matthews in Hurtado that the authorities notwithstanding, due process of law must permit within its compass novel modes of criminal prosecution, because, said Matthews, the common law must grow "with the new and various experiences of our situation and system." Otherwise, he warned, American jurisprudence would be stamped with "the unchangeableness attributed to the laws of the Medes and the Persians." [54] Thus wrapped in the mantle of progressivism, the rule of Hurtado issued forth that a state might abolish the grand jury system of trial by jury without violating the due process clause of the Fourteenth Amendment. Although history did not justify that decision, the principle of federalism might have.

Harlan, dissenting, expressed Shaw's sentiments in saying: "It is difficult, however, to perceive anything in the system of prosecuting human beings for their lives, by information, which suggests that the State which adopts it has entered upon an era of

---

[51] 8 Gray 365–366, 368–369 (1857).

[52] Fifth Amendment: "No person shall be held to answer for a capital or otherwise infamous crime, unless on a presentment or indictment of a grand jury, except in cases arising in the land or naval forces, or in the militia when in actual service in time of war or public danger . . ."

[53] See DeJolyer v. Commonwealth, 314 Mass. 626, 627–628 (1943).

[54] 110 U.S. 516, 529, 531 (1884).

progress and improvement in the law of criminal procedure." [55] In conclusion, then, when in *Jones v. Robbins* Shaw crystallized antiquity, he knew how to distinguish change from progress; knew, too, that platitudes about the laws of the Medes and the Persians did not justify the abrogation of established procedures that protected personal rights.

V

In summing up the constitutional limitations enforced against the state legislature by the Shaw Court in cases where statutes were invalidated, one finds that the limitations were primarily concerned with the protection of civil liberties. The legislature was also checked when it sought to divest or substantially impair rights vested by contract. But in addition to the contract clause, the limitations comprised the right to be free from unreasonable searches and seizures; the right to trial by jury under equal operation of the laws, upon determination of probable cause for trial by a grand jury, with the crime plainly set forth and with an opportunity to meet the witnesses face to face and defend one's self; the right to an unfettered avenue of appeal on grounds of law; and the right to vote.[56]

There were only four cases in which the Court checked the legislature exclusively in behalf of property rights. These were the three contract clause cases and the case involving special legislative confirmation of an illegal private sale of land.[57] None of the four involved statutes of general operation, and in none did the Court subordinate the public interest to vested interests. In

[55] *Ibid.*, at 553. The logical consequence of the Hurtado rule is to be found in the dictum of the majority in Maxwell v. Dow, 176 U.S. 581, 603 (1900), where it was said, *per* Peckham, J.: "Trial by jury has never been affirmed to be a necessary requisite of due process of law." See also the dictum in Jordan v. Massachusetts, 225 U.S. 167, 176 (1912), where it was said, *per* Lurton, J.: "The requirement of due process does not deprive a state of the power to dispense with jury trial altogether." Justice Harlan, again dissenting in Maxwell v. Dow, drew this conclusion: "If, then, the 'due process of law' required by the Fourteenth Amendment does not allow a state to take private property without just compensation, but does allow the life or liberty of the citizen to be taken in a mode that is repugnant to the settled usages and the modes of proceeding authorized at the time the Constitution was adopted and which was expressly forbidden in the national Bill of Rights, it would seem that the protection of private property is of more consequence than the protection of the life and liberty of the citizen" (176 U.S. 581, 614, 1900).

[56] Warren v. Mayor & Alderman of Charlestown, 3 Gray 84 (1854).

[57] Commonwealth v. New Bedford Bridge, 2 Gray 339 (1854); Commonwealth v. Essex Co., 13 Gray 239 (1859); Central Bridge Corp. v. City of Lowell, 15 Gray 106 (1860); and Sohier v. Mass. General Hospital, 3 Cush. 483 (1849).

a fifth case, Latimer's,[58] which was unreported and not decided by the full bench, the right of trial by jury, protected by the legislature, was suspended by the Court; but the decision affected only fugitive slaves and was governed by a precedent of the Supreme Court of the United States.[59]

The remaining cases in which the Shaw Court voided an act of the legislature all clearly come under the rubric of civil liberties, each involving judicial protection against impairment of some procedural right affirmed by the Massachusetts Declaration of Rights.[60] For the sake of comparison, it is interesting to note that in the Supreme Court of the United States, judicial review developed out of an enthusiasm for protecting private property from legislative interference, and the decisions were often in opposition to the public good. As one scholar has pointed out, in the entire history of the national Court down to the Civil War, there was but one case, a minor one, in which a civil right was protected against legislative action.[61] In Massachusetts the strongest impetus to the growth of judicial review originated in the Shaw Court's propensity to safeguard the procedural rights of accused persons.

It is part of Chief Justice Shaw's greatness that he should have exercised a commendable restraint in cases of government controls in the economy, yet allowed himself to be comparatively zealous in guarding the Massachusetts Declaration of Rights. If he erred in enforcing constitutional limitations, it was on the side of personal rights. Unfortunately he did not go for enough in this direction, choosing rather to exercise judicial self-restraint in the blasphemy and segregation cases.

[58] Commonwealth v. Coolidge, *Law Reporter* 5:482 ff. (1843).

[59] Prigg. v. Pennsylvania, 16 Pet. 539 (1842).

[60] Fisher v. McGirr, 1 Gray 1 (1854); Warren v. Mayor & Alderman of Charlestown, 3 Gray 84 (1854); Sullivan v. Adams, 3 Gray 476 (1855); Jones v. Robbins, 8 Gray 329 (1857); Robinson v. Richardson, 13 Gray 454 (1859). To this list should be added Commonwealth v. Anthes, 5 Gray 185 (1855) because the decision, while avoiding a declaration of unconstitutionality, had the effect of voiding the statute.

[61] Benjamin F. Wright, *The Growth of American Constitutional Law* (Boston, 1942), pp. 77–78, citing Webster v. Reid, 11 How. 437 (1851), in which an act of the Iowa territorial legislature, providing that in certain cases the territorial court should decide matters of fact without a jury, was held repugnant to the Seventh Amendment.

16

THREE DECADES OF LAW
AND SOCIETY

Résumé and Conclusions

A society reveals itself in its law. Its points of growth and the interests it values may be disclosed even in the decision of a seemingly technical and insignificant legal question. For example, one case confronted Shaw with the question of a railroad employee's competency to testify as to the delivery of goods allegedly not delivered by his company. A common-law rule of evidence which had "existed for ages" would have excluded the testimony of an agent in behalf of his principal. But the Chief Justice made an exception to that rule, stating with more candor than is characteristic of judges that if the rule were followed, "business would be greatly impeded." The decision shows that the law reflected the needs of a new industry, the railroad. It shows too that the law was vitally concerned with the future of a recently emergent form of business, the corporation, for as Shaw said, to follow the old rule "would nearly prevent the operations of corporate companies, who must act entirely through various classes of officers and agents." [1]

The ultimate question of legal history is, how does the law of a given time and place meaningfully connect with the society of which it is a part? In the United States the question is all the more pressing because, as was noted by Burke, Tocqueville, and Dicey, Americans are the most legal-minded of people. Accordingly, American legal history should show in striking fashion how law is shaped by and in turn shapes the thought and experience of the American people. Tocqueville, a jurist in his own country, was

---

[1] Draper v. Worcester & Norwich RR., 11 Metc. 505, 508 (1846).

astonished to discover that "Scarcely any question arises in the United States which does not become, sooner or later, a subject of judicial debate . . ." [2] In the guise of legal disputes between private parties, matters of high policy involving great stakes are referred ultimately to the courts for decision. Thus the opinions of judges are often political, economic, and social events, as well as legal events.

The relation of the individual to the state and of the states to the nation; the role of the government in the economy; the private and public interests deemed important enough to secure in permanent and authoritative form; the comparative valuation placed on different activities and goals, and on liberty and order; the points of tension, growth, and power; and prevailing conceptions of rights, duties, and liabilities: all are exposed in the law.

For thirty years, Lemuel Shaw sat as Chief Justice, during an age which he said was remarkable for its "prodigious activity and energy in every department of life." [3] America was being transformed by the rise of railroads, steam power, the factory system, and the corporate form of business. A more complex society, urban and industrial, was superseding the older rural, agrarian one. Only a pace behind the astonishing rate of economic change came the democratization of politics and of life. The federal system lumbered toward its greatest crisis. During this time Shaw delivered what is probably a record number of opinions for a single judge: two thousand and two hundred, enough to fill about twenty volumes if separately collected.

At the time of his appointment to the bench, American law was in its formative period. Whole areas of law were largely uncultivated, many unknown, and few if any settled. Although Shaw was not writing on a completely clean slate, the strategy of time and place surely presented an unrivaled opportunity for a judge of strength and vision to mold the law.

In estimating the significance of Shaw's career it would be a mistake to search for the ways in which he altered the direction of social change, for that begins outside the law. Moreover, judges

[2] Alexis de Tocqueville, *Democracy in America* (translated by Henry Reeve, var. eds.), I, ch. 16. In the Bowen translation, the passage reads: "Scarcely any political question arises in the United States that is not resolved, sooner or later, into a judicial question" (New York: Vintage Books, 1954, ed. by Phillips Bradley), I, 290.

[3] Lemuel Shaw, "Profession of the Law in the United States." Extract from an Address Delivered before the Suffolk Bar, May, 1827. *American Jurist* 7:56, 65 (Boston, 1832).

are in an unfavorable position to act as social engineers or innovators. They must wait until litigous battle casts up an issue for decision. Usage demands that they speak only to that issue in its legal character, that they do not unburden themselves on the subject at large, and that they stifle their personal preferences as to matters of wisdom or policy. In the course of deciding a given case, they can repair decayed parts of the legal structure or do some remodeling, but an architectural change takes a generation of decisions. Individual judges do well to keep the law in a state of good preservation so that it may be a place where social tensions are neutralized and the present may meet with and learn from the past.

But great judges like Shaw, who revitalize the law so that it may fulfill its function, can channel and legitimatize social change in as reasoned a way as is possible. This is surely a vital and civilizing task. Willard Hurst has remarked that the great judges have had an ability "to express the times or foretell the generation to come." They were the ones who "saw better where the times led and took their less imaginative, less flexible, or less courageous brethren in that direction with a minimum of waste or suffering." [4] Hurst might have been describing Shaw.

One of the major themes of his life work was the perpetuation of what Oscar and Mary Handlin have called "the commonwealth idea" [5] — essentially a quasi-mercantilist concept of the state within a democratic framework. In Europe where the state was not responsible to the people and was the product of remote historical forces, mercantilism served the ruling classes who controlled the state. In America men put the social-contract theory into practice and actually made their government. The people were the state; the state was their "Common Wealth." They identified themselves with it and felt that they should share, as of right, in the advantages that it could bring to them as a community. The state was their means of promoting the general interest.

A theory of the general interest was common. Shaw expressed it in his address to the Suffolk Bar in 1827 in language he was later to repeat from the bench. Speaking of the "theory of free government," he declared:

[4] James Willard Hurst, *The Growth of American Law* (Boston, 1950), p. 18.
[5] Oscar Handlin and Mary F. Handlin, *Commonwealth. A Study of the Role of Government in the American Economy: Massachusetts, 1774–1861* (New York, 1947), p. 31.

It regards men as by nature social, and endowed with powers adequate to enable them, by the establishment of government, to provide for defining and securing their social rights, and under a natural obligation to respect those of others, and it presupposes that all power resides originally in the whole people as a social community, that all political power is derived from them, is designed to be exercised solely for the general good, and limited to the accomplishment of that object; that no powers are, or ought to be, vested in the government, beyond those which are necessary and useful to promote the general security, happiness, and prosperity; and that all powers not delegated remain with the people.[6]

The Commonwealth idea precluded the laissez-faire state whose function was simply to keep peace and order, and then, like a little child, not be heard. The people of Massachusetts expected their Commonwealth to participate actively in their economic affairs. As the Handlins point out, they found "manifestly erroneous" the notion that the economy should be left to its own devices, that the people individually, rather than their government, "are the judges of their interests." That principle was considered "subversive to the end and aim of all governments; and . . . utterly impracticable." [7]

Where risk capital feared to tread or needed franchises, powers of incorporation, or the boost of special powers like eminent domain, the duty of the state was to subsidize, grant, and supervise the whole process in the interests of the general welfare. But regulation was not restricted to those special interests which had been promoted by government aid. Banks, insurance companies, liquor dealers, food vendors, and others were all subjected to varying degrees of control, though the public trough had not been open to them. As the Handlins say, "Massachusetts observors conceived of the beneficent hand of the state as reaching out to touch every part of the economy." [8]

The Commonwealth idea profoundly influenced the development of law in Massachusetts. It was largely responsible for the

[6] Shaw, "Profession of the Law," *American Jurist*, 7:61; and see *A Charge Delivered to the Grand Jury for the County of Essex . . . May Term, 1832* (Boston, 1832), p. 4.

[7] "Public Interests," *Boston Commercial Gazette*, Sept. 23, 1819, quoted by Handlin and Handlin, pp. 54–55.

[8] Handlin and Handlin, p. 54. For the experience of other states, see Louis Hartz, *Economic Policy and Democratic Thought: Pennsylvania, 1776–1860* (Cambridge, 1948), and James Neal Primm, *Economic Policy in the Development of a Western State: Missouri, 1820–1860* (Cambridge, 1954). For the colonial period through the Revolution, see Richard B. Morris, *Government and Labor in Early America* (New York, 1946).

direction taken by the law of eminent domain, for the development of the police power, and for the general precedence given by the courts to public rights over merely private ones. As employed by Shaw, the Commonwealth idea gave rise to legal doctrines of the public interest by which the power of the state to govern the economy was judicially sustained.

The idea "that some privately owned corporations are more public in character than others," as Edwin Merrick Dodd noted, "had already begun to emerge in judicial decisions before 1830." [9] The grant of powers of eminent domain to early turnpike and canal companies had been upheld on ground that they were public highways, although privately owned. The mill acts, which originated as a means of promoting waterpowered gristmills, had also been sustained in early decisions on ground that a public purpose was served. In this respect, the work of Theophilus Parsons and Isaac Parker, Shaw's predecessors, provided him with useful precedents in support of legislation that advanced both the Commonwealth idea and industrial interests.

On the other hand, the earlier judges regretted the extension of the old gristmill acts to new manufacturing corporations. Shaw, by contrast, warmly accepted the mill acts because he believed that industrialization would bring prosperity and progress to the Commonwealth. Accordingly he declared that "a great mill-power for manufacturing purposes" was, like a railroad, a species of public works in which the public had a great interest. He even placed "steam manufactories" in the same class as waterpowered mills, as devoted to a public use, although the former were never granted powers of eminent domain. [10] His opinions show reason for believing that he would have sustained far reaching factory regulation if he had had the opportunity. In such a case, which never arose, the Commonwealth idea would have explained his support of the legislature.

Certainly the Commonwealth idea underlay those remarkably prophetic opinions of Shaw's that established the basis of the emerging law of public utilities. The old common law of common calling had considered only millers, carriers, and innkeepers as "public employments"; it "knew no such persons as the common road-maker or the common water-supplier." [11] The "common

---

[9] Dodd, *American Business Corporations Until 1860* (Cambridge, 1954), p. 44.

[10] See Palmer Co. v. Ferrill, 17 Pick. 58 (1835) and Hazen v. Essex Co., 12 Cush. 475 (1853).

[11] E. M. Dodd, p. 161.

road-maker," that is, the turnpike, bridge, and canal companies, were added to the list of public employments or public works while Shaw was still at the bar. But it was Shaw who settled the legal character of power companies, railroads, and water suppliers as public utilities, privately owned but subject to regulation for the public benefit. He would have included even manufacturers and banks. The Commonwealth idea left no doubt as to whether the state would master or be mastered by its creatures, the corporations, or whether the welfare of the economy was a matter of public or private concern.

Indeed the police power may be regarded as the legal expression of the Commonwealth idea, for it signifies the supremacy of public over private rights. To call the police power a Massachusetts doctrine would be an exaggeration, though not a great one. But it is certainly no coincidence that in Massachusetts, with its Commonwealth tradition, the police power was first defined and carried to great extremes from the standpoint of vested interests. Shaw's foremost contribution in the field of public law was to the development of the police-power concept.

The power of the legislature "to trench somewhat largely on the profitable use of individual property," for the sake of the common good, as Shaw expressed the police power in *Commonwealth v. Alger*,[12] was consistently confirmed over thirty years of his opinions. Three decades later, when judges were acting on the supposition that the Fourteenth Amendment incorporated Herbert Spencer's *Social Statics*, the ideas expressed in Shaw's opinions seemed the very epitome of revolutionary socialism. Shaw's name was revered, but the implications of his police-power opinions were politely evaded. In the period between Shaw and the school of Holmes and Brandeis, American law became the graveyard of general-welfare or public-interest doctrines, and doctrines of vested rights dominated.

The trend toward legal Spencerianism was so pronounced by the end of the nineteenth century that legal historians concentrated on a search for the origins of doctrines of vested rights, almost as if contrary doctrines had never existed. When touching the pre-Civil War period, it is conventional to quote Tocqueville on the conservatism of the American bench and bar, to present American law almost exclusively in terms of Marshall, Story, and Kent, and to emphasize that the rights of property claimed the very warmest affections of the American judiciary. So familiar is

[12] 7 Cush. 53 (1851).

this view of our legal history that we may summarize it with a paraphrase of Tennyson's "Northern Farmer, New Style":[13]

> Proputty, proputty, proputty, proputty
> That's what the judges and historians say.

If, however, the work of the state courts were better known, this view might be altered. But Gibson and Ruffin and Blackford are little more than distinguished names, their work forgotten. Shaw's superb exposition of the police power is respectfully remembered, but it is usually treated as exceptional, or mistreated as an attempt to confine the police power to the common-law maxim of *sic utere tuo ut alienum non laedas*.

Shaw taught that "all property . . . is derived directly or indirectly from the government, and held subject to those general regulations, which are necessary to the common good and general welfare." [14] Dean Pound, in discussing the "extreme individualist view" of the common law concerning the rights of riparian property owners, says the common law asked simply, "was the defendant acting on his own land and committing no nuisance?" [15] But Shaw believed that the common law of nuisances, which was founded on the *sic utere* maxim, inadequately protected the public, because it was restricted to the abatement of existing nuisances. He believed that the general welfare required the anticipation and prevention of prospective wrongs from the use of private property. Accordingly he held that the legislature might interfere with the use of property before its owner became amenable to the common law. So a man could not even remove stones from his own beach if prohibited by the legislature, nor erect a wharf on his property beyond boundary lines fixed by it. Even if his use of his property would be "harmless" or "indifferent," the necessity of restraints was to be judged "by those to whom all legislative power is intrusted by the sovereign authority." Similarly the "reasonableness" of such restraints was a matter of "expediency" to be determined by the legislature, not the court. The simple expedient of having a precise statutory rule for the obedience of all was sufficient reason for a finding of constitutionality.[16]

---

[13] See Henry Steele Commager, "Joseph Story," in A. N. Holcombe *et al.*, *Gaspar G. Bacon Lectures on the Constitution of the United States* (Boston, 1953), p. 58, where the paraphrase omits "historians."

[14] Commonwealth v. Alger, 7 Cush. 53, 83–84 (1851).

[15] Roscoe Pound, *The Spirit of the Common Law* (Boston, 1921), pp. 53–54.

[16] Quotations are from Shaw's opinions in the Alger case and in Commonwealth v. Tewksbury, 11 Metc. 55 (1846).

Thus Shaw, using the Commonwealth idea, established a broad base for the police power. He carried the law's conception of the public good and the power of government to protect it a long way from the straitjacketing ideas of Kent and Story. Their position may be summed up in Blackstone's language that "the public good is in nothing more essentially interested than the protection of every individual's private rights." [17]

A review of a few other decisions of the Shaw Court on the police power will illustrate that the Chief Justice's Alger opinion was more than rhetoric. The authority of the legislature to shape private banking practices in the public interest was unequivocally sustained in two sweeping opinions. In one, Shaw said that a statute intended to prevent banks from "becoming dangerous to the public" was attacked as unconstitutional on the authority of Marshall, Story, and Kent. The statute allegedly operated retroactively against the bank in question; constituted a legislative assumption of judicial power because it required the Supreme Judicial Court to issue a preliminary injunction against banks on the findings of a government commission; and violated the contract clause by providing for a perpetual injunction against the further doing of business, in effect a revocation of the charter. Rufus Choate probably never argued a stronger case. But Shaw sustained the statute and the injunction, peppering his opinion with references to the paramountcy of "the great interests of the community," the duty of the government to "provide security for its citizens," and the legitimacy of interferences with "the liberty of action, and even with the right of property, of such institutions." [18]

In a second bank case of the same year, 1839, the Court refused "to raise banks above the control of the legislature." The holding was that a charter could be dissolved at the authority of the legislature, under the reserved police power, without a judicial proceeding. [19]

It has been said that from the standpoint of the doctrine of vested rights the most reprehensible legislation ever enacted was the prohibition on the sale of liquor. Such legislation wiped out the value of existing stocks and subjected violators to criminal sanctions, their property to public destruction. Similarly, buildings used for purposes of prostitution or gambling might, on the authority of the legislature, be torn down. The question presented

[17] Quoted by Pound, *Spirit of the Common Law*, p. 53.
[18] Commonwealth v. Farmers & Mechanics Bank, 21 Pick. 542 (1839).
[19] Crease v. Babcock, 23 Pick. 334 (1839).

by such statutes was whether the police power could justify uncompensated destruction of private property which had not been appropriated for a public use. The power of the Commonwealth over the health and morals of the public provided Shaw with the basis for sustaining legislation divesting vested rights.[20] On half a dozen occasions, the Wynehammer doctrine of substantive due process of law was repudiated in such cases.

Regulation of railroads was another subject for the exercise of the police power, according to the Shaw Court. The same principles that justified grants of eminent domain to railroads, or to canals, bridges, turnpikes, power companies, and water suppliers, also provided the basis for sustaining controls over their rates, profits, and services. Railroads, said Shaw, were a "public work, established by public authority, intended for the public use and benefit . . ."[21] The power to charge rates was "in every respect a public grant, a franchise . . . subject to certain regulations, within the power of government, if it should become excessive."[22]

These dicta by Shaw became holdings at the first moment the railroads challenged the "reasonableness" of the rates and services fixed by government railroad commissions. "Reasonableness" was held to be a matter for determination by the legislature or the commission to which it delegated its powers. Those powers, in turn, were broadly construed. The Court would not interfere with the regulatory process if the railroads had the benefit of notice, hearing, and other fair procedures.[23] Due process of law to the Shaw Court meant according to legal forms, not according to legislation which the Court approved or disapproved as a matter of policy.

A final illustration will show the scope of the police power as conceived by the Shaw Court. It was held, in an opinion by the Chief Justice, that because the right to use land washed by tidewaters was a public rather than a private right, the government could validly authorize the uncompensated flooding of a tidemill owner's property, destroying much of his business.[24] This decision rode roughshod over every doctrine of vested rights.

[20] Commonwealth v. Blackington, 24 Pick. 352 (1837); Fisher v. McGirr, 1 Gray 1 (1854); Brown v. Perkins, 12 Gray 89 (1858); Commonwealth v. Howe, 13 Gray 26 (1859). These are the leading cases among dozens.
[21] Worcester v. Western RR., 4 Metc. 564, 566 (1842).
[22] Roxbury v. B. & P. RR., 6 Cush. 424, 431–432 (1850).
[23] B. & W. RR. v. Western RR., 14 Gray 253 (1859), and L. & W. C. RR. v. Fitchburg RR., 14 Gray 266 (1859).
[24] Davidson v. B. & M. RR., 3 Cush. 91 (1849). See also Baker v. Boston, 12 Pick. 183 (1831).

The owner had the misfortune to be located where the "mere regulation of a public right, and not a taking," in Shaw's words, had caused his ruin. Here was a harsh application of the Commonwealth idea based on the theory that the owner's loss had been inflicted by the government for the greater good of the community; moreover, that he was compensated by sharing with others in the advantages which derived from regulations of the public rights. As for compensation in the form of damages, it was a case of *damnum absque injuria*.

II

The latitudinarian attitude of the Shaw Court toward the police power was unquestionably influenced by the strong tradition of judicial self-restraint among Massachusetts judges. Although they never questioned their power to hold a statute unconstitutional, they exercised that power only in rare and clear-cut cases. Theoretically, the explanation for such restraint was the doctrine of separation of powers. The courts would not invalidate an act whose wisdom they doubted on grounds of policy if it were passed within the compass of the legislature's delegated powers. Why Theophilus Parsons and Isaac Parker should have adhered so scrupulously to this rule when the federal judiciary and some other state courts did not is hard to understand, unless judicial self-restraint was an outgrowth of the Commonwealth idea.

Shaw carried on the tradition of the Massachusetts judiciary in good faith. When he became Chief Justice, there were only two reported cases in which enactments had been held void by the Supreme Judicial Court. One related to an unimportant and expired act of Congress; the other to a special resolve of the Massachusetts legislature which suspended the statute of limitations in favor of a particular creditor.[25] During the thirty years that Shaw presided, there were only ten cases, one unreported, in which the Supreme Judicial Court voided legislative enactments.

Four of these cases in no way related to the police power. One involved a special legislative resolution confirming a private sale that had divested property rights of third persons without compensation.[26] The second concerned an act by which

---

[25] Wetherbee v. Johnson, 14 Mass. 412 (1817); Holden v. James, 11 Mass. 396 (1814). A third precedent of 1799 had been unreported and was "lost." See *supra*, p. 266.

[26] Sohier v. Mass. General Hospital, 3 Cush. 483 (1849).

Charlestown was annexed to Boston without providing the citizens of Charlestown with representative districts and an opportunity to vote.[27] The third, an unreported case decided by Shaw sitting alone, involved the "personal liberty act," by which the state sought to evade Congress' Fugitive Slave Law.[28] Here Shaw felt bound by the national Constitution and by a decision of the Supreme Court of the United States. In the fourth case he invalidated a state act which dispensed with the ancient requirement of grand jury proceedings in cases of high crimes.[29] In each of these four, the decisions are above any but trifling criticism.

Of the six cases bearing on the police power, three involved legislation egregiously violating procedural guarantees that are part of our civil liberties.[30] The statutes in question had validly prohibited the sale of liquor. But they invalidly stripped accused persons of virtually every safeguard of criminal justice, from the right to be free from unreasonable searches and seizures to the rights that cluster around the concept of fair trial. Shaw's decisions against these statutes, like his decisions insuring the maintenance of grand jury proceedings and the right to vote, were manifestations of judicial review in its best sense. There were also dicta by Shaw on the point that the legislature cannot restrain the use of property by ex post facto laws, by bills of attainder, or by discriminatory classifications.

Thus the limitations placed upon the police power by the Shaw Court were indispensable to the protection of civil liberties. The only exception to this generalization consists of the limitation derived from the contract clause of the United States Constitution. But there were only three cases during the long period of Shaw's Chief Justiceship in which this clause was the basis for the invalidation of statutes. In each of the three, the statutes were of limited operation and the decisions made no sacrifice of the public interest. The legislature in one case attempted to regulate in the absence of a reserved power to alter or amend public contracts; the Court left a way open for the legislature's purpose to be achieved under common law.[31] In the other two cases, regulatory powers had been reserved but were exercised in particularly faithless and arbitrary ways: to increase substantially the obliga-

[27] Warren v. Mayor and Alderman of Charlestown, 3 Gray 84 (1854).
[28] Commonwealth v. Coolidge, *Law Reporter* 5:482 ff. (1843).
[29] Jones v. Robbins, 8 Gray 329 (1857).
[30] Fisher v. McGirr, 1 Gray 1 (1854); Sullivan v. Adams, 3 Gray 476 (1855); and Robinson v. Richardson, 13 Gray 454 (1859).
[31] Commonwealth v. New Bedford Bridge, 2 Gray 339 (1854).

tions of a corporation for a second time, in effect doubling a liability which had been paid off; and to repeal an explicit permission for another corporation to increase its capitalization in return for certain services rendered.[32] The legislature in all three cases had passed a high threshold of judicial tolerance for governmental interference with the sanctity of contracts. The decisions were hardly exceptional, considering the facts of the cases and their dates — between 1854 and 1860, after scores of similar decisions by Federalist, Whig, and Jacksonian jurists alike in state and federal jurisdictions.

The striking fact is that there were so few such decisions by the Shaw Court in thirty years. Handsome opportunities were provided again and again by litigants claiming impairment of their charters of incorporation by a meddlesome legislature. But the Court's decisions were characterized by judicial self-restraint rather than an eagerness to erect a bulwark around chartered rights. In that sense the three cases wherein statutes were voided for conflict with the contract clause were exceptional.

Generally the attitude of the Court was typified by Shaw's remark that "immunities and privileges [vested by charter] do not exempt corporations from the operations of those laws made for the general regulation . . ."[33] He habitually construed public grants in favor of the community and against private interests. When chartered powers were exercised in the public interest, he usually interpreted them broadly; but when they competed with the right of the community to protect itself or conserve its resources, he interpreted chartered powers narrowly. To be sure, he held that the police power could in certain respects be contracted away in return for some public benefit to be gained by the contract. But he did not permit the public control over matters of health, morals, or safety, nor the power of eminent domain, to be alienated by the contract clause.

In the face of such a record it is misleading to picture state courts assiduously searching for doctrines of vested rights to stymie the police power. Certainly no such doctrines appeared in the pre-Civil War decisions of the Supreme Judicial Court of Massachusetts, except for the one doctrine derived by John Marshall from the contract clause and so sparingly used by Shaw. The sources from which vested-rights doctrines were derived by

---

[32] Commonwealth v. Essex Co., 13 Gray 239 (1859); Central Bridge Corp. v. Lowell, 15 Gray 106 (1860).

[33] Commonwealth v. Farmers & Mechanics Bank, 21 Pick. 542, 556 (1838).

others — the higher law, natural rights, the social compact, and other sources of implied, inherent limitations on majoritarian assemblies — were invoked by Shaw when he was checking impairments on personal liberties or traditional procedures of criminal justice.

If this picture does not fit the stereotype of conservative Whig jurists, the stereotype may need revision. True enough, Shaw was capable of warning against the "encroachments of a wild and licentious democracy" or against the "irregular action of mere popular will."[34] He could applaud the restraints fixed by a well-balanced constitution, call for the "best members" of society to direct the government, and exalt the virtues of private property and the sanctity of chartered rights. Such rhetoric, however, was rare in his judicial utterances and was far outweighed by his affirmations of the power of government to "promote the general security, happiness, and prosperity" of the whole community.

On the great issue which has historically divided liberals from conservatives in politics — government controls over property and corporations — Shaw supported the government. Even when the Commonwealth idea was being eroded away by those who welcomed the give-away state but not the regulatory state, Shaw was still endorsing a concept of the police power that kept private interests under government surveillance and restraint. He would not permit the Commonwealth idea to become just a rationale for legislative subventions and grants of chartered powers, with business as the only beneficiary. To Shaw, government aid implied government control, because the aid to business was merely incidental to the promotion of the public welfare. No general regulatory statute was invalidated while he was Chief Justice.

III

The idea of individualism was expressed in the law cheek by jowl with the Commonwealth idea, but it was an individualism that differed from that associated with the laissez-faire state of the *fin de siècle*. It did not imply an absence of restraints upon private economic enterprise, though it did imply that individuals were economically self-sufficient. In constitutional law, individualism meant that a man's natural rights to life, liberty, and property could not be fettered by the state except by due process of law; nor could property be appropriated to any use but a public one

[34] Shaw, "Charge to the Grand Jury, 1832," p. 4; and "Profession of the Law," p. 62.

and then only upon just compensation. The more aggressive individual rights, such as freedom of speech, press, and religion were also safeguarded. In criminal law, individualism was apparent in the most fundamental of premises: a crime may be committed only by a free moral agent who acts voluntarily, is accountable for his conduct, and is the object of retributive justice.

The individualism of both criminal and constitutional law derived from the incorrigibly individualistic common law, which placed an unlimited valuation upon personal liberty and property. The common law knew society only as so many John Does and Richard Roes, which is to say that it had scant regard for society collectively. Social and economic problems were reflected in the common law merely as conflicts of personal interest between contending parties. They might possess an unequal status and power; their case might involve great and grave social interests. But to the common law, indifferently neutral and, in the hands of lesser judges, generally oblivious to public policy, the parties were theoretically interchangeable personalities to be dealt with on equal terms and with scant regard for others. The system made for impartial justice and protected the rights of persons and property; but its justice was sometimes harsh or indifferent to the general good.[35]

The hero of the common law was the property-owning, liberty-loving, self-reliant, reasonable man. He was also the hero of American society, celebrated by Jefferson as the freehold farmer, by Hamilton as the town merchant, by Jackson as the frontiersman. Between the American image of the common man and the common law's received ideal of Everyman there was a remarkable likeness.

In Shaw's time social conditions provided a congenial climate for the burgeoning of this individual in law and in society. America enjoyed an open class system in which power was fluid and plural, and everyone, including the industrial worker, lusted after capitalistic success. Where "the mentality of an independent entrepreneur" prevailed, as Professor Hartz observed, "two national impulses are bound to make themselves felt: the impulse towards democracy and the impulse towards capitalism."[36] Both

[35] See Pound, *Spirit of the Common Law*, pp. 13–15, 18–20, 27–28, and 37.
[36] Louis Hartz, *The Liberal Tradition in America* (New York, 1955), p. 89.

made the "extreme individualism"[37] of the common law acceptable.

Individualism and the Commonwealth idea were by no means incompatible, despite certain logical inconsistencies. The common law itself punished the injurious use of property by individuals, a fact which Shaw made a point of departure for expansion of the police power. The corporation, an individual in contemplation of law, although soulless, represented the collective enterprise of many individuals, as did the labor union. And both were smiled upon by the common law as construed by Shaw. Yet the corporation also represented a threat to strictly individualistic enterprisers, and on their behalf a grant of incorporation was accompanied by public governance of corporate organization and policy.

It was also on behalf of individuals, and the community too, that the common law frowned upon monopolies and sought to preserve a free competitive market. When, for example, the South Boston Iron Company bought out a shareholder at a price conditioned upon his bond that he would never thereafter engage in the iron business, the Shaw Court found a violation of a common-law rule that "bonds in restraint of trade are void." This rule the Court said was "suited to the genius of our government and nature of our institutions. It is founded on great principles of public policy and carries out our constitutional prohibition of monopolies and exclusive privileges." [38]

The Court enumerated five specific considerations to prove the "unreasonableness" of contracts in restraint of trade.[39] The first, quite interestingly, protected individuals from themselves:

1. Such contracts injure the parties making them, because they diminish their means of procuring livelihoods and a competency for their families. They tempt improvident persons, for the sake of present gain, to deprive themselves of the power to make future acquisitions. And they expose such persons to imposition and oppression.

The other considerations, enumerated by the Court, equally reflected the values and spirit of the time:

2. They tend to deprive the public of the services of men in the

[37] Pound, *Spirit of the Common Law*, p. 15.
[38] Alger v. Thacher, 19 Pick. 51, 53 (1837) *per* Morton, J.
[39] *Ibid.*, at 54.

employments and capacities in which they may be most useful to the community as well as themselves.

3. They discourage industry and enterprise, and diminish the products of ingenuity and skill.

4. They prevent competition and enhance prices.

5. They expose the public to all the evils of monopoly.

The fifth consideration, declared the Court, "especially is applicable to wealthy companies and large corporations, who have the means, unless restrained by law, to exclude rivalry, monopolize business and engross the market. Against evils like these, *wise laws protect individuals and the public,* by declaring all such contracts void." [40] The "wise laws" of this case were judicial, not legislative, in character, but constituted state action nonetheless. The relationship between the Commonwealth idea and individualism is clear enough.

The common law did not often protect individuals from themselves, from monopolies, or from anything. It tended more strongly to express its individualism not by tenderness but by harshly and uncompromisingly treating men as free-willed, self-reliant, risk-and-responsibility-taking individuals. The consequences of such an attitude were, as Dean Pound noted, a strict insistence upon full and exact performance of all duties legally undertaken, without allowance for accident or extenuating circumstances and without mercy for defaulters. If a man were tricked or coerced into a legal transaction, said Pound, the law might permit him to sue for the wrong, but declined to set aside the transaction. "If he could not guard his own interests, he must not ask the courts, which were only keeping the peace, to do so for him. . . . In other words, it held that every man of mature age must take care of himself. He need not expect to be saved from himself by legal paternalism. . . . When he acted, he was held to have acted at his own risk with his eyes open, and he must abide the appointed consequences." [41] One might add that the spirit of the common law was epitomized in the maxim, "Let the buyer beware" (*caveat emptor*).

The spirit manifested itself daily in the Shaw Court in commercial law and in the law of private contracts. But its most important manifestation, from the standpoint of social consequences, was in cases of railroad and industrial accident, which fell within the compass of tort law. Here the fierce individualism

---

[40] *Ibid.* Italics added. This was a common-law case not involving any statute.
[41] Pound, *Spirit of the Common Law*, p. 19.

of the common law, even though reflecting the self-reliance that America so highly valued, was devoid of humane considerations. No doubt the law could not have been expected to reward fools for their foolishness. Shaw would not allow damages to a man whose fingers were frozen when he left the warmth of a stalled train to walk out in the cold in search of an inn, rather than wait with the other passengers for a rescue sleigh. The Chief Justice was right in ruling that because passengers can take care of themselves, the liability of a common carrier toward them is less than that toward goods entrusted to the carrier's care by a shipper. Yet when an accident occurred despite all precaution, Shaw held railroads liable for damage to freight but not for injuries to passengers. They took the risk of accidents that might occur regardless of due care.

The rigorous individualism of the common law was especially noticeable in the emergent doctrine of contributory negligence, of which Shaw was a leading exponent.[42] That doctrine required a degree of care and skill which no one but the mythical "prudent" or "reasonable man" of the common law could match. A misstep, however slight, from the ideal standard of conduct, placed upon the injured party the whole burden of his loss, even though the railroad was also at fault and perhaps more so. Comparative rather than contributory negligence would have been a fairer test, or perhaps some rule by which damages could be apportioned.

Probably the furthermost limit of the common law's individualism in accident cases was expressed in the rule that a right to action is personal and dies with the injured party. This contributed to the related rule that the wrongful death of a human being was no ground for an action of damages. But for the intervention of the legislature, the common law would have left the relatives of victims of fatal accident without a legal remedy to obtain compensation. It would also have made it more profitable for a railroad to kill a man outright than to scratch him, for if he lived he could sue.

The fellow-servant rule was the most far-reaching consequence of individualism in the law as Shaw expounded it. The rule was that a worker who was injured, through no fault of his own, by the negligence of a fellow employee, could not maintain a claim of damages against his employer. Shaw formulated this rule at a strategic moment for employers, because as industrialization expanded at an incredible pace, factory and railroad acci-

---

[42] Brown v. Kendall, 6 Cush. 292 (1850); Shaw v. B. & W. RR., 8 Gray 45 (1857).

dents multiplied frighteningly. Since the fellow-servant rule threw the whole loss from accidents upon innocent workers, capitalism was relieved of an enormous sum that would otherwise have been due as damages. The encouragement of "infant industries" had no greater social cost.

The fellow-servant rule was unmistakably an expression of legal thinking predicated upon the conception that a free man is one who is free to work out his own destiny, to pursue the calling of his choice, and to care for himself. If he undertakes a dangerous occupation, he voluntarily assumes the risks to which he has exposed himself. He should know that the others with whom he will have to work may cause him harm by their negligence. He must bear his loss because his voluntary conduct has implied his consent to assume it and to relieve his employer of it. On the other hand, there can be no implication that the employer has contracted to indemnify the worker for the negligence of anyone but himself. The employer, like his employees, is responsible for his own conduct, but cannot be liable without fault.

On such considerations Shaw exempted the employer from liability to his employees, although he was liable to the rest of the world for the tortious acts which they committed in the course of their employment. It is interesting to note that Shaw felt obliged to read the employee's assumption of risk into his contract of employment. This legal fiction also reflected the individualism of a time when it was felt that free men could not be bound except by a contract of their own making.

The public policy which Shaw confidently expounded in support of his reading of the law similarly expressed the independent man: safety would be promoted if each worker guarded himself against his own carelessness and just as prudently watched his neighbor; to remove this responsibility by setting up the liability of the employer would allegedly tend to create individual laxity rather than prudence. So Shaw reasoned. It seems not to have occurred to him that fear of being maimed prompted men to safety anyway, or that contributory negligence barred recovery of damages, or that freeing the employer from liability was no inducement to employ only the most careful persons and to utilize accident-saving devices. Nor, for all his reliance upon the voluntary choice of mature men, did it occur to Shaw that a worker undertook a dangerous occupation and "consented" to its risks because his poverty deprived him of real choice. For that matter, none of these considerations prompted the legislature to supersede the common law with employers' liability and workmen's compensation acts until many decades later. Shaw did no violence to the spirit of his age by the fellow-servant rule, or by the rules he applied in other personal injury cases, particularly those involving wrongful death. In all such cases his enlightened views, so evident in police-power cases, were absent, probably because government action was equally absent.

IV

Shaw's controversial rulings on the law of homicide, which he expressly based on common-law principles, were similarly influenced by pervasive individualism. The cardinal principle of criminal jurisprudence is that a crime is the act of a voluntary and responsible agent who freely choses between the lawful and the unlawful. From this standpoint, guilt, like sin, is personal because each man is the captain of his own conduct. As in the theory behind the fellow-servant rule, the law pictured personal action as the result of the exercise of free will tempered by prudent considerations of consequences. As Shaw put it, "a person must be presumed to intend all the natural, probable, and usual consequences of his own acts." [43] Since he is thus responsible for his conduct, he must curb his passions and his malice, or assume the risk of punishment.

On the basis of these views Shaw ruled that the law implies malice, making out a case of murder, where one person intentionally kills another and nothing beyond the intentional killing is shown. Since the "wilful and voluntary act of destroying the life of another is . . . the greatest wrong which can be done," Shaw held, the burden of rebutting the presumption of malice by proving extenuating circumstances falls upon the defendant. Accountable for his actions, he must account for them or pay the price of the exaggerated respect which the law has for him. This respect was expressed in the presumption that he is a self-governing will, knows right from wrong, and therefore must have acted maliciously when without apparent provocation he violently assailed a fellow being with a dangerous weapon likely to kill.

Shaw has been unjustly criticized from his own time to ours for this rule of implied malice and its corollary, that the burden is upon the defendant to disprove malice by showing facts that will reduce the crime to manslaughter. The critics fail to appreciate not only that this rule of law was of long standing in Anglo-

[43] Commonwealth v. Webster, 5 Cush. 295, 305 (1850).

American jurisprudence, but that Shaw construed it in its most liberal light. Where others had implied malice from the mere fact of killing alone, he annexed several crucial conditions before permitting the implication. Not the least of these was the condition that the prosecution must first prove beyond reasonable doubt that the accused, a rational and responsible individual, had intentionally committed the homicide. Moreover, the disclosure of evidence showing extenuating circumstances required the prosecution to prove malice as well, rendering the rule of implied malice inoperative. Shaw construed the law as fairly as possible in favor of the accused.

His most notable contribution to the substantive criminal law was his exposition of the criminal responsibility of the insane. Nowhere in that field of law was the individualism with which it was imbued more sharply etched. For the criminal law as Shaw expounded it assumed that mental disease virtually robbed its victim of his individualism, or, more properly put, of the capacity for acting as a free moral agent. Theoretically an insane person could not even commit a crime since he could not possess the requisite guilty state of mind if at the time of the act he did not know what he was doing or that it was wrong. Such was the law as Shaw adopted it from England. But he further individualized the knowledge that one must have before being held responsible for having acted maliciously: that is, he insisted upon a knowledge by the accused of his interrelationships with others and an ability to apply "to his own case" an abstract understanding of the difference between right and wrong or the nature of an act.

Moreover Shaw perceived that a mentally diseased person may possess such knowledge and understanding and yet be irresponsible for his acts, both psychologically and legally. For in law or psychology one cannot be accountable for his conduct if he cannot control it. He must, that is, possess volition as well as knowledge before he can be said to possess a criminal intent. It was Shaw who added to the criminal law of insanity the volitionary element which ordinarily enters into the *mens rea* of a crime.

Without volition the essence of individualism is absent, because as Shaw put it, the loss of volition, like the loss of knowledge, makes an act the result of a mind incapable of choosing, ungoverned by will, and involuntary. Accordingly, Shaw formulated a test of "irresistible impulse" to supplement earlier tests of insanity which, based on purely cognitive elements, had ignored the volitional ones. The irresistible impulse test, which Shaw constructed from the best opinion that the medical science of his day could offer, represented his belief that the law as he found it had not sufficiently recognized the incapacity of the mentally diseased to control their own conduct. His exposition of the criminal irresponsibility of the insane accorded with both the individualism and the growing humanitarianism of his day.

In another area of the criminal law, that dealing with conspiracies, Shaw seems on first glance to have run counter to individualist doctrines. He held, in what is probably his best-known opinion, that a combination of workers to establish and maintain a closed shop by the use of peaceable coercion is not an indictable conspiracy even if it tends to injure employers. Shaw also indicated that he saw nothing unlawful in a peaceable, concerted effort to raise wages.

But other judges had been persuaded by the ideology of individualism, or at least used its rhetoric, to find criminality in trade-union activity and even in unions per se. Combination, labor's most effective means of economic improvement, was the very basis of the ancient doctrine of criminal conspiracy and the denial of individual effort. The closed shop was regarded as a hateful form of monopoly by labor, organized action to raise wages as coercion, and both regarded as injurious to the workers themselves, as well as to trade and the public at large. When so much store was placed in self-reliance, the only proper way in law and economics for employees to better themselves seemed to be by atomistic bargaining. Unions were thought to impede the natural operation of free competition by individuals on both sides of the labor market. Or so Shaw's contemporaries and earlier judges had believed.

Individualism, however, has many facets, and like maxims relating to liberty, the free market, or competition, can be conscripted into the service of more than one cause. If self-reliance was one attribute of individualism, the pursuit of self-interest was another. As Tocqueville noted, where individualism and freedom prevail, men pursue their self-interest and express themselves by developing an astonishing proclivity for association. As soon as several Americans of like interest "have found one another out, they combine," observed Tocqueville.[44] Shaw too noted the "general tendency of society in our times, to combine men into bodies and associations having some object of deep interest common to

[44] *Democracy in America* (Vintage edition), II, ch. 5, p. 116.

themselves . . ." [45] He understood that freedom meant combination.

When the question arose whether it was criminal for a combination of employees to refuse to work for one who employed nonunion labor, Shaw replied in the disarming language of individualism that men who are not bound by contract are "free to work for whom they please, or not to work, if they so prefer. In this state of things, we cannot perceive, that it is criminal for men to agree together to exercise their acknowledged rights, in such a manner as best to subserve their own interests." [46]

He acknowledged that the pursuit of their own interests might result in injury to third parties, but that did not in his opinion make their combination criminal in the absence of fraud, violence, or other illegal behavior. To Shaw's mind the pursuit of self-interest was a hard, competitive game in which atomistic individuals stood less chance of getting hurt by joining forces. He also seems to have considered bargaining between capital and labor as a form of competition whose benefits to society, like those from competition of any kind, outweighed the costs. Finally, he was fair enough to believe that labor was entitled to combine if business could, and wary enough to understand that if the conspiracy doctrine were not modified, it might boomerang against combinations of businessmen who competed too energetically. Thus Shaw drew different conclusions from premises which he shared with others concerning individualism, freedom, and competition. The result of his interpretation of the criminal law of conspiracies was that the newly emerging trade-union movement was left viable.

But the corporate movement was left viable too, a fact which helps reconcile the fellow-servant and trade-union decisions. To regard one as "anti-labor" and the other as "pro-labor" adds nothing to an understanding of two cases governed by different legal considerations, on the one hand tort and contract, on the other criminal conspiracy. The fellow-servant case belongs to a line of harsh personal injury decisions that were unrelated to labor as such. To be sure, labor was saddled with much of the cost of industrial accidents, but victims of other accidents hardly fared better. The fellow-servant decision also represented a departure of the maxim *respondeat superior* which might impose liability without fault; while the trade-union decision, intended

---

[45] "Charge to the Grand Jury, 1832," pp. 7–8.
[46] Commonwealth v. Hunt, 4 Metc. 111, 130 (1842).

in part to draw the fangs of labor's support of the codification movement, represented a departure from Hawkins's conspiracy doctrine which might impose criminality on business as well as labor.

Despite the conflicting impact of the two decisions on labor's fortunes and the fact that they are not comparable from a legal standpoint they harmonize as a part of Shaw's thought. He regarded the worker as a free agent competing with his employer as to the terms of employment, at liberty to refuse work if his demands were not met. As the best judge of his own welfare, he might assume risks, combine in a closed shop, or make other choices. For Shaw, workers possessed the same freedom of action enjoyed by employers against labor and against business rivals. Although the fellow-servant and trade-union decisions had the effect of dividing two loaves, the baker fashioned them from similar ingredients, legal ones excepted.

v

Individualism's most glorious chapter in history is related to the procedural side of the criminal law. It was here that the historic contest for the "liberties of the subject" had been fought for and won. Many of the "rights of Englishmen" which the embattled farmers of 1776 claimed were rights held against the state by persons criminally accused. Professor Chafee calls them collectively "human rights" and finds among criminal procedures "the most important human right in the Constitution" — the writ of habeas corpus. Liberty of speech and worship, he adds, "will go on somehow, despite laws, but not liberty of the person." [47]

Criminal justice signified procedural justice: habeas corpus; immunity from arbitrary search, arrest, and imprisonment; fair public trial after indictment and presentation of charges; immunity against self-incrimination; confrontation of accusers and representation by counsel; regularized judicial proceedings and the right of appeal; and the whole complex of rights which are loosely epitomized by the phrase "by the law of the land" or due process of law. All were hallowed as both natural rights and common-law rights of individuals, and were doubly secured by bills of rights in written constitutions. Criminal procedure is accordingly saturated with the theory and practice of individualism.

[47] Z. Chafee, *How Human Rights Got Into the Constitution* (Boston, 1952), pp. 44 and 51.

Shaw believed that his greatest duty was "to apply the sustaining arm of the law to the support of right, liberty, and justice, to every individual, however humble." [48] His contemporaries knew him as a zealous defender of cherished procedures. No doubt the presence of the Supreme Judicial Court and its readiness to enforce the procedural rights of individuals rendered abortive many a legislative or lower-court impropriety. Then too the nisi prius sessions of the high court, its hearings en banc in capital cases, as well as its appellate opinions, made criminal justice a day-to-day reality.

Few cases came before Shaw involving what he regarded as "a proceeding subversive of the rights of the subject." [49] But he watched for such cases carefully. Despite his high tolerance for legislative enactments and his many rules of construction for avoiding a declaration of unconstitutionality, he placed in a special category statutes "which in their operation are in danger of encroaching private rights," by which he meant the rights appertaining to criminal justice. His interpretation of such statutes would not be "according to any presumed intention of the legislature not expressed"; rather, the statute itself "must on its face, be conformable to the constitution." [50] When construing the provisions of "a bill of rights," he said, "we are to look at the spirit and purpose of them as well as the letter." They were "so obviously dictated by natural justice" that he found them to be "obligatory upon the consciences of legislators and judges, without any express declaration . . ." [51] Thus, despite the fact that the state Declaration of Rights made no mention of the common law's grand jury system of trial by jury, Shaw read into the law-of-the-land clause an inherent limitation upon the legislature against abolishing that system in cases of infamous punishment.

In four of the nine reported cases in which the Shaw Court invalidated statutes, the grounds were legislative violation of some right of the criminally accused.[52] The four cases involved virtually every right from arrest to trial and appeal. In another case Shaw technically avoided a declaration of unconstitutionality but in effect nullified a statute which he construed as a threat to prin-

[48] Shaw, *An Address Delivered at the Opening of the New Court House in Worcester, Sept. 30, 1845* (Worcester, 1845), p. 9.

[49] Fisher v. McGirr, 1 Gray 1, 30 (1854).

[50] *Ibid.*, at 39–40.

[51] Jones v. Robbins, 8 Gray 329, 340 (1857).

[52] *Ibid.*; Fisher v. McGirr, 1 Gray 1 (1854); Sullivan v. Adams, 3 Gray 476 (1855); and Robinson v. Richardson, 13 Gray 454 (1859).

ciples underlying trial by jury.[53] The statute had empowered juries to decide the law as well as the facts of a case, rather than take the law from the trial judge. This, Shaw ruled, would prevent the right of appeal on grounds of law and would create uncertainty in law and inequality in its operation. Although he twisted the statute beyond recognition by holding that it must be construed to be merely declaratory of the common law, he was motivated by a laudable desire: to preserve "a government of laws and not of men" so that historic personal liberties would endure undiminished. Except for fugitive slaves, "every individual, however humble," knew that Shaw stood for exact and constant observance of the principles of criminal justice.

VI

The blemishes on Shaw's record of devotion to civil liberties lay outside the field of procedural rights. They are his opinions on blasphemy and racial segregation. In a time that still sanctioned slavery, the right of Negro children to sit side by side with whites in public schools was yet to be established — and even today is controversial. The Kneeland blasphemy case, however, involved the great historic rights of conscience and expression. Considering that Kneeland had merely expressed a disbelief in, or at worst, a simple denial of, God's existence, Shaw's finding of blasphemy grossly abridged freedom of speech, press, and religion.

Yet his opinion outraged only the transcendentalist reformers, some of the old dissenter sects, and the Jacksonian leaders who counted Kneeland as a colleague. By contrast, the general public and particularly the men of substance who dominated Massachusetts opinion, appplauded Shaw's distinctions between liberty and "license" and between freedom of religion and irreligion. Shaw spoke for them, the Whigs, the Congregationalists, and proper Unitarians who blenched at Parker and Emerson, and the merchants and lawyers. They praised their constitution's Declaration of Rights, but in reading its safeguards to freedom of utterance they followed Blackstone rather than Paine or Jefferson.

Shaw himself advocated that the "spirit and purpose" of the Declaration of Rights should control its reading, but he departed from this proposition in Kneeland's case. Despite his defense of the rights of the criminally accused, he did not appreciate that a criminal prosecution, like that against Kneeland, even if procedurally perfect, could be as much an instrument of oppression

[53] Commonwealth v. Anthes, 5 Gray 185 (1855).

as unreasonable searches or the abolition of the grand jury system. As Chief Justice, Shaw followed public opinion on heretics and free thinkers instead of upholding their rights.

The other decision blemishing his support of civil rights established the precedent for the "separate but equal" doctrine that became the legal linchpin of racial segregation. Shaw's opinion was probably motivated less by personal prejudice against Negroes than by judicial self-restraint and a corresponding high regard for the school committee, which laid down the rule for separate schools. The Chief Justice disavowed any consideration by the Court of the "expediency" of the school committee's exercise of its power to make all "reasonable" rules for the classification of students. But when a government agency, in the face of a constitution with an equality-of-rights clause, classifies the legal rights of citizens on the basis of race, the reasonableness of its rule is questionable; and the self-restraint of the Court is an abdication of judicial responsibility.

Shaw contented himself with the thought that prejudice was "not created by law, and probably cannot be changed by law," and more than likely would be fostered by "compelling colored and white children to associate together in the same schools." [54] The remark was destined to become a cliché in opinions of this kind, but experience had already denied its validity. At the time of the case, segregated schools had already been abolished in Massachusetss, excepting Boston, with the most successful results. Indeed, Boston's schools provided the state's last legal refuge for the prejudice of color. Various other legal inequities which had been based on race had recently been eliminated. The "civilization of the age," as Charles Sumner put it, demanded the abolition of segregated schools in Boston. A few years later, the legislature provided that "no distinction shall be made on account of race, color or religious opinions of the applicant or scholar." But Shaw's opinion, though no longer valid in his own state, had a noxious influence on American constitutional law for a century. Not until 1954 was its doctrine repudiated by the United States Supreme Court.

The rights of heretics and of free Negroes posed serious problems reflecting the tensions of American society, but none could compare with the tragic and terrible problem of slavery itself. Its shadow fell across the whole Union; inevitably it cast up issues in the guise of legal questions upon which Shaw had to pass

[54] Roberts v. City of Boston, 5 Cush. 198, 209 (1849).

judgment. That he hated slavery is unquestionable. The west-ward spread of this "great and acknowledged evil" he called a "crime and a disgrace." He believed that if it were not gradually and voluntarily abolished, a "great national calamity" threatened.[55] He did all that he thought he could, consonant with his judicial obligations, to "take the weaker side," as Whittier said of Rantoul, "and right the wronged, and free the thrall."

While Shaw was Chief Justice, all slaves whom fate brought to Massachusetts were guaranteed liberty, except for runaways. Whether they were brought by their masters who were temporarily visiting the Commonwealth or were just passing through, or whether they were cast up by the sea, they were set free by Shaw's definition of the law. Bound by neither precedent nor statute, he made that law. The principle of comity, he ruled, could not extend to human beings as property: because slavery was so odious and founded upon brute force it could exist only when sanctioned by positive, local law. There being no such law in Massachusetts, Shaw freed even slave seamen in the service of the United States Navy if they reached a port within his jurisdiction.

The abolitionists who at first lavished their praise on Shaw were quick to revile him for his fugitive-slavery decisions. He returned their disesteem for several reasons. Their plan for immediate emancipation was in his mind impractical and most dangerous to Southern society. Their lawlessness, with which he had considerable personal experience, cut deeply across his grain. In a speech of 1845, he warned against those who "would seek to destroy the respect of the community for the law and its administration, without which the dearest rights of humanity would be without protection." A bad law, he declared, should be corrected only by legislative action, but "so long as it remains in force, it is to be respected as the law, and because it is the law, not grudgingly and reluctantly, but with honesty and sincerity, because any departure from this fundamental rule of conduct, would put in jeopardy every interest and every institution which is worth saving."[56] The first statute he ever voided was a state enactment obstructing Congress' Fugitive Slave Act.[57]

This decision had been dictated by a precedent of the highest

[55] Shaw, "Slavery and the Missouri Question," *North American Review*, 10:138, 147, 153 (Jan. 1820).
[56] Shaw, *Address at Opening of Court House*, pp. 12–13.
[57] Commonwealth v. Coolidge, *Law Reporter*, 5:482 ff. (1843).

court of the nation. Undoubtedly Shaw's rendition of fugitive slaves was consistent with the obligations of his judicial office to support the Constitution and Congressional acts sustained by the Supreme Court. When he gave the leading opinion on the constitutionality of the Fugitive Slave Act of 1850, he was upholding "law and order," as well as following "the duty of all judges." But he was also doing what he thought best for "the peace, happiness, and prosperity of all the states," that is, for the Union.[58]

The fugitive slavery issue imperiled the very security of the Union. But Shaw's love for that Union outweighed even his concern for those whom he once said had been robbed of all the blessings and rights of life. The Fugitive Slave Law was a sectional compromise, a "peace measure," calculated to maintain national harmony. Shaw would do nothing to violate the North's pledge to remand fugitives. As he saw the matter, it was a case of "political and moral necessity" that the pledge be honored.

Significantly he remained an old-line Whig when most others of his background pledged themselves to the new Republican banner. In 1860 he supported the Constitutional Union Party, the heir of the traditional party of compromise. "Impelled by no motive save love of country," he joined a group of conciliationists who dreaded to see "the great union . . . broken," its people "shedding fraternal blood in civil war."[59] Their program called for Massachusetts to appease the South by repealing all personal liberty laws. Thus Shaw retreated from the cause of human freedom at the approach of the "national calamity."

VII

His conservatism tended to crop out in many of the notable social issues of his day — for example, fugitive slavery, segregation, blasphemy, and the fellow-servant rule. The church-state issue also revealed this conservatism. Lucifer's influence was not more noticeably prevalent in states where the rights of conscience were secured by a disestablishment of religion. However, Shaw, a devout Unitarian who believed that religion secured the moral character and good order of society, opposed any change in the state constitutional requirement that all citizens attend public worship and be taxed for its support.

His opinion in the Brookfield case, that a church could not

[58] Sims's Case, 7 Cush. 285, 310, 318–319 (1851).
[59] "Address. To the Citizens of Massachusetts." Reprinted in George T. Curtis, *A Memoir of Benjamin Robbins Curtis*, I, 329–335.

exist independently of a territorial parish, gave continued judicial support to the parish system upon which the Commonwealth's establishment of religion was based.[60] For it was the parish, a subdivision of the state, that collected taxes for religion and policed church attendance, thereby linking church and state in a manner violative of conscience. On the other hand, by subordinating the church to the parish, which elected the minister, Shaw made it possible for the ancient principle of congregationalism to fulfill its democratic promise by vesting the governance of the church in its parishioners instead of in the minority who had been admitted to church membership.

Religious liberty was also advanced by the Brookfield decision in another manner. The Trinitarian Congregationalists, once the virtually exclusive beneficiaries of the territorial parish system, suffered heavy losses in the eastern parishes to the Unitarians and belatedly discovered that the Baptists and other dissenters had a just cause in demanding complete separation of chuch and state. An 1833 constitutional amendment to this effect (an unintended and indirect consequence of his Brookfield decision), was unwelcome to Shaw, whose confidence in the conservative social values of religion led him to prefer an establishment.

His conservatism also manifested itself in certain common-law cases where the public interest had not been defined by statute. Here the law was shaped to meet the press of business needs; nothing illustrates this better than the personal injury cases and the variety of novel cases to which railroad corporations were parties. As has been noted, the roar of the first locomotive in Massachusetts signaled the advent of a capitalist revolution in the common law, in the sense that Shaw made railroads the beneficiaries of legal doctrine. To be sure, he believed that he was genuinely serving the general interest, calculating that what was good for business was good for the Commonwealth.

The legislature itself fostered this notion by conferring special privileges and powers on railroads and other enterprises, on ground that they acted in the name of the public or served the public interest. Of course, regulation went hand in hand with promotion. When the legislature intervened against the unbridled use of property, corporate or personal, on the theory that neither the common law nor the automatic market adequately insured the stake of the many, Shaw stanchly sustained the legislature. The

[60] Stebbins v. Jennings, 10 Pick. 172 (1830).

name of no nineteenth-century judge is more deservingly associated with the public interest than his.

It was when he had a free hand, in the absence of government action, that the character of his conservatism displayed itself: he construed the law so that corporate industrial interests prevailed over lesser, private ones. An individual farmer, shipper, passenger, worker, or pedestrian, when pitted against a corporation that in Shaw's mind personified industrial expansion and public prosperity, risked a rough sort of justice, whether the issue involved tort or contract. Shaw strictly insisted that individuals look to themselves, not to the law, for protection of life and limb. That insistence, together with his belief that rapid growth of manufactures and transportation heralded the coming of the good society, tended to minimize the legal liabilities of business. This was especially striking in cases of industrial accident and personal injury cases generally. His opinions went a long way to accentuate the inhumantiy of the common law in the area of torts, and, simultaneously, to spur capitalist enterprise. Here was the one great area of law in which he failed to protect the public interest. He might have done so without checking rapid industrialization, since the cost of accidents, if imposed on business, would have been shifted to the public by a hike in prices and rates.

VIII

It would be misleading and scarcely informative to conclude an analysis of Shaw's views by calling him a conservative. Moreover, his conservatism, to use favorite adjectives of historians, was on the whole enlightened, constructive, and moderate. He was certainly not a black-letter common-law judge, nor was he insulated against the liberalizing currents of his time. His inordinate faith in progress and his receptivity to change could not permit him to indulge in the blind intransigence of those who walked "in the same steps with their fathers, because their fathers walked in them . . ." He scorned lawyers "educated in a profound reverence for things established, who could never think of questioning the authority of a black-letter maxim . . ." Warning that it was "useless to regret the existence of changes which are now irrevocable," he urged the bar to give "the spirit of the age" its due by bringing the law abreast of the "rapid progress" being made everywhere else.[61]

While Story and Kent, steeped in the crusty lore of the Year

[61] Shaw, "Profession of the Law," *American Jurist* 7:64–66 (1832).

Books, were wailing to each other that they were the last of an old race of judges and that Taney's Charles River Bridge decision meant that the Constitution was gone,[62] Shaw was calmly noting that property was "fully subject to State regulation" in the interest of the "morals, health, internal commerce, and general prosperity of the community . . ."[63] At the age of eighty, in an opinion which is a little gem in the literature of the common law, he gave fresh evidence of his extraordinary talent for keeping hoary principles viable by adapting them "to new institutions and conditions of society, new modes of commerce, new usages and practices, as the society in the advancement of civilization may require."[64]

Shaw, a reformer of law, found objectionable the efforts of many of the Universal Social Reformers like Ripley, Parker, Kneeland, and Phillips. But he shared the premises of others who, like Mann, Howe, Dix, and Pierpont, fought for public schools, for better care of society's unforunates, and for temperance. While the rich growled about having to pay for the education of the children of the poor, Shaw used his high office to state that because free government must rest upon the general intelligence of the people, "a system of general education, therfore, by means of free schools, maintained at common expense, and to which every child of the Commonwealth may have access . . . is . . . indispensable . . ."[65] His defense of trade-union activities, in a common-law decision, and his stand on the police power of the government to regulate society for the general good also suggest that he was not hidebound in his social views.

Compared to such Whig peers as Webster, Story, and Choate, Shaw was quite liberal in many respects. Indeed his judicial record is remarkably like that one might expect from a jurist of the Jacksonian persuasion. Marcus Morton, during ten years of service as Shaw's associate, found it necessary to dissent only once, in Kneeland's case. No doubt the inherited legal tradition created an area of agreement among American jurists that was more influential in the decision-making process than party differences. Yet it is revealing that many of Shaw's opinions might conceivably have been written by a Gibson, but not by a Kent. It was not

[62] Charles River Bridge v. Warren Bridge, 11 Peters 420 (1837). See Carl B. Swisher, *Roger B. Taney* (New York, 1936), pp. 377–379, and John T. Horton, *James Kent* (New York, 1939), pp. 293–295.

[63] Commonwealth v. Kimball, 24 Pick. 359, 363 (1837).

[64] Commonwealth v. Temple, 14 Gray 69, 74 (1860).

[65] "Charge to the Grand Jury, 1832," pp. 15–16.

just the taught tradition of the common law which Shaw and Gibson shared; they shared also taught traditions of judicial self-restraint, of the positive state, and the "Commonwealth idea," a term that is meaningful in Pennsylvania's history as well as in Massachusetts'.[66]

But personality makes a difference in law as in politics. It oversimplifies to say, as Pound has, that the "chiefest factor in determining the course which legal development will take with respect to any new situation or new problem is the analogy or analogies that chance to be at hand . . ." [67] There are usually conflicting and alternative analogies, rules, and precedents from among which judges may choose. The direction of choice is shaped by such personal factors as the judge's calculation of the community's needs, his theory of the function of government, his concept of the role of the court, inexpressible intuitions, unrecognized predilections, and perhaps doting biases. It is difficult to name a single major case decided by Shaw which might not have gone the other way had another been sitting in his place.

Shaw interpreted the received law as he understood it, and his understanding was colored by his own presuppositions, particularly in respect to those interests and values he thought the legal order should secure. Few other judges have been so earnestly and consciously concerned with the public policy implicit in the principle of a case.

Much of his greatness lay in this concern for principle and policy. "It is not enough," he observed, "to say, that the law is so established . . . The rule may be a good rule . . . But some better reason must be given for it than that, so it was enacted, or so it was decided." [68] He thought it necessary to search out the rule which governed a case; to ask "upon what principle is it founded?" and to deliver a disquisition on the subject, with copious illustrations for the guidance of the future. From the bench he was one of the nation's foremost teachers of law.

His opinions did not overlook the question *"cui bono?"* which, he believed, "applies perhaps, with still greater force to the laws, than to any other subject." [69] That is why he fixed "enlightened public policy" at the root of all legal principles, along with "rea-

<hr />

[66] See generally Louis Hartz, *Economic Policy and Democratic Thought: Penn-sylvania, 1776–1860* (Cambridge, 1948).

[67] *Spirit of the Common Law*, p. 12.

[68] "Profession of the Law," p. 66.

[69] *Ibid.*

son" and "natural justice." [70] He understood that American law was a functioning instrument of a free society, embodying its ideals, serving its interests. It is not surprising, then, that he tended to minimize precedent and place his decisions on broad grounds of social advantage. Justice Holmes, attributing Shaw's greatness to his "accurate appreciation of the requirements of the community," thought that "few have lived who were his equals in their understanding of the gounds of public policy to which all laws must be ultimately referred." [71] To be sure, he made errors of judgment and policy. Yet the wonder is that his errors were so few, considering the record number of opinions which he delivered, on so many novel questions, in so many fields of law.

Perhaps his chief contribution was his day-by-day domestication of the English common law. He made it plastic and practical, preserving its continuities with what was worthwhile in the past, yet accommodating it to the ideals and shifting imperatives of American life. The Massachusetts Bar made a similar evaluation of his work when honoring the "old Chief" upon his resignation. The Bar, speaking through a distinguished committee, declared:

It was the task of those who went before you, to show that the principles of the common and the commercial law were available to the wants of communities which were far more recent than the origin of those systems. It was for you to adapt those systems to still newer and greater exigencies; to extend them to the solution of questions, which it required a profound sagacity to foresee, and for which an intimate knowledge of the law often enabled you to provide, before they had even fully arisen for judgment. Thus it has been that in your hands the law has met the demands of a period of unexampled activity and enterprise; while over all its varied and conflicting interests you have held the strong, conservative sway of a judge, who moulds the rule for the present and the future out of the principles and precedents of the past. Thus too it has been, that every tribunal in the country has felt the weight of your judgments, and jurists at home and abroad look to you as one of the great expositors of the law.[72]

Time has not diminished the force of this observation. As Professor Chafee has noted, "Probably no other state judge has so deeply influenced the development of commercial and constitu-

[70] Norway Plains Co. v. Boston & Maine RR., 1 Gray 263, 267 (1854).

[71] Oliver Wendell Holmes, *The Common Law* (Boston, 1881), p. 106.

[72] Address on Chief Justice Shaw's Resignation, Sept. 10, 1860, Supplement, 81 Mass. 603.

tional law throughout the nation. Almost all the principles laid down by him have proved sound . . ." [73]

He was sound in more than his principles. Like John Quincy Adams, his fellow Bay-Statesman whom he resembled in so many ways, he made his name a synonym for integrity, impartiality, and independence. Towering above class and party, doing everything for justice and nothing for fear or favor, he was a model for the American judicial character. And none but an Adams could compare with Shaw in his overpowering sense of public service and devotion to the good of the whole community. His achievement as a jurist is to be sought in his constructive influence upon the law of our country and in the fact so perfectly summed up in a tribute to him on his death: life, liberty, and property were safe in his hands.

[73] Zechariah Chafee, Jr., "Lemuel Shaw," *D.A.B.*

APPENDIX

SAMUEL PUTNAM (1768–1853) *1814–42*. Harvard, 1787. Unitarian.
Studied under Theophilus Bradbury, later Judge of the Massachusetts
Supreme Judicial Court. Admitted to bar in 1794. Practiced in Salem.
Teacher of Joseph Story. Federalist. Representative to General Court,
1812; state senator, 1808–09; 1813–14. Early expert on commercial
law. [Frank W. Grinnell, "A Glimpse of the Life of an Essex County
Judge. Samuel Putnam," *Massachusetts Law Quarterly* 8:1–8 (November 1922).]

SAMUEL SUMNER WILDE (1771–1855) *1815–50*. Dartmouth, 1789.
Unitarian. Studied law under David L. Barnes, U.S. District Court
Judge. Admitted to bar in 1792. Practiced in Maine district. Federalist.
Presidential elector, 1800, 1808. State Councillor, 1814. Member of
Hartford Convention, 1815. Influenced development of criminal law.
[J. Gardner White, "Samuel Sumner Wilde," *Memorial Biographies
of the New-England Historic Genealogical Society* (Boston, 1881), II,
368–388.]

MARCUS MORTON (1784–1864) *1825–40*. Brown, 1804. Studied
law at Tapping Reeve's law school in Litchfield, Conn. Admitted to
bar in 1807. Practiced in Taunton. Democrat. Congressman, 1817–
21. Lieutenant-governor of Massachusetts, 1824–25. Perennial candidate for governor, 1828–43, elected 1839 and 1842. Championed
farmer and worker classes. Advocate of civil liberties. Collector of
Port of Boston, 1845–48. Joined Free-Soil Party in 1850's. Overseer of
Harvard for thirty-two years. [Scott H. Paradise, "Morton, Marcus,"
D.A.B.]

CHARLES AUGUSTUS DEWEY (1793–1866) *1837–66*. Williams, 1811.
Congregationalist. Studied law under his father, Daniel Dewey, Judge
of Massachusetts Supreme Judicial Court. Admitted to bar in 1814.
Practiced in Williamstown and Northampton. Whig. Two terms as
representative to General Court, one as state senator. U.S. District Attorney, 1830–37. Trustee of Williams College for over forty years.
[Maria Dewey, "Charles Augustus Dewey," *Memorial Biographies of
the New-England Historic Genealogical Society* (Boston, 1905), VI,
178–180.]

SAMUEL HUBBARD (1785–1847) *1842–47*. Yale, 1802. Congregationalist. Studied law under Charles Jackson, later Judge of the Massachusetts Supreme Judicial Court. Admitted to bar in 1806. Practiced in Maine District and Boston. Director, then President of Suffolk Bank, 1818–42. Federalist-Whig. Representative to General Court, 1816–18, 1820–21, 1831; state senator, 1823–24, 1838. Member of Massachusetts Constitutional Convention, 1820. Temperance leader. Trustee of Phillips Andover Academy, 1823–43; trustee of Dartmouth College, 1829–47. [Elizabeth G. Buck, "Samuel Hubbard," *Memorial Biographies of the New-England Historic Genealogical Society* (Boston, 1880), I, 86–101.]

RICHARD FLETCHER (1788–1869) *1843–53.* Dartmouth, 1806. Baptist. Studied law under Daniel Webster. Admitted to bar in 1811. Practiced in Portsmouth, N.H. and Boston. Excelled as trial lawyer. Advocated strict construction of corporate charters, equal rights for Negroes, and the fellow-servant rule. Whig. Congressman, 1836–37; declined renomination. Trustee of Dartmouth, 1848–57. [H. W. H. Knott, "Fletcher, Richard," *D.A.B.*]

CHARLES EDWARD FORBES (1795–1881) *1848.* Brown, 1815. Studied law under Elijah H. Mills of Northampton. Admitted to bar in 1818. Practiced in Northampton. Whig. Representative to General Court, 1825, 1835. County attorney, 1826. Master in Chancery, 1835. Commissioner for codifying common law, 1836. In later years an advocate of Darwinism. [Conrad Reno, *Memoirs of the Judiciary and the Bar of New England* (Boston, 1900, 3 vols.), I, 620–621.]

THERON METCALF (1784–1875) *1848–65.* Brown, 1805. Studied law at Tapping Reeve's law school in Litchfield, Conn. Admitted to bar in 1807. Practiced in Dedham. Editor of *Dedham Gazette,* 1813–19. Founded private law school, 1828. For many years county attorney. Federalist-Whig. Representative to General Court, 1833–34; state senator, 1835. Reporter to Supreme Judicial Court, 1840–47. Contributed to law journals, edited several English works, indexed Massachusetts statutes, and wrote *Law of Contracts,* 1867. [Charles Fairman, "Metcalf, Theron," *D.A.B.*]

GEORGE TYLER BIGELOW (1810–78) *1850–67.* Harvard, 1829. Gave up teaching career to study law under Charles G. Loring. Admitted to bar in 1834. Practiced in Boston. Whig. Representative to General Court, 1840–45; state senator, 1847–48. Judge of Court of Common Pleas, 1848. Chief Justice of the Supreme Judicial Court after Shaw, 1860–67. Fellow of Harvard. [George B. Chase, "Memoir of George Tyler Bigelow," *Proceedings,* Massachusetts Historical Society, 2nd ser., 5:458–482 (April 1890).]

CALEB CUSHING (1800–79) *1852–53.* Harvard, 1817. Unitarian. Admitted to bar, 1821. Three terms in General Court. Son-in-law of Judge Wilde. Congressman, 1834–43. Orthodox Whig until about 1843. Thereafter a leading Democrat, and an uncompromising advocate of Southern views and national expansion. Twice defeated for Massachusetts governorship. Attorney general to Presidents Pierce and

Appendix 339

Buchanan. Republican after outbreak of Civil War. Diplomat. Nominated by Grant as Chief Justice of United States but not confirmed. [Claude M. Fuess, "Cushing, Caleb," *D.A.B.*]

BENJAMIN FRANKLIN THOMAS (1813–78) *1853–59*. Brown, 1830. Unitarian. Admitted to bar in 1833. Practiced in Worcester. Whig. Representative to General Court, 1842. U.S. Commissioner in Bankruptcy, 1843. Judge of Probate, 1844–48; resigned for lucrative private practice. Republican. Congressman, 1861. Defeated for reëlection because of conservatism on slavery question. For the same reason, he was not confirmed when nominated to Chief Justiceship of Massachusetts Supreme Judicial Court in 1868. [Richard Olney, "Memoir of Benjamin F. Thomas," *Proceedings*, Massachusetts Historical Society, 2nd ser., 14:297–302 (Oct. 1900).]

PLINY MERRICK (1794–1867) *1853–67*. Harvard, 1814. Studied law under Levi Lincoln the Younger. Admitted to bar in 1817. Practiced in Worcester and Taunton, where he was a partner of Marcus Morton. County district attorney, 1832–43. Judge of Court of Common Pleas, 1843–48; 1851–53. President of Worcester & Nashua Railroad, 1848–50. Senior counsel for defense in celebrated Webster-Parkman murder case, 1850. Democrat of inconstant loyalty. Four years a Worcester selectman. Representative to General Court, 1827; state senator, 1850. For a time edited Worcester *National Aegis*. [Charles Fairman, "Merrick, Pliny," *D.A.B.*]

EBENEZER ROCKWOOD HOAR (1816–95) *1859–69*. Harvard, 1814 (A.B.) and Harvard Law School, 1839 (LL.B.). Early prominence at the bar. Lay Unitarian leader. "Conscience Whig," organizer of Free-Soil Party, abolitionist leader. Judge of Court of Common Pleas, 1849–55. Attorney general to President Grant. Served on commission to settle *Alabama* claims. Congressman, 1873–75. Long eminent in Republican politics. For thirty years an Overseer of Harvard or member of the corporation. [George E. Haynes, "Hoar, Ebenezer Rockwood," *D.A.B.*]

BIBLIOGRAPHY

I. SHAW MANUSCRIPTS

Shaw Papers, 1607–1861. Massachusetts Historical Society.
Shaw Collection. Boston Social Law Library.

These manuscript collections are a source of disappointment. They consist primarily of deeds, briefs, mortgages, receipts, and other documents. There are also a few manuscript charges and speeches, some clippings, personal effects, account books, and at the Social Law Library, Shaw's manuscript notes, handsomely bound, of the cases argued before him — revealing no more than the published *Massachusetts Reports*. There are hundreds of letters to Shaw, most of them from members of the legal profession, concerning the business of the Court and legal trivia. Of the few letters written by Shaw, the majority are to members of his family, and, on the whole, are of minor value. A careful search of the manuscript collections of many of his contemporaries, such as Edward Everett and Joseph Story, turned up no noteworthy letters by Shaw.

II. ADDRESSES AND ARTICLES BY LEMUEL SHAW

An Address Delivered at the Opening of the New Court House in Worcester, Sept. 30, 1845 (Worcester, 1845). Pamphlet.
A Charge Delivered to the Grand Jury for the County of Essex, May Term 1832 (Boston, 1832). Pamphlet.
A Concise View of Some of the Facts and Arguments Respecting Another Bridge, to South Boston. Respectfully Addressed to the Citizens of Boston (N.d., 1824? Authorship uncertain). Pamphlet.
A Discourse Delivered before the Officers and Members of the Humane Society of Massachusetts, 11 June, 1811 (Boston, 1811). Pamphlet.
Memorial to Congress against the Tariff Law of 1828, by Citizens of Boston (Boston, 1829). Pamphlet.
"Profession of the Law in the United States. Influence of the Form of Government and Political Institutions upon the Law and Its Professors." Extract from an Address Delivered before the Suffolk Bar, May, 1827. *American Jurist and Law Magazine* (Boston), 7:56–69 (Jan. 1832).
"A Sketch of the Life and Character of the Hon. Isaac Parker, Late Chief Justice of this Court. An Address Delivered before the Bar of Berkshire, by Lemuel Shaw C.J., September term 1830, at Lenox," Appendix, 9 Pickering 567–578 (1830).
"Slavery and the Missouri Question," *North American Review and Miscellaneous Journal* (Boston), 10:137–168 (Jan. 1820).

III. CONTEMPORARY ESTIMATES OF SHAW

Aldrich, Emory P. "Professional and Judicial Life of Lemuel Shaw," *Memorial Biographies of the New-England Historic and Genealogical Society* (Boston, 1880–1907, 9 vols.), 230–247.

Proceedings of the Bench and Bar, Sept. 10, 1860, on Chief Justice Shaw's Resignation, Supplement, 15 Gray 599–608.

Proceedings of the Bench and Bar, April 9, 1861, on Chief Justice Shaw's Death, Supplement, 16 Gray 598–606.

Shaw, Samuel S. "Lemuel Shaw, Early and Domestic Life," *Memorial Biographies of the New-England Historic and Genealogical Society* IV, 200–229.

Thomas, Benjamin F. "Sketch of the Life and Judicial Labor of Chief-Justice Shaw," *Proceedings,* Massachusetts Historical Society (Boston), 2nd ser., 10:50–67 (Sept. 1867).

IV. LATER ESTIMATES OF SHAW

Beale, Joseph H. "Lemuel Shaw," *Great American Lawyers,* ed. by W. D. Lewis (Philadelphia, 1907, 9 vols.), III, 453–490.

Chafee, Zechariah, Jr. "Shaw, Lemuel," *Dictionary of American Biography.*

Chase, Frederic Hathaway. *Lemuel Shaw, Chief Justice of the Supreme Judicial Court of Massachusetts, 1830–1860* (Boston, 1918).

Feller, A. H. "Lemuel Shaw," *Encyclopedia of the Social Sciences.*

MacLean, Arthur W. "Lemuel Shaw and His Influence on American Jurisprudence," *Temple Law Quarterly,* 4:148–156 (March 1930). (Misleading title; a mere summary of Chase's biography.)

Proceedings of the Bench and Bar on the Centennial Anniversary of Chief Justice Shaw's Appointment. 272 Mass. 591–608 (1930).

Proceedings at the Meeting of the Bar at the Birthplace of Chief Justice Shaw in West Barnstable, Mass. August 4, 1916. (Pamphlet, n.d.)

V. MASSACHUSETTS REPORTS

The official reports of the cases decided by the Supreme Judicial Court began with the. cases of the 1804 law terms. Shaw's opinions begin in 9 Pickering and end in 15 Gray. The volumes are here listed in the order of their appearance, under the names of the successive reporters.

Williams, Ephraim. *Reports of Cases Argued and Determined in the Supreme Judicial Court of Massachusetts. 1804–05* (Boston, 1804–05).

Tyng, Dudley Atkins. *Reports of the Cases Argued and Determined in the Supreme Judicial Court of Massachusetts. 1806–22* (Exeter and Boston, 1806–22), 16 vols.

Pickering, Octavius. *Reports of Cases Argued and Determined in the Supreme Judicial Court of Massachusetts. 1822–39* (Boston, 1824–41), 24 vols.

Metcalf, Theron. *Reports of Cases Argued and Determined in the Supreme Judicial Court of Massachusetts. 1840–1847* (Boston, 1840–51), 13 vols.

Cushing, Luther S. *Reports of Cases Argued and Determined in the Supreme Judicial Court of Massachusetts. 1848–53* (Boston, 1850–60), 12 vols.

Gray, Horace, Jr. *Reports of Cases Argued and Determined in the Supreme Judicial Court of Massachusetts. 1854–61* (Boston, 1855–71), 16 vols.

VI. MASSACHUSETTS STATUTES

Acts and Resolves, Public and Private of the Province of Massachusetts Bay (Boston, 1869–1922), 21 vols.

Laws of the Commonwealth of Massachusetts from November 28, 1780 to February 28, 1807 (Boston, 1807), 3 vols.

Laws of the Commonwealth of Massachusetts Passed at the Several Sessions of the General Court Holden in Boston, 1809 . . . 1812 (Boston, 1812).

Laws of the Commonwealth of Massachusetts, 1812 ff., sessional (Boston, 1812 ff.).

Private and Special Statutes of the Commonwealth of Massachusetts from February 1806 to February 1814 (Boston, 1823).

Resolves of the General Court of the Commonwealth of Massachusetts, 1806 ff., sessional (Boston, 1806 ff.).

Revised Statutes of the Commonwealth of Massachusetts, Passed November 4, 1835. Printed under the Supervision of Theron Metcalf and Horace Mann (Boston, 1836).

Supplements to the Revised Statutes, ed. by Theron Metcalf and L. S. Cushing (Boston, 1844).

The General Laws of Massachusetts from the Adoption of the Constitution to February, 1822, ed. by Theron Metcalf, under the Supervision of Asahel Stearns and Lemuel Shaw, Commissioners (Boston, 1823), 2 vols.

VII. OTHER PUBLIC RECORDS

Bemis, George, ed. *Report of the Case of John W. Webster* (Boston, 1850).

Bigelow, George T. and George Bemis, eds. *Report of the Trial of Abner Rogers, Jr.* (Boston, 1844).

Debates and Proceedings of the Massachusetts Constitutional Convention of 1853 (Boston, 1853), 3 vols.

Journal of Debates and Proceedings in the Convention of Delegates, Chosen to Revise the Constitution of Massachusetts, Nov. 15, 1820–Jan. 9, 1821. Reported for the *Boston Daily Advertiser* (Boston, 1853, 2nd ed.).

Journal of the Massachusetts House of Representatives, XXXI–XXXV. (MSS, Massachusetts Archives, State House Library.)

Kneeland, Abner. *Speech of Abner Kneeland Delivered Before the Full Bench of Judges of the Supreme Court, In His Own Defense, for the Alleged Crime of Blasphemy. Law Term, March 8, 1836* (Boston, 1836).

Lawson, John D., ed. *American State Trials* (St. Louis, 1921, 20 vols.), XIII.

(Parker, Samuel D.). *Report of the Arguments of the Attorney of the Commonwealth at the Trials of Abner Kneeland, for Blasphemy, in the Municipal and Supreme Courts, in Boston, January and May, 1834* (Boston, 1834).

Phillips, Willard. *Preliminary Report of the Commissioners to Reduce So Much of the Common Law as Relates to Crimes and Punishments, and the Incidents Thereof, to a Written and Systematic Code* (Boston, 1839).

Phillips, Willard and Samuel B. Walcott, eds. *Report of Penal Code of Massachusetts, Prepared (by the) . . . Commissioners "to Reduce . . . the Common Law as Relates to Crimes . . . to a Written and Systematic Code"* (Boston, 1844).

Pickering, Charles and William H. Gardiner, eds. *Report of the Trial by Impeachment of James Prescott* (Boston, 1821).

Report of the Minority of the Committee of the Primary School Board, on the Caste Schools of the City of Boston with some remarks (by Wendell Phillips) on the City Solicitor's Opinion (Boston, 1846). Pamphlet.

Report of a Special Committee of the Grammar School Board, presented August 29, 1849, on the petition of sundry colored persons praying for the abolition of the Smith School (Boston, 1849).

Reports of the Annual Visiting Committees of the Public Schools of the City of Boston. City Document No. 28 (Boston, 1846).

Story, Joseph, *et al. Report on Codification of the Common Law. Report of the Commissioners Appointed to Consider and Report upon the Practicability and Expediency of Reducing to a Written and Systematic Code the Common Law of Massachusetts or any Part Thereof* (Boston, 1837).

(Sumner, Charles). *Argument of Charles Sumner, Esq. against the Constitutionality of Separate Colored Schools, in the Case of Sarah C. Roberts vs. The City of Boston. Before the Supreme Court of Mass., Dec. 4, 1849* (Boston, 1849). Pamphlet.

The Trial of Thomas Sims (Boston, 1851).

VIII. CONTEMPORARY LAW JOURNALS

American Jurist and Law Magazine (Boston, 1829–43), 28 vols.
American Law Magazine (Philadelphia, 1843–46), 4 vols.
The Monthly Law Reporter (Boston, 1838–66), 27 vols.
United States Law Intelligencer and Review (Providence and Philadelphia, 1829–31), 3 vols.

IX. NEWSPAPERS

Baltimore Gazette, 1830.
Boston Courier, 1851.
Boston Daily Advertiser, 1830, 1840, 1842, 1861.
Boston Post, 1842.
Boston Statesman, 1830.
Columbian Centinel (Boston), 1799, 1830, 1836, 1842.
The Commonwealth (Boston), 1851.
Daily Atlas (Boston), 1832, 1842, 1850.
Daily Evening Transcript (Boston), 1836, 1851, 1861.
Daily Evening Traveller (Boston), 1861.
Emancipator and Free American (Boston), 1842–1843.
The Liberator (Boston), 1832–1855.
Mercantile Journal (Boston), 1836.
National Intelligencer (Washington, D.C.), 1851.
New England Palladium (Boston), 1830.
The Puritan Recorder (Boston), 1851.

X. LEGAL TREATISES

Angell, Joseph K. *A Treatise on the Law of Common Carriers* (Boston, 1849).
Angell, Joseph K. and Samuel Ames. *A Treatise on the Law of Private Corporations* (Boston, 1832).
Bailey, W. F. *Treatise on the Law of Personal Injuries, Including Employer's Liability, Master and Servant and Workmen's Compensation Acts* (Chicago, 1912, 5 vols.), II.
Baty, T. *Vicarious Liability* (Oxford, 1916).
Beach, Charles F. *Treatise on the Law of Contributory Negligence* (New York, 1885).
Bishop, Joel P. *Commentaries on the Criminal Law* (Boston, 1856–58), 2 vols.
Blackstone, Sir William. *Commentaries on the Laws of England, in Four Books,* ed. by Edward Christian (London, 1793–1795, 12th ed.), 4 vols.
Buck, Edward. *Massachusetts Ecclesiastical Law* (Boston, 1866).
Carson, Hampton L. *The Law of Criminal Conspiracies and Agreements as Found in the American Cases* (Philadelphia, 1887).

Cooley, Thomas M. *A Treatise on Constitutional Limitations* (Boston, 1903, 7th ed.).

Freund, Ernst. *The Police Power* (Chicago, 1904).

Glueck, S. Sheldon. *Mental Disorder and the Criminal Law* (Boston, 1927).

Greenleaf, Simon. *A Treatise on the Law of Evidence* (Boston, 1842–1843, 3 vols.), I.

Hall, Jerome. *General Principles of Criminal Law* (Indianapolis, 1947).

Hay, Gustavus. *The Law of Railroad Accidents in Massachusetts* (Boston, 1897).

Hilliard, Francis. *The Law of Torts and Private Wrongs* (New York, 1859).

Holmes, Oliver Wendell. *The Common Law* (Boston, 1881).

Hurd, John Codman. *The Law of Freedom and Bondage in the United States* (Boston, 1862), 2 vols.

Kenny, Courtney S. *Outlines of Criminal Law* (American ed., New York, 1907).

Michael, Jerome and Herbert Wechsler. *Criminal Law and Its Administration* (Chicago, 1940).

Mott, Rodney L. *Due Process of Law* (Indianapolis, 1926).

Nichols, Philip. *The Law of Eminent Domain* (Boston, 1917, 2nd ed.), 2 vols.

Pierce, Edward L. *A Treatise on American Railroad Law* (New York, 1857).

Prosser, William L. *Handbook of the Law of Torts* (St. Paul, 1941).

Redfield, Isaac F. *A Practical Treatise upon the Law of Railways* (Boston, 1858, 2nd ed.).

Shearman, Thomas G. and Amasa A. Redfield. *A Treatise on the Law of Negligence* (New York, 1869).

Story, Joseph. *Commentaries on the Constitution of the United States* (Boston, 1858, 3rd ed., 2 vols.), II.

———. *Commentaries on the Law of Agency* (Boston, 1846, 3rd ed.).

Thayer, J. B. *A Preliminary Treatise of Evidence at the Common Law* (Boston, 1898).

Tiffany, Francis B. *Death by Wrongful Act* (Kansas City, Mo., 1913, 2nd ed.).

Wharton, Francis. *A Treatise on the Law of Homicide* (Philadelphia, 1875).

Weihofen, Henry. *Mental Disorder as a Criminal Defense* (Buffalo, 1954).

Wigmore, John H. *A Treatise on the Anglo-American System of Evidence* (Boston, 1923, 2nd ed.), 5 vols.

Wright, R. S. *The Law of Criminal Conspiracies and Agreements* (American ed., Philadelphia, 1887).

Zollman, Carl. *American Church Law* (St. Paul, 1933).

XI. BOOKS

Adams, Charles Francis. *Richard Henry Dana* (Boston, 1891, 3rd ed.), 2 vols.

Amory, Cleveland. *The Proper Bostonians* (New York, 1947).

Amory, Thomas C. *Life of James Sullivan* (Boston, 1859, 2 vols.), II.

Annual Reports, Presented to the Massachusetts Anti-Slavery Society, by Its Board of Managers (Boston, 1833–1853), 21 vols.

Auman, Francis R. *The Changing American Legal System* (Columbus, 1940).

Bailey, Hollis R. *Attorneys and Their Admission to the Bar in Massachusetts* (Boston, 1907).

Bearse, Austin. *Reminiscences of Fugitive-Slave Law Days in Boston* (Boston, 1880).

Beecher, Lyman. *Autobiography and Correspondence,* ed. by Charles Beecher (New York, 1864), 2 vols.

Bell, Charles H. *The Bench and Bar of New Hampshire* (Boston, 1894).

Birrell, Augustine. *Four Lectures on the Law of Employers' Liability at Home and Abroad* (London, 1897).

Boudin, Louis. *Government by Judiciary* (New York, 1932, 2 vols.), II.

Bowditch, Vincent I. *Life and Correspondence of Henry Ingersoll Bowditch* (Boston, 1902), 2 vols.

Brown, Samuel G. *The Life of Rufus Choate* (Boston, 1891, 6th ed.).

Burgess, George. *Pages from the Ecclesiastical History of New England, 1740–1840* (Boston, 1847).

Butler, Benjamin F. *Autobiography of Personal Reminiscences. Butler's Book* (Boston, 1892).

Chadwick, John W. *William Ellery Channing* (Boston, 1903).

Chafee, Zechariah, Jr. *How Human Rights Got Into the Constitution* (Boston, 1952).

Channing, William Henry. *The Life of William Ellery Channing* (Boston, 1899).

Clark, Joseph S. *Historical Sketch of the Congregational Churches, 1620–1858* (Boston, 1858).

Commager, Henry S. *Theodore Parker* (Boston, 1936).

Commons, John R. *et al.,* eds. *Documentary History of American Industrial Society* (Cleveland, 1910–1911, 11 vols.), III and IV.

———. *History of Labour in the United States* (New York, 1918), 2 vols.

Cooke, George W. *Unitarianism in America* (Boston, 1902).

Curtis, Benjamin R., Jr., ed. *A Memoir of Benjamin Robbins Curtis* (Boston, 1897), 2 vols.

Curtis, Charles P. *It's Your Law* (Cambridge, 1954).

Darling, Arthur B. *Political Changes in Massachusetts, 1824–1848* (New Haven, 1925).

Davis, William T. *Bench and Bar of the Commonwealth of Massachusetts* (Boston, 1895), 2 vols.

———. *History of the Judiciary of Massachusetts* (Boston, 1900).

———, ed. *The New England States, Their Constitutional, Judicial, Educational, Commercial, Professional, and Industrial Development* (Boston, 1891, 3 vols.), III.

Derby, John Barton. *Political Reminiscences, Including a Sketch of the Origin and History of the "Statesman Party" of Boston* (Boston, 1835).

Dewey, Davis R. *State Banking before the Civil War* (Washington, D.C., 1910).

Dexter, Henry M. *The Congregationalism of the Last Three-Hundred Years* (New York, 1880).

Dodd, Edwin Merrick. *American Business Corporations until 1860* (Cambridge, 1954).

Dunning, Albert. *Congregationalists in America* (Boston, 1894).

Ellis, George. *A Half-Century of the Unitarian Controversy* (Boston, 1857).

Emerson, Edward W. and Waldo E. Forbes, eds. *Journals of Ralph Waldo Emerson* (Boston, 1912, 10 vols.), VIII.

Foner, Philip S. *History of the Labor Movement in the United States* (New York, 1947).

Frankfurter, Felix. *The Commerce Clause* (Chapel Hill, 1937).

Freund, Ernst. *Standards of American Legislation* (Chicago, 1917).

Frothingham, Louis A. *A Brief History of the Constitutional Government of Massachusetts* (Boston, 1916).

Frothingham, Octavius B. *Theodore Parker* (New York, 1880).

Fuess, Claude M. *Rufus Choate, The Wizard of Law* (New York, 1928).

(Garrison). *William Lloyd Garrison, 1805–1879, The Story of His Life, Told by His Children* (New York, 1885, 4 vols.), II.

Greenslet, Ferris. *The Lowells and Their Seven Worlds* (Boston, 1946).

Gregory, Charles O. *Labor and the Law* (New York, 1946).

Handlin, Oscar and Mary F. Handlin. *Commonwealth, A Study of the Role of Government in the American Economy: Massachusetts, 1774–1861* (New York, 1947).

Hart, Albert B., ed. *Commonwealth History of Massachusetts* (New York, 1927–1930, 5 vols.), IV.

Hartz, Louis. *Economic Policy and Democratic Thought: Pennsylvania, 1776–1860* (Cambridge, 1948).

———. *The Liberal Tradition in America* (New York, 1955).

Harvey, Peter. *Reminiscences and Anecdotes of Daniel Webster* (Boston, 1890).

Higginson, Thomas Wentworth. *Cheerful Yesterdays* (Boston, 1899).

Hoar, George F. *Autobiography of Seventy Years* (New York, 1903), 2 vols.

Holdsworth, William S. *A History of English Law* (London, 1903 ff., 14 vols.), IV, XI, and XIII.

Horton, John T. *James Kent, A Study in Conservatism* (New York, 1939).

Howe, Mark DeWolfe. *Readings in American Legal History* (Cambridge, 1949).

Hurst, James Willard. *The Growth of American Law* (Boston, 1950).

Irving, H. B. *A Book of Remarkable Criminals* (London, 1918).

Kirkland, Edward C. *Men, Cities and Transportation* (Cambridge, 1948), 2 vols.

Krout, John A. *The Origins of Prohibition* (New York, 1925).

Lauer, Paul E. *Church and State in New England* (Baltimore, 1892).

Lerner, Max. *The Mind and Faith of Justice Holmes* (Boston, 1943).

Lieberman, Elias. *Unions before the Bar* (New York, 1950).

Longfellow, Samuel. *Life of Henry Wadsworth Longfellow, with Extracts from His Journals and Correspondence* (Boston, 1936 ed., 2 vols.), II.

Loring, James Spear. *The Hundred Boston Orators* (Boston, 1853).

MacGill, Caroline. *A History of Transportation in the United States before 1860* (Washington, 1917).

McCabe, Joseph, ed. *Biographical Dictionary of Modern Rationalists* (London, 1920).

McDougall, Marion G. *Fugitive Slaves (1619–1865)* (Boston, 1891).

McLaughlin, Andrew C. *Constitutional History of the United States* (New York, 1935).

Meyer, Jacob C. *Church and State in Massachusetts, 1740–1833* (Cleveland, 1930).

Morison, Samuel Eliot. *A History of the Constitution of Massachusetts*. Reprinted from the Manual for the Constitutional Convention of 1917 (Boston, 1917).

———. *Life and Letters of Harrison Gray Otis* (Boston, 1913), 2 vols.

Morris, Richard B. *Fair Trial* (New York, 1952).

———. *Government and Labor in Early America* (New York, 1946).

———. *Studies in the History of American Law* (New York, 1930).

Morse, James K. *Jedidiah Morse, A Champion of New England Orthodoxy* (New York, 1939).

Parker, Edward G. *Reminiscences of Rufus Choate* (New York, 1860).

Parker, Theodore. *The Trial of Theodore Parker for the "Misdemeanor" of a Speech in Faneuil Hall Against Kidnapping* (New York, 1864).

Pearson, Edmund. *Murder at Smutty Nose and Other Murders* (New York, 1926).

Pearson, H. G. *The Life of John A. Andrew* (Boston, 1904, 2 vols.), I.

Pierce, Edward L. *Memoir and Letters of Charles Sumner* (Boston, 1893, 4 vols.), III.

Platner, John W., *et al. The Religious History of New England* (Cambridge, 1917).

Pound, Roscoe. *The Formative Era of American Law* (Boston, 1938).

———. *Interpretations of Legal History* (New York, 1923).

———. *The Spirit of the Common Law* (Boston, 1921).

Robinson, Mrs. W. S., ed. *"Warrington" Pen-Portraits: A Collection of Personal and Political Reminiscences, from 1848–1876* (Boston, 1877).

Punchard, George. *History of Congregationalism from about A.D. 250 to the Present Time* (Boston, 1881, 5 vols.), V.

Quincy, Josiah. *A Municipal History of the Town and City of Boston* (Boston, 1852).

Reno, Conrad. *Memoirs of the Judiciary and the Bar of New England for the Nineteenth Century* (Boston, 1900), 3 vols.

Right and Wrong in Boston, No. 1, Report of the Boston Female Anti-Slavery Society (Boston, 1836, 2nd ed.).

Right and Wrong in Boston in 1836, (Third) Annual Report of the Boston Female Anti-Slavery Society (Boston, 1836).

Robinson, William A. *Jeffersonian Democracy in New England* (New Haven, 1913).

Sanborn, Franklin B. and William T. Harris, *A. Bronson Alcott: His Life and Philosophy* (Boston, 1893, 2 vols.), I.

Schlesinger, Arthur M., Jr. *The Age of Jackson* (Boston, 1945).

Shannon, Fred. *America's Economic Growth* (New York, 1940).

Shepard, Odell, ed. *The Journals of Bronson Alcott* (Boston, 1938).

Sprague, Henry H. *City Government in Boston: Its Rise and Development* (Boston, 1889).

Stephen, James F. *History of the Criminal Law of England* (London, 1883), 3 vols.

Stokes, Anson P. *Church and State in the United States* (New York, 1950, 3 vols.), I.

Story, William W. *Life and Letters of Joseph Story* (Boston, 1851, 2 vols.), II.

Swisher, Carl Brent. *Roger B. Taney* (New York, 1936).

Taylor, P. E. "The Turnpike Era in New England" (MS dissertation, Yale Library, 1934).

Warren, Charles. *A History of the American Bar* (Boston, 1911).

———. *History of the Harvard Law School* (New York, 1908, 3 vols.), I and II.

———. *Jacobin and Junto, or Early American Politics as Viewed in the Diary of Dr. Nathaniel Ames, 1758–1822* (Cambridge, 1931).

Warren, Edward. *The Life of John Collins Warren* (Boston, 1859), 2 vols.), I.

Washburn, Emory. *Judicial History of Massachusetts* (Boston, 1840).

Willard, Joseph A. *Half a Century with Judges and Lawyers* (Boston, 1895).

Willis, William. *A History of the Law, the Courts and the Lawyers of Maine* (Portland, 1863).

Wilson, Henry. *History of the Rise and Fall of the Slave Power in America* (Boston, 1872–1877, 3 vols.), II.

Windsor, Justin, ed. *Memorial History of Boston Including Suffolk County, Massachusetts, 1630–1880* (Boston, 1880–1881, 4 vols.), IV.

Worthington, Erastus. *The History of Dedham . . . to 1827* (Boston, 1827).

Wright, Benjamin F. *The Contract Clause of the Constitution* (Cambridge, 1938).

———. *The Growth of American Constitutional Law* (Boston, 1942).

XII. ARTICLES, ESSAYS, PAMPHLETS, ETC.

Allison, William H. "Abner Kneeland," *Dictionary of American Biography.*

Berman, Edward. "Employers' Liability," *Encyclopedia of the Social Sciences.*

Billington, Ray A. "Burning of Charlestown Convent," *New England Quarterly,* 10:3–24 (March, 1937).

Blaney, J. M. "The Term, 'Police Power'," *Central Law Journal,* 59:486 ff. (Dec. 16, 1904).

Bohlen, Francis H. "Voluntary Assumption of Risk," *Harvard Law Review,* 20:14–34 (1906).

Buck, Elizabeth G. "Samuel Hubbard," *Memorial Biographies of the New-England Historic Genealogical Society,* I, 86–101.

Burdick, Francis M. "Is the Law the Expression of Class Selfishness?" *Harvard Law Review,* 25:349–359 (1912).

"The Case of Thomas Sims," *Monthly Law Reporter* (Boston), 14:1–16 (1852).

Chase, George B. "Memoir of George Tyler Bigelow," *Proceedings, Massachusetts Historical Society,* 2nd ser., 5:458–482 (April 1890).

Cohen, Morris R. "The Process of Judicial Legislation," *American Law Review,* 48:176 ff. (1914).

Commager, Henry Steele. "The Blasphemy of Abner Kneeland," *New England Quarterly,* 8:29–41 (March 1935).

———. "Joseph Story," in Holcombe, Arthur N., *et al. Gaspar G. Bacon Lectures on the Constitution of the United States* (Boston, 1953), pp. 33–94.

"The Congregational Churches of Massachusetts," *Spirit of the Pilgrims,* 1:57–74 (Feb. 1828).

Cooke, Reverend Parsons. *Remonstrance Against an Established Religion in Massachusetts* (Boston, 1831). Pamphlet.

———. *Unitarianism an Exclusive System, or the Bondage of the*

Churches . . . Planted by the Puritans (Boston, 1828). Pamphlet.

Corwin, Edward S. "The Basic Doctrine of American Constitutional Law," *Selected Essays on Constitutional Law* (Chicago, 1938, 5 vols.), I, 101–127.

———. "The Doctrine of Due Process of Law before the Civil War," *Selected Essays on Constitutional Law* (Chicago, 1938, 5 vols.), I, 203–235.

Cushman, Robert E. "Ten Years of the Supreme Court: 1937–1947," Part V. "Civil Liberties," *American Political Science Review*, 42:42–52 (Feb. 1948).

Dennis, Samuel K. "Maryland's Antique Constitutional Thorn," *University of Pennsylvania Law Review*, 92:34–52 (Sept. 1943).

Dewey, Maria. "Charles Augustus Dewey," *Memorial Biographies of the New-England Historic Genealogical Society*, VI, 178–180.

"Difficulties in Parishes," *Christian Examiner* (Boston), Vol. 9. No. 40 (Sept. 1830), pp. 4–5.

"The Exiled Churches of Massachusetts," *Congregational Quarterly* (Boston), 5:216–240 (July 1863).

Fairman, Charles. "Merrick, Pliny," *Dictionary of American Biography*.

———. "Metcalf, Theron," *Dictionary of American Biography*.

Fuess, Claude M. "Cushing, Caleb," *Dictionary of American Biography*.

Goudy, H. "Two Ancient Brocards," *Essays in Legal History*, ed. by Paul Vinogradoff (London, 1913), 215–229.

Grinnell, Frank W. "A Glimpse of the Life of an Essex County Judge. Samuel Putnam," *Massachusetts Law Quarterly* (Boston), 8:1–8 (Nov. 1922).

———. "Constitutional History of the Supreme Judicial Court of Massachusetts from the Revolution to 1813," *Massachusetts Law Quarterly*, 2:359–552 (May 1917).

Hale, Robert L. "The Supreme Court and the Contract Clause: II," *Harvard Law Review*, 57:621–674 (May 1944).

Hastings, W. G. "The Development of Law as Illustrated by the Decisions Relating to the Police Power of the State," *Proceedings of the American Philosophical Society*, 39:359–554 (Sept. 1900).

Hay, Gustavus, Jr. "Death as a Civil Cause of Action In Massachusetts," *Harvard Law Review*, 7:170–176 (Oct. 1893).

Haynes, George E. "Hoar, Ebenezer Rockwood," *Dictionary of American Biography*.

(Henshaw, David). *Review of the Prosecution Against Abner Kneeland for Blasphemy*. By a Cosmopolite (Boston, 1835). Pamphlet.

Hobbs, Marland C. "Statutory Changes in Employers' Liability," *Harvard Law Review*, 2:212–230 (1888).

Holbrook, Stewart. "Murder at Harvard," *The American Scholar*, 14:425–435 (Autumn 1945).

Holdsworth, William S. "The Origin of the Rule in *Baker v. Bolton,*" *Law Quarterly Review,* 32:431–437 (Oct. 1916).

Howe, Mark DeWolfe. "Juries as Judges of Criminal Law," *Harvard Law Review,* 52:582–616 (Feb. 1939).

Howe, Samuel Gridley. "Atheism in New England," *The New England Magazine* (Boston), 7:500–509 (Dec. 1834), and 8:53–62 (Jan. 1835).

Howie, Wendell D. "One Hundred Years of the Liquor Problem in Massachusetts," Appendix "B" to the Report of the Special Commission on the Regulation of the Liquor Traffic in Massachusetts. House Document No. 1300. Reprinted in *Massachusetts Law Quarterly,* 18:76–284 (March 1933).

"Insanity and the Criminal Law. A Critique of *Durham v. United States,*" Symposium in *University of Chicago Law Review,* 22:317–404 (Winter 1955).

Karpman, Benjamin. "Criminality, Insanity, and the Law," *Journal of Criminal Law and Criminology,* 39:584–605 (Jan.–Feb. 1949).

Keedy, Edwin R. "Insanity and Criminal Responsibility," *Harvard Law Review,* 30:535–560, and 724–738 (1917).

Knott, H. W. H. "Fletcher, Richard," *Dictionary of American Biography.*

Laski, Harold J. "The Basis of Vicarious Liability," *Yale Law Journal,* 26:105–135 (Dec. 1916).

"Latimer's Case," *Law Reporter* (Boston), 5:481–497 (March 1843).

"The Law of Carriers' Notices," *Monthly Law Reporter* (Boston), 15:241–264 (1852).

Lenhoff, Arthur. "Development of the Concept of Eminent Domain," *Columbia Law Review,* 42:596–638 (1942).

"Letters on the Introduction and Progress of Unitarianism in New England," *Spirit of the Pilgrims* (Boston), 3:507–509 (Oct. 1830).

Levy, Leonard W. "The 'Abolition Riot': Boston's First Slave Rescue," *New England Quarterly,* 25:85–92 (March 1952).

———. "Chief Justice Shaw and the Church Property Controversy in Massachusetts," *Boston University Law Review,* 30:219–235 (April 1950).

———. "Chief Justice Shaw and the Formative Period of American Railroad Law," *Columbia Law Review,* 51:327–348 and 852–865 (March and Nov. 1951).

———. "Fallacies in the Law of Segregation," *New Republic,* 128:16–17 (March 23, 1953).

———. "Jim Crow Schools on Trial," *The New Leader,* 36:6–8 (Nov. 30, 1953).

———. "Satan's Last Apostle in Massachusetts," *American Quarterly,* 5:16–30 (Spring 1953).

———. "The 'Separate but Equal' Doctrine," *The New Leader,* 36:8–10 (Feb. 2, 1953).

Levy, Leonard W. "Sims' Case: The Fugitive Slave Law in Boston in 1851," *Journal of Negro History*, 35:39–74 (Jan. 1950).

Levy, Leonard W. and Harlan B. Phillips. "The *Roberts* Case: Source of the 'Separate but Equal' Doctrine," *American Historical Review*, 56:510–518 (April 1951).

Nelles, Walter, "Commonwealth v. Hunt," *Columbia Law Review*, 32: 1128–1170 (Nov. 1932).

Olney, Richard. "Memoir of Benjamin F. Thomas," *Proceedings*, Massachusetts Historical Society, 2nd ser., 14:297–302 (Oct. 1900).

Paradise, Scott H. "Morton, Marcus," *Dictionary of American Biography*.

(Parker, Isaac). "Reply to the Reverend Parsons Cooke," *Christian Examiner* (Boston), 5:277–283 (July–Aug. 1828).

Parker, Joel. "The Law of Homicide," *North American Review and Miscellaneous Journal* (Boston), 62:178–204 (Jan. 1851).

Pound, Roscoe. "The Economic Interpretation and the Law of Torts," *Harvard Law Review*, 53:365–385 (1940).

———. "Discussion of Report on 'Insanity and Criminal Responsibility'," *Journal of Criminal Law and Criminology*, 2:544 (1911).

Reik, Louis E. "The Doe-Ray Correspondence," *Yale Law Journal*, 63:183–196 (1953).

"Remarks on a 'Letter to the Reverend Parsons Cooke'," *Spirit of the Pilgrims* (Boston), 1:67–72 (Dec. 1828).

"A Review of the Brookfield Case," *Spirit of the Pilgrims* (Boston), 5: 402–406 (July, 1832).

"Review of the Rights of the Congregational Churches," *Spirit of the Pilgrims* (Boston), 2:370–403 (July 1829).

"Review of the 'Vindication of the Rights of the Churches'," *Christian Examiner* (Boston), 5:298–316 (May–June 1828).

"Revision of the Laws of Massachusetts," *American Jurist*, 13:344–378 (April 1835).

Robinson, William A. "The Washington Benevolent Society in New England," *Proceedings*, Massachusetts Historical Society, 49:274–286 (1916).

Rosenthal, James. "Massachusetts Acts and Resolves Declared Unconstitutional by the Supreme Judicial Court of Massachusetts," *Massachusetts Law Quarterly*, 1:301–318 (Aug. 1916).

Sayre, Francis B. "Criminal Conspiracy," *Harvard Law Review*, 35: 393–427 (Feb. 1922).

———. "Mens Rea," *Harvard Law Review*, 45:974–1026 (1932).

Seavey, Warren Abner. "Speculations as to 'Respondeat Superior'," in *Harvard Legal Essays* (Cambridge, 1934), 433–465.

A Statement of Reasons Showing the Illegality of That Verdict upon Which Sentence of Death Has Been Pronounced against John Webster. By a Member of the Legal Profession (New York, 1850). Pamphlet.

"Third Article in the Declaration of Rights," *Spirit of the Pilgrims* (Boston), 4:624–648 (Dec. 1831).

"The Trial of Peter York," *Monthly Law Reporter* (Boston), 7:497–521 (March, 1845).

Ward, Andrew H. "David Henshaw," *Memorial Biographies of the New-England Historic and Genealogical Society,* I, 492.

Warren, Charles. *"Volenti Non Fit Injuria* in Actions of Negligence," *Harvard Law Review,* 8:457–471 (1895).

"The Webster Case," *Monthly Law Reporter* (Boston), 13:1–16 (1850).

Whitcomb, Mary R. "Abner Kneeland: His Relations to Early Iowa History," *Annals of Iowa,* 3 Ser., 6:340–363 (1904).

White, J. Gardner. "Samuel Sumner Wilde," *Memorial Biographies of the New-England Historic and Genealogical Society,* II, 368–385.

Winfield, Percy H. "Death as Affecting Liability in Tort," *Columbia Law Review,* 29:239–254 (March 1929).

Witte, Edwin E. "Early American Labor Cases," *Yale Law Journal,* 35:825–837 (May 1926).

Woodward, Julian L. "Changing Ideas on Mental Illness and Its Treatment," *American Sociological Review,* 16:454 ff. (Aug. 1951).

TABLE OF CASES*

* Numbers following colons refer to pages in the present volume.

INDEX